Christian Democracy in Western Germany

THE CDU/CSU IN GOVERNMENT AND OPPOSITION, 1945–1976

GEOFFREY PRIDHAM

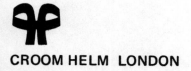

CROOM HELM LONDON

© 1977 Geoffrey Pridham

Croom Helm Ltd, 2-10 St John's Road, London SW11

British Library Cataloguing in Publication Data

Pridham, Geoffrey
    Christian democracy in Western Germany.
    1. Christlich-Demokratische Union – History
    I. Title
    329.9'43   JN3971.A98 C4567 1977b

    ISBN 0-85664-508-7

41,515

Printed and bound in Great Britain by
REDWOOD BURN LIMITED
Trowbridge & Esher

CONTENTS

CONTENTS

PREFACE

The idea for this book arose from an initial study of the CDU/CSU as the new Opposition in West Germany in the early 1970s, and of the nature of Government/Opposition roles in the political system of that country. In a wider sense, it drew on earlier research on confession as a factor in German political development and a general interest in the study of German political parties.

I wish to express my warmest thanks to the German Academic Exchange Service (DAAD) for providing me with substantial grants for three-month visits to the Federal Republic in both 1973 and 1976. The publication of this book would not have been possible without the generous financial support in this respect of the Social Science Research Institute of the Konrad Adenauer Foundation and the University of Bristol publications committee, for which I gratefully offer my thanks. During my several research visits to West Germany, I have received the unfailing assistance and co-operation of many organisations and individuals from the CDU/CSU, which are generally acknowledged in the Note on Sources and List of Interviews at the end of this book, as well as the encouragement of friends and acquaintances from different political persuasions. I should like in particular to mention in this connection Dr Hildegard Schlüter and the staff of the *Bundesgeschäftsstelle der CDU* in Bonn, the staff of the Bundestag Library and press archives, officials of the *Landesverbände* of the CDU and also Sigrid Lanzrath of Inter Nationes, Wolfgang Dexheimer, Klaus Sieveking, the late Rudolf Ullner, William E. Paterson, Gordon Smith and Peter Hüttenberger. I should also like to thank the Konnertz family, the Hasselbach family and Hans and Ruth Baumann for their hospitality during the summer of 1976, as well as that of Herbert and Eva Imlau, Dieter and Gisela Denneberg, Klaus and Dorothea Sieveking and Helga Becker on many occasions during past years. It is hoped, however, that the interpretation in this book will be accepted by them all as an attempt at academic impartiality.

My greatest individual debt is to Pippa, my wife, for her general encouragement over the years in writing this book, but in particular for her work in editing and criticising all draft chapters during the final months of revising and completing the manuscript. Her perceptive comments and insistence on clarifying many points have made an invaluable contribution to this work. Some credit must also be due to her for conceiving the title of the book.

Finally, I should like to acknowledge the help received from Mrs Anne Merriman in producing the final typescript and agreeing to do so somewhat at short notice, and to thank Mrs Jan Nicholas for typing the early chapters.

The bibliography at the back consists of selected publications on the subject of the book for further reading, although the detailed sources used are mentioned at the end of each chapter. A distinction has been made in each chapter between the Explanatory Notes and the Source References, the former serving to elaborate points in the text for the general reader and the latter indicating to the specialist the location of material used.

Bristol   Geoffrey Pridham
March 1977

INTRODUCTION: THE CDU/CSU AND THE WEST GERMAN PARTY SYSTEM.

A strictly national approach to the study of political parties has its recognisable limitations, but also its merits, if viewed within the wider framework of comparative politics. The latter has the advantage of providing, by way of categorisation, a reasonably accurate conceptual grasp of the nature and activities of political parties both in relation to each other and within the context of their respective party systems.[1] In offering empirical generalisations on how party systems may develop, the comparative angle therefore adds a useful and necessary perspective on how political parties function at the national level.

However, a very detailed study of a particular political party has inevitably to base its approach on the national context, and in doing so further contributes in an important way to the study of comparative politics. There are two principal but related reasons for pursuing a national approach. First, political parties are instruments for the exercise of power especially in Western democracies, which usually feature highly developed party systems. The focus of their organisation and activities is within the national political system, although the formulation of external policy may lead to international links with like-minded parties. However, even attempts to integrate ideologically related political parties at the European level with a view to direct elections to the European Parliament have encountered the problem that such parties work essentially from a national base.[1] The national approach is therefore a fundamentally important factor in assessing the role of political parties at a comparative level.

Secondly, each country has its own historical, cultural and socio-economic differences, which determine the environmental setting of political parties and must therefore affect their composition, outlook and structure, although parties of course often do in turn have an impact on their own environment. The influence of the national political environment on parties can best be analysed in two ways: externally in relation to socio-political conditions whereby the party's electoral appeal and ideological orientation must harmonise with the particular 'values' of the society in question; and internally whereby the structure of the party must accord with the structure of the political system. For example, the two main Christian Democratic parties in Western Europe

11

since the Second World War — the Italian *Democrazia Cristiana* (DC) as well as the West German Christian Democratic Union and Christian Social Union (CDU/CSU) — have witnessed similarities of experience and development. As new movements after the War they grew out of a mood of anti-Fascism/Nazism and they both enjoyed a position of political dominance in their respective countries during the first decade and a half which followed.[2] However, the particular socio-political feature of the West German version of Christian Democracy has been its inter-confessional character based on its response to the traditional division between Catholics and Protestants in German political history. Moreover, the strong regional roots in the political environment of West Germany, expressed through its federal political system, have limited the possibilities for internal cohesion in the CDU/CSU. Just as the CDU is itself federal in structure so there is a separate Christian Democratic party for Bavaria, the CSU, reflecting the strong sense of regional identity in that state. It follows that the nature of the party in question is formed by its response to political developments in the country concerned. At the same time it is conditioned by national constitutional rules.

The starting-point for a close examination of a political party must accordingly be the national party system. Two basic and interconnected approaches for evaluating the nature of a party system may serve as a point of departure: first, the historical dimension focusing on the relationship between party and state; and second, the type of party system under which it may be classified.

The first criterion is especially relevant when looking at the Federal Republic of Germany, for it is generally agreed that the most significant new development marking the evolution of its political system has been the pivotal role acquired by political parties and the party system in the representative institutions of the post-war state.[3] This special feature of West Germany, underlined by the formation of its party system preceding the re-establishment of its political sovereignty a few years later, involved a break with past patterns of German political development. German political parties had previously had little direct experience of responsibility in the state in a democratic form, for under the Empire they had been largely excluded from executive government, while during the Weimar Republic the parties had failed to establish a viable role in government because of their fragmentation and because of the impact of economic and social developments. The one-party state of the Third Reich was a radically different system from any that had preceded it, so that its total collapse in 1945 opened the way for a new development in the party-state relationship. This relationship has been characterised since the nineteenth century by a peculiarly German outlook in political thought, divorcing the concepts of 'party' and 'state', thus producing a 'dualism' between these two concepts. As a result of the successful founding and development of the West German party system, these historical 'conditions' have weakened in both practice and theory. Their place has been assumed by the experience and the concept of the 'party state' (*Parteienstaat*), a stronger version of the idea of 'party government', whereby the political parties not only hold the strategic positions in the political decision-making process but also permeate the activities of public life in general. A special measure of the importance of the party system for the operation of the political system in West Germany is the extent to which its uniformity throughout the country has provided a 'nationalising' influence within its federal system,[4] while at the same time retaining its identity at the regional level.

The second criterion concerning the type of party system is particularly interesting in its application to West Germany, because of the change which has occurred during the generation since the Second World War. All party systems change in their structure over time. Such change may result from a long-term alteration in the electoral strengths of the various parties concerned following new socio-political trends, or from adjustments in the constitutional rules (notably electoral systems) favouring one party against others; or from the impact of major political or economic events and splits and re-formations in the case of individual parties. The West German party system has been noted for its change, and also the speed with which it has taken place. It developed initially as a multi-party system but one with dominant elements (i.e. CDU/CSU and SPD), and in this sense was qualitatively different from the (literal) multi-party system of the Weimar Republic. During the 1950s there was a consolidation on the centre-right leading to the dominant position of the CDU/CSU, whereby that party's absorption of the smaller conservative parties was facilitated by a revision of the electoral system raising the minimum qualification for representation in the Bundestag. This bias in the party system towards the CDU/CSU gradually weakened during the course of the 1960s with the loss of its dominant status, once the impetus it had gained from the period of socio-economic and political reconstruction had been absorbed. Of the three main parties, the CDU/CSU was the least able to adjust to changing conditions in the 1960s, while the SPD benefited from new socio-political developments and closed the gap between its own electoral strength and that of the

CDU/CSU. The new formation of forces on the centre-left, marked by the SPD/FDP coalition initiated in 1969, led to a changed situation creating a new balance in the party system, though one without the possibility of a ready alternation in power between the main parties. This has been called a 'two-and-a-half party system', for its main distinguishing feature from a two-party system is that a change of power normally occurs not through a straightforward replacement of one major party by another, but through the medium of a third smaller party in coalition (i.e. the FDP). This transformation of the West German party system has featured an electoral consolidation in favour of both the CDU/CSU and SPD, so that together they have acquired 80-90 per cent (and recently more than 90 per cent) of the total vote in Bundestag elections since 1957. During the period 1945-1976 major splits have not happened in the main parties except in the FDP in the mid-1950s, and with the loss of its conservative support from the late 1960s.

One important aspect of the transformation of the West German party system has been the emergence of *Volksparteien*, or political parties whose overriding motivation is electoral and which appeal substantially across political and social cleavages. Such traditional cleavages in Germany had been significantly reduced by the end of the Second World War,[5] so that the development of a different type of party from the predominantly sectional ones of the Weimar Republic became more possible. The main contribution to the party system of these *Volksparteien* − the CDU/CSU from the earlier 1950s, and the SPD increasingly from the early 1960s − has been their role as forces of political integration through the aggregation of different groups in West German society, a function particularly important in view of the tenuous roots of the new political system after the War. In the case of the CDU/CSU, the first example in Germany history of a democratic *Volkspartei*, its principal importance was in mobilising under one political banner different forces of the centre-right, which had traditionally been divided or even antagonistic. This new unity especially of the middle classes forged by the CDU/CSU − of which a special feature was its relatively successful attempt to overcome the historical political division between Catholics and Protestants − was the first important departure in the reconstruction of German party political patterns after the War. During its period of dominance, and especially in the 1950s, the CDU/CSU enlarged this new political unity, and presented an attractive political formula for meeting the demands of different groups in society during the reconstruction period. The political dominance of the CDU/CSU produced a reaction on the part of its main rival, the SPD, which took a deliberate decision (symbolised by the Godesberg Programme of 1959) to remould itself as a *Volkspartei*.[6] This produced in turn a reaction on the part of the CDU/CSU and consequent efforts to reform itself, once the SPD displaced it as the main governing party of the Federal Republic.

There are different approaches for analysing an individual political party. One may focus on how it organises its own affairs (its general internal structure, nature of leadership and various functions); on its ideological character (policy and goal orientation); or, on how it governs the country and responds to political developments (the historical approach). All three approaches are viable, although each has by itself its obvious limitations of scope. The compulsion to adopt all these approaches in examining the CDU/CSU is strong, because of the absence of a comprehensive and up-to-date academic study on the subject in either English or German.[2] Every study must, however, have its particular scope of interest. The author's main approach has been historical, centering on the Government/Opposition dimension. It has then focused on the importance of this for the nature and development of the CDU/CSU, in terms of its form of leadership, internal relations and cohesion, organisational structure, political activities, ideological character and electoral appeal. The emphasis, for instance, is not on the content of CDU/CSU governmental policies as such, but rather on how the CDU/CSU was instrumental in the formulation of such policies. The book therefore concentrates more on the 'internal' aspects of the CDU/CSU than on its 'external' aspects, though both are discussed substantially in relation to the Government/Opposition dimension. One principal feature of this dimension needs to be emphasised in the case of West Germany. While the author's starting point for this study was an interest in the CDU/CSU as a new Opposition after 1969, it must be pointed out that there is a basic difference between the West German and British models of the Government/Opposition relationship, deriving from the former's federal system and its different attitudes to the role of Opposition. While Federal-*Land* relations are discussed in this book, the author has chosen, however, to treat the particular question of *Land* politics as such only marginally.

The book is structured in two parts, the first looking at the development of the CDU/CSU in both Government and Opposition (the historical approach), and the second focusing on the composition and structure of the CDU/CSU and considering its different aspects such as organisation, membership, its auxiliary organisations, the CSU and its electoral appeal and campaigns (the thematic approach). The Government/Opposition dimension is carried into the second part, where the effects of both roles are examined more closely in relation to its organisational features.

One particular difficulty has been the treatment of the CSU, for it is essentially a separate (and in many ways different) political party from the CDU in spite of their common alliance for thirty years. This point was emphasised by the growing divergence between these parties during the author's research on the book for over four years during 1972-1977. The CSU is therefore discussed together with the CDU in the historical examination of their role in Government and Opposition in the first part, but their particular relationship as well as the character of the CSU's own leadership and organisational structure are covered separately as a chapter in Part Two. For the sake of convenience, the term 'party' is frequently used in reference to the CDU/CSU as a whole in Part One, although this is strictly not an accurate description of the organisational character of Christian Democracy in West Germany.

Notes

[1]   For a special discussion of this problem, see the chapter by Geoffrey Pridham and Pippa Pridham in Stanley Henig/John Pinder (eds.), *European Political Parties* (forthcoming, 1978), on transnational parties.
[2]   Certain special aspects of the CDU/CSU have been covered at different times. The early CDU (during the Occupation period) was analysed by Arnold Heidenheimer (1960) and the two books of H.G. Wieck (1953 and 1958), as well as in a short study by Gerhard Schulz (1955). Heidenheimer also wrote several articles on aspects of the CDU during the 1950s, in addition to the useful work by Jürgen Domes (1964) on the Bundestag *Fraktion* during that decade. Two informative academic studies have recently appeared in German on the CSU by Alf Mintzel (1975) and Günter Müchler (1976), as well as the introductory outline study of the CDU by Helmuth Pütz (1971, revised 1976). There has also appeared a study of the CDU/ CSU *Fraktion* in the Bundestag during 1969 to 1972 by Hans-Joachim Veen (1973 and 1976), again in German. No comprehensive scholarly political biography of Adenauer has yet appeared. (For details of these various publications, see bibliography at the end of this book.)

References

1.   See Jean Blondel, *An Introduction to Comparative Government* (1969); and L.D. Epstein, *Political Parties in Western Democracies* (1967).
2.   See Geoffrey Pridham, 'Christian Democracy in Italy and West Germany: a comparative analysis' in M. Kolinsky/W. Paterson (ed.), *Social and Political Movements in Western Europe* (1976), pp. 142-174

3. Peter Merkl, *Party Government in the Bonn Republic* in G.C. Byrne and K.S. Pedersen, *Politics in Western European Democracies* (1971), pp. 167-176; and Karl Dietrich Bracher, 'Das Bonner Parteiensystem' in Bracher (ed.), *Nach 25 Jahren: eine Deutschland-Bilanz* (1970), pp. 254-276.
4. Gordon Smith, 'West Germany and the Politics of Centrality' in *Government and Opposition,* Autumn 1976, pp. 387-407.
5. Gerhard Loewenberg, 'The Remaking of the German Party System' in M. Dogan and R. Rose, *European Politics: A Reader* (1971), pp. 259-279.
6. See W.E. Paterson, 'Social Democracy — the West German Example' in M. Kolinsky and W. Paterson (eds.), *op. cit.,* pp. 211-242

PART ONE:
THE DEVELOPMENT OF THE CDU/CSU

1 THE OCCUPATION PERIOD: THE FORMATION OF THE CDU/CSU (1945-1949)

The first significant stage in the consolidation of the post-war party system in West Germany was the regrouping of Catholic and conservative political forces under the banner of Christian Democracy. German party development since the late nineteenth century had consisted of four principal political tendencies — the Social Democratic/Marxist, the Catholic political, the Liberal and the Conservative — but the degree to which each of these tendencies had been expressed in an organisational form through an identifiable political party had varied considerably. The Social Democratic Party (SPD) had represented exclusively the first tendency until the establishment of the German Communist Party (KPD) after the First World War, just as the Centre Party together with the separate Bavarian People's Party (formed in 1918) catered for the interests of German Catholics in politics. A fissiparous organisational history had characterised the two remaining tendencies with the Liberal one weakened by the antagonism of progressive and conservative streams and the Conservative tendency equally represented by various rival political parties. This disunity among the non-Catholic middle-class electorate in Germany had facilitated the success of the Nazi Party in attracting mass voting support in the last years of the Weimar Republic.

Christian Democracy was a new political tendency, since although the Catholic political tradition still provided its core element it sought to broaden its base by including the former Conservative tendency and to some lesser extent the Liberal one too. Unlike the SPD which was refounded after the Second World War as a continuation of the pre-1933 party, the CDU/CSU was built on the support of two or three different political tendencies from the past. This radical departure from previous patterns of German party development was made possible by conditions after the collapse of the Third Reich. The Nazi state had of course disrupted the traditional party system, but its effect was less powerful on the two left-wing parties, where the remnants of an organisational network found an outlet in either underground activity or exile abroad, than on the parties of the right. The latter had been discredited by their compromises with Nazism, even affecting the behaviour of the Centre Party, during the last year before the estab-

lishment of Hitler's dictatorship. The common experience of Nazi
tyranny had drawn certain groups closer together, most notably Catholics
and Protestants, which had politically been hostile during the Weimar
Republic and before. Finally, the impact of socio-economic change
with the collapse of some traditional social structures as a consequence
of the Nazi regime[1] made it less likely that under a new democratic
system social divisions would be expressed as sharply as they had been
in pre-1933 Germany through political divisions.

The new tendency of Christian Democracy in post-war Germany
must first be examined in both its ideological and organisational forms
before any appraisal can be made of its success in establishing itself
politically during the years of Occupation. In looking at the ideology
of the very early CDU/CSU, two salient questions must be considered:
the extent to which different political tendencies were moulded together
in one new political movement; and, how far the CDU/CSU was in
fact ideological in its political outlook.

(a)   The Ideological Motivation behind Christian Democracy

Early Christian Democratic leaders inevitably viewed themselves as the
initiators of a new political movement. The phrase 'Die Neugestaltung
des deutschen Lebens' ('The Reshaping of German Life') was frequently
used in their speeches and quoted in the first proclamations of Christian
Democratic groups during 1945-6. A certain crusading fervour, illustrated
by such themes of party meetings as 'The CDU as a Work for God in
the Service of the Cross', reflected a mood of religious revival immediately after the German defeat in the Second World War, but in a wider
sense the party was responding to a general desire for national self-
purgation following the Nazi tyranny. CDU leaders attempted to channel
the sense of guilt into something positive by claiming they would lead
Germany to a better future, a promise contained in the 'Frankfurt
Principles' (September 1945), the manifesto of the CDU group founded
in the city of that name:

> We want a new Germany. A completely different one. . .different
> from that which existed before 1933 or before 1914. We simple do
> not wish to continue from where our predecessors had to leave
> off. . . [2]

The emphasis on the need to made a decisive break with the past and
the belief that Christian Democracy posed the only radical alternative
for Germany was illustrated by the following declaration made by

Lambert Lensing, first chairman and co-founder of the CDU in West-phalia, in September 1945:

> We are on the point of committing an act revolutionary in Germany,
> namely to attempt forming a united Christian political front. . .The
> belief in unity is overwhelming in our ranks and has made a clear
> breakthrough. Where complete agreement does not yet exist, we will
> strive and fight for it. We should not however flatter ourselves
> that with the founding of this party all will be mobilised who,
> we believe, belong to us. . .The concentration of forces must first
> of all take place. We are beginning this task because we believe that
> the past twelve years have welded us together, and we did not draw
> lessons from it.[3]

The predominantly utopian and moralistic tone of such early pronounce-ments suggests a freshness of approach typical of a political party in the initial stage of its existence with its need to differentiate itself from other political forces by establishing its own programme or 'philosophical' identity. Viewed more closely, the emerging principles of the new Christian Democracy already revealed signs of that 'loose-ness' and diversity of its ideology visible in later years. As one French commentator remarked at the time with some exaggeration, 'this party is socialist and radical in Berlin, clerical and conservative in Cologne, capitalist and reactionary in Hamburg and counter-revolutionary and particularistic in Munich'.[4]

Christian democracy was in its infancy an ideological patchwork, if only because it was basing itself not only on formerly divergent political tendencies but also on different regional political traditions. But any attempt to develop an integrated political approach would have occasioned serious problems of cohesion, for Christian Democracy had been created as a political movement as a result largely of a series of uncoordinated regional and local initiatives. The dispute over such a fundamental question as the name of the new party drew attention to the lack of cohesion among Christian Democrats immediately after the War. The term 'Union' in the CDU's name was apparently recommended by Andreas Hermes,[5] the co-founder of the party in Berlin, who through his experiences in the Resistance formed this preference as it would 'give the new entity a special appearance as a democratic counterpart to "the movement" of an authoritarian kind'.[6] There was a sense too of wanting to distance the CDU from the party development of the Weimar Republic, for the term implied the combination of different political tendencies and social groups even though 'Union' was generally understood to refer to the cooperation in politics of Catholics and Protestants. Nevertheless, several early regional and local groups of Christian Democrats chose their own names independently and settled on the title 'Party', such as the Christian Democratic Party established in Frankfurt in September 1945, the *Christlich-Demokratische Aufbaupartei* (Christian Democratic Reconstruction Party) formed by Hans Schlange-Schöningen in Schleswig-Holstein and the *Badische Christlich-Soziale Volkspartei* in south-west Germany.

Differences of opinion arose over the title 'Christian' on the grounds that it implied a monopoly of those values and beliefs and involved the use of Christ's name for political reasons and its adoption offended (anti-clerical) liberal circles in north Germany,[7] but generally the differences over the party's name seemed to represent variations on a like-minded theme. Official agreement on the title 'Christian Democratic Union' was reached at the nationwide conference of Christian Democratic leaders held at Bad Godesberg in December 1945. This decision placed a pressure on regional groups to adopt the common name, even though a few recalcitrant groups failed to conform for a time like the Baden party which finally renamed itself in the summer of 1947. Only in Bavaria did the regional formation of Christian Democrats adhere to a separate name, for in the view of the CSU's first chairman Josef Muller the name 'Christian Social Union' 'corresponded more to our conception of social evolution deriving from a Christian sense of responsibility in cultural, economic and above all social policy than the idea Christian Democratic'.[8]

Outside Bavaria, in which the CSU remained as a separate political party, the name 'Christian Democratic Union' acquired both a positive symbolic meaning and sufficient flexibility to provide a common umbrella under which the different political tendencies and regional groups could unite.[1] Christian Democratic ideology could not be characterised as a coherent body of political thought or interpretation comparable to the ideologies of the left, but even so certain conspicuous features or leitmotivs were perceptible in the original *Unionsgedanke* (concept of the Union). It is important to select these leitmotivs for individual mention, even though they did not represent a composite whole and to some extent overlapped.

1.   *Anti-Nazism: The Third Reich Viewed as the Highpoint of Atheism and Materialism*

Incipient Christian Democracy was fervently anti-Nazi, although less from a political ideological standpoint than a moralistic view. Typical of the pronounced anti-Nazi tone of CDU declarations during 1945-6 was the opening paragraphs of the *Kölner Leitsätze* (The 'Guiding Principles' of the Cologne CDU) issued in June 1945:

> National Socialism has plunged Germany into a catastrophe which is without parallel in her long history. It has covered the German name in the eyes of the whole world with shame and humiliation. All this would not have overwhelmed us if wide circles of our nation had not let themselves be governed by an avaricious materialism. In this way far too many fell victim to National Socialist demagogy, which promised each German a paradise on earth.[9]

The Neheim-Hüsten Programme of the British Zone CDU similarly called in March 1946 for the 'purging of National Socialist thinking', and like other statements of the party at the time totally rejected the values of Nazism because of its devaluation of individual human life and thought and its general effect on German society. The Ahlen economic programme of the CDU in the British zone (February 1947) was influenced by the belief that many abuses of the Nazi state had derived from the political misuse of the capitalist system. By 1948-9, however, anti-Nazi sentiments had virtually disappeared from the text of party programmes. This change reflected the growing pragmatism of the CDU's outlook towards the end of the decade.

2. *Christian Principles as the Basis of Political Life*

The full adoption of these principles was presented as the only real solution for Germany's future following the Third Reich. Just as the Neheim-Hüsten Programme advocated the 'return to the fundamentals of Christian culture of the West, the essence of which is the high view of the dignity of the person and the value of each individual being', so it continued:

> . . .the Christian outlook on life must again replace the materialistic outlook, and instead of the principles resulting from materialism must come the principles of Christian ethics. They must be the determining factor in the rebuilding of the state and in fixing the limits of its power, in the rights and duties of individuals, for economic and social life, for our culture and for the relationship between peoples.[10]

This general adherence to Christian values formed the basis for political cooperation between the two confessions of Catholicism and Protestantism after the War, particularly as the emphasis lent to them in party programmes was welcomed by leaders of both churches as an important move to combat the trend of secularisation in the postwar world.

3.   The Creation of a 'Confessional Bridge'

The most prominent motive behind the founding of the Christian Democratic movement was the desire to erase confession as a divisive factor in German politics by establishing, through the medium of a new political party, a unity between Catholics and Protestants never before achieved. This motive was based on a reassessment of political and religious realities: that the common threat to both religious communities posed by the Nazi system and the changed character of German society after the Third Reich meant that the real antagonism now lay between Christians and heathens rather than Catholics and Protestants, since the persecution had welded both denominations together. As Leo Schwering, first chairman of the Rhineland CDU, commented, 'the close collaboration of Catholics and Protestants, which occurred in the prisons, dungeons and concentration camps, brought to an end the old conflict and began to build bridges'.[11] The idea of confessional harmony in politics had been first advocated by Adam Stegerwald, the former Prussian Prime Minister and Christian Trade Unionist, who in his famous speech at the Essen Congress of Christian trade unions in November 1920 had proclaimed:

> What is needed is a union of the constructive forces in both the Catholic and Protestant camps . . . a strong Christian-national people's party, which the Protestants cannot create by themselves because they lack the necessary unity . . . and the Catholics also are too weak to organise themselves.[12]

Stegerwald was generally acknowledged by Christian Democrats as the father of the *Unionsgedanke*, and lived just long enough after the War to see others attempt to carry his ideas into practice. The year 1945 provided the long-sought opportunity for initiating a movement combining both confessions. The idea was linked to discussion about whether or not to refound the old Centre Party. The arguments against the latter possibility were outlined in a memorandum produced by Karl Zimmerman, a co-founder of the Cologne CDU, in November 1945.

Viewing the course of German politics over the past century, Zimmermann claimed that the Centre Party was now a thing of the past because it was seen by Protestants as a Catholic Party and was a reminder of the trauma of Bismarck's assault on the influence of the Catholic Church in the *Kulturkampf* of the 1870s. 'We are standing on the threshold of a new epoch with completely new religious and political relationships, and these demand a new formula for the political tasks of German Catholics.'[13] He pointed out that the Protestant Church was no longer closely associated with the state as it had been traditionally under the Hohenzollern monarchy, and that during the Nazi dictatorship it had not been a question of 'one confession or the other, but of the existence of the Christian faith in Germany altogether'.[14]

4. The Desire to Break Out of the 'Confessional Ghetto'

The arguments in favour of uniting the two confessions in politics were reinforced by party considerations, for it had been widely regarded as a major problem by Centre Party leaders that Roman Catholic voters, who were their only support in Weimar, had formed a minority of the German electorate until 1933, and even then not all Catholics had supported the Centre Party. This problem was very uppermost in Leo Schwering's mind, when he recorded in his diary on 10 April 1945, following discussions with similarly concerned members of the old party, that

> . . . we argued moreover that the Centre Party had for decades found itself in the Catholic ghetto. Only 36% of Catholics belonged to its camp. Where were the other 64% hiding? It was clear that the majority of Catholics had looked for and found another political home. That was an intolerable state of affairs and above all disquieting because this number was constantly declining and was sinking even further, so therefore the moment for assessing the situation had arrived since this minority had become alarming. Either one must fatalistically bend to this law, which was concealed in this diminishing number, or do something else, for the situation so far would be intolerable in the long run. In whatever way one might debate this subject, it is evident that something new must be created. If this does not happen, we shall have rejected the signal of fate at an important hour.[15]

The fact that CDU leaders, like Adenauer himself, made strenuous efforts to win the co-operation of Protestant political figures and activists, and with it the chance to appeal to the Protestant majority in the electorate, reveals how much they considered this the crucial step in establishing Christian Democracy as a political force in post-war Germany.

5.   *The Desire to Bridge the Divisions of German Society*

For many party leaders, the name 'Union' served not only a confessional purpose but also a social purpose. This motive of CDU/CSU founders derived not from any particular confessional doctrine but had a general appeal. It formed the basis of the Christian Democrats' claim that they represented a political force with broad appeal or *Volkspartei*. This wish to create a socially unifying force was for instance voiced by the group of Protestant leaders who established the party in Wuppertal. Pastor Hermann Lutze, a co-founder of the party there, said in his speech in August 1945 on the purpose of founding a Christian Democratic party:

> It would be an unutterable misfortune for our people, if our common Christian outlook did not have the power to overcome antagonisms . . . Everything therefore depends on whether we can establish links with the working class. The Christian Democratic party ought not to be simply a middle-class party, for the Christian worker must feel that his rights are just as much spoken for as any other class.[16]

6.   *The Desire to Simplify the Party System*

A further consideration which influenced the founders of the CDU/CSU was the turbulent history of the German party system. Memories of the Weimar Republic were of a period of many small parties riven with strife and confusion, quite apart from the economic chaos and the rise of a totalitarian movement. The importance of overcoming this political inheritance was mentioned by Ernst Lemmer[2] in an interview as one of his principal reasons for establishing the new party:

> . . . we thought in terms of a few large parties. The Weimar democracy was wrecked by the splintering of parties. We wanted parties which could really support the state. From this came the notion of concentrating democratic circles from the Christian camp, across confessions, in one large party of the progressive centre.[17]

Christian Democracy was presented as a momentous opportunity for breaking with former political patterns. This motive had much in common with the desire to heal social and confessional divisions, for in the Weimar Republic such divisions had featured in the structure of the party system. It also reflected a traditional German aversion to party political divisiveness.

7. The Formation of a 'Bourgeois Counterweight' to Socialism

The aim to consolidate the German party system also had its partisan reasons. The determination on the part of many early Christian Democrats to establish, in the words of Leo Schwering, a 'spiritual dam' against the 'socialist and collectivist ideas bursting forth everywhere'[18] was another stimulus to initiating a plan for a grand bourgeois party of all political forces 'to the right of Social Democracy'. This motive stemmed from a defensive concern about the superiority of the SPD's (and the KPD's) organisation and propaganda and the speed with which these two parties resumed their political activities immediately after the War. It was a compelling reason behind the founding of Christian Democratic groups in conservative Protestant areas, such as Westphalia where according to Lambert Lensing 'the rapid formation of the socialist parties after the collapse forced us to become active'.[19] In the Kiel area too, where former activists of the Weimar liberal bourgeois parties, the German Democratic Party (DDP) and the German People's Party (DVP), joined together in the name of Christian Democracy, the same concern was the starting-point for their activities.[20] This motive was uppermost also in traditional strongholds of the left. Gerd Bucerius from Hamburg announced that it was the 'hope of the CDU' there to become 'the great bourgeois party which could as a mass party face the socialists'.[21]

8. The Concept of Freedom and Opposition to Communism

The Christian Democratic idea of freedom, meaning in particular individual freedom in relation to the state, arose initially as a reaction to the Third Reich although it inevitably acquired anti-Communist overtones in the course of time. As the Guiding Principles of the CSU stated in December 1946:

> The Union rejects dictatorship and collectivism in all shapes and forms. Democracy is for us more than a form of government; it is an attitude of life, which has as its basis respect for human personality. Such a real democracy remains always aware of the rights of the minority when exercising the will of the majority . . . Each democracy

is presented with the danger of self-dissolution in that freedom is cast aside from the fear of dictatorship. Even more dangerous are those demagogues who under the cover of democracy attempt to establish their absolute power. Between both dangers lies real political freedom, for which we engage ourselves.[22]

The anti-Communist interpretation of the freedom concept was associated especially with the name of Adenauer, who had written in his famous letter of 21 August 1945 to his friend Karl Scharnagl, mayor of Munich: 'I beg you and the other gentlemen to bear in mind continually in your deliberations that only this planned concentration of all forces with a Christian and democratic basis can protect us from the dangers emanating from the East'.[23] The anti-Communist motive became more prominent during the time Adenauer was rising in the party and the growing impact of the Cold War on German politics in the late 1940s. It related to the idea of Christian values in politics, for as Adenauer argued at the 1948 congress of the British Zone CDU:

> When we examine the question whether we are entitled, indeed are obliged, to conduct politics on the basis of the Christian outlook, and glance across the German frontiers and see how things look in the world, then we find that in large areas an anti-Christian spirit rules which is the cause of present circumstances. Quite a large part of the world today is dominated by Soviet Russia . . . In this enormous area with several hundred millions of people there rules a thoroughly anti-Christian spirit — but not only that, for the fight against Christianity is willed there and carried out systematically.[24]

9.   *The Application of Christian Socialism*

The progressive leitmotiv in Christian Democratic ideology was represented by the advocates of progressive Catholicism who proposed ideas for the reform of German society after the War. They included Christian trade unionists and former left-wing Centre Party members and had as their centres of activity the three cities of Cologne, Frankfurt and Berlin with the Rhineland CDU as their main regional stronghold. Their chief emphasis was on giving a 'social content' to Christian Democracy, as became apparent in the first programmatic expression of these ideas in *Kölner Leitsätze* (June 1945). This declaration was formulated at a conference of Cologne CDU leaders held at the Dominican monastery of Walbaberg near Cologne under the guidance of Father Eberhard

Welty, the author of several works on Catholic philosophy. The 'Cologne Principles' proclaimed:

> Social justice and social love should protect a new people's community, which knows how to combine the God-given freedom of the individual and the claims of the community with the demands of the common good. Therefore we are advocating a real Christian socialism, which has nothing in common with false collectivist aims which fundamentally contradict the essence of man. It is however our firm will to set up a social order which accords just as much with the democratic tradition of the German past as with the breadth and spirit of Christian natural law.[25]

While this approach drew on principles of Christian socialism, it was motivated politically by the need for reordering political forces after the War. There was at an early stage vague discussion in a few cities of the formation of a progressive centre party bringing together some Social Democrats with left-wing Catholics from the old Centre Party and Christian trade unionists. This idea was favoured by the Frankfurt group of Catholic intellectuals led by Karl-Heinrich Knappstein, Walther Dirks and Eugen Kogon, whose programme the *Frankfurter Leitsätze* was presented under the title 'Socialism based on Christian Responsibility'.[26] In the Cologne CDU, such speculation was stimulated by the thought that with Germany's likely improvement in the coming years there was the need to build an obstacle to the threat from Communism.[27] The Ahlen economic programme of the British Zone CDU (February 1947), which sought a compromise between private capitalism and state socialism, was the highpoint of these Christian socialist tendencies, but the trend in the party from 1948 was in an economically conservative direction, which ensured the success of Erhard's plans in 1949. The ideas of progressive Catholics had never attracted wide support and were regarded with suspicion in Protestant circles. Adenauer's tart comment at a conference of party leaders in 1946 that the word 'socialism' had associations with class struggle and was 'not applicable' even with a Christian outlook[28] proved to be more representative of feeling in the party as a whole.

10. *The Principles of the Social Market Economy*

Whereas progressive ideas had featured centrally in the discussion among Christian Democrats over economic policy alternatives in the immediate aftermath of the War, the new concept of the social market economy became the vehicle for Christian Democratic economic ideas from 1948. Its exponent was Ludwig Erhard, later Federal Minister for Economic Affairs, who persuasively explained the principles of the social market economy at the congress of the British Zone CDU in August 1948, again at a session of its executive committee the following February, and received the support of Adenauer. It became adopted as the party's official policy in the *Düsseldorfer Leitsätze* in July 1949. The essential features of his proposals were a principled objection to the values of a planned economy, restraining the excesses of private capitalism through the independent control of monopolies, free competitive production and social justice for everyone.[29] Erhard saw this as a departure from the old-style free economy, for he underlined that his new form of market economy would reward individual achievement but at the same time protect economically weak elements in society.

11.   The Concept of Federalism

The question of the structure of the future West German state provoked serious ideological conflict within the CDU/CSU. The cause of federalism was championed most ardently by the Bavarian CSU, which drew on a strong sense of regional identity. The CSU's declaration of principles in 1946 had proclaimed:

> We are federalists from conviction and experience. We reject the centralistic unity-state as much as sterile separatism . . . The German federal state, which we are striving for, should arise from the voluntary union of the individual *Länder*.[30]

The most pronounced advocate of federalism was Hans Ehard, later Bavarian Minister-President, who viewed it as the basis of what he called an 'organic democracy'. Sympathy for federalist ideas was also voiced among South-West German leaders of the CDU, who combined with the CSU to form a discussion forum called the Ellwangen Circle for the purpose of combating 'Prussian' tendencies among North German Christian Democrats,[31] for the latter diverged over the degree of federalism necessary. Federalist ideas gained a certain force among South German party leaders from their concern at the growing importance of the British Zone CDU in the whole party, and were sufficiently strong to compel the latter to comply with some of their proposals over the Basic Law in 1949.

It is clear from this analysis of the key elements in the early ideology of Christian Democracy that they were often individually characteristic of different tendencies in various areas of Germany. In some cases, like Christian Socialism and federalism, they conflicted with other viewpoints elsewhere in the CDU/CSU. The most commonly held features of its ideology were the idea of working on the basis of Christian principles, the importance given to the concept of freedom and, where applicable, the wish to form a 'confessional bridge' between Catholics and Protestants. Generally speaking, the overriding feature of its early ideology was the firm belief in the CDU/CSU that Christian Democracy was a new and modern political force, which would offer Germany the best chance of departing from her recent past and moving to the future.

It was also evident from the composition of Christian Democratic ideology at this stage that its many diverse strands were not closely linked. Strictly it was a misnomer to refer to a 'Christian Democratic ideology', for it lacked that essential feature of an ideology, a coherent interpretation of politics expressed through a distinguishable programme. The many CDU/CSU declarations during the 1945/8 period were not so much programmatic enunciations as statements of principle and concepts about the future. They provided at best vague political guidelines. This ideological incohesion later facilitated the CDU/CSU's appeal to diverse electoral groups. Typical of Adenauer's own cynical view of party programmes was his remark in 1949 that they have 'no eternal value', followed by his suggestion that Erhard's ideas on the social market economy should be reprinted as election publicity.[32] When Adenauer became party leader, the utopian content typical of early CDU/CSU declarations had gradually been replaced by the espousal of concrete policy ideas. This reflected a changed outlook in the party expressed in the following comment of a CDU newspaper in South Württemberg, the *Schwäbische Zeitung*, which illustrates the incorporation of pragmatism as a conservative value:

We ought to have the courage to profess ourselves conservative people open to all demands of our time. That means the freedom to solve present needs by means of practical measures taking each case on its merits without being encumbered by a party doctrine . . . The Union can accomplish such a policy without a programme. It enjoys the real freedom of acting if it remains conscious of its conservative basis.[33]

The CDU/CSU had developed into a centre-right conservative political force of an unprecedented kind in the history of political tendencies in

German politics, containing as it did Catholic political and liberal elements as well as traditional conservative ones. But it was not a consciously ideological political force, even though certain of its ideological motivations — notably its anti-Communism and the social market economy — remained uppermost, because its ideological values did not knit together into a cohesive political outlook.

(b)   The Founders of the New Party

The crucial initial test of the CDU/CSU's prospects as a viable political force was the willingness of the surviving leaders of the Weimar parties, who were still politically influential, to promote its interests. Many such leaders remained, for the Weimar Republic had collapsed only just over a decade before. Old party allegiances among conservative circles reappeared in 1945 after the years of hibernation under the Nazi regime, and it was not clear in that year what the outcome would be. But the tragedy of Weimar and the trauma of the Third Reich provided an overwhelming impetus for Christian Democratic initiatives in many politically decisive areas of the country, and for overcoming a cautious reluctance elsewhere.

By far the most important rival political force of the CDU was the Centre Party, which was refounded after the War in North-Rhine Westphalia as a continuation of the Weimar party.[34] Both parties wished to control the Catholic electorate, but the CDU had two advantages: first, many former parliamentary deputies and functionaries of the Weimar Centre Party were motivated by the aforementioned ideological considerations and took the initiative in influential Catholic areas in establishing local groups of the CDU; and secondly, they acted rapidly within months or even weeks of Germany's capitulation. Cologne was a potential focal point for this competition for Catholic votes, because it had been one of the main political and organisational centres of the old Centre Party and because of its influence on developments elsewhere in the Rhineland. Leo Schwering, co-founder of the CDU in that city, commented as follows in his account of the early party:

> We had to attack as quickly as possible and at the decisive place, in Cologne, the former leading city of the Centre Party, and in the bastions of the Centre Party in the Rhineland and Westphalia. There lived here 70 per cent of its old loyal voters. If we succeeded in weakening the Centre Party decisively, then the struggle in the rest of Germany would be settled in favour of the new party.[35]

The desire to establish a party with a broad political base including Protestants was the decisive consideration here. The Cologne initiative taken as early as June 1945 was successful,[3] and was followed swiftly by similar moves in Aachen and Bonn. Schwering, for instance, was able to make use of personal contacts he had made during the Nazi period as an intermediary between opposition circles of Catholic workers and the Kolpinghaus, the Catholic workingman's association, in Cologne.

In several rural districts of Westphalia, the CDU faced stronger resistance from supporters of the refounded Centre Party. These remained strongholds of that party for a while, but after some hesitation a number of prominent regional Centre Party leaders from Weimar times decided to back the CDU. Joseph Kannengiesser, former general secretary of the Centre Party in north Westphalia, was initially seen as general secretary of the refounded Centre Party, but left it to work for the Christian Democratic effort in Westphalia. Johannes Gronowski, formerly a leader of the Centre Party *Fraktion* in the Prussian Landtag, joined with other leading Centre Party members, with whom he had maintained contact during the Third Reich, to support the CDU in Westphalia.[36]

Such defections to the CDU were influenced by its general success in establishing itself. The CDU was able to make fast progress in the Rhineland, for example, because it enjoyed a ready-made organisational network there owing to the fact that so many district executive secretaries of the Weimar Centre Party and other Weimar Catholic organisations had worked for the CDU as soon as it was refounded.[37] What finally clinched the contest in favour of the CDU over the Centre Party generally in North-Rhine Westphalia was the former's superior propaganda machine which began to show its effectiveness in elections from 1947, the latter's unimpressive leadership personnel and further defections to the CDU. The absorption of the Centre Party by the CDU in North-Rhine Westphalia, the most populous state in the Western Occupation zones after the War, provided the CDU with a strong political and organisational base in the country.

A similar preference for the CDU shown by the vast majority of pre-1933 Centre Party leaders was a very influential factor in other Catholic regions of the country. In Lower Saxony, for example, old Centre Party circles opted swiftly for the CDU in the districts of south Oldenburg, Osnabrück and Hildesheim.[38] Examined more closely at the grass-roots level, the response to the CDU here depended as much on local historical and political traditions as it did on the support of influential activists.[4]

In the Rhineland-Palatinate, the CDU faced the problem of the reluctance of Catholic circles to discard their former allegiance to the Centre
Party. This difficulty illustrated that the common experience of Nazism
did not inevitably bring Catholics and Protestants together. Old confessional antagonisms reappeared after the War in Trier and Rhine Hesse
(including the city of Mainz) in the context of local political traditions
to make the situation less open to a new initiative.[39] Eventually,
the success of the CDU in other regions of Germany influenced trends
in the Rhineland-Palatinate, where the CDU's Landtag election triumph
in 1947 finally settled that problem.

The initiation of a Christian Democratic party in Bavaria followed a
different course from anywhere else in Germany, and resulted in the
formation of a separate party from the CDU. The Christian Social
Union (CSU) had as a basis the Weimar Bavarian People's Party (BVP),
the equivalent there of the Centre Party. Many prominent BVP figures,
such as Fritz Schäffer (BVP chairman, 1929-33) and Anton Pfeiffer
(its general secretary, 1928-33), co-founded the CSU. The problem in
Bavaria was not a contest of different tendencies represented by an old
and a new party, but the development of such a contest within the CSU
itself. It failed for some years to integrate both those who wanted to
model it as a reformed BVP or Catholic party and others led by Josef
Müller, the CSU's first chairman, who sought to direct it towards inter-
confessional cooperation in line with Christian Democratic groups
elsewhere in Germany. The problem was complicated with the rise at the
end of the 1940s of the Bavarian Party (BP), which for a brief time
enjoyed success as a regionalist Catholic movement aimed at exploiting
discontent with the CSU.[a]

While a distinct sense of commitment to change accounted for the
various Christian Democratic initiatives, some conflict arose between
ideological motivation and traditional local or regional political attach-
ments. Once again, the CDU's ability in overcoming these difficulties
owed much to the response of influential personalities and groups
towards the new party. Such problems were particularly apparent in
Protestant regions. Here the CDU did not face a direct contest with one
traditional party, as over the control of the Catholic electorate, but
rather the problem of amalgamating different and sometimes conflicting
political forces which until 1933 had represented the right-of-centre,
involving a test of the CDU's integrative capacity to unite across confessional barriers and attract conservative bourgeois circles. The CDU

a   See below chapter 10, pp. 322 and 329-30.

was successful in forming a viable political base in most Protestant regions, except where there was an entrenched Liberal tradition such as in parts of Lower Saxony, Württemberg and Baden chiefly because of anti-clerical feelings. Anti-socialist solidarity was usually sufficient to knit these various bourgeois groups together even if at first rather loosely. In Berlin, a city with a strong left-wing tradition, members of the former German Democratic Party (DDP) allied with those of the Centre Party to set up the CDU.[5] In Hamburg, also a stronghold of the SPD, the local CDU owed its existence less to former Centre Party activists (a minority element there during Weimar) than to the initiative of local citizens' associations like the 'non-party' *Vaterstädtischer Bund* (Native City Association), a number of prominent figures in Hanseatic society, a group of independent city councillors and generally to to support from high bourgeois circles.[40] In other areas, leading members from the pre-Nazi national conservative DNVP provided the crystallising force: Hans Schlange-Schöningen, formerly a Reich Minister of Agriculture, was the leading light of the Christian Democratic founding group in East Holstein; Friedrich Holzapfel, mayor of Herford (1945-8) helped to initiate the CDU in Westphalia; and Robert Lehr, formerly DNVP mayor of Düsseldorf (1924-33), was a co-founder of the CDU there. An implicit factor assisting the establishment of these CDU groups was the ineffectiveness of traditional bourgeois parties in Weimar and the loss of their political credit, especially because of its compromises with Nazism during 1930-3.

The success of these initiatives followed therefore from a combination of varied local circumstances exploited and developed within the general framework of the variegated ideological motives which inspired Christian Democracy. In areas where confessional attitudes affected political affiliation, the success in bridging the religious divide owed as much to the interest of leading (Protestant) politicians in forming a confessional bridge as it did to the readiness of former Centre Party leaders to be conciliatory on the basis of common Christian principles. A meeting of leading Protestants in Düsseldorf at the end of 1945 expressed concern about the political dangers of a confessional split, and the nature of their deliberations, somewhat theological in tone, revealed a strong ideological attraction for the tenets of Christian Democracy.[41] In the Ruhr city of Essen the idea of inter-confessional cooperation germinated among a group called the Wattenscheid Circle formed during the War, consisting of figures like Gustav Heinemann (later mayor of Essen, 1946-9), who had played a part in the Resistance to Nazism, and a senior police official who had warned Catholics and Protestants of actions by the Gestapo.[42] Sometimes the initiative for founding a CDU group was taken by Protestant circles. A prominent case was the founding of the CDU in Wuppertal, where the stimulus came from Otto Schmidt, a Protestant lawyer who had been attracted by National Socialism at the beginning of the Third Reich but later broke with it, and his long-time friend Pastor Hermann Lutze, who had been close to the anti-Nazi Confessional Church and was a strong advocate of a 'Christian party'.[43] The Wuppertal group was influenced by the ideas of the Barmen Declaration of 1934, in which the newly established Confessional Church of Protestants had opposed the totalitarian claims of the Nazi regime and its intention to form a Reich Church. This group had difficulties at first with reconciling traditional confessional feelings, so they attempted to allay doubts among broader Protestant circles by the deliberate avoidance of Catholic terminology in CDU declarations.[44] The closest approximation to a Protestant political party during the Weimar period had been the CSVD (literally: Christian Social People's Service), many of whose activists now played an influential role in representing the Protestant interests in the CDU during negotiations with former Centre Party circles in Lower Saxony and north Württemberg. In Hanover, for example, two Protestant figures played an important part in founding the CDU there — Adolf Cillien, a member of the Lutheran Church consistory who became the first local chairman of the CDU there, and Arnold Fratzscher, who had been a CSVD leader in Mecklenburg and a lay representative at the synods of the Confessional Church.[45]

It was clear from these various initiatives that ideological considerations were crucial, but alone were not decisive. For instance, the attitude of Church leaders was basic to the success of uniting and integrating the confessions. The declared preference for the CDU by several prestigious figures in the Catholic Church gave some impetus to the new party. Bishop Galen of Münster, a focus of moral opposition to the Nazi regime during the War, exercised his influence among the cautious conservative population in Westphalia in favour of the CDU so that Leo Schwering, the Cologne party leader, attributed to him much of the credit for swinging opinion there against the Centre Party.[46] Other Catholic Church leaders who lent their name to the cause of the CDU were Archbishop Frings of Cologne in the Rhineland and Paul Simon, provost of Paderborn cathedral, in Westphalia. The picture among Protestant Church leaders was one of greater reserve towards the CDU. Ecclesiastical figures who showed the greatest willingness to support a political alliance of Protestants with Catholics predictably had been active in the Confessional Church. A prominent example was Bishop Otto Dibelius of Berlin, who in a letter written in December 1945 claimed that 'the Evangelical Church today finds understanding and positive support almost only from the Christian Democratic Union of Germany' even though the Church could not ally itself with any one party.[47] But although the Treysa Conference of German Protestant churches (August 1945) had given its blessing to 'the endeavours already set in motion in many places to erase political conflict between Protestantism and Catholicism', several prominent religious voices expressed hostility about such an alliance, notably Karl Barth, the eminent theologian and spiritual leader of the Confessional Church:

> . . . if we were to co-operate with them, we should always be at a disadvantage — whereas we would seek to be guided by the Word of God in practical political questions, the Catholics would make their decisions on the basis of natural law and would take us for a ride before we had reached a conclusion in our deliberations.[48]

This 'cultural' Protestant view of mistrust towards the experiment of the CDU was not generally representative of Protestant ecclesiastical opinion in Germany, although it helped to sway feelings away from the initial outlook of open-mindedness, by drawing attention to memories of 'political Catholicism' in that country and feelings that the new confessional cooperation might deteriorate in the course of time.

Despite the varied opinions among the ecclesiastical elites, the early CDU/CSU gained sufficient positive approval from influential church leaders to make its idea of a 'confessional bridge' seem a reasonable possibility. Indeed, the support it received from such quarters acted as a temporary substitute for non-existent party organisation in winning public support. At this stage, the CDU/CSU had the characteristics of a political movement rather than a political party, with little organisational structure and identified by its attachment to certain (albeit variegated) political values. There was no central directing force, although several cities like Cologne, Berlin and Munich were prominent focal points for early Christian Democratic activity. The only factor which unified the different regional and local groups during 1945-6 was their attachment to the concept of Christian Democracy.

(c)   The CDU/CSU Begins to Establish its Political Position

The CDU/CSU had been formed as a loose political grouping with a variegated ideological base and owed its existence to different regional and local initiatives with little coordination. The Bavarian CSU remained as a separate political party from the CDU although in alliance with it, while the latter did not become a national party in the institutional sense of acquiring a formal organisation co-ordinating its regional branches until 1950. In looking beyond the initiatives of 1945-6, the question remains how the CDU/CSU managed to consolidate itself politically in the later 1940s. It faced then two main political rival forces: the reestablished SPD, already well-organised and optimistic about becoming the ruling party in post-war Germany; and the smaller parties of the right, which because of Allied licensing policy did not materialise until the end of the decade although they then presented a temporary but serious challenge to the unconsolidated CDU/CSU. In spite of the momentum generated by the prompt and appealing initiatives of its founders, the CDU/CSU faced many problems in converting public opinion to its cause. One must therefore examine to what extent the grass-roots supported the direction given by the founders of Christian Democracy, and what formative influences moulded the character of the CDU/CSU. These questions will be discussed with reference to: the efforts by the CDU/CSU to establish a 'confessional bridge' in politics; attempts to build a party organisation; the impact of Allied occupation policies; its early electoral performance; and developments in the party leader-ship.

In trying to create an enduring political alliance between Catholics and Protestants, the Christian Democrats were defying traditional trends in German political opinion. The antagonism between Catholics and Protestants had historical roots reaching back to the Reformation and Counter-Reformation. They had been revived by Bismarck's attack on the Catholic Church in the 1870s, and had thereafter been expressed in party political terms by the formation of the Catholic Centre Party in opposition to this threat. Up to the Third Reich, confession had been the single most influential voting determinant in electoral patterns in Germany. While members of both churches' elites were conscious of the unifying effect of the Third Reich experience for the two confessions, rank-and-file Catholics and Protestants did not necessarily view the problem in the same light. While the Catholic Church hierarchy gave its general blessing to the new party, local Catholic priests did not automatically accept the advice of their bishops to do the same. In some localities of West-phalia the clergy showed a preference for the refounded Centre Party at first, and even as late as October 1947 the Rhineland CDU complained that 'the connection between the new Centre Party and a row of Catholic priests' residences is unmistakable'.[49]

The attitude of local priests had to be related to the local environment in which they worked. Confessional feelings were still deeply engrained especially in areas of mixed religious communities. The early records of the south Württemberg CDU noted the following on the problem of overcoming traditional Catholic antagonisms towards Protestants:

> Let us have no illusions about it, for there predominates in all parts of the country in all zones plenty of mistrust between Catholics and Protestants. And this mistrust is growing instead of diminishing. It is not surprising with regard to the Protestants, for the English radio for example has presented the CDU as the 'Catholic party' to its countrymen. Centre Party people of the oldest and most renowned provenance are likewise busily engaged. The examples of this are legion. On the other hand, for a great number of the oldest Catholics the Protestant is at best a co-Christian . . . They look down at the poor Protestant brother rather compassionately and reckon politically that they can put him neatly in second place. Protestant voting fodder for a successor party to the Centre Party! However much this attitude towards the CDU is basically wrong, some circles are partial to it. Our task is therefore to disperse this mistrust, to demonstrate the genuine loyalty of both confessional blocs to each other in practice and to undo the hope of the enemies of the CDU for a split.[50]

The attitudes mentioned by the writer inhibited the efforts of the CDU to build a confessional alliance at the local level, although sometimes it was simply a problem of making the idea intelligible to ordinary people. Paul Bausch, a co-founder of the CDU in Württemberg, discovered that the aim of a 'confessional bridge' appeared too 'intellectual' in localities he visited with a colleague:

> During that time I went with Josef Andre to completely Catholic villages in the district of Aalen. In one village inn many people were assembled including a number of Catholic priests from the surrounding area who had come to hear about what was to be done.

I presented to the meeting the view that we had to make a totally
new start and that we should be guided by the Word of God . . .
Then I attempted to elucidate the aims and principles of our new
party. Afterwards we sat together and discussed the matter. Josef
Andre sat at the neighbouring table with the priests and I heard
exactly what was said. Afterwards I entered into conversation with
the priests. They told me I should really not have spoken about
matters that came within their competence. They said they were
astonished, as a layman should simply not concern himself with
theological questions. I soon noticed that for these gentlemen
the whole idea was new and unusual.[51]

Caution and suspicion of the new accounted for the initial reluctance
by ordinary Catholics to espouse the CDU, influenced as they were,
especially in smaller communities, by the attitude of the priests.
Ultimately, the influence of the Catholic bishops counted with the
priests, although they could not compete with entrenched local
viewpoints. Such reluctance was even more apparent among ordinary
Protestants because of the greater reserve of Evangelical church
leaders towards the new party. As one member of the church
consistory in Stuttgart, an early supporter of the CDU there,
described the situation in north Württemberg:

It all depends on what experiences the members of the Protestant community have with the Catholic Church. Where
there exists ill-will or conflict, the willingness to vote CDU
declines appreciably and especially in united areas one
frequently hears the comment: 'On no account can we continue voting for the CDU'. At the same time there are
communities where convinced Protestants see without
question their party as the CDU, above all where their
associations play a leading role.[52]

The problem of this confessional alliance in relation to the political
position of the new party received much attention in CDU leadership
circles during these first years after the War. Konrad Adenauer, chairman of the British Zone CDU, had taken considerable pains to woo
Protestants, but had to confess his concern about the frequent lack of
response he had met. In an address to the Rhineland party executive
in December 1947, he touched on this matter:

There are some grounds for concern about the relationship of both confessions to each other. Negotiations have already taken place . . . but there will be further discussions in which I am participating. Those between the representatives of the Evangelical Church and of the CDU are not proceeding very satisfactorily. This is for me, as a Catholic, completely incomprehensible. I await this first conference with the gentlemen of the Evangelical Church with a certain apprehension, because in effect I do not understand the whole thing. I was recently in Marburg for a discussion and could observe a certain guarded attitude among the Protestant circles. This resistance which is due to the SPD can be noticed everywhere. And we must naturally respect the opinion of certain Protestant theological groups that they would lose the Church's influence on the working classes, if they associated too strongly with the CDU . . . [53]

The leaders of the CDU attempted to mitigate the problem of such attitudes by paying strict attention to 'confessional arithmetic' in appointments to internal positions even to the extent of overproportional representation, in the hope of attracting more Protestants into the party. The executive committee of the Hesse CDU, for example, consisted of a Catholic chairman and a Protestant deputy chairman while the 16 ordinary members were divided equally between the two confessions.[54] Catholic political leaders like Karl Arnold (CDU minister-president in North-Rhine Westphalia from 1947), Joseph Gockeln (another prominent figure in that state's politics), Leo Schwering and Adenauer himself made demonstrative gestures of goodwill and cooperation, while party reports abounded at this time with proud references about the consideration given to Protestants in leading positions in the CDU. An illustration of the importance which party leaders placed on the fair representation of both confessions was the 1947 membership report of the Rhineland CDU that 'in the Landtag elections of April 1947 26 per cent of the nominated CDU candidates were Protestant, of the elected CDU deputies 19.3 per cent are Protestant'[55] in this predominantly Catholic region. Despite these efforts, the 'confessional bridge' sought by the Christiam Democrats had not yet been firmly established. That development came in the 1950s once the CDU/CSU was a governing party.

The CDU found it necessary to strengthen its public appeal by attempting to coordinate its activities, but it remained in an embryonic institutional state during the Occupation years. The CDU was not during this time a national party in the basic organisational sense, for it had no administrative structure, it elected no national party chairman nor did it possess a national executive organ responsible for policy discussion or even a national party headquarters. Nevertheless, a sense of urgency inspired party activists, who organised local and regional election campaigns from 1946, to present a viable and strong alternative to other parties, especially the SPD. Modest steps were taken to set up some formal channels of coordination, but these were weak due to the autonomy of the regional associations of the CDU and the lack of responsibility to any central body. There was as yet no pressure from a national election to do otherwise, and also the struggle between various leaders to become the dominant figure in the CDU meant that any attempt by any one of them to initiate a central organisation was checkmated by his rivals.

The first national conference of CDU leaders took place at Bad Godesberg in December 1945 and resulted in the opening of a secretariat for the British Zone CDU in Düsseldorf, as well as agreement on the formation of a zone co-ordination committee in Frankfurt am Main. There was some reluctance in implementing the latter decision because of the independence of the CDU and CSU groups from the various Occupation zones, but a further meeting of CDU/CSU representatives at Königstein (February 1947) made the final decision to form the Working Association of the CDU/CSU (*Arbeitsgemeinschaft der CDU/CSU*) as a so-called 'steering organ' but really with no influence on party policy. The resolution stipulated that the CDU or CSU from each of the four Occupation zones would have equal representation on its co-ordination committee and that five working committees on agriculture, constitutional matters, refugee questions, economic and social problems and cultural issues should be formed.[56] An interzonal office was opened shortly afterwards in Frankfurt, administered by a general secretary who was Bruno Dörpinghaus, business manager of the CDU in Hesse since 1945.

There being no effective central party machine, the burden of organisational work and decisions devolved to the regional branches of the CDU. It was not therefore surprising to encounter much variation in the state of party organisation throughout the country. Certain common problems did however present themselves to party organisers everywhere. The CDU lacked in its early years an experienced reservoir of activist personnel, it met difficulties in attracting membership and it was frequently short of the necessary facilities.

Unlike the SPD, which could count on its pre-1933 organisational tradition and network, the CDU had to start with the rudiments of

party organisation. It had relied in the beginning on the enthusiasm of
its founders and often on their previous experience as members of
Weimar parties, but their forte was not usually organisational talent.
Local party activists came from multifarious political backgrounds,
which meant that habits of party solidarity had not had time to
develop. There was such a shortage of organisational expertise that new
party members were surprised to find themselves appointed to offices
in the CDU. Even people who were not party members at all were
occasionally given positions. The most serious deficiency was in party
speakers. Leo Schwering observed that 'in Westphalia one heard the
complaint that trained speakers were wanting; the lacuna of 1933-45
made itself disastrously evident, and it could only be closed through
systematic training.'[57] Some effort was devoted to reducing this
shortage by instituting courses for party speakers, but again the
success of this depended on the efficiency of the particular regional
organisation.

One special problem facing the CDU was the strong aversion
prevalent among the middle classes towards joining a political party
as such, an attitude which derived from the stigma attached to the
word 'party' through its automatic association with the Third Reich
period. The bourgeoisie had, more than other sections of the
population, been politically scalded through their involvement in the
Nazi movement, and were regularly reminded of this unpleasant fact
by the denazification programme of the Occupation authorities
which attempted to root out former members of the NSDAP. The
CDU obviously saw the middle classes as the main source of its
membership, but it found their inhibition about the party label
virtually insurmountable. One young party worker in Bad
Godesberg commented:

> It was very difficult to acquire members. At the urging of my
> former class-teacher, headmaster Schiefer, I was sent to recruit
> members. Priests of both denominations had given Schiefer the
> names of people who were approachable. I said to them that the
> SPD was ahead by a short lead. Some of them replied they were
> fed up and wanted to think long and hard about joining in. Most
> of them rejected the idea, and only a small number were ready
> to cooperate.[58]

The CDU sought to overcome this deep-rooted feeling by persistent
publicity. Circulars issued by regional party offices were full of

exhortations such as the following from the Rhineland CDU in May 1946:

> Recruitment is impeded by a widespread mood which shows
> little inclination to become the 'member' of a party – at every
> suitable opportunity in large public meetings of the party it must
> be pointed out how important it is that the CDU can show as many
> registered members as possible.[59]

A further organisational problem encountered by the CDU was the
lack of basic facilities like office equipment, publicity materials and
a party press. Naturally, the other political parties were inflicted with
similar difficulties, although the SPD already possessed some expertise
here from former times. The CDU had no party press worthy of the
name, so it had to rely on semi-independent newspapers which
shared its viewpoint. Even their support was questionable, for as the
regional office of the Rhineland CDU complained in May 1946: 'So
far no help from the press; "our" newspapers are colourless, they make
little or no propaganda for the party.'[60] The shortage of paper in the
years after the War helped to cripple the party's own publicity efforts
such as issuing pamphlets, leaflets and posters. The scarcity of basic
amenities was illustrated by the regional headquarters of the Rhineland
CDU, which still possessed only one typewriter, at the end of
1947, and had only recently acquired a motor-car for party use.[61] One
fundamental reason for these difficulties was the party's inability to meet
the vast expense involved in creating an organisational infrastructure
at a time of general scarcity. Matters were not helped by the immediate
hardship caused by the currency reform of 1948, which had the effect
of reducing party membership and blighting the circulation of party
newspapers and other publications.[62]

The CDU had therefore to function with a minimum of organisation
in most areas of Germany. It really had no party machine (*Apparat*) in
the sense that this implied a certain degree of political professionalism,
so that party activists had to rely on the willing support of lay confessional associations and also, when forthcoming, the readiness of
priests to use their influence in their localities. The extent of the
organisational disarray did however vary across the country, depending
on the availability of experienced activists and the energy of key
personalities in the regional party offices.

The best organised regional branch in the three Western zones was
the Rhineland CDU, which used the available talent of former Centre
Party activists to institute a system of 39 district party secretariats,

which was fortified by the training of those party secretaries not versed in this kind of work. Regular contact was maintained between them and the headquarters of the Rhineland CDU in Cologne, run by Dr Hans Schreiber whose efficiency as regional business manager had been proven in his stint as local secretary for the Centre Party in Düsseldorf during the Weimar period. Schreiber was assisted by a group of 12 permanent party officials including one deputy business manager, a treasurer, an archivist, a specialist in youth questions and somebody responsible for propaganda. The tasks envisaged for the Rhineland party headquarters included the registration of members, the compilation of organisation reports and frequent visits by members of its staff to supervise the activities of the district branches.[63] This case was untypical of the CDU then, and was the only instance of something akin to a party machine.

The third factor influencing the general development of the CDU/ CSU was the impact on it of Allied occupation policy and of general political conditions in occupied Germany. The view of the Western Allies on political parties consisted of a desire to school Germans in the ways of democratic politics allowing them to manage their internal affairs, but also a determination to keep a watchful eye in case of the emergence of unwelcome tendencies. Political parties were in the words of one contemporary British observer 'expected to behave like goldfish in a bowl, although, as the good faith of the main political figures was thought to be established, the regulations were less rigidly observed'.[64] The occupation policy towards political activity and the granting of party licences differed however from zone to zone. The US authorities were the most forthcoming in encouraging party activity by the Germans, while the British were accused by CDU circles of showing a partiality in favour of the SPD since there was a Labour Government in power in Britain. No doubt this feeling was exacerbated by Adenauer's rough treatment when he was dismissed as Mayor of Cologne in 1945 by the British authorites, although the British attitude stemmed less from a conscious discrimination against the CDU than from a general concern that German conservatives might once again provide a cover for a revival of nationalist politics. Leo Schwering complained after his experience of contacts with British officers that 'the Germans could not avoid the impression that they were in a school'.[65] The belief persisted among CDU leaders that they were singled out for special scrutiny by the British, for as Arnold Fratzscher commented in the case of Lower Saxony 'he who did not support the SPD, or in the beginning also the KPD, was regarded as a "conservative" and closely scrutinised to see whether he was sufficiently progressive'.[66] In the Soviet zone, the Christian Democratic organisation with its focal point in the city of Berlin spread rapidly at first under the energetic leadership of Andreas Hermes and later Jakob Kaiser, acquiring 200,000 members by June 1946 based in Saxony, Thuringia, Mecklenburg, Brandenburg as well as Berlin.[67] But Kaiser's hopes for creating a 'bridge policy' between East and West Germany by acting as the liaison between party leaders of all zones were dashed, when the Soviet authorities replaced their early encouragement of party activity by plans aimed at establishing a Communist regime in their zone and deposed Kaiser as chairman of the Eastern zone CDU in 1947.

Western Allied policy did not substantially hinder the progress of the CDU, even though there were differences of approach between the occupation zones in the granting of licences for political parties. The only serious obstruction came from the French authorities in south-west Germany, who opposed the formation of a zonal party organisation out of a wish to discourage centralism. As a result , the CDU developed there as a collection of regional organisations (*Landesverbände*), whose lack of solidarity was further increased by rivalries based on traditional provincial loyalties as in areas of Baden and areas of Württemberg. While the French authorities discouraged the reestablishment of the Centre Party because they saw it as 'centralistic' and 'Prussian', their interference in the formulation of party programmes and in one case their encouragement of a provincial party — the Baden Christian Social People's Party, which did not adopt the title CDU until 1948 — in place of a CDU organisation slowed down the formation of the CDU in their zone.[68]

Another problem for the CDU was the divisive effect on party organisation and intra-party co-operation of the boundaries between the three Occupation zones, and the boundaries of the states (*Länder*) within these zones. Since the CDU was a new party, it had to take more note of the realities of these boundaries than the SPD which had previously operated on a national level in Germany, and was not so inhibited by them. The importance of the *Land* boundaries as an obstacle to party cohesion was least serious in the British Zone, where, as Adenauer pointed out at a meeting of the Rhineland CDU executive in Devember 1947:

> . . . we have a good co-ordination in the Zonal Committee in contrast to the situation in the American Zone, where there are

considerable divergencies. So far there is lacking in that case the common superstructure: Bavaria, Hesse and Baden-Württemberg are all a law unto themselves. The picture in those places is not what we imagine. As far as the coordination of all zones in the Working Association (*Arbeitsgemeinschaft*) is concerned, the state of affairs is not satisfactory. The blame for this lies in the diverse mentality in the zones. A further reason is that the General Secretariat in Frankfurt/Main is not correctly staffed, or else does not perform correctly. But for the time being nothing can be changed. We must await the outcome of the London Conference. There is nevertheless the most urgent need to form closer party ties within the *Länder*.[69]

Another aspect of Occupation conditions was simply the poor state of communications in Germany. War destruction had devastated most systems of transport, while normal amenities like the telephone and the postal systems were also badly affected so the party had to rely heavily in the early days on contacts at the personal level.[6] These conditons helped to explain the independent and unco-ordinated character of the Christian Democratic organisation after the War.

The acid test of the CDU/CSU's political strength was of course its appeal to the electorate. Some party leaders viewed the prospect of elections with apprehension particularly as they lacked any elaborate organisation to mobilise public support. As Paul Bausch of the Württemberg CDU remarked about the elections to the Constituent Assembly there in July 1946: 'nobody knew how the Protestant population would react to the formation of this new party which was cooperating with the Catholic world'.[70] This indicated the question of how far pre-1933 voting patterns would reassert themselves and hinder the purpose of the CDU in unifying the conservative and progressive middle classes. The new party possessed one decisive advantage in that the Allied system of licensing political parties restricted the number of competitors in the first elections after the War. Apart from the CDU/CSU and the SPD, only the Liberals and Communists were allowed to present candidates while extremists or splinter parties were not usually permitted to function. Since these last were most likely to depend on support from conservative voters, the potential political base of the CDU/CSU was thus artificially widened. The only major right-of-centre rival was the Liberals, who gained substantial support in some areas but generally suffered from developing their organisation even later than the

Christian Democrats.

The first regional elections were held in June 1946 for constituent assemblies in Bavaria, Hesse and Württemberg-Baden. The results for the CDU/CSU were impressive, especially in Bavaria where the CSU won an absolute majority of 58.3 per cent while the CDU gained 37.3 per cent and 40.9 per cent respectively in Hesse and Württemberg-Baden. The Landtag elections which followed during 1946-7 confirmed the CDU/CSU as the dominant party of the right, for it emerged as the strongest single party in the four states of Bavaria (52.3 per cent), North-Rhine Westphalia (37.6 per cent), the Rhineland-Palatinate (47.2 per cent) and Württemberg-Hohenzollern (54.2 per cent). In the other state elections the SPD became the largest party with the CDU in second place, although the CDU faced close rivalry in Lower Saxony where a regional party won a high vote.[71] The total vote of the CDU/CSU in these state elections was over 6½ million (37.7 per cent), giving it a marginal lead over the SPD with its 35 per cent of the vote. The CDU/CSU generally performed substantially better in the Catholic regions of western and southern Germany, but its relatively strong showing in Protestant regions nevertheless represented the beginnings of an electoral breakthrough. For example, the CDU's vote of 34.1 per cent in Schleswig-Holstein and 26.7 per cent in Hamburg compared very favourably with the 1 per cent vote and 1.5-2 per cent acquired respectively by the Centre Party in these areas throughout the Weimar period.

This relatively strong electoral position of the CDU/CSU as a force of the moderate right contained a hidden vulnerability. In the next year or two, the Allies allowed other political parties to perform on the electoral stage. Some of them succeeded in attracting the less committed voters from the CDU/CSU like the German Party (DP) in areas of north Germany and (dramatically so) from the CSU in the case of the Bavarian Party (BP). The FDP also began to establish a national party organisation, so that with the increased competition for conservative voters it seemed for a time as if the trend was towards a multi-party system, although one with two leading parties within it. In the 1949 Bundestag Election, the CDU/CSU became the strongest parliamentary group with 31 per cent of the vote (139 seats out of a total of 402) compared with 29.2 per cent for the SPD (131 seats). Among the ten other groups in the Bundestag, the Liberals gained 11.9 per cent, the Communists 5.7 per cent, while the Centre Party won the support of no more than 3.1 per cent of the electorate.[72]

Finally, the leadership situation of the CDU/CSU was becoming clear. This process was accelerated by the party's important role in the Economic Council, formed in 1947 to promote the economic union of the American and British zones, and by its role in the Parliamentary Council, which in 1948-9 formulated the Basic Law for the new Federal Republic. In both cases, the CDU/CSU formed the largest political grouping and together with other right-of-centre parties, including the Liberals, acquired key positions. This advantage led in the former case to the 'discovery' of Ludwig Erhard, director for economic affairs, and in the latter instance accorded Konrad Adenauer national prominence because of his election to the presidency of the Parliamentary Council. Even before this time Adenauer had been methodically consolidating his position inside the party. His political base during the Occupation period was the chairmanship of the British Zone, to which he had been elected early in 1946. He rapidly moved into the limelight in this zonal party, which soon became renowned as the best organised regional group of the new CDU. The British Zone consequently acquired a dominant political weight in the party, particularly as its principal rival the Berlin CDU was already suffering from the constrictive Soviet attitude towards political activity. Until then the Berlin CDU had been the base for Jakob Kaiser, whose forceful ideas on making the CDU a progressive force conflicted directly with those of Adenauer. Other possible rivals to Adenauer presented a much less serious challenge, for they either lacked his tactical finesse as did Hans Schlange-Schöningen, provisional chairman of the north German CDU, who alienated Catholic opinion by his ambitions to make the party a national conservative force, or they suffered from the lack of solidarity within their own political base, as did Josef Müller in Bavaria.[73]

By the time of the inauguration of the Federal Republic in 1949 the CDU/CSU had assumed many of its distinguishing political and structural characteristics. The CDU/CSU was not a mass-organised party for it lacked a formal unified structure, which was impossible to establish in the face of the jealous independence of its different regional associations. The CDU/CSU was in fact loose-associational in character and its activities were conducted largely by a non-professional activist elite. Three special political features had already become apparent in the three western zones of the party during the four years of the Occupation. First, the CDU/CSU showed a low level of intra-party coordination because it lacked any organisational tradition as it was a new party and because it was moulded structurally by the new and unique federal system which was emerging in

West Germany. Secondly, the CDU/CSU had developed from the ideologically-motivated party of its birth into a more pragmatic political force. Such a change was perhaps inevitable considering the various political tendencies contained within the CDU/CSU, for any emphasis placed on a party ideology would have created further problems of cohesion. The move towards the more cautious approach of pragmatism was promoted by the conservative political mood in Germany occasioned by the threat from Communism and the Cold War from 1948, and by a marked aversion to political ideology in general as a reaction to totalitarianism of both the left and the right. This qualitative change in the CDU/CSU's character was confirmed by the assumption of effective leadership by the pragmatic Adenauer-Erhard team, which led the party into the Bundestag Election of 1949. Thirdly, the CDU/CSU was already showing characteristics of the voter-orientated party it was to become in the 1950s. The variety of ideological trends which it incorporated allowed the CDU/CSU an electoral flexibility which the other political parties could not enjoy. Moreover, the party had achieved remarkable success in the early elections after the War with only a bare minimum of organisation, although with support from external influences notably the Churches.

The development of the political strength of the CDU/CSU was assisted by two major historical factors. The Third Reich had broken the chain of continuity whereby Catholic voters during Weimar had expressed a clear preference for the Centre Party, and, additionally, the division of Germany, consummated with the formation of both the Federal Republic and the German Democratic Republic in the Eastern Zone in 1949, deprived the SPD of many of its former Weimar strongholds. Therefore, the developments during the Occupation period continued to give the CDU/CSU a relatively sound basis for its future as the leading political party of the 1950s in West Germany, although it remained for the advantages it acquired as governing party to consolidate and strengthen its position. The vacuum of the formal party leadership was soon to be filled by Konrad Adenauer, whose recognised qualities as leader and whose country-wide appeal were to provide the new party with its most important single integrating force. This development helped to ensure the CDU/CSU's political position and to determine its role in the 1950s as the 'Chancellor's party'.

Notes

[1]   See the comment of Arnold Heidenheimer, the historian of the early
CDU, on the party name that 'Catholics could regard it as the political
arm of their network of religious and lay organisations and as the protector of Catholic social and cultural interests. Practising Protestants
viewed it as the symbol of a worthwhile alliance with the stronger Catholics, and as the protector of common values against the atheistic left.
Liberals could accept it as embodying basic liberal values within the
supporting framework of a non-sectarian interpretation of the Western
cultural tradition. Bourgeois elements could accept it for its avoidance
of any mention of socialism. Those attracted to concepts of social
solidarity, whether Catholic trade unionists or Prussian conservatives,
could accept it in terms of a movement seeking to encompass, and
reconcile, the claims of all social groups and classes' (*Adenauer and the
CDU* (1960), pp. 35-6).

[2]   A co-founder of the Berlin CDU and former Reichstag deputy of one
of the smaller liberal parties (German Democratic Party – DDP) before
1933. As former secretary of the liberal trade unions, he had played a
leading part in the futile effort to bolster middle-class support for the
Weimar Republic.

[3]   The initiative in founding the CDU in Cologne was led among others by
Peter Josef Schaeven, former executive manager of the Cologne Centre
party from 1914 to 1933, and Theodor Scharmitzel, who had been a
former Landtag deputy of the Centre Party and general secretary to
the Windthorst League, a Catholic interest association. Leo Schwering
himself had been a Centre Party deputy in the Prussian state parliament
from 1921-32, and now became first chairman of the Rhineland CDU.

[4]   In Lower Saxony, the situation varied almost from district to district.
In the district of Duderstadt, a Catholic enclave near the East German
border, the CDU owed its initiation to two Christian trade unionists,
while in neighbouring Protestant districts non-socialist circles opted
instead for a separate Liberal party. The role of local notables was underlined by the case of the CDU in the district of Vechta, where the new
party overcame initial difficulties through the backing it received
from Dr Siemer the district administrator (see the account of Arnold
Fratzscher, later General Secretary of the CDU in Hanover, in *Die CDU
in Niedersachsen, Demokratie der ersten Stunde* (1971), pp. 16-19,
25-7).

[5]   The circle of founders of the Berlin CDU numbered twelve, of whom
seven had belonged in the Weimar Republic to the Centre Party, four
to the DDP and one was a conservative without any former party
allegiance (H.G. Wieck, *Die Entstehung der CDU und die Wiedergründung
des Zentrums im Jahre 1945* (1953), pp. 208-9).

[6]   According to Josef Kannengiesser, the situation at least in the Osnabrück
area was ameliorated by the use of radio announcements: 'The means
of conveying news were difficult and transport conditions hopeless,
but the tidings of a new party reached the open-minded and attentive
ears of men in the countryside partly from Osnabrück, partly from
Westphalia and partly through the first radio announcements about
the founding of a Christian Democratic party in the Rhineland and in
Westphalia' (report undated on the early years of the CDU in Osnabrück
and in Emsland, Archiv Bundesgeschäftsstelle der CDU, Bonn, file 20
(Geschichte)).

54 Christian Democracy in Western Germany

References

1. See Ralf Dahrendorf, *Society and Democracy in Germany* (1967) and David Schoenbaum, *Hitler's Social Revolution* (1966).
2. Quoted in H.G. Wieck, *Die Anfänge der Christlichen Demokraten und der Liberalen in Hessen, Rheinland-Pfalz, Baden und Württemberg im Jahre 1945* (1954), p. 60.
3. Quoted in Ernst Deuerlein, *CDU/CSU 1945-1957: Beiträge zur Zeitgeschichte* (1957), p. 49.
4. *L'Ordre*, 21 September 1946.
5. Leo Schwering, *Vorgeschichte und Enstehung der CDU* (1952), p. 24.
6. Deuerlein, *op. cit.*, p. 63.
7. H.G. Wieck, *Die Entstehung der CDU und die Wiedergründung des Zentrums im Jahre 1945* (1953), pp. 168-73.
8. Quoted in Deuerlein, *op. cit.*, pp. 59-60.
9. Leo Schwering, *Fruhgeschichte der Christlich-Demokratischen Union* (1963), p. 215.
10. *Ibid.*, appendix, p. 223.
11. *Ibid.*, p. 24.
12. Quoted in Arnold Heidenheimer, *Adenauer and the CDU* (1960), p. 7.
13. Karl Zimmerman, *Warum nicht Zentrum, sondern Sammlung der Christlichen Demokraten Deutschlands*, Nachlass Schwering, Stadtarchiv Köln.
14. *Ibid.*
15. Diary of Leo Schwering, 10 April 1945, pp. 95-6, Stadtarchiv Köln.
16. Ulrich Föhse, *Entstehung und Entwicklung der Christlich-Demokratischen Union in Wuppertal, 1945-50* (mimeograph, 1970), p. 18.
17. 'Die neue CDU – eine Reichsparti? Gespräch mit Ernst Lemmer' in Albert Wucher (ed.), *Wie kam es zur Bundesrepublik?* (1968), p. 61.
18. Schwering, *Vorgeschichte*, p. 34.
19. Lambert Lensing on the early CDU in Westphalia in *Westfalenpost*, 14 May 1948.
20. H.G. Wieck, *Die Entstehung der CDU*, p. 173.
21. *Die Zeit*, 21 February 1946.
22. 'Die dreissig Punkte der Union' in *Gründungsurkunde der CSU* (1971), p. 8.
23. Quoted in Klaus Dreher, *Der Weg zum Kanzler: Adenauers Griff nach der Macht* (1972), p. 279.
24. Konrad-Adenauer-Stiftung (ed.), *Konrad Adenauer und die CDU der britischen Besatzungzone* (1975), p. 585.
25. Schwering, *Frühgeschichte*, pp. 215-16.
26. Gerhard Schulz, 'Die CDU – Merkmale ihres Aufbaus' in *Parteien in der Bundesrepublik: Studien zur Entwicklung der deutschen Parteien bis zur Bundestagswahl 1953*, Schriften des Instituts für Politische Wissenschaft, vol. 6 (1955), p. 45.
27. Schwering, *Frühgeschichte*, p. 69.
28. Konrad-Adenauer-Stiftung, *Konrad Adenauer und die CDU*, p. 43.
29. *Ibid.*, p. 50.
30. *Die dreissig Punkte der Union*, p. 7.
31. H.G. Wieck, *Christliche und Freie Demokraten in Hessen, Rheinland-Pflaz, Baden und Württemberg, 1945/46* (1958), pp. 192-94.
32. Konrad-Adenauer-Stiftung, *op. cit.*, p. 858.
33. *Schwäbische Zeitung*, 2 April 1948.
34. For a full discussion of the refounding of the Centre Party in North-Rhine Westphalia, see Peter Hüttenberger, *Nordrhein-Westfalen und die Entstehung seiner parlamentarischen Demokŗatie* (1973), pp. 72-96.

35. Schwering, *Frühgeschichte*, p. 13.
36. Wieck, *Die Entstehung der CDU*, pp. 108-9.
37. Schwering, *Frühgeschichte*, p. 194.
38. Karl Buchheim, *Geschichte der Christlichen Parteien in Deutschland* (1953), p. 448.
39. Wieck, *Christliche und Freie Demokraten*, pp. 61-68.
40. BGS, *Dokumentation: die Geschichte der CDU* (1972), p. 25; Gerhard Schulz, *op. cit.*, p. 61.
41. Peter Egen, *Die Entstehung des Evangelischen Arbeitskreises der CDU/CSU* (Ph.D. thesis), p. 24 ff.
42. Hüttenberger, *op. cit.*, p. 55.
43. Wieck, *Die Entstehung der CDU*, p. 90.
44. Föhse, *op. cit.*, p. 50.
45. Buccheim, *op. cit.*, pp. 448-9; Arnold Fratzscher, *Die CDU in Niedersachsen* (1971), passim.
46. Schwering, *Frühgeschichte*, pp. 119-20.
47. Wieck, *Die Entstehung der CDU*, p. 209.
48. Paul Bausch, *Lebenserinnerungen und Erkenntnisse eines schwäbischen Abgeordneten* (1970), p. 144.
49. Report of the Rhineland CDU Landessekretariat, *Die Zusammensetzung unseres Mitglieder-Bestandes*, 5 October 1947, Nachlass Schwering, Stadtarchiv Köln.
50. Memorandum of the south Württemberg CDU quoted in Wieck, *Christliche und Freie Demokraten*, p. 181.
51. Bausch, *op. cit.*, p. 145.
52. Quoted in Wieck, *Christliche und Freie Demokraten*, p. 166-67.
53. Minutes of meeting of Rhineland CDU Landesvorstand, 5 December 1947, Haupstaatsarchiv Düsseldorf, RWV 26, No. 75a.
54. Wieck, *Christliche und Freie Demokraten*, pp. 54-5.
55. Report of Rhineland CDU Landessekretariat, 5 October 1947, *op. cit.*.
56. Wieck, *Christliche und Freie Demokraten*, p. 195.
57. Schwering, *op. cit.*, p. 204.
58. Quoted in Dreher, *op. cit.*, pp. 273-74.
59. Report of Rhineland CDU, 11 May 1946, Nachlass Schwering.
60. *Ibid.*
61. Annual Report of Rhineland CDU for 1947, Archiv BGS, A 32d, Teil XI.
62. Annual Report of Rhineland CDU for 1948, *ibid.*
63. See reports of Rhineland CDU, 5 November 1945 and 11 May 1946, Nachlass Schwering.
64. M. Balfour and J. Mair, *Four-Power Control in Germany and Austria, 1945-46* (1956), p. 203.
65. Schwering, *op. cit.*, p. 169.
66. Arnold Fratzscher, *op. cit.*, p. 25.
67. Werner Conze, *Jacob Kaiser – Politiker zwischen Ost und West, 1945-49* (1969), p. 84.
68. Wieck, *Christliche und Freie Demokraten*, pp. 114-19.
69. Minutes of meeting of Rhineland CDU Landesvorstand, 5 December 1947, *op. cit.*
70. Paul Bausch, *op. cit.*, p. 148.
71. Heino Kaack, *Geschichte und Struktur des deutschen Parteiensystems* (1971), pp. 182-7.
72. *Ibid.*, p. 196.
73. For fuller discussion of the early CDU leadership, see Arnold Heidenheimer, *Adenauer and the CDU* (1960).

2 THE PERIOD OF ADENAUER'S ASCENDANCY: THE PARTY IN THE SHADOW OF THE CHANCELLOR (1949-1959)

The political heyday of Christian democracy in Western Germany in the 1950s was obviously linked with the period of Adenauer's ascendancy as Federal Chancellor. Building on its innate appeal already acquired in the later 1940s, growing support for the CDU/CSU followed to a large extent from the Adenauer Government's policy successes, which were most notable in the prominent areas of foreign and economic affairs. The party achieved electoral victories in 1953 (45.2 per cent) and 1957 (50.2 per cent) which were unprecedented in German history. The CDU/CSU came to assume the role of the dominant political force in the new Federal Republic within less than a decade of its founding after the War. This chapter discusses the role of the party during the Adenauer Governments of the 1950s and seeks to answer the question: what impact did this success and early governmental responsibility have on its character and development?

The nature of the leading role played by the CDU/CSU in the new West German state may be appreciated in the context of two models of dominant party theory. Maurice Duverger's three criteria for a dominant political party of continuous supremacy of electoral appeal, identification with prevailing political-cultural norms and recognition by public opinion of this supremacy are partly applicable.[1] The CDU/CSU's electoral support was not at first certain because of the appeal of smaller parties of the right in Landtag elections during 1950-2, but its stability was assured at the national level from 1953. Its electoral supremacy was underlined by the difference between its vote and that of the next largest party the SPD (16.4 per cent in 1953; 18.4 per cent in 1957). This strength of electoral support together with the impact of the Government's policy successes helped to explain the public's recognition of the CDU/CSU's dominance, in answer to Duverger's third point. The second criterion is more difficult to measure, although the influence acquired by the CDU/CSU from its long and continuous period in office since the inception of the new state and its ability to represent the conservative outlook of post-war West German political society would tend to support this thesis. Arnold Heidenheimer's more specific criteria for locating a dominant-party situation also help to highlight the nature of the CDU/CSU's dominance.[2] The association between party and the state applies in this period, as continuing CDU/CSU governments encouraged economic growth after the War and helped to lift West Germany out of the mire of national disgrace. Similarly, the party was associated with national security, perhaps best illustrated by Adenauer's firm commitment to the Western alliance with its defence against Communism. Because of their political dominance and the credit given to them for the achievement of the 'economic miracle', Christian Democratic governments were able to some extent to harmonise different socio-economic interests. Heidenheimer's fourth criterion of the use of constitutional rules of the game to buttress such dominance cannot be argued too strongly, even taking into account Adenauer's periodic efforts to devalue the status of the parliamentary opposition. Finally, the integrative and publicity function performed by a charismatic leader was exemplified in a classic manner by Adenauer.

While the CDU/CSU's dominance of the West German party system during the 1950s is unquestionable, the question remains of evaluating the importance of the party as distinct from and in relation to the Adenauer Government. It is a difficult one to answer because the party played a subordinate role to both the Government and Chancellor and was often politically indistinguishable from them. However, it is important to attempt to answer it because it throws light on the nature of the CDU/CSU as a political party during this time. Contemporary views, from different standpoints, of the CDU/CSU generally agreed on its position as essentially that of 'the party of the government' rather than governing party, described it as an association for the election of the Chancellor (*Kanzlerwahlverein*) and above all underlined its political and psychological dependence on the figure of Adenauer. Even the daily newspaper *Christ und Welt*, one friendly towards the CDU/CSU, remarked at the end of the 1950s that Adenauer's political weight had concealed many weaknesses in the party for it appeared 'as if people in the Union regarded the existence of Adenauer as a sufficient substitute for hard organisational work'.[3] Academic analyses of the party's role in relation to the Government have indicated the former's peripheral rather than central influence in policy-making during this period. According to Arnulf Baring in his enlightening study of Adenauer's methods of decision-making in foreign policy, the Chancellor's 'chief means in the formation of Chancellor Democracy was the bureaucratic machine of the Chancellor's Office' while the 'still rudimentary party machine played a quite inferior role'.[4] Heidenheimer commented similarly that Adenauer viewed his position as party chairman as ancillary to that of Chancellor, the former as the 'crutch' of the latter.[5]

These views while generally describing the CDU/CSU's external features nevertheless avoid certain internal complexities in the relationship between party leaders and members. The CDU/CSU had a loose organisational structure and little individual political weight during the 1950s, but that did not mean that it remained a static entity throughout the decade. Discontent with Adenauer's role as paterfamilias of the CDU/CSU did begin to express itself towards the end of the 1950s in the form of proposals for the reform of leadership positions and pressure for change in secondary personnel. The decade culminated in the first serious disaffection in the CDU/CSU with Adenauer over his attitude to the choice of Federal President in 1959. What also must be investigated is how much the development of the political independence of the party was obstructed by the leadership and in particular Adenauer or was inhibited by prevalent attitudes among party activists, notably their antipathy towards the creation of a party machine and the reluctance of regional party leaders and organisers to countenance any diminution of their strong position in the CDU/CSU hierarchy. Heidenheimer concluded with some reason in 1958 that while the CDU/CSU was 'little more than a loosely-coordinated alliance of Christian Democratic *Land* parties as late as 1949, it has now become a powerful instrument for the exercise of national power, with its members and components held in harness by a firm Chancellor'.[6] To what extent therefore was the party such a 'powerful instrument'; and what effect did this have on its nature?

Some direct examination of the CDU/CSU's internal development is necessary in order to answer such a question. This will illustrate some essential characteristics of West German Christian Democracy which became delineated during this period, and will also help to explain the slow reaction of the CDU/CSU in response to even greater external pressures for change which multiplied in the 1960s. For reasons of analytical convenience the internal features of the CSU are discussed elsewhere,[a] so that this chapter will concentrate on the impact of government responsibility on the CDU as well as the role of the party in office. Following Duverger's hypothesis that modern political parties may be characterised by their anatomy,

a   See below chapter 10.

the different levels of authority and activity in the CDU will be examined in turn, looking at the national institutional (the creation of the CDU as a national party) through the parliamentary (the relationship between the CDU/CSU Bundestag *Fraktion* and the Government) to the extra-parliamentary (the relationship between the national leadership, regional party leaders and activists in general), with, finally, a discussion of Adenauer's loss of authority following his stillborn candidacy for the Presidency in 1959.

(a)   Adenauer's Election as Chancellor and the Establishment of the CDU as a National Party

The first factor of importance in assessing the role of the CDU as the dominant political force in government during the decade of the 1950s concerns the nature of its birth as a national political organisation. The CDU together with the CSU in a coalition with two smaller right-of-centre parties became the leading party in office at the outset of the Federal Republic, exactly one year before its formal constitution as a political party with a national leadership structure and organisation. The CDU had already, under the authority of Adenauer, begun to establish its position and reputation as the dominant governing force before it had time to develop any separate identity as a political party. Indeed, the assumption of governmental responsibility early in its history fundamentally influenced the character of the CDU. Control of the government and enjoyment of the fruits of power with all its attractions of patronage and advantages pertaining to electoral appeal very easily became the basis for party solidarity, which in turn explained among other things the weakness of its organisational structure through lack of necessity during the 1950s. The key feature harmonising internal party relationships was the decisive role of the party leader. By the time CDU delegates assembled to form a national organisation at the Goslar Congress (October 1950), they saw before them in the words of one observer 'not only an outstanding party leader, but moreover also a statesman'.[7] Adenauer had already the year before demonstrated his overriding political authority by the leading role he played in the formation of the first Federal Government.

In certain respects the formation of the first national Cabinet in 1949 was more easily accomplished compared with later ones because of the absence at the time of a formal parliamentary organisation, for the CDU/CSU Bundestag *Fraktion* has not yet been officially constituted, and there were of course no national party

organs. Consequently, Adenauer in particular as well as other leading
Christian Democrats were allowed a greater freedom of manoeuvre
than would otherwise have been the case in the decisive consultations
following the Bundestag Election on 14 August which led to the
formation of a right-of-centre government including the CDU/CSU, the
FDP, and the German Party (DP). As the CDU/CSU had emerged
from the election with the largest single group of seats in the forthcoming Bundestag, it enjoyed from the start the initiative in forming
a cabinet. This advantage held by the Christian Democrats was underlined by the disappointment of Kurt Schumacher, the SPD chairman,
and his party with their own election result.

The first major problem was the one most easily settled. Adenauer's
accepted position as the patriarch of the Christian Democrats, his
chairmanship of the influential British Zone CDU and his reputation
gained earlier in the year as President of the Parliamentary Council
made his nomination as CDU/CSU Chancellor candidate inevitable.
No serious alternative was even voiced. Adenauer himself took the
initiative in proceeding to internal party consultations over the
future government by calling an informal gathering of selected party
leaders at his own home in Rhöndorf on 21 August, one week after
the election, to discuss this question. Adenauer had in fact requested
Aloys Zimmer, the party's election campaign manager, to send out
invitations for the meeting only two days after the election. The list
of participants was dominated by regional CDU chairmen and
leaders, whose attachment to their *Land* party positions meant that
they had little personal interest in the composition of the Federal
Government, but also included members of Adenauer's staff.[1] The
absence from the Rhöndorf Conference, as it later became known, of
obstreperous party leaders who might have tried to counter
Adenauer's wishes was obvious. The CSU was represented not by its
chairman, Hans Ehard, whose relations with Adenauer were strained,
but by the young Franz-Josef Strauss (then responsible for CSU party
organisation); while Adenauer's old rival, Jakob Kaiser, did attend
but had long ceased to challenge Adenauer's authority in the party.
One of Adenauer's most persistent opponents in the CDU, Karl
Arnold (Minister-President of North-Rhine Westphalia) was not
even invited. The occasion was shrewdly stage-managed by Adenauer,
who produced a testimonial from his doctor declaring that he could
assume the burdens of the Chancellorship for one or two years, and
who showed his gift for hospitality with a splendid meal and an
impressive assortment of wines, and made certain that the occasion

would enjoy generous publicity from the press. There was no murmur of opposition to the idea that Adenauer should be nominated for the Chancellorship. The legitimacy of this gathering as a decision-making body was later questioned even in CDU/CSU circles, particularly as it hardly included any deputies elected to the new Bundestag. Despite this, it marked a crucial stage in the formation of the Government and provided Adenauer with an occasion to exercise his commanding authority as effective leader of the CDU/CSU.[8]

The question of the form of coalition produced more difficulties in subsequent consultations, because opinion inside the CDU/CSU was divided. Adenauer's determined preference for a right-of-centre coalition with the FDP obviously carried much weight in view of his role as undisputed Chancellor candidate, but he had to face a strong body of opinion in the CDU which favoured a grand coalition with the SPD. Adenauer had chosen to face the issue in a direct manner at the Rhöndorf meeting by interpreting the election result ideologically: while only 8 million voters had supported a socialist economy (SPD and KPD), 13 million had in his view rejected this in favour of the social market economy offered by the CDU/CSU and, by association, the other parties of the right including the FDP. He pointed to the model of the coalition between Christian and Free Democrats on the Frankfurt Economic Council, and further stressed the need for a strong opposition in the Bundestag to counter the danger of an extra-parliamentary one. Strong objections to his interpretation of the choice were not raised at the meeting, simply because the main protagonists of a grand coalition apart from Kaiser were not present. Erhard's arguments there against a coalition with the SPD for reasons of economic policy carried much weight because of the strong respect in the party for his abilities as economic manager.[9]

The main argument in favour of a grand coalition was that the work of reconstruction could best be achieved by the co-operation of the two main parties. Since CDU/SPD coalitions were in office in most of the *Länder* at the time, it is surprising that support for this form of coalition was so weak at the Rhöndorf meeeting. Many of its participants had apparently not thought out this problem in terms of Federal politics, so that the surprise element at the meeting worked to Adenauer's advantage. Any second thoughts were disrupted a few days later when the SPD made it bluntly clear that they considered a coalition with the CDU/CSU out of the question by the outrageousness of its demands if they participated in one, including control of the Economics Ministry, the main source of contention with the CDU/CSU. This alienated some pro-grand coalition circles in the latter. Adenauer clinched the matter in a public statement he made on 5 September. He admitted that 'his negotiations with the party leaders had not included a meeting with Dr Schumacher', thus indicating the impossibility of co-operation between the two antagonists, and stressed that the voters who had returned a majority which supported a free economy would have regarded a grand coalition as 'a great swindle of the parliamentary system'. In response to suggestions that the appointment of Erhard as Economics Minister might be balanced by selecting a Social Democrat as his Secretary of State, the prospective Chancellor likened such a position to 'having two horses each pulling its own way at different ends of a cart'. In his view no progressive work would be possible, for he preferred 'to have a straight policy'.[10]

The FDP leadership gave its assent to a coalition with the CDU/CSU on the basis of generally agreed policy positions but only after the Christian Democrats agreed to support the FDP chairman, Theodor Heuss, as Federal President. Coalition negotiations occurred speedily, thus reducing the chance for further internal party disputes, so that Adenauer could soon present a cabinet of thirteen ministers including six from the CDU, two from the CSU, three from the FDP and two from the German Party. On 15 September, Adenauer was elected Chancellor of West Germany after a close vote.

The formation of the first Adenauer Government in 1949 may be considered an ideological milestone in the history of the CDU/CSU, because it indicated clearly the conservative orientation of the party which continued to underpin its basic outlook for its long-term future as the party of government. The manner of the government formation illustrated not only Adenauer's strong position in his party but also his exclusive method of operating, and it was made all the more possible by the lack of organised opposition in the CDU/CSU to his plans. Although the abrasive attitude of the SPD made a grand coalition unlikely, its advocates inside the CDU/CSU did not present their case well.

Their relative silence at this crucial moment ultimately reflected the recent declining influence of progressive Christian Democrats within the party. Jakob Kaiser, who had made his peace with Adenauer, was rewarded with a Cabinet post (Minister for All-German Affairs), but other major figures of the progressive CDU/CSU were excluded. Its figurehead Karl Arnold remained in silent disapproval as head of the *Land* Government in North-Rhine-Westphalia, but much of the criticism from this wing was expressed *ex post facto*.

A meeting of the Social Committees of the CDU/CSU in the summer of 1949 had brought to the surface the ideological divide between Adenauer and themselves, but any conflict was submerged by the election campaign which followed. Adenauer's speedy formation of his Government ensured against its reappearance. Having won his case for the form of coalition in Bonn, he chose to make some concessions to the progressive wing by, for instance, appointing Anton Storch, a prominent Christian trade unionist, as Federal Minister of Labour. Nevertheless, there ensued some controversy over the choice of personnel (whether conservative or progressive) for the posts of State Secretary and even heads of departments in that ministry.[11] A meeting of leaders of the progressive wing was held in Düsseldorf on 2 October, because 'the events in Bonn and the course they represent have called forth deep concern and uncertainty in the ranks of the Catholic workers' movement'.[12] Karl Arnold was present and so were Johannes Albers, chairman of the Social Committees, and Carl Spiecker, long an advocate of a 'party of the centre' based on the Catholic working class. The main speaker was Joseph Gockeln, President of the *Landtag* for North-Rhine Westphalia. He argued that 'the new state is brittle' and that its interests came before party warfare between the CDU/CSU and the SPD. Adenauer's interpretation of the election result and his stress on the need for a strong opposition were dismissed in favour of a trial period during which both parties could prove their worth at governing.[13] This minority view inside the party had no effect on developments in Bonn, although it did pose a warning of possible future tension in the party. However the progressive wing swallowed its objections and reluctantly supported the Adenauer Government, while Arnold remained as a critic of Government policy during the years which followed.

These signs of muffled discontent within the CDU were a further reason for giving the party some national institutional backbone as a means of binding it more closely to the new Government's course, and possibly lending it a more integrated character. The conduct of the CDU/CSU's campaign for the Bundestag Election in 1949 had already exposed many organisational deficiencies which derived from the lack of any satisfactory national co-ordination of activities. The CDU had no official central campaign office or even election programme and uncertainty was created by the absence of responsible national party organs, not to mention the independent line taken by the Bavarian CSU, which rejected Adenauer's suggestion to form a common electoral management committee.[14] The

General Secretariat of the *Arbeitsgemeinschaft der CDU und CSU*
based in Frankfurt had in fact made administrative arrangements for
election meetings and distributed publicity material, but despite the
enthusiastic efforts of Aloys Zimmer, Herbert Blankenhorn and Bruno
Dörpinghaus it failed to overcome the basic problem of reluctant
cooperation between the CDU's different regional associations.[15] It also
did not have the means available to conduct an efficient campaign,
such as the lack of personnel, so that the accumulation of many small
organisational mistakes produced a campaign which floundered.

The election result was nevertheless sufficient to support the
CDU/CSU's claims to national political office, but the party clearly
needed to develop a national organisation to strengthen its political
position in the future. With this question in mind, a meeting of *Land*
party chairmen was fixed to meet at Königswinter on 11 May 1950
to set in motion the process of forming a national party structure
for the CDU. The meeting decided in principle to establish a national
party, agreed on the first CDU national congress for the autumn and
unanimously elected Adenauer as provisional CDU chairman. Some
indication of the future structural nature of the party was given in the
final statement of the meeting that 'the organisation on a united
German basis shall be determined by the federative principles which
guided the CDU during the construction of the Federal Republic'.[16]
This reflected the organisational weight within the CDU of the
regional associations, who were determined not to cede any significant measure of their authority.

Adenauer recognised the power of the *Land* party chairmen and
consulted with them over arrangements for the congress. He nevertheless used his position as interim chairman to influence preparations.
A further meeting of *Land* party chairmen was called at Königswinter on 11 September 1950 to discuss party organisation and settle
the date and venue of the congress. After an introductory discourse
by Adenauer on matters of national policy and the achievements of
his Government, the participants turned to organisational matters.
They emphasised the need for better co-ordination of party forces
to check the 'drifting apart' in the CDU whereby 'everyone conducted his own policy'. Attention was drawn to the role of CDU
auxiliary organisations, like the Young Union and the Social Committees, when Adenauer commented that even though their independence should be respected they 'must be and remain components
of the CDU'. It was decided to leave this matter to a committee of
eight, who would negotiate a solution with the various auxiliary

organisations 'in the sense of a possibly close alliance of the organisations with the party'.[17] A lively debate ensured on the choice of meeting-place. The Berlin representatives argued in favour of their own city to show that the CDU 'does not forget the people in the East', but this proposal was rejected after a vote and the final choice settled on Goslar in the Harz as this would be 'as close as possible to the Eastern zone'. A committee was appointed to arrange the programme for the congress.[18]

The Goslar Congress of 20-22 October 1950 had two main purposes: the inauguration of a national party organisation, its immediate and official aim, and the publicity value of a meeting of the whole party. There were present almost 1,000 delegates — 386 with voting rights and 600 guest delegates.[19] To an observer the latter of the two aims of the Congress was the more apparent. Adenauer had played the role of disinterested mediator and conciliator at the session with the *Land* party chieftains behind the closed doors, but now with a large public audience he could indulge his gifts as a charismatic leader. After Adolf Cillien, chairman of the Hanover CDU acting as host, had opened the Congress, the Federal Chancellor strode onto the platform to the sounds of Beethoven's 'Egmont' Overture and, following a welcome from Cillien to representatives of foreign Christian Democratic parties, delivered a major speech on 'Germany's Place and Task in the World'. The theme of his speech was that the two super powers, the USA and USSR, were ideologically opposed and that the conviction of his party was that 'the Christian outlook, its chosen basis for domestic and foreign policy, is essential for the struggle against Bolshevism'.[20]

Adenauer had a special reason for dwelling on national security affairs. The German rearmament issue had arisen with the outbreak of the Korean War earlier in the year following American pressure for a West German contribution to NATO, and in the very same week as the Goslar Congress the Pleven Plan for a European Defence Community, including the Federal Republic, was announced. Shortly before the Congress one of Adenauer's ministers, Gustav Heinemann, had resigned from the Cabinet over the issue, having been alienated by the manner of Adenauer's consultations with the Western foreign ministers in New York, since he had not first discussed the matter with the Cabinet. The issue was a sensitive one in Germany in view of her recent past. Further controversy had been fanned by a sharp attack on Adenauer's implicit support for rearmament by Martin Niemöller, a prominent figure in the Protestant Church and a noted anti-militarist. Adenauer's fear was that an ensuing wave of criticism might weaken the CDU's appeal among Protestant voters, for Heinemann as President of the Church's Synod was a highly respected figure among Protestants. Fortunately for Adenauer, Heinemann not being an aggressive character chose not to appear at the Congress and test feeling among the party for his case. Adenauer decided therefore to go on to the attack and concentrated his speech on Niemöller, whose outspokenness he blamed for inflicting 'the most serious damage on the reputation of the German people at home and abroad'. He denied emphatically that his Government had ever committed itself to German remilitarisation, assured the delegates that any final decision would lie with the German Bundestag and asserted that 'the Federal Government, the Bundestag and I personally will do everything within our power to see that the militarist thinking, which found its most bitter expression during the National Socialist time, will never return under any circumstances'.[21] Niemöller's views failed to draw support at the Congress from Protestant delegates, who passed a declaration expressing their solidarity with Adenauer's Government: 'We range ourselves behind the policy of the Federal Chancellor and his Government, which alone has been empowered by the people to speak in the name of all Germany'.[22] The delegates generally responded well to Adenauer's speech. According to one foreign correspondent: 'The crowded audience gave Dr Adenauer a warm-hearted reception and his speech was throughout enthusiastically acclaimed; no sentence was more loudly cheered than his words "We belong to the West and not to Soviet Russia"; significantly, he drew cheers when, referring to the Western Powers' decision to reinforce their troops in Germany, he said: "The reinforcements will mean burdens for us, but rather burdens than destruction." '[23]

The other speeches from the platform followed an ideological or even cosmic pattern rather than dealing with concrete matters of Government or party policy. Professor Hans Erich Stier from Münster, a member of the *Landtag* in North-Rhine Westphalia, spoke at considerable length on 'The Historical Mission of the CDU', while Dr Mathilde Gantenberg, a State Secretary from Mainz, complemented it with a discourse on the party's 'Cultural-Political Mission'. Several Government ministers spoke, such as von Brentano on European affairs, while Dr Erhard was listened to with respect when he addressed the Congress on his economic policy. The proceedings were dominated by set speeches from party leaders in the form of pro-grammatic monologues, which left little time for discussion from the floor. According to one observer, the programme of 'the conference was consciously so arranged that the possible controversial questions of internal policy remained in the background'.[24]

The elections to the party leadership were predictable. Adenauer was officially elected CDU party chairman by 302 votes out of 335, with 22 abstentions, four 'no' votes and a handful of votes divided among other names. Friedrich Holzapfel and Jakob Kaiser both received strong support as the two party vice-chairmen. The exception to these smooth proceedings was the question of creating the post of a party executive secretary, who would be primarily in charge of party organisation. The proposal which had Adenauer's blessing was that Kurt Georg Kiesinger, a 46 year-old Bundestag deputy from South Württemberg, should fill this position. Opposition to the proposal arose out of two objections: the fear that such a decision might lead to too much centralisation in the party; and the political background of the candidate, who had been a member of the NSDAP during the Third Reich. Opposition to Kiesinger's candidacy was led by the Berlin contingent, comprising 96 delegates, which won enough support among delegates to achieve a moral victory in the vote, which Kiesinger technically won but with a high rate of abstentions.[2] The matter was officially left open to await the recommendations of a five-man committee on party organisation and the establishment of a party headquarters in Bonn.[25]

The CDU had now been established as a national party, but the difficulties in coming to terms with its organisational consequences remained. Heinrich von Brentano, chairman of the CDU/CSU *Fraktion* in the Bundestag, had expressed the hope that 'the Congress will be in the position to provide for the CDU Bundestag *Fraktion* the face of a large and functionable party organisation, the absence of which has always been felt by the *Fraktion* as a painful deficiency'.[26] Brentano's wish was not to be met. The draft statutes of the CDU presented to the Goslar Congress by the leadership and adopted without discussion emphasised the role of the Party Federal Committee (*Parteiausschuss*), which consisted of delegates from the regional organisations (*Landesverbände*) and the Soviet Zone, the *Land* party chairmen, the chairman of the Bundestag *Fraktion*, the chairmen of the *Fraktionen* in the *Land* parliaments, the Federal Party Executive and five representatives from the Refugees' Committee.[27] This Party Committee, whose composition was clearly weighted in favour of the *Land* party leaders, was given the power of selecting the ordinary members of the Federal Party Executive

(*Bundesvorstand*), for only the party chairman and his two deputies
were elected by the Party Congress. The electoral orientation of the
CDU was reflected in the provision in article four of the 1950
Statutes that the number of delegates each *Land* party organisation
should send to the Party congress was based on the results of the
previous Bundestag Election, one delegate for every 25,000 CDU
voters in the *Land* concerned, rather than on the size of its membership. Similarly, the number of representatives for each *Landesverband*
on the Party Committee was based on the calculation of one for
every 100,000 CDU voters.[28]

The other main provision in the 1950 Statutes concerned the
formation of a CDU national headquarters (*Bundesgeschäftsstelle*).
This should be responsible to the Party Executive, but would be
financed chiefly through contributions from the *Landesverbände*.
Once again, the federal structure of the CDU was reinforced showing
that the concentration of party organisers was to be found on the
Land level. Nothing further was said in the Statutes about the role
or organisation of the party headquarters in Bonn. These matters
were simply postponed. After the Goslar Congress, the Party Executive
appointed a committee to decide on the organisation of the headquarters. Aloys Zimmer, one of the members of this committee,
wrote to *Land* chairmen on 3 November 1950 urging them to 'draw
conclusions from the party Congress' particularly in implementing
provisions for party organisation.[29] Four days later, Zimmer wrote
to the same as well as to the chairmen of the *Fraktionen* in the *Land*
parliaments asking them to keep the national party office informed of
all important motions and legislative initiatives,[30] but their reaction
was unresponsive. Progress in setting up the national party headquarters was slow. It did not come into operation until the spring of
1952, when Bruno Heck was made Federal Business Manager (*Bundesgeschäftsführer*) of the CDU. Temporary arrangements before then
included an office in the Blücherstrasse run by Heinz Lubbers, editor
of the party publication *Deutschland-Union-Dienst,* to concentrate on
publicity and propaganda.[31]

The Goslar Congress served more the function of demonstrating
solidarity behind the policies of the Adenauer Government
than of marking an important stage in the development of the CDU's
party organisation. The main official purpose of the Congress, that
of announcing the birth of the CDU as a national party, was achieved,
but this involved little significant structural change in the party. The
CDU was still essentially a loose-associational party, for the creation of

national party organs and a national headquarters were only a small step in the direction of central co-ordination, for the strong position of the regional associations was written into the formal party structure. The contemporary view of the Goslar Congress was justifiably of a triumph for Adenauer. In the words of the *Neue Zürcher Zeitung,* the acclamation for Adenauer from the delegates 'formed the external confirmation that the line which the Chancellor follows with his often criticised "lonely decisions" finds ultimately the concurrence of his party friends'.[32]

(b) Government Policy and the Party: the CDU/CSU Fraktion in the Bundestag

Adenauer's underlying attitude towards internal relations of the CDU/CSU had already become apparent at the outset of his Chancellorship: he recognised the entrenched position of the regional 'party barons' and their predominance in the party organisation in return for their support of his unquestioned authority in the field of national policy-making. It was a mutually satisfactory arrangement as Adenauer himself entertained little enthusiasm for a centralised party machine, since its development would have resulted in a new constraint on his freedom of manoeuvre as party leader. The national organs of the CDU, which slowly established themselves during the 1950s, posed little serious check on his authority.[b] Although Adenauer faced few extra-parliamentary party pressures in areas where the Federal Government had the exclusive right of policy-making, the influence of the CDU/CSU Bundestag *Fraktion,* the only national party organ for want of any effective alternative, could not be discounted. The discussion of 'Chancellor Democracy' during the 1950s has concentrated on the position of the Chancellor in relation to his Cabinet and individual ministers,[3] so that a discussion of Adenauer's relationship with other national party politicians will throw further light on the nature of his leadership.

The predominance of the *Fraktion* in the party hierarchy was illustrated by the high proportion of Bundestag deputies who were members of party executive organs, showing that not only was the parliamentary elite superior in authority to the extra-parliamentary organisation but also exerted a great influence within it.[4] Members of the *Fraktion* depended for their national political careers to a large extent on Adenauer's electoral appeal, so that ultimately the success of

b   See below chapter 7 (a), especially pp. 250-51.

his policies and his public authority as Chancellor determined the strength of his party position, yet paradoxically the greater the size of the *Fraktion* – it increased from 139 in 1949 to 243 in 1953 and 270 in 1957, as a result of Adenauer's victories in the latter two years – the more unwieldy it became to manage. While the first Bundestag *Fraktion* had been relatively unversed in national affairs, there developed in it over time a body of experienced parliamentarians, whose willingness to comply with Adenauer's policies became more considered and less automatic. The political weight of the *Fraktion* increased during the 1950s, so that an examination of its role during this period must focus on its influence in policy-making vis-à-vis Government and Chancellor, the state of its cohesion and degree of solidarity and the extent to which it developed its own independent leadership.

In view of its predominant role in the party hierarchy, the Bundestag *Fraktion* acted as a 'clearing station' for particular interests incorporated in the CDU and CSU which in turn reflected their nature as *Volksparteien,* political parties which appealed across a variety of interests and classes while at the same time representing them individually. Since it therefore assumed a decisive responsibility for integrating the CDU/CSU at the national level, the *Fraktion's* role in performing as the main channel for internal party pressure groups and for promotion to ministerial office must be considered.

A Chancellor-designate needs the votes of his backbenchers for his election to office, which is the first major task of a new Bundestag. The 'Chancellor election', which is a separate act from general support for his Government team, allows disaffected backbenchers to express their feelings through the secrecy of the ballot-box. In fact, no Chancellor candidate elected since 1949 has acquired the full support of the nominal majority for his Government.[5] Once elected the new Chancellor is in a strong constitutional position as a result of the provisions of the Basic Law concerning a constructive vote of no-confidence.[6] Nevertheless, Adenauer was required to take more account of party pressures during the formation of his Government. Such pressures were applied on Adenauer, who received delegations from *Fraktion* sub-groups, which represented different economic and political interests within the party, during the course of coalition negotiations.[7] The political strength of these sub-groups lay in their individual cohesion and size as well as the degree of powerful economic interests they represented. While Adenauer was troubled little in 1949 by such considerations, because of the absence then of structural articulation in the party, his later Government formations were more

complicated affairs for the *Fraktion* asserted more influence over
ministerial appointments as the 1950s progressed. In 1953 Adenauer
had to acknowledge for the sake of his majority the demands of
his coalition partners, the FDP and the German Party (DP), which
allowed him to balance these demands against those from his own
party.[33] Four years later, he found with the formation of a virtually
Christian Democratic government, with only the small DP (17 seats)
to consider, that pressures from within the CDU/CSU had more
influence and weight.[8] The *CSU-Landesgruppe* in particular was
more self-assertive in 1957, for it demanded and acquired a formal
'*Fraktion* pact' and increased the number of CSU Cabinet ministers
from three to four.[34] On both occasions, however, Adenauer failed
to implement all his plans for creating new ministerial posts largely
because of *Fraktion* opposition. These internal pressures were
exerted specifically over the choice of ministerial personnel, who consequently reflected not only different economic interests, but also
the balance of strong regional attachment within the CDU/CSU,[9]
and not over the political form of the coalition. Jacob Kaiser had
been the sole advocate of a grand coalition in 1953, but the CDU
Federal Executive had already confirmed its preference for a continuation of the centre-right coalition.[35] For all this assertion by
his *Fraktion*, Adenauer remained the key figure in Government
formations and ultimately could rely on the loyalty of his backbenchers.[36] In 1961, when Adenauer's political position was in
decline for his party had lost electoral support and he was forced to
negotiate with an intransigent FDP, he was once more able to play
off pressures from his own party against those from the FDP and
vice versa.[10] These various instances proved that pressure from
within the main Government-supporting *Fraktion* had to be taken
into account the more the Government's majority was concentrated
in the one party.

Although Adenauer's repeated election and therefore longevity
as Chancellor may be attributed in the short-term sense to his
political skills or room for manoeuvre within his own party, it must be
remembered that he was dealing with a *Fraktion* which, interest
pressures apart, showed a relatively low degree of political independence. A high proportion of CDU/CSU deputies, especially in the
first legislative period or two, were content with coupling a rather
passive role as backbencher with the respected position back home of
local notable. There was also a sizeable group of deputies, including
those with no strong ministerial ambitions, who concentrated on

being active backbenchers through committee work as long as they felt they were playing a consultative role in the formulation of policy. The likely tension point between Chancellor and Bundestag deputies was hence located among those backbenchers, especially prominent members of the CDU/CSU rank-and-file, whose career interests and aspirations could not be ignored. Adenauer was partial to pliable colleagues round the Cabinet table. This could not be universally applied, as in the case of ministers representing coalition partners or those from his own party who demonstrated their unquestionable authority in their own special field (most prominently, Ludwig Erhard as Minister of Economic Affairs, 1949-63). Noted CDU politicians like Hermann Ehlers, Eugen Gerstenmaier and Kurt-Georg Kiesinger found an outlet in the Bundestag presidency or important committee chairmanships, but they nevertheless remained a source of irritation within the party elite. Adenauer otherwise used the patronage of diplomatic posts abroad as a convenient channel for neutralising career ambitions, including those of some party figures outside the Bundestag.[11] His only other method of dealing with inconvenient political ambitions lay simply in ignoring the claims of certain non-strategic party leaders, and in doing so counted on the resources of his authority as Chancellor to neutralise their influence.

The *Fraktion* as a body remained essentially outside the limited circle of influential policy-makers chosen by Adenauer. This circle included some Cabinet ministers on the basis of their expertise or indispensability like Erhard (Economics), Gerhard Schröder (Interior), Fritz Schäffer (Finance) and Franz-Josef Strauss (Defence), the latter two being strong figures in the CSU; the *Fraktion* chairmen — Heinrich von Brentano (later Foreign Minister),[12] and from 1955 Heinrich Krone,[13] both of whom were loyal and close supporters of Adenauer; a changing group of individual deputies, who for a time enjoyed Adenauer's favour; and finally, his advisers in the Chancellor's Office, most notably Hans Globke who was State Secretary there (1953-63), having already served in the Office as a department head from 1950.[14] The obvious source of organised resistance to Adenauer's exclusive manner of policy-making would have been the *Fraktion* Executive (*Fraktionsvorstand*), but this was not noted for its political profile during the 1950s, largely because both von Brentano and Krone were unwilling to present an independent stance and preferred to voice their criticisms in confidence to Adenauer.[15] They both in any case belonged to the group of Adenauer's close advisers, and were at different times appointed to Cabinet posts. The low political profile of the *Fraktion* Executive also followed from the generally unassertive political line taken by its other component members. For instance, the 21 members of the *Fraktion* Executive in 1952 included only five who counted politically — Eugen Gerstenmaier, Kurt-Georg Kiesinger, Robert Pferdmenges (Adenauer's confidant), Robert Tillmanns (chairman of the West Berlin CDU) and Helene Weber (a prominent figure in Catholic welfare organisations from North-Rhine Westphalia) — but of these only Gerstenmaier and Kiesinger had ambiticus ideas in Adenauer's chosen field of foreign affairs.[37]

The distance of the *Fraktion* as a whole, and even its leadership, from the CDU/CSU power structure in government naturally presented problems of potential friction, although these never assumed dangerous proportions during the 1950s because of Adenauer's virtually unchallengeable political position and also because of the nature of personal relations and composition of *Fraktion* personnel already described. One or two of Adenauer's advisers were selected as objects of disapproval of the secretiveness of power relations round the Chancellor, but such instances of disaffection did not lead to changes of staff in the Chancellor's Office if only because of Adenauer's tenacity in supporting his close associates. Felix von Eckhardt, Adenauer's press chief as head of the Federal Press and Information Office, recognised pressures coming from the CDU/CSU *Fraktion* to relieve him of his position and attempted to pacify feelings by arguing somewhat unconvincingly that his field of activity was limited:

> I endeavoured fruitlessly during both my periods of office, that is during all my almost ten years, to make it clear to party politicians that the scope of influence of my office was restricted to the field of domestic policy and did not cover party political matters.[38]

Attacks on Globke increased in the mid-1950s because of his past Nazi associations, and some of them originated in CDU circles among those who blamed Globke for the Chancellor's 'mistakes' since his illness in the winter of 1955, such as the loss of the FDP from the coalition and the collapse of the Arnold government in North-Rhine Westphalia in 1956.[39] Adenauer consistently refused to withdraw his support from Globke, whom he defended publicly on several occasions on grounds of competence. No groups in the *Fraktion* were willing to make a major issue out of the 'Globke affair', because of the ultimate dependence of his Bundestag deputies on Adenauer as a public figure, and a reluctance to undermine his position especially when ill.

Other friction between the Government and backbenchers might have been reduced through regular consultation by the former of the latter, but this did not occur. Adenauer's personal relations with the *Fraktion* as a whole showed scant consideration for backbench opinion. His first meeting with the new CDU/CSU *Fraktion*, on 1 September 1949, had revealed something of his condescending attitude towards his parliamentary supporters. The meeting had been preceded by a conclave of the deputies from Württemberg who wanted to push their regional interests inside the *Fraktion*. Adenauer had somehow got wind of this, for as Paul Bausch, one of the group concerned, put it, 'a directing hand had already thwarted our plans'.[40] All deputies were required to sit in strict alphabetical order — name plates had even been fixed on each desk — so that immediate discussions among cliques during the meeting were frustrated. Adenauer entered the meeting and at once broached the matter. According to Bausch:

> This large man rose up, opened the meeting and declared with the most deadly serious face, just as if something terrible had happened, roughly the following: Much to his regret it was not possible to open the deliberation with the *Fraktion* before one disagreeable occurrence, which had happened in one of the Federal states, had been cleared up. Deputies, who had been elected in the *Land* concerned, had taken it on themselves to make decisions which only this *Fraktion* was in a position to make. He could not endure it when this *Fraktion* was browbeaten over its right to take decisions.[41]

Adenauer's remarks were followed by a long and complete silence. Some of the Württemberg deputies tamely requested that they should have some determining influence over the composition of the *Fraktion* executive, but Adenauer simply remarked that 'we do not want anything unjust', ignored the matter otherwise and passed without further protest to the agenda of the meeting.[42]

Adenauer seemed to have a personal authority which made itself felt instinctively, even when there was some conflict. Bausch himself, who had never before met the Chancellor in person, commented in a eulogistic fashion afterwards: 'Through his clarity of aim, his sense of justice, his political passion and his fighting spirit Adenauer had stolen the hearts of the best of the *Fraktion*.'[43] On bigger issues, adulation was not sufficient to make the Chancellor's exclusive manner of decision-making bearable, though even here his towering political authority allowed Adenauer a strong measure of freedom with regard to his party. Adenauer's somewhat authoritarian attitude explained his impatience with party political bickering.[16] He was able to follow his inclination because of the element of confidentiality which surrounds foreign policy-making, the field in which he chose to make himself master, but all the more because he came to symbolise to some degree the international confidence in the new Federal Republic which developed during his Chancellorship. There were a number of structural reasons too why Adenauer could exercise the upper hand in this area of policy. Until 1955, when the Federal Republic assumed full responsibility for her external relations, foreign and defence questions were handled by the Allied High Commission, and this involved direct dealings with the Chancellor's Office. During these regular consultations with the High Commission, Adenauer represented the Federal Government in person and was accompanied by an adviser from the Chancellor's Office in preference to a Cabinet minister.[44] This situation therefore enhanced further the authority of Adenauer over his ministers, not to mention his parliamentary deputies.[17]

Adenauer's reluctance to inform and consult with his parliamentary colleagues was particularly noticeable over his *Westpolitik* treaties, establishing West Germany as a member of the Western security system and as a partner in the process of European integration. His unwavering view that 'theirs is not to reason why' but to comply was shown in his belief that an effective way of avoiding the influence of parliamentarians was by not informing them of the contents of the treaties before signature.[45] However, Adenauer was forced over the controversial matter of the European Defence Community (EDC), which would initiate German rearmament and so aroused strong public misgivings, to show a more flexible position because of pressure from the *Fraktion*. He was compelled on this occasion to meet Brentano, Gerstenmaier and other representatives of the *Fraktion* in the form of a special committee on the subject, as a result of which some detailed alterations were made in the text of the EDC treaty.[46] Strong misgivings were also felt in the *Fraktion* over Adenauer's negative attitude to Stalin's proposals for German reunification in 1952, but they were never openly expressed.[47] Adenauer managed to neutralise or compromise with criticisms of his plans for the EDC in spite of considerable domestic controversy over the issue, and the treaty was ratified with full party support early in 1954. There was nevertheless some disquiet in the *Fraktion* about Adenauer's methods of operating.[18] Some party figures such as Hermann Ehlers (a vice-chairman of the CDU and Bundestag President) held reservations about Adenauer's European policy because they feared that it would reduce the chances of German reunification, but like him they supported the policy even if only half-heartedly.[48]

During the crucial years of the early and mid-1950s, when Adenauer was establishing his Western policy and hence the basic future foreign-policy orientation of the Federal Republic, he did not have to contend with serious opposition to either the ideas or conduct of his policy in his party (except sporadically over the EDC) because this did not take the form of organised opposition in the *Fraktion*. By the late 1950s, the picture was beginning to change because Adenauer's mounting age (he was now in his eighties) encouraged thoughts that he was not infallible and because political frustrations were coming to a head.

One such occasion was the disaffection expressed half-openly in the *Fraktion* over the management of foreign-policy debates in the Bundestag early in 1958. The foreign policy debate in January 1958 brought this smouldering resentment to a head, for the CDU/CSU *Fraktion* was quite unprepared and accordingly incapable of responding to the violent and impressive attacks on Adenauer's foreign policy by Gustav Heinemann, his old opponent now with the SPD, and Thomas Dehler the FDP leader. The ineptness of the *Fraktion* leadership, not helped by the placid approach of its chairman Heinrich Krone, was much publicised in the press and even criticised in some pro-CDU papers, This bitter experience was not easily forgotten, for in March, when another foreign policy debate was in the offing, Kurt-Georg Kiesinger took it on himself in his capacity as chairman of the Bundestag Foreign-Policy Committee to postpone the debate because of lack of preparations. Kiesinger had acted while Adenauer and Krone were away from Bonn. On Adenauer's return, tension erupted at a meeting of the *Fraktion* at which there were personalised remarks. Adenauer turned on Kiesinger sharply for his decision to postpone the debate without consulting him. Some deputies stood up to defend Kiesinger's action and demand better treatment from the Government. There followed an exchange of accusations after which Kiesinger left the meeting in protest.[49] Personal disappointment and

rivalry were connected with this event,[19] although in this particular
case internal party sensitivities over foreign questions were already
aroused at the time by the provocative manner in which Gerstenmaier (now Bundestag President)[20] had introduced discussion in an
interview with *Der Spiegel* of a German peace treaty as a way of
facilitating German reunification.[50] Gerstenmaier's individualistic
line was regarded as a challenge to the assumptions behind Adenauer's
Western policy, but he made no substantial impact for the habits
of maintaining the appearance of external solidarity in the CDU/CSU
asserted themselves. Calming statements were issued to the press by
Krone and other CDU leaders, including one from Kiesinger that
'objective differences of opinion' within the *Fraktion* now no longer
existed. A preparatory commission of two dozen CDU/CSU deputies
was appointed to make arrangements for the foreign policy debate,
while Adenauer invited leading members of the *Fraktion* along to the
Palais Schaumburg for lengthy discussions about possible lines to take
in the debate. The Chancellor succeeded in smoothing over the personal
feelings which had arisen.[51]

By the end of the decade, as illustrated, the *Fraktion* had become
more restive. Cases of revolt against Adenauer's foreign policy positions
had been the exception rather than the rule during the 1950s, for
the *Fraktion's* turnout in votes on foreign and defence issues was high
and its solidarity behind Adenauer was in this respect very strong, as
Domes has shown for the second and third legislative periods (1953-
61).[52] The same was also true of the first legislative period.[53] Yet
Domes's conclusion that the CDU/CSU deputies acted effectively as
a 'Yes-Man *Fraktion*' over foreign and defence questions cannot be
accepted without some explanation or even qualification, as also
with Markmann's assertion that 'the *Fraktion* supported its leader
single-mindedly'.[54] The impressive solidarity behind Adenauer's
external policies was a result not only of the power structure surrounding the Chancellorship as he had developed it, but also of several general
features and attitudes in the CDU/CSU, both in the *Fraktion* and outside it, which need to be mentioned in order to complete the picture
of the party's relation to Government policy.

First, Adenauer's pro-Western foreign policy with its marked
clarity of purpose of establishing his country's credit as a Western
partner drew on the resources of a strong ideological commitment in
the CDU/CSU to anti-Communism and Western cultural values.[c]

c   See above chapter 1 (a), pp. 29-30.

This commitment was most strong among Catholic politicians like von Brentano, Kiesinger and other foreign spokesmen of the CDU/CSU who like Adenauer revealed a strong desire for friendly relations with France. It was weak among a few prominent Protestant Christian Democrats like Ehlers and Gerstenmaier, but their influence was either not exercised on this matter or it failed to make any imprint on the party as a whole, where a widespread but passive adherence to 'European' positions was evident.

Secondly, foreign relations was the policy area where the CDU was by far the most cohesive. The divisions which existed in the party between the progressive and conservative wings over matters of economic and social policy were not a relevant factor in foreign policy attitudes. This unity owed something to the ideological factor already discussed, but it arose from two other causes: the interest-group tendencies within the *Fraktion* were not essentially interested in foreign-policy making; and loyalty to Adenauer which accepted him as the architect of West Germany's new international status. According to Heidenheimer, 'for the overwhelming majority of relatively inexperienced and uncommitted Christian Democratic deputies, who saw their own political futures increasingly tied to the public state of confidence in Adenauer, there was no alternative but to stand solidly behind the Chancellor'.[55] Unity over foreign policy therefore acted as a necessary balance to the divisions which tended to appear sometimes over domestic issues. This unity was strengthened by Adenauer's personal emphasis on the importance of foreign policy issues during the 1950s. It was much easier for a loose-associational party like the CDU to integrate over foreign policy, because its national parliamentary elite was inclined to act as a body of 'the Chancellor's faithful' (*Kanzler-Getreuen*), but also because this area of policy encouraged a deferential attitude in the party.

Thirdly, the degree of discipline within the two main *Fraktionen* in the Bundestag (the SPD as well as the CDU/CSU) was extremely high in the 1950s. Gerhard Loewenberg concluded in a study on this subject made in the early 1960s that 'the voting behaviour of Bundestag deputies confirms the effectiveness of party discipline', and that 'the fact remains that when the most controversial issues are decided on the floor of the Bundestag, the deputies vote in party blocs; the discipline is so extensive that it allows little opportunity for a deputy to develop an individual voting record'.[56] Officially, the CDU/CSU group in the Bundestag applied no *Fraktionszwang* (rules of compulsion to vote the party line), but there was a significant difference between the theory and the reality. The absence of such rules could be explained by the CDU outlook, which saw coerced discipline as a property of Marxist parties, for as Heinrich von Brentano proclaimed at the party Congress in 1953: 'Our *Fraktion* was never the extended arm of a party rigidly organised and structured according to totalitarian principles.'[57] The *Fraktion* rules of procedure obliged deputies who had 'misgivings' about party policy to 'express their differing viewpoint promptly to the *Fraktion* and its chairman', but the same rules circumscribed this implied freedom considerably by demanding that deputies who intended to present bills, resolutions, interpellations and parliamentary questions submit them for examination by the *Fraktion* secretariat beforehand.[58] In practice a great deal of pressure was applied on recalcitrant members of the CDU/CSU *Fraktion*.[21]

Fourthly, the dominance of the *Fraktion* Executive over the CDU/CSU deputies was an important final reason for the party's solidarity over foreign policy in the Bundestag. This obviously followed from the third reason, but there were other reasons too. A high proportion of ordinary deputies were, especially in the early years of the Bundestag, not very knowledgeable about foreign affairs, for their greater concern was to represent certain interests at the national level. The comment of the *Weser-Kurier* (a pro-SPD paper) that 'most of them are no "politicians", but very upright average citizens or local notables, who find pleasant not political passion but the honour of belonging to the Parliament'[59] had a ring of truth, although in the course of time more and more deputies became experienced enough to speak on foreign affairs. This process was slow because the rate of personal continuity in the CDU/CSU *Fraktion* was much lower than was the case with the SPD, due to the influx of many new members after the election successes of 1953 and 1957 and to the fact that only a few deputies remained from the first legislative period.[60]

The *Fraktion's* solidarity behind the Government was less strong in domestic affairs, reflecting as this did the diversity of political outlook contained within the CDU/CSU and the strength of organised sub-group activity within the *Fraktion* itself.[d] CDU/CSU deputies were more assertive than passive over social and economic issues, and therefore less submissive to Government policy decisions than was the case over foreign policy. Whereas deviationists over foreign policy

d   See pp. 70 and 106 (note 7).

were isolated, bloc deviation rather than individual deviation
occurred over social questions. This was most noticeable among
the progressive wing of CDU deputies — the *Arbeitnehmergruppe* -
which on ten occasions during the first Bundestag sided with the SPD
on such matters as the creation of a Federal unemployment insurance
office, the question of the death penalty and a labour-management
law.[61] The independent behaviour of this sub-group was also apparent
during the second and third legislative periods, such as with the split
in the *Fraktion* over the law on unemployment insurance in 1956.
It was less pronounced in the case of other sub-groups.[62]

The Adenauer Government had to take into account such pressures,
so that it could be said the CDU/CSU *Fraktion* took some active
part in the formulation of domestic policy, although one which was
still decidedly secondary to that of the Chancellor and his Cabinet.[22]
The Government was most vulnerable to the influence of the *Fraktion*
under certain conditions: when interest-group activity through the
Fraktion was very strong; when there were differences inside the
Cabinet and ministers, while recognising Cabinet discipline, nevertheless sought support from organised groups in the *Fraktion* (such as
ministers of Labour who spoke for the interests of the progressive
wing); and when there was strong opposition from the public.[63]
The pressure of public opinion could be used especially when the CDU/
CSU lost support in Landtag elections, as often happened mid-term
during the Government's period in office. This however touches on
the Federal/*Land* dimension, and will be discussed in the next chapter.

Fraktion solidarity was in any case less likely in the more complicated area of domestic policy-making, in which, unlike foreign
affairs, it was not feasible to contain the circle of those who exercised
power and influence. The pressure of interest groups in the broader
context of the federal system and the lower degree of confidentiality
of the policy-making process made that necessary. In the field of
domestic policy the *Fraktion* was simply demonstrating the CDU/
CSU's *Volkspartei* character as a parliamentary filter for different
socio-economic viewpoints, and was performing a natural function
in a parliamentary democracy even one under the patriarchal
guidance of Adenauer. Adenauer in any case chose primarily
questions of foreign affairs for confidence in his leadership, and here
he found a generally willing instrument for the ratification of his
policies. The key to Adenauer's success with his *Fraktion* was his
undisputed political authority through the 1950s. Only when his
authority showed signs of weakening in 1959 did the prospects for

a more politically independent role for the CDU/CSU *Fraktion* appear
possible, but before turning to that development, Adenauer's
relations with the party outside the parliament must first be considered.

(c)   The Party in the Country: the Role of CDU Congresses

At the outset of the Adenauer era, the CDU was a loosely organised
'coalition of interests' held together politically by a common
loyalty to the Adenauer Government. Organisational power in the
party remained however in the control of its regional associations
(*Landesverbände*). Both Adenauer and the regional 'party barons' had
seemed at the time of the Goslar Congress in 1950 to co-operate in
the face of their similar dislike of a strong national party organisation.
But the question remained open how far the different motives
behind these similar positions complemented each other, or whether
there was potential scope for conflict the more Adenauer required the
CDU as a political base for supporting his policies. In other words,
could such a fine distinction be made between political and organisational interests in the CDU? An examination of this problem throws
significant light on relations between party leaders and activists, and
on the state of cohesion in the CDU as a political movement.

The essential starting point for a discussion of the extra-parliamentary
character of the CDU must be the federal political system of West
Germany. As already shown, the structure of the CDU was itself
federal, for like the federal structure of the state it had developed from
its regional units upwards. Since the Basic Law provided for the
formulation of much domestic policy in conjunction with the *Länder*
and in several important cases for their exclusive right of legislation,
it followed that *Land* governments offered an important outlet
for political activity by regional party leaders if they chose not to
confine themselves to matters of party administration. Indeed,
the CDU had established a leading position in regional government
(in North-Rhine Westphalia and the Rhineland-Palatinate, as well as
in the case of the CSU in Bavaria) well before Adenauer's rise to the
Chancellorship.

Early tension between Adenauer and regional party leaders
appeared over the former's desire that *Land* parties of the CDU
should conform to the Bonn formula of a right-of-centre coalition,
because the Government required a substantial majority for its
policies in the Bundesrat which consisted of selected ministers
from the *Land* governments. Any alternative coalition might weaken
the solidarity of that majority. It was also in Adenauer's eyes unthink-

able in view of the SPD's intransigent opposition to many of his
policies in the Bundestag that a regional party should coalesce with
the Social Democrats, although this was the case in many *Länder* in
the late 1940s. By 1950, many of these grand coalitions had ended
mainly over differences between the parties concerning *Land*
politics, but pressures were exerted by national leaders against those
regional party politicians who persisted in a governmental alliance
with the SPD. The two cases of Werner Hilpert in Hesse and Günther
Gereke in Lower Saxony, both deputy minister-presidents in
coalitions led by the Social Democrats, illustrated the weakening
effect such conflicts of loyalty could have on the CDU's political
strength at the regional level.[23]Adenauer's most prominent rival,
Karl Arnold, however remained as Minister-President in North-Rhine
Westphalia until 1956, and refused in the face of much pressure
from Bonn to form a right-of-centre coalition in Düsseldorf until
after the *Land* election of 1954. The example of Arnold demonstrated
that where a regional party chieftain could count on strong loyalty
from within his own party base he could contend with blandishments
and threats from the Federal Chancellor.

Direct conflict between Adenauer and the regional 'party barons'
arose when he attempted to encroach on *Land* party interests.
Whenever this occurred, it illustrated Adenauer's inability to impose
his will against entrenched regional party interests. The unsuccessful
efforts by Felix von Eckhardt, Adenauer's press spokesman, to
determine nominations for CDU candidates in electoral districts
exposed the resentment at the regional and local party levels at
interference from above in organisational matters. The newly
formed Federal party headquarters in Bonn (*Bundesgeschäftsstelle* —
BGS) learned very quickly not to follow Adenauer's example of
meddling with the *Landesverbände's* interests. In his election report
of 1953, the CDU Business Manager Bruno Heck commented
defensively that:

> . . . the establishment of means whereby the BGS can be kept
> in continuous contact will not be used to give the BGS political
> weight. That is not its job. Quite the contrary, for there is no
> sense in trying to maintain the fiction of a political section
> within the BGS.[64]

This underlined the fact that organisational and political interests
could not be strictly distinguished from each other at the regional

level of party activity. It was also not unusual for CDU deputies
in the Bundestag to couple their support for the Federal Government's national policies with opposition in their other capacity as
local chairmen to efforts by the Bonn party elite to influence party
politics within their domain.

Instances of interference by national leaders in organisational
questions at the regional level were not a regular feature of party
life, in fact they were exceptional. The most serious conflict arose
over policy matters, particularly in the domestic field where the
Federal Government had restricted scope for manoeuvre, notably in
the area of education policy-making which was exclusively directed
by the *Länder*. The Federal Government could therefore only
influence the direction of education policy. In fact, the formulation
of education policy within the CDU was subject to numerous
influences and pressures extending from 'the local branch to the top
Federal leadership, from the simple member to the occupant of a
leadership position, from a senior civil servant to the minister of
education, from the education-policy expert to the representative
of interests in an association of the CDU'.[65] Even the Roman
Catholic Church and the teachers' associations could have an
important say in education policy.[66] Most of these influences
operated at the *Land* level, for that was where these policy
decisions were taken.

Adenauer was not satisfied with this minimum control by the
Federal Government and became more and more openly critical
of the federal structure in relation to education policy, attacking
the Bundesrat in his speech to the CDU Congress in 1956, claiming
that federalism had gone too far in this case. Before specifically
mentioning educational policy matters, he accused *Land* governments,
including those of the CDU, of conducting what he called 'party
politics':

I am a convinced federalist. I am not a centralist, but everything
must be weighed up against each other. The federalistic tendencies
of the Basic Law, which were chosen by the Occupation authorities
in order to keep the central power as weak as possible and so to
create a weak Germany, go rather too far in my opinion. The
whole legislative work is endlessly slowed down and complicated
because of this. When we created the Basic Law in the Parliamentary
Council . . . we never believed that the *Länder* would carry on
party politics in the Bundesrat. At that time we are prisoners of

the illusion that the *Länder* governments would detach themselves
from the struggle of parties . . . [67]

This outburst of Adenauer's against 'educational federalism'
(Kulturföderalismus) which implied a basic criticism of the constitutional structure of the Federal Republic and therefore trod
on dubious ground, aroused little sympathy and some disquiet in
the CDU. A member of the Federal Education Committee of the
CDU, Hellmust Lauffs, wrote to Josef Hofmann, the Committee's
chairman, in May 1956 about Adenauer's remarks at the party
Congress the month before: 'It ought not to happen again that
highest party authorities should issue declarations on education
policy without any previous advisory comments, and thereby use
formulations which lead to misunderstanding.'[68] At the Congress
itself, Adenauer's speech in which he had named certain *Land*
governments caused sufficient rancour that Kai-Uwe von Hassel,
the Minister-President of Schleswig-Holstein, felt compelled to
calm ruffled feelings by suggesting in his address at the final rally
two days later that the main aim in education policy was to find a
balance between uniformity and diversity. This would accord with
the principle of federalism, because it would avoid 'both extremes —
centralism and particularism'.[69]

Adenauer's remarks were expressed in a provocative manner,
although he felt he had good reasons for deploring the lack of
satisfactory co-ordination and co-operation within the CDU as a
whole over education policy. Indeed many education specialists
in the party found this a continuous source of irritation and dissatisfaction. There was no effective co-ordination in this field
between national party leaders on the one hand and *Land* party
organisations and *Fraktionen* in the regional parliaments on the
other, in spite of continuous efforts made by the CDU's Federal
Education Committee to influence and control matters. Only in 1959
was a decision taken to hold sessions of the Committee together
with education-policy experts from the Bundestag and Landtag
Fraktionen of the CDU and CSU.[70] The reason for the delay of
this initiative and the real cause of the conflict between Adenauer
and regional party leaders was the jealous attitude of the latter
towards the protection of their powers and privileges in regional
government from any Federal interference. Other instances of such
conflict over domestic policy issues were less dramatic than that over
education, although they illustrated that the divisions within the CDU/

CSU over the nature of federalism apparent when the Basic Law was formulated[e] were as strong as ever.[24] These few examples emphasised how much the process of domestic policy-making was determined by the federal system of West Germany, for it had to take into account internal party pressures at different geographical levels as well as those deriving from interest groups and the different levels of governmental authority. This picture corresponded too with the lower degree of cohesion in the Bundestag *Fraktion* of the CDU/CSU over domestic compared with foreign issues.[f]

Adenauer sought and more easily found unanimous party support for his decisions on foreign and European affairs, where he and his government had the exclusive right of policy-making. The Chancellor acquired full backing from his party over West Germany's entry to the Council of Europe in 1951, membership of the European Coal and Steel Community introduced by the Schuman Plan of 1950 and later signature of the Treaty of Rome of 1957 creating the EEC. The only strong opposition to these decisions was voiced individually by Ludwig Erhard on economic grounds.[71] Erhard's objections to what he called 'supranational dirigisme' and his preference for a free-trade area found a sympathetic audience among industrial circles, but although a popular figure he had no strong political base in the CDU so that Adenauer was able to use his authority as party leader to overwhelm the CDU with his enthusiasm for the European cause.[72] The CSU although a separate political party was still involved for most of the 1950s in establishing its position in Bavarian politics and showed little interest during this decade in developing a separate profile in foreign policy.[g] The real test of party solidarity in foreign affairs came over the one issue which occasioned the most domestic political controversy, namely the project introduced in 1950 to create a European Defence Community (EDC) and with it initiate West German rearmament. Adenauer went to some extraordinary lengths to ensure support for his policy of joining the proposed EDC, especially as the SPD Opposition chose to make an emotional issue out of it and harnessed public opinion, unhappy over Germany's recent past, in several *Land* elections during the early 1950s.

e See above chapter 1(a), p. 32
f See above chapter 2(a), pp. 79-80
g See below chapter 10(a), pp. 307 ff.

In order to counter the Opposition's successful mobilisation of
popular feelings on the EDC at the grass-roots. Adenauer needed the
publicity services of his party to transmit support for his policy to
the local level, for the official publicity machine in Bonn was inadequate
for this task. Here he found himself dependent on the CDU *Landesverbände* for the organisation of mass publicity. The Federal party
headquarters had only limited means and staff at its disposal, and
was not in a position to conduct a massive publicity drive or cope
with other publicity problems arising from the EDC issue. This
weakness of the national party organisation was underlined in a
circular letter written by Bruno Heck to *Land* business managers of
the CDU on 3 June 1952. In view of the forthcoming creation of
a European army, it was to be expected that applications to join the
ranks of the new German units would be made through the CDU. As
it was not possible for the Federal headquarters to deal with a rush of
applications, Heck requested that each *Landesverband* should assume
the responsibility for 'scrutinising them conscientiously'. Larger
Landesverbände were recommended to appoint an official who would
'handle the applications for the Office Blank [25] on the level of the
Landesverband'.[73] Shortly before the final vote on the Paris Treaties
in the Bundestag early in 1955, Adenauer sent a personal letter to all
Land business managers as well as all Bundestag and Landtag deputies
of the CDU goading them into a final spurt of publicity to offset the
SPD's exploitation of public concern about the issue:

> The representatives of the Christian Democratic Union must
> with all determination confront this attempt of the SPD. I
> therefore ask you to put all your power in the coming weeks into
> the service of instructing our people about the dangerous illusions
> of the Opposition, and about the aims and intentions of our
> policy. The *Land* organisations of our party will approach you in
> the next days to discuss with you your practical involvement
> in the context of this action of enlightenment.[74]

Adenauer insisted that the EDC Treaty should restore West German
sovereignty and settle the country's participation in the Western
defence alliance, and with his determined efforts to push through his
policy he managed to use his authority in the party to overcome
remaining doubts among the party rank-and-file which were occasioned
by the arousal of public feelings on the subject. In so doing Adenauer
could count on the deferential and passive attitude among party

members that elected leaders and representatives should in foreign affairs be left free to decide which policies should be pursued.[75] Adenauer's domestic difficulties over the EDC did not originate from any lack of internal party unity or solidarity over the issue, for even the public opposition of Martin Niemöller, a former leader of the Confessional Church and now church president in Hesse, and Gustav Heinemann, Adenauer's former Minister of the Interior,[h] failed to shake party loyalty to Adenauer, even though other CDU leaders had initially feared the influence of these two figures on Protestant Christian Democrats.[26] The main threat to the acceptance of the EDC came from trends in the politics of certain *Länder* and their effect on the stability of the Government's majority in the Bundesrat, whose approval was necessary for the passage of the EDC treaty. In 1952 the new Federal state of Baden-Württemberg had been born out of the four different regions, which previously had formed south-west Germany. This merger had brought to the surface old antagonisms between Badeners and Württembergers, and with it divisions within the Baden CDU into moderate and uncompromising groups. These divisions in the regional CDU occasioned a slump in its vote in the *Landtag* election which followed in March of that year, thereby allowing the formation in Stuttgart of an FDP/SPD/BHE coalition led by Reinhold Maier, the FDP leader in the new *Land*. These events seriously affected the Government's majority in the Bundesrat before the EDC Treaty came up for approval, for the new *Land* government held the balance there and so endangered Adenauer's policy plans. Maier was determined to side with the SPD in blocking the Treaty. Meanwhile, Adenauer had been trying to influence the formation in Lower Saxony of a CDU coalition with the refugee party, the BHE, in view of the insecurity of the SPD-led government in Hanover under Heinrich Kopf. Since Lower Saxony was one of the larger states, its five representatives in the Bundesrat under CDU direction would have secured a majority there for the Federal Government. These attempts at interference from Bonn proved unsuccessful and were abandoned, when Reinhold Maier after weeks of hostile pressures against him changed his position in the spring of 1953 and withdrew his opposition to the Treaty.[76]

The issue of the European Defence Community had absorbed West German attention for nearly four years, from the presentation of the Pleven Plan in October 1950 until the French rejection of the

---

h   See above chapter 2 (a), pp. 65-66.

Treaty in the National Assembly in August 1954.[27] These years of
the early 1950s were also the period during which the CDU/CSU,
although the leading governing party of the Federal Republic, had
not yet established its strong position as majority party. Adenauer's
hope that electoral support for his party at the regional level would
substantiate support for his policies at the Federal level did not
materialise. *Land* election results during 1950 to 1952 showed a
decisive swing against the CDU/CSU in almost all cases, bringing it an
average loss of more than 6 per cent compared with its national
vote of 31 per cent in the Bundestag Election in 1949. The SPD's
average gain of 5 per cent reflected public uncertainty about
Adenauer's foreign policy at that time, but it also was the first
occasion of one general feature that was to characterise *Land*
elections in future, namely a trend against the principal governing
party between national elections because of less mobilisation of its own
voters compared with those of the Opposition. The appearance of
several new minor parties and their impressive impact in several state
elections also introduced a fluidity in the balance of party strengths
on the right of the political spectrum. The Refugees' Party (BHE)
founded in 1950 and the neo-Nazi Socialist Reich Party (SRP) scored
high votes in certain areas like Schleswig-Holstein in July 1950
(BHE 23.4 per cent, CDU 19.7 per cent) and Lower Saxony in May
1951 (SRP 11 per cent, BHE 14.9 per cent), but their success was only
a temporary phenomenon.[77] They were able to capitalise on discontent
especially among refugees, because West Germany was still in a state
of economic readjustment to post-war conditions. At the same time,
several of the older smaller parties like the German Party (in coalition
with the CDU/CSU in Bonn) and the Centre Party (the CDU's main
rival for Catholic voters) lost heavily in these elections.

The party system began to consolidate itself, chiefly to the
advantage of the CDU/CSU, from the mid-1950s. The turning-
point came with the Bundestag Election of 1953, when the CDU/
CSU was able to exploit the advantages of incumbency and
acquire substantial gains from the smaller parties. Posing as the
architect of national security and the new economic stability,
the CDU/CSU scored the remarkable breakthrough of a 45.2 per
cent vote (a gain of 14.2 per cent over 1949), giving it an absolute
majority of seats in the Bundestag. This unprecedented achievement
in German electoral history accounted for in part by the party's
strong appeal for the first time among Protestant voters, had a
stabilising effect on the party systems even though a swing against

the party in national government remained as before a feature of
state election. The CDU/CSU pursued its electoral cannibalism
at the cost of the smaller parties, most of which disappeared
gradually from the political scene as a result of a combination
of ideological and personal rifts, financial scandals and the lack
of political issues to exploit. The revision of the electoral law
by the Bundestag Election of 1957 finally put paid to their chances,
for the new requirement that a party must acquire 5 per cent
of the national vote in order to qualify for Bundestag representation directly affected the smaller parties, because most of them
had based their appeal on regional rather than countrywide
support.

The establishment of its electoral supremacy by the CDU/CSU,
further enhanced by Adenauer's triumph of winning an absolute
majority of the national vote in 1957, had important consequences
for party unity. Adenauer's authority as leader was strengthened,
while his party's electoral success helped to contain the problems of
internal cohesion evident in the early 1950s. One suitable way of
evaluating the quality of relations between party leaders and activists
in the CDU during the decade of the 1950s is to examine the
official forum in which they met, although this approach has limitations, which will emerge. CDU Congresses usually took place
annually, and lasted about three days. In theory the CDU Congress
(*Parteitag*) had the right to 'determine the basic lines of the policy
of the CDU' and 'to receive the responsible reports of the Party
Executive and the Party Committee, and make a decision on them'
(CDU Statutes of 1950). The reality was quite different during
this period, for policy was rarely discussed on these occasions.
In addition to electing the party leadership, the Congresses performed
the function of a mystic communion between Chancellor and
followers. Adenauer's long oration on his Government's policies was
the highlight of the event, while the presence in force of Federal
ministers as well as *Land* minister-presidents and their cabinets on
the rostrum underlined the CDU's importance as a governing party.
Yet the role of the party Congress was not exclusively as a vehicle
for publicising Adenauer's policies, for it could also act as an agent
for promoting internal party solidarity, stimulating developments in
party organisation and even in exceptional cases reflecting tensions
in the party. It is therefore useful to look individually at the different
functions of CDU Congresses, and in so doing to acquire some flavour
of the internal character of the CDU and throw further light on the

nature of Adenauer's party leadership:

1.   *The Inauguration of Election Campaigns*

Many of the CDU Congresses during the 1950s took place before Federal and *Land* elections, and were consciously geared to boosting party morale and presenting a united and confident front to the electorate. The prospect of *Land* elections could influence the venue of a Congress, as with the 1954 Congress in Cologne (held a month before the elections in North-Rhine Westphalia) and the 1958 Congress in Kiel (only one week before the elections in Schleswig-Holstein). At the 1954 Congress, the meeting of the Federal Party Executive on the first day specifically discussed the line to be followed during the forthcoming *Land* election, and Karl Arnold, the Minister-President, addressed the plenary session on the third day on 'The Importance of the *Land* of North-Rhine Westphalia'. The mobilisation purpose of these gatherings of the party faithful was most clearly evident at the Hamburg Congress in April 1953, which for all practical purposes was an 'electoral congress' with a view to setting the scene for the Bundestag Election campaign the following September. The emphasis placed on electoral success featured prominently in speeches made by party leaders. The first paragraph of Adenauer's opening address to the CDU Congress in the following year dwelt on the party's recent triumph in the Bundestag Election, in which 'the German people handed over to the Christian Democratic Union the claim and the right to leadership!'.[78] Election success solidified Adenauer's position in the party, but equally election reverses could affect the mood of delegates and provoke concern about the Chancellor's advancing age and his ability to continue with the affairs of state. The 1951 Congress in Karlsruhe, for instance, met against the background of CDU losses in recent *Land* elections and press rumours that some sort of post-mortem would be conducted. The CDU was among other things accused of fatigue. Adenauer met the problem frontally in a stirring speech to the assembled delegates. According to one observer,

He put his prepared text in his pocket, took off — symbolically speaking — the dignified Chancellor's coat and rolled up the shirtsleeves of the party politician right to the top. He who believed that the CDU was in a state of decline, so he said, was making a basic mistake. Never has the party been so vigorous and internally united as today. During the powerful applause which greeted these words, the Chancellor shouted out: 'This party Congress was the opening phase of the election campaign of 1953. And this election we are going to win!'[79]

The 1958 Congress by contrast took place after the CDU/CSU's unprecedented win of an absolute majority in the Bundestag Election of 1957. According to the then *Times* correspondent, delegates were 'converging on Kiel to pay homage to the father-figure of post-war Germany' for 'the resounding victory in last year's federal elections remains a warm memory'. Also a CDU government had been returned to power in North-Rhine Westphalia, following the party's success in the *Land* election two months before. Adenauer appeared to be at the acme of his career. *The Times* commented piquantly: 'Millions of middle-class Germans will sleep more soundly in their feather beds after this congress.'[80]

2. Publicity for the Policies of the Federal Government

The Congresses were regarded by the CDU leadership as an occasion for reinforcing party solidarity behind the Chancellor's policies. The Hamburg Programme of 1953 presented to the Congress of that year opened with the words: 'Under the Chancellorship of Konrad Adenauer, the Christian Democratic Union has in the last four years led the German people away from hunger, distress and deadly isolation . . .'.[81] Similarly, Adenauer wrote about the forthcoming Congress in Hamburg in 1957: 'We will render account there on whether we have fulfilled what we promised before the Bundestag Election of 1953.'[82] CDU Congresses closed almost invariably with an acclamatory ratification of Adenauer's foreign policies, on which his speeches tended to concentrate. Deviationists particularly over foreign policy were treated with little respect. An attack on the Chancellor's Saar policy by the Berlin deputy Friedensburg at the Cologne Congress in 1954 produced not only an interjection from Adenauer, but also the telling comment from Wilhelm Johnen, president of the Congress, that:

At this moment, when the foreign-policy debate of our Congress is taking place, the eyes of the people at home and abroad are directed at us (Lively applause). May I therefore ask you to be aware of the fact that everyone who speaks is being heard at home and abroad, and that each false utterance against the policy of the Chancellor, and with it of the CDU, could perhaps cause enormous damage.[83]

Sometimes, party Congresses were used to publicise the 'correct' picture of a particular Government policy which might be in dispute. Adenauer held three mass rallies in West Berlin on the evening of his arrival there for the Congress in 1952 to dispel the belief that the CDU was ultimately opposed to German reunification. The monopolistic role of Adenauer and his ministers at Congress did mean that internal party democracy, in the sense of active participation in policy formulation by the rank-and-file of CDU delegates, was very low. Adenauer influenced the preparation of Congress agendas, so that the main time was given to set speeches by party leaders preferably dealing with the fundamentals rather than specifics of policy. Many of them sounded like prepared lectures,[28] and there was little time left for open discussion and certainly not for the airing of views on controversial issues of the day. In spite of the prominence of the rearmament issue at the time of the 1956 Congress, there was a noticeable absence of any provision for debating it there — on the contrary, the Bundestag *Fraktion* had already made the decision to introduce national service shortly before the Congress opened. The Hamburg Programme, the last important CDU programme until the Berlin Programme of 1968, was drawn up by committees of the Federal Party Executive and presented to the 1953 Congress for its acceptance without debate. The lack of discussion of policy matters at this Congress provoked some criticism from within the party. Shortly afterwards, the CDU *Land* party executive in Hamburg met to discuss a report on the Congress:

> Especially emphasised was the absence of a genuine discussion — a criticism, which the past Congresses also experienced, without this state of affairs being changed up to now. In Hamburg once again any discord and any fruitful exchanges were missing; during the discussions the ministers stood in the foreground and not the delegates, who had to keep strictly to the five-minute speaking time.[84]

This criticism expressed behind closed doors did not, however, take the form of an open protest.

3. The Promotion of Internal Party Solidarity

If party solidarity was usually demonstrated to an impressed public, how much did Congresses also reinforce party solidarity? Adenauer was invariably presented by contemporary observers as the 'clamp between the many groups which together form the CDU'.[85] Party Congresses provided regular evidence through the 1950s of a charismatic relationship between the Chancellor and his party followers, which could be described as a sort of 'emotional integration' within the party. Adenauer's entries at Congresses were usually preceded by a number of brief 'warming-up' speeches and then a hushed pause. He would then stride in to the accompaniment of loud ovations. Adenauer's charisma was most vividly illustrated at the Hamburg Congress in 1953. He arrived a day late, having only just returned from his first visit to the USA. As an avid reader of newspapers, Adenauer had kept an eye in particular on the West German press coverage of his tour, for its domestic effect, which he saw as symbolic of his country's new international respectability and acceptance as a partner by other Western democracies. He flew back direct to Hamburg, and was greeted at the airport by almost the whole Federal Cabinet. Adenauer drove straight to his hotel to prepare for his appearance at the Congress. The scene of his reception there was described as follows by a newspaper reporter:

> As the Chancellor appeared the floodlights lit up, the delegates rose up and accorded their chairman continuous ovations. Upright and self-confident, Dr Adenauer strode past the rows waving again and again to all sides, here and there exchanging a handshake. For a while a proud smile rested on his face, on which otherwise the exertions of the last weeks still were noticeable. After a few words of greeting from the Congress president, the Chancellor stepped up to the microphone.[86]

Adenauer's speech, which concentrated as expected on his American visit, said in reference to his visit to the Arlington National Cemetery in Washington: 'I want to explain the ceremony to you in detail in order to give you an impression of the extent to which Germany counts for something again.'[87] Adenauer generally spoke in straightforward, simple sentences, but this kind of oratory and his sense of political timing had a powerful effect on the audience of CDU delegates. They consisted largely of local notables from lower or upper middle-class backgrounds, who felt a certain veneration when they found themselves face-to-face with the national figures of the party (*Parteiprominenz*). Party solidarity was therefore strongly associated in the eyes of Congress delegates with the figure of Adenauer as leader of West Germany and with his policies. This association was further enhanced by the decor of Congresses, such as the tendency to display the German eagle and the national colours behind the rostrum. Party solidarity as reinforced by the Congresses contained therefore a very strong personal and Government-oriented element.

4.   *An Occasional but Rare Outlet for Party Dissatisfaction*

Because of the strong governmental orientation of CDU Congresses, they did not provide a ready outlet for party dissatisfaction. One instance did occur, however, during the 1950s at the Congress at Stuttgart in 1956, but significantly this case illustrated that Adenauer's authority was not really under challenge, for it arose from a concern over Adenauer's political future on health grounds. The Chancellor's illness the previous autumn had forced a postponement of the Congress planned for 1955, but uneasiness over the party's dependence on his seeming fragility of health lingered on until the delayed Congress took place in April 1956. There followed the unprecedented stand taken against Adenauer over a change in the Party Statutes. Adenauer chose to make it clear that his position was not to be disputed, for on the second day he addressed himself to the party with his usual aplomb: 'As long as God gives me vitality and strength, it depends on you whether Khruschev succeeds or fails in reaching his objective.'[88] As a foreign correspondent noted about Adenauer: 'He is an aged 80, and the delegates could be excused their private thoughts about his eventual successor; no one cared to mention the matter in open debate.'[89] Although the prospects for the 1957 Bundestag Election did not at this time seem good, it was in any case too late to consider a change in the leadership. The occasion for the mini-revolt at the 1956 Congress was the proposed change in the Party Statutes of 1950 to allow for the election of four instead of two party vice-chairmen. The motion was presented by the delegates from North-Rhine Westphalia and introduced with a masterly speech from Josef-Hermann Dufhues of the Westphalian CDU, arguing that the party should respond to the 'forces' which could overthrow the CDU-led *Land* government in Düsseldorf[29] by promoting Karl Arnold, the ex-Minister-President, as a party leader. It was further understood that the creation of more deputy chairmen, together with the enlargement of the Party Executive, would lighten Adenauer's burden as party leader. The proposed elevation of Arnold, Adenauer's old party rival, to a national party position inspired him to oppose the motion obstinately within the party Federal Committee, but after an even vote the question was put to the plenary session, which decided through secret ballot in favour of the motion by 239 votes to 227. Four party vice-chairmen were elected, including Arnold.[90] This flicker of independence from the party was interpreted by most press reports as a 'defeat' for Adenauer, although it was more like a gesture of defiance. The Congress, as on previous occasions, expressed its full support for the policies of the Chancellor, who in his final speech showed himself in good form with his dry sarcastic partisan humour.[91]

5.   The Encouragement of Developments in Party Organisation

This was another function of party Congresses which proved to have little influence. During the early 1950s little interest was shown in matters of party organisation, but as the decade progressed some party leaders began to display a special concern for structuring and strengthening party organisation. At the 1956 Congress, uncertainty about the CDU's chances in the Bundestag election the following year had led to the appointment of a three-man collegium within the Federal Party Executive, consisting of Kiesinger, Meyers and Schröder, to concentrate on party work and to act as a 'general staff' for the election campaign.[92] Franz Meyers, formerly Minister of the Interior in the Arnold *Land* government, used his appointment in 1956 to devote time to encourage some changes by employing young graduates as party officials. At the Kiel Congress in 1958, Meyers paid special attention to weaknesses of party organisation and the problem of party membership in his report on behalf of the Federal Executive.[93] Bruno Heck, CDU Business Manager, made regular appeals for an increase in party membership, and in September 1956 Adenauer lent his name to a membership drive with a letter addressed to every party member (his *Kanzlerbrief*) urging the need for the 'application of all forces' in preparation for the 1957 Bundestag election. Those members who were most successful in wooing new adherents to the party would be given an invitation to come to Bonn 'so that I can talk with them about their experiences'.[94]

Although Adenauer was not generally interested in strengthening party organisation, his *Kanzlerbrief* indicated that his concern over party membership was motivated exclusively by thoughts

about the electoral future of the CDU. This was not surprising in
a party leader with certain authoritarian tendencies, for his overriding
ambition was that his (in particular foreign) policies should succeed,
and that meant without the complication of any questioning of
them within his party. Internal party democracy was therefore
virtually non-existent in the CDU during the 1950s, as the pronounced
executive-dominated character of party Congresses showed. There
was little recognition at them that ideological conflicts were
legitimate, for different internal party groups did not exercise any
significant political weight through their voting power, nor was
there any institutional provision for policy discussion. The Kiel
Congress in 1958, which witnessed some debate over domestic
issues, showed that Congresses could demonstrate policy involvement.
Indeed, there were signs of a cautious growth of independence
within the CDU by the end of the decade, if only because the political
ambitions of the next generations of party leaders, which had been
hibernating under Adenauer's ascendancy, were now beginning to
awaken. Gerhard Stoltenberg, chairman of the Young Union,
expressed this attitude when he pointed out in 1958 that the CDU
could not for ever depend on 'an exceptional party chairman' and
that party organisation had to be strengthened.[95]

The development of a viable national party organisation was held
back during the 1950s not only because it was a taboo subject with
Adenauer, but also because the chairmen of the *Landesverbände*, who
were a considerable organisational power in the land of Christian
Democracy, could also use their political weight in internal party
matters to check any such development. Both Adenauer and the
regional 'party barons' formed a basis of co-operation, though at
times it was an uneasy one, since their common interest was the
electoral success of their party. Any major change in this weighted
balance in the party leadership, where Adenauer was the unquestion-
ably dominant figure at the national level, was only likely to come
eventually from a serious decline in the CDU/CSU's electoral appeal.
In fact, the beginning of this change occurred unexpectedly for quite
another reason, as Adenauer's blatant manoeuvrings over his candidacy for the Federal Presidency in 1959 brought to the surface a
concern about his advanced age, which until then had remained in
closed circles, occasioned doubts about his political judgement and
therefore cast a shadow across his authority in the party. All these
developments in the late 1950s reflected in turn on the state and
nature of party cohesion in the CDU.

(d) The Crisis over Adenauer's Presidential Candidacy, 1959

Adenauer's 58-day candidacy for the Federal Presidency in 1959 was the first principal stage in his political decline, for the manner in which it was conducted weakened his authority as party leader. Theodor Heuss had occupied the position of Federal President since 1949, and was shortly to retire in the early autumn of 1959, having completed his second five-year term in office. The situation concerning candidates was an open one, and speculation about various possibilities had been abundant since 1958. The SPD Opposition found no difficulty in settling on the respected figure of Carlo Schmid, a leading figure in the establishment of the Federal Republic, but the question remained who would be the Government's candidate. This became a controversial political issue because it was linked by most influential CDU politicians, including Adenauer himself, with the even more problematical issue of who would succeed him as Chancellor — the 'crown prince' question, until then undiscussed. This was the key to Adenauer's own attitude and behaviour during the crisis which followed, which caused uproar and dismay within his party. The crisis may be divided chronologically into two stages: the period from 7 April, when Adenauer declared that he would stand for President, until the first week of June when he withdrew his candidacy; the weeks following which saw the public quarrel between Adenauer and Erhard terminating in a truce on 23 June.

The crisis brought into the open internal party pressures and personal conflicts in the CDU, which were normally thrashed out behind closed doors. The question of Adenauer's presidential candidacy and its consequences is therefore an interesting case study of how power and influence flowed inside the CDU. It was a turning-point because the Chancellor's political position was never the same again. The crisis will be analysed to show how it exposed relationships within the CDU/CSU, and affected the party itself and Adenauer's authority within it.

Adenauer's agreement on 7 April 1959 to become the presidential candidate of the CDU/CSU was a sudden announcement, but it followed much internal party manoeuvring involving certain important figures in the *Fraktion* and the Chancellor's closest political advisers. Some tension had been caused late in February, when the Selection Committee of the CDU/CSU, consisting of twelve members (including the CDU chairman — i.e. Adenauer — and four vice-chairmen, the CSU chairman and a few *Land* Minister-Presidents and Federal ministers), had under Adenauer's guidance suggested Ludwig Erhard, the Federal Minister of Economics, as their candidate. This was a blatant move by Adenauer to remove his most likely successor as Chancellor, whom he considered on political grounds unsuitable for the post. Erhard's initial reaction was one of amazement and surprise. According to a telephone interview with a newspaper, he said:

> I have not yet decided . . . consultations with the Federal Chancellor are necessary beforehand . . . If this is the unanimous view and the general wish, then I will find it difficult to withdraw from the candidacy . . . All the same I had not believed that it would come to me with such abruptness.[96]

A unanimous view on this matter did not exist inside the party. The *Fraktion* resented being presented with a fait accompli by the Selection Committee and voiced strong objections to Erhard's candidacy for President, not on the grounds of the latter's suitability as President but because the *Fraktion* viewed Erhard as the party's main alternative to Adenauer as a vote-winner. Erhard's transfer to the neutral position of head of state would deprive the CDU/CSU of his future electoral services. As was confirmed during the months which followed, the *Fraktion's* main concern was to retain Erhard as 'a guarantee against electoral accidents'[97] in the event of Adenauer's death or resignation. Heinrich Krone, chairman of the *Fraktion*, collected signatures from a clear majority of the deputies for a letter of protest against the nomination of Erhard.[98] Adenauer's plan was therefore foiled. Shortly afterwards, on 3 March, Erhard, aware of party feeling about his candidacy, announced that he had decided not to stand for President.

Adenauer's own candidacy for the Presidency was promoted by a small circle of parliamentary leaders, who like others in the CDU/CSU were growing concerned at the 83-year old Chancellor's apparent disinclination to broach the subject of his successor. Adenauer's electoral triumphs of 1957 had stilled the doubts felt in the party during 1955-6 about his continuing political capacity on health grounds, but the problem still remained. The vacancy in the Villa Hammerschmidt caused by Heuss's forthcoming retirement seemed to offer a dignified solution to the succession question. That was the view of older CDU politicians like Heinrich Krone (*Fraktion* chairman and a loyal colleague of Adenauer) who were concerned with continuity and party unity, both of which they believed could be disturbed by a sudden political vacuum. Some younger party leaders, like Eugen Gerstenmaier, President of the Bundestag, and Kai-Uwe von Hassel, Minister-President in Schleswig-Holstein, were less concerned with political niceties and argued that changing times demanded Adenauer's resignation as Chancellor.[99] They were also disturbed by Adenauer's 'juggling with candidates' for the Presidency over the previous months, which prompted them to consider that the only means of countering his devaluation of the highest office in the state was if the supreme Christian Democrat himself were to assume that position.[30][100] After much hesitation Adenauer was in fact persuaded to announce his own candidacy for the Presidency on 7 April, after some of his closest advisers, including Robert Pferdmenges and Hans Globke (who produced a meticulous report arguing that Adenauer would by no means suffer political castration if he became head of state), had requested him to show consideration for his age and health.[101] These consultations had been so confidential that, when the news was broken to the *Fraktion*, it was at first taken aback and then expressed approval. The reaction of the press and the public to Adenauer's sudden announcement was a mixture of surprise and pleasure. The Chancellor's decision was seen as a fitting climax to a distinguished political career.

Although Adenauer had been persuaded to stand for President, he was not firmly convinced by this decision. His equivocal behaviour during the weeks which followed reflected this, for he appeared doubtful about his decision on different occasions, and dropped sly hints in semi-private that he was reconsidering his position — such as his announcement to a Cabinet meeting on 14 May that his candidacy was '90 per cent no longer certain'.[102] Rumours seeped out to a tense *Fraktion*, already frustrated with the unrelieved struggle for succession. One foreign correspondent observed on 24 May that there was growing pressure for an early decision from CDU/CSU Bundestag deputies, who themselves had the ultimate responsibility of electing the new Chancellor, for the dispute had 'grown markedly sharper in the past few days and members fear that it will become even more bitter if it is allowed to drag on'.[103] Adenauer's original hesitation to stand was developing into an obstinate reluctance to continue with his candidacy. Apart from the belief that he had been hood-winked over the extent of the powers of the President, Adenauer's determination to preserve continuity for his foreign policy strengthened his desire to have the decisive influence over the choice of his successor as Chancellor. His decision to remain as Presidential candidate there-fore depended finally on whether he could have his own way over this matter.

In this highly charged situation, a conflict emerged between Adenauer's preferred choice as Chancellor candidate and the inclinations of his parliamentary party. Adenauer's selection of Franz Etzel, the Federal Minister of Finance, as his heir, was on grounds of policy agreement and personal compatibility. This would have suited his needs on becoming head of state, for, as Adenauer stressed, a 'relationship of confidence' between Chancellor and President was important for harmonious government, although in fact his wish went further to the extent of wanting to maintain a dominant influence. Support for Etzel within the *Fraktion* was by no means insignificant, for at the end of May a count of the majority of deputies indicated that just on 100 would vote for him, while about 120-150 preferred Erhard.[104] However, Etzel's lack of a popular image was reflected in an opinion poll taken during April, after Adenauer's endorsement of Etzel, showing that only three per cent of the voters favoured Etzel as Chancellor, while 53 per cent supported Erhard.[105] The well-informed weekly *Christ und Welt* commented, in a study of the mood at the CDU grass-roots, that members of the party were 'in a situation of doubt more for Erhard than for Etzel'.[106] This hesitation reflected doubts about Erhard's political leadership skills as opposed to his economic expertise and electoral appeal, for sceptics among the CDU/CSU deputies were not happy about Erhard's qualifications because he had shown 'no great affinity or even passion for the political metier'.[107]

This was ironically Adenauer's own contention, which he baldly stated in his letter to Krone on the withdrawal of his candidacy, that Erhard was a good economist but 'no politician', and that he did not trust his ideas or his competence in foreign affairs. These doubts about Erhard the politician accounted for his absence among the names considered as successors to Adenauer as CDU chairman. Adenauer, who on his assumption of the presidential office would have to relinquish all his political posts, once again had his preferred candidate in Heinrich Krone, but the latter soon found strong rivals in Franz Meyers, Minister-President in North-Rhine Westphalia, and Kurt-Georg Kiesinger, Minister-President in Baden-Württemberg.[108] Meanwhile, Erhard showed no enthusiasm for serving under Etzel as Chancellor, so that the *Fraktion* was faced, in the words of one commentator, 'with the possibility that if it votes for Herr Etzel it may lose Professor Erhard altogether — a prospect too horrible to be contemplated with an election only two years away'.[109] Erhard

none the less remained the probable choice, so that the situation
reached by the beginning of June was that the *Fraktion* preferred
him for electoral reasons, while Adenauer opposed him for personal
and policy reasons.

Adenauer's way out of this political cul-de-sac was an assertion in
an arbitrary manner of his Chancellor authority. Adenauer's
announcement on 5 June of his decision to forego his candidacy for
President because of the 'seriousness' of international affairs produced
an atmosphere of crisis within the *Fraktion*. There were rumours of
a possible revolt, and a determination to show 'the unscrupulous
old man' just where his limitations lay was expressed in some
quarters. A meeting of the *Fraktion* Executive took place in the
Bundestag on the morning of 5 June. Adenauer met bitter criticism
of his conduct, in response to which he very coolly dared those
present to take the ultimate step of overthrowing him: 'It is not a
question here that I want to become Federal Chancellor — I am that
already — if you don't like that, then you can propose a constructive
vote of no-confidence against me.'[110] During the afternoon there was
a three-hour closed session of the whole *Fraktion*. Objections were
voiced about Adenauer's lack of respect for the party, for the
Government and for public opinion, yet the meeting closed with an
official statement declaring the *Fraktion's* solidarity with Adenauer
and 'respecting' his decision to remain Chancellor.[111]

The *Fraktion* had when the crunch came bent to Adenauer's iron
will to remain in office, for it still basically preferred the incumbent
Adenauer to a Chancellor Erhard, at least in the present situation,
despite all that had happened. The *Fraktion* had, however, become
more aware of its potential power during this contretemps by
insisting on its right to select the Chancellor successor it wanted.
The second state of the 'crisis', which followed during the middle
weeks of June, further illustrated this new realisation in the *Fraktion*.
This 'June crisis' witnessed the unveiling to the full glare of publicity
of the troubled relationship between Adenauer and Erhard, which
had been at the basis of the crisis over Adenauer's presidential
candidacy.

Following Erhard's return from the USA, a meeting between
the two antagonists was only arranged after mediation by Heinrich
Krone, who insisted that some arrangement between them was
'essential for the Union'. but it produced no reconciliation, although
the *Fraktion* issued a 'declaration of honour' greeting the Chancellor's
statement that any 'disqualification' of the Economics Minister was

'far from his thoughts'.[112] Since both men concerned appeared
together at this session of the *Fraktion*, it seemed that a reconciliation
was at hand, but this assumption proved mistaken only a few days
later when *The New York Times* published an interview with
Adenauer, who repeated his doubts about Erhard's political capa-
bilities. Krone officially deplored these remarks and advised
Adenauer to remain absent from a meeting of the *Fraktion* on
19 June. On the way to the meeting, Erhard told journalists waiting
outside the Bundestag that Adenauer was 'damaging the reputation
of Germany and destroying the party'.[113] The mood among CDU/
CSU deputies was, according to one of the journalists, 'black enough
to storm the nearby Chancellory gates'.[114] One deputy expressed a
commonly felt concern about the Bundestag Election due in 1961:
'So far the Adenauer-Erhard team of the CDU/CSU has guaranteed
election successes — what will now happen if the enmity is not at
least concealed outwardly?'[115] After several unsatisfactory efforts at
mediation, which merely produced a lukewarm letter from the
Chancellor to Erhard, Krone and Pferdmenges used all their powers
of persuasion on Adenauer to write Erhard the assurance of respect
for his achievements that he wanted.[116] Following this, Erhard
agreed to continue serving as minister in Adenauer's Government,
and so the quarrel was at least to outward appearances finally
concluded.

The Adenauer/Erhard crisis had important long-term consequences
for relationships within the CDU/CSU. However, the *Fraktion* had
ultimately demonstrated its loyalty to Adenauer even in the midst of
the crisis, and there never was any chance of an organised rebellion
among its members, for, although the question of a constructive
vote of no-confidence against Adenauer was raised by a few deputies,
they gained hardly any support in the *Fraktion* at large.[117] The press
speculated about splits in the party and a possible 'national secession'
under Erhard, but these rumours came to nothing.[118] Yet, despite
its actual submission to Adenauer's will, the *Fraktion's* cool attitude
towards Adenauer's behaviour had encouraged a sense of independence
that was likely to grow in the course of events.

The three months had imposed severe strains on the party's
solidarity behind Adenauer — in fact, the main victim of the crisis
was Adenauer's own prestige and authority, both inside the CDU/CSU
and among the public. Most *Landesverbände* hardly surprisingly
revealed a negative attitude towards the affair. The Hamburg CDU
executive had resolved on 5 June to urge the Bundestag *Fraktion*

executive to demand that Adenauer remain by his original decision to stand for President. The CSU chairman, Hanns Seidel, commented in Munich that he 'respected' the Chancellor's decision but that he was 'not enthused by it'; while Kai-Uwe von Hassel, Minister-President of Schleswig-Holstein, remarked more bluntly that the decision was 'extremely unpopular'.[119] Even pro-CDU newspapers like the *Kölner Rundschau* and the *Frankfurter Neue Presse* referred to a 'black day for German history' and proclaimed that Adenauer had done a disservice to German democracy.[120]

The reaction at the local levels of the party was a mixture of sharp criticism and depression. CDU leaders in Bonn were accused of spending too much time arguing exclusively about the leadership issue and ignoring other party matters. There had not been sufficient consultation through the party channels, so that demands for more inner party democracy began to be heard.[121] Heinrich Krone had received many letters 'expressing annoyance' with Adenauer;[122] while Bundestag deputies returning from spending weekends back in their constituencies reported that reactions 'around the country' to the 'incomprehensible Bonn game' were 'extremely negative', and that not only the protagonists but also the party and 'Bonn' as a whole had been thoroughly discredited.[123] The district party leader in Wiedenbrück (Westphalia) wrote a report on 9 June to the CDU headquarters in Bonn and to the Bundestag *Fraktion* on the mood in his locality after Adenauer's withdrawal from the presidential election. This accurately portrayed feelings in the CDU at the time:

> One can generally speak of a mood of depression, perplexity, yes even of distinct enragement. Everywhere where our prominent members appear in public, they are accosted about the events, even by persons who are otherwise politically uninterested. The undersigned has not been made aware of any single voice of approval and understanding for the step of the Federal Chancellor. All CDU voting circles of whatever position, age or religion label this step of the Federal party chairman as destructive both for the prestige of the office of Federal President and of the state, but especially also for the party and its future electoral chances. Generally, one is of the opinion that now is the right time between the elections to entrust Herr Minister Erhard with the Chancellor's office. Herr Minister Etzel is considered too little known . . . A few of our colleagues take the view that the

CDU *Fraktion* should propose a constructive vote of no-confidence against the Herr Federal Chancellor. The fact that the Herr Federal chairman was, so it seems, simply not prepared to take into consideration the overwhelming majority of the *Fraktion* and the mood inside the Christian Democratic Union is criticised to the effect that the Herr Federal chairman has peculiar ideas about inner party democracy.[124]

Fear of the electoral effects of the crisis was featured prominently in an on-the-spot report published by *Christ und Welt* on 15 October from two electoral districts: Marburg in Hesse, and Olpe in North-Rhine Westphalia. Some party officials in Marburg were evasive, although they emphasised the need for party unity and did indicate their disgust with recent events. On the possibility of an electoral setback, the party district leader in Olpe commented, in answer to the question whether everything had been forgotten: 'No, not in the CDU and also not among the Catholic people here in the district; the people are sour; we fear not gains by the Opposition, but numerous electoral abstentions out of anger.'[125]

Criticism of Adenauer was widespread at all levels of the CDU. Although initial anger over his behaviour passed, the memory of the crisis remained. Many party functionaries redeclared their solidarity with the Chancellor when he made it clear that he was determined to stay in office, but his charismatic relationship with his party had suffered a blow from which it never recovered. Up to that time Adenauer had been viewed as a leader with shrewd political instincts and a statesmanlike judgement of his country's future. His authority, which had to a large extent held the party together, was being seriously questioned for the first time. Ironically, Adenauer's criticism of his probable heir apparent, Erhard, for lacking the qualities of a 'political animal' had been verified by Erhard's actions during the crisis itself. This added to the pessimistic mood in the party about its future in relation to the leadership problem. Consequently, the blow to the charismatic element of Adenauer's leadership was accompanied by growing demands for party reform with a more structured organisation and more internal democratisation.

Notes

[1]   They included among others CDU regional chairmen like Werner Hilpert
        (Hesse), Carl Schröter (Schleswig-Holstein), and Adolf Cillien
        (Hanover) as well as Peter Altmeier (Minister-president of the Rhineland-
        Palatinate), Johannes Gronowski from Westphalia and the president
        of the Bavarian Landtag. Others included Herbert Blankenhorn
        from Adenauer's staff and Adenauer's confidant Robert Pferdmenges,
        the Cologne banker. The most prominent member of this list was
        Ludwig Erhard, direction of economic affairs on the Economic
        Council. (The list is in the possession of the Chancellor Adenauer
        House Foundation at Rhöndorf — its details are published in Klaus
        Dreher, *Der Weg zum Kanzler: Adenauers Griff nach der Macht*
        (1972), p. 237.)

[2]   According to Johann Baptist Gradl, a leader of the Berlin delegation,
        the main reason for the opposition of the Berlin party members was
        one of principle, for 'Kiesinger's association with National Socialism
        would have been bad for the party then'. As General Secretary,
        Kiesinger 'would have been effectively head of the party', as Adenauer
        was busy as Chancellor. Adenauer had nevertheless insisted in Kiesinger's
        candidacy, but following the large abstention in the vote as well as
        the strong vote against, pressure was put on Kiesinger to withdraw
        in spite of his slight majority. (Interview with the author in Bonn,
        September 1974.)

[3]   An exception has been the useful work by Jürgen Domes, *Mehrheits-
        fraktion und Bundesregierung, Aspekte des Verhältnisses der
        Fraktion der CDU/CSU im zweiten und dritten Deutschen Bundestag
        zum Kabinett Adenauer* (1964). More recently, K.D. Bracher has
        paid attention to the question of Chancellor and party in his study,
        Die Kanzlerdemokratie in Richard Löwenthal and Hans-Peter Schwarz.
        *Die Zweite Republik, 25 Jahre Bundesrepublik Deutschland — eine
        Bilanz* (1974), pp. 179-202.

[4]   In the CDU Federal Party Executive *(Bundesvorstand)* of 1956, 24
        of its 49 members (almost half) were Bundestag deputies and in 1960
        the proportion rose to nearly 60 per cent (34 out of 59 members).
        MdBs were less conspicuous in the CSU Party Executive *(Landes-
        vorstandschaft)* with 13 out of 62 members in 1956 and 17 out of 64
        members in 1960. 45 MdBs belonged in 1956 and 70 in 1960 as
        members of *Land* party executives of the CDU, while 53 of the 543
        chairmen of CDU district branches in 1960 were also active as
        members of the Bundestag. In total, 42 per cent of the CDU/CSU
        Fraktion in the second Bundestag and 55 per cent in the third
        Bundestag held leadership positions in the organisations of the
        two parties (Jürgen Domes, *Mehrheitsfraktion und Bundesregierung*,
        p. 47).

[5]   Adenauer was elected by 202 deputies (out of a nominal majority of 208)
        in 1949, by 305 (out of 336) in 1953 and by 274 (out of 287) in 1957.

[6]   Article 67 of the Basic Law states that 'the Bundestag can express its lack
        of confidence in the Federal Chancellor only by electing a successor
        with the majority of its members and by requesting the Federal President
        to dismiss the Federal Chancellor'. This provision, which in effect
        amounted to a further 'Chancellor election', was intended to prevent
        unstable alliances against the incumbent head of government during his
        four-year term of office. In fact it was not used until 1972.

[7]   For a discussion of these sub-groups, see Jürgen Domes, *op. cit.*, pp. 33-40. They included among others the employees' group (*Arbeitnehmergruppe*), the entrepreneurs' group (*Unternehmer-Abgeordneten*), the representatives of agriculture (*Arbeitsgemeinschaft Landwirtschaft und Ernährung*) and the refugee element (*Arbeitsgemeinschaft vertriebener Abgeordneter*). Domes lays special emphasis on the role of the CSU deputies from Bavaria (who organised themselves as the *CSU-Landesgruppe*) because of their regional consciousness.

[8]   This was illustrated by the number of official coalition discussions Adenauer conducted on both occasions. In 1953, 28 such discussions were held of which 17 were with the *Fraktionen* of the smaller parties and 11 with the CDU/CSU *Fraktion*. There were 26 coalition discussions in 1957, as many as 20 of them with the CDU/CSU *Fraktion* (Jürgen Domes, *op. cit.*, p. 91).

[9]   In 1953, out of eleven CDU/CSU ministers in the Cabinet four came from North-Rhine Westphalia, three from Bavaria and one each from Baden Württemberg, Lower Saxony, Rhineland-Palatinate and West Berlin. The 16 CDU/CSU ministers appointed in 1957 were comprised as follows: six from North-Rhine Westphalia, four from Bavaria, two from Baden-Württemberg and one each from Lower Saxony, Hesse, the Rhineland-Palatinate and West Berlin (Jürgen Domes, *op. cit.*, p. 88).

[10]   Peter Merkl explains the operation of an 'equilibrium system' of the different political and economic interests inside the CDU/CSU as the main reason for Adenauer's continuation as Chancellor in 1961 in spite of his general loss of political authority. See his interesting study, 'Equilibrium, Structure of Interests and Leadership: Adenauer's Survival as Chancellor' in *American Political Science Review*, 1962, pp. 634-50.

[11]   Two such cases were Hans Schlange-Schöningen (co-founder of the CDU in North Germany and an advocate of a grand coalition in 1949) who became West German envoy to London in 1950, and Friedrich Holzapfel, a vice-chairman of the CDU and Bundestag deputy from 1949, who was appointed West German envoy to Switzerland in 1952. Lesser known party leaders were sometimes awarded with a consulate abroad for their loyal service (see Arnulf Baring, *Aussenpolitik in Adenauers Kanzlerdemokratie* (dtv, 1971), vol. II, p. 42).

[12]   Heinrich von Brentano, born 1904, was chairman of the CDU/CSU Bundestag *Fraktion* 1949-55 and Foreign Minister 1955-61. He was particularly known as a strong 'European', having been vice-president of the Consultative Assembly of the Council of Europe 1950-5.

[13]   Heinrich Krone, born 1895, was chairman of the *Fraktion* 1955-61, and also became a deputy chairman of the CDU. He had been a prominent figure in the Centre Party during the Weimar Republic as both its deputy general secretary and a Reichstag deputy 1925-33. He helped to found the CDU in Berlin after the Second World War.

[14]   Without political ambitions of his own, Hans Globke acted as the Chancellor's right-hand man and functioned as his continuous and accurate source of information. Globke's powerful position was shown during Adenauer's illness in 1955, when his proximity to the Chancellor allowed him to take charge of the everyday affairs of the Government. Globke's mastery of the detailed business of the Chancellor's office even extended to briefing Adenauer on party matters, on which Globke often proved to be a more regular and reliable source of information than the CDU Executive itself (see the feature story on Globke in *Der Spiegel*, 4 April 1956, pp. 15-25).

[15] For a valuable source on Heinrich von Brentano's relations with Adenauer, see their correspondence published in Arnulf Baring (ed.), *Sehr verehrter Herr Bundeskanzler: Heinrich von Brentano im Briefwechsel mit Konrad Adenauer, 1949-64* (1974).

[16] Paul Bausch, now a member of the *Fraktion* Executive, once complained to Adenauer about the lack of information on the Government's policy intentions and requested that the Chancellor should participate more regularly in sessions of the *Fraktion*. Adenauer retorted: 'I will tell you why I am so unwilling to come to meetings of the *Fraktion*, for only criticisms of the Government are practised there, and you, Herr Bausch, you are one of the spokesmen of the critics!' In response to Bausch's further remark that 'we deputies' could not properly defend Government policy in public if not kept in touch with the motives of this policy by the head of Government, Adenauer seemed impressed and indicated that he would try and attend more regularly (Paul Bausch, *Lebenserinnerungen und Erkenntnisse eines schwäbischen Abgeordneten* (1970), p. 171).

[17] In the absence of formal ministries for external relations, special agencies (*Dienststellen*) were set up in the Chancellor's Office to cover foreign and defence questions. In 1955, in accordance with the Federal Republic's full acquisition of sovereignty, a Ministry for Foreign Affairs was established in Bonn. Adenauer took a strong interest in its formation, exercised a decisive influence on personnel appointments within it and appointed as Foreign Minister his confidant Heinrich von Brentano, who shared Adenauer's European convictions and because of his conciliatory nature was unlikely to emerge as a political rival. Adenauer kept an equally tight reign over the creation of a Federal Defence Ministry in the same year, ensuring for instance that the Bundestag was only marginally concerned with the matter (Arnulf Baring, *Aussenpolitik in Adenauers Kanzlerdemokratie* (dtv, 1971), vol. I, pp. 93 & 67-8).

[18] Several times during his tenure of the *Fraktion* chairmanship (1949-55) Heinrich von Brentano complained privately to Adenauer about the *Fraktion* being kept in the dark. In May 1952 he wrote to remind Adenauer: 'I am perfectly clear about the difficulties which arise especially from the limitations of time; but these difficulties are not in my view a sufficient explanation of why your own *Fraktion* are not brought up-to-date with information soon after. I do not wish to revert to my objections against the complete exclusion so far of deputies of the Bundestag from the whole work of the treaty from the beginning. These objections are already known to you.' (Quoted in Baring, *Aussenpolitik*, vol. I, p. 269.) There was no major alteration in Adenauer's behaviour, for he chose not to appear before the new foreign-policy working group of the *Fraktion* formed in 1953 and even obstructed the setting up of a foreign-policy committee by the CDU party organisation (*ibid.*, vol. II, pp. 28-9).

[19] Kiesinger had been Krone's chief opponent for the election to the *Fraktion* chairmanship in 1955, following von Brentano's promotion as Foreign Minister, but he had lost decisively (by 83 votes to Krone's 122). Kiesinger's desire for national office had been frustrated when Adenauer passed him over for a Cabinet post in 1957 on the grounds of 'confessional arithmetic', because there were already enough Catholics in the Cabinet. Press speculation had tipped him strongly for either the Ministry of All-German Affairs or of Justice. At the

end of 1958, Kiesinger chose the opportunity of election as Minister-President in Baden-Württemberg to leave Bonn for *Land* politics.

[20]   Eugen Gerstenmaier had been elected Bundestag President in 1954, a post he held until 1969. With his vigourous personality he played a prominent role in the CDU as one of its leading Protestant figures and as a party 'theoretician'.

[21]   A few cases illustrate this pressure which was sometimes exerted through the party organisation. The CDU deputy Matthias Mehs from the Rhineland-Palatinate was the one member of the *Fraktion* to oppose West German membership of the Council of Europe in 1950. This was explained by the CDU as evidence that the *Fraktion* 'refused to force the opinions of its members into one single mould', but when Mehs persisted in his anti-European line and objected to the EDC, he was disowned by his local party branch and not renominated for the Bundestag Election in 1953. Another CDU deputy Nellen carried on a feud with the *Fraktion* leadership over defence policy from 1956, and became known as 'the black sheep in the Christian party'. After a year of this, his electoral district distanced itself from his position and the CDU compelled him not to write articles for Opposition periodicals. (A: Heidenheimer, *Foreign Policy and Party Discipline in the CDU* in *Parliamentary Affairs,* winter 1959-60, pp. 72-3; and *NZZ,* 23 January 1958.)

[22]   See the case study of the Law for the Furtherance of Wealth Formation among Employees, promoted by the *Arbeitnehmergruppe,* which passed the Bundestag during the third legislative period and illustrated the participation in the decision-making process of organised internal party interests (Jürgen Domes, *Mehrheitsfraktion und Bundesregierung,* pp. 136-51).

[23]   Both men proved obdurate in the face of strong pressure from Bonn. Hilpert was urged by Erich Koehler, the CDU President of the Bundestag, to 'think on the Federal level' for 'great political decisions lie in the balance', and 'we simply must create a parallelogram of power between the Government coalition in the Bundestag and that in the Bundesrat'. Hilpert was subjected to intrigues against him within the Hesse CDU organised by Koehler, but these were only successful after the public divisions in the party contributed to its loss of votes in the *Land* election of November 1950. Hilpert then had no alternative but to resign, and was then replaced as chairman of the Hesse CDU by the more pliable Wilhelm Fay. Gereke proved to be a more eccentric case of internal party intransigence. He had already won Adenauer's disapproval by his open preference in 1949 for Karl Arnold as Federal Chancellor, following which he had entered a coalition with the Lower Saxony SPD in 1950. Gereke's main weakness was that he did not enjoy the full confidence of his own regional party, which was further alienated when he took the surprising step of visiting East Berlin for the ostensible purpose of promoting trade relations between the DDR and Lower Saxony. Gereke's visit was viewed with 'displeasure' by the Bonn cabinet, and he was roundly attacked by the press service of the CDU. The Lower Saxony CDU then replaced Gereke by a new chairman. Gereke left the CDU for the refugee party the BHE, and later went to live in East Germany. (See Arnold Fratzscher, *Die CDU in Niedersachsen* (1971), pp. 86-91.)

[24]   Adenauer proposed, for instance, in 1950 to create a stand-by police service to strengthen national security as the *Land* control of

the police system inhibited speedy action in the event of foreign attack. His plan was rejected by several CDU/CSU-led regional governments on the grounds that it transgressed the division of competences between the *Bund* and the *Länder*. Hans Ehard, as Minister-President of Bavaria a pronounced federalist, opposed fervently any attempts by Adenauer to circumvent the consent of the Bundesrat over legislative matters.

[25] The Office Blank (*Dienststelle Blank*) was a sub-department in the Chancellor's Office in Bonn responsible for defence affairs until the creation of a West German Defence Ministry in 1955. The Office was named after its head, Theodor Blank, who later became the first Minister of Defence.

[26] CDU leaders felt sensitive about the influence of these two respected Protestant figures, because the party had not yet firmly established its desired 'confessional bridge' between Catholic and Protestant voters. A meeting took place at the end of 1950 between Niemöller and various CDU leaders, including Friedrich Holzapfel and Robert Tillmanns, both prominent Protestant leaders in the party, but the latter's efforts to prevent the controversy coming to a head proved fruitless. Niemöller was determined to make an issue out of re-armament and called on Protestant voters to support the SPD in the Hesse Landtag election of November 1950, but his stand was generally criticised by Protestant bishops. Heinemann's challenge proved in the end equally abortive. He spoke out against rearmament at public meetings while still a member of the CDU, and for a time attracted enough attention for some CDU leaders to consider counter-action necessary. In 1952 Heinemann finally broke with the CDU to form his own party, the Pan-German People's Party (GVP), but this never had any electoral impact.

[27] West German sovereignty and hence the end to Allied occupation together with her membership of NATO were nevertheless settled without the EDC arrangement a few months later by the London Agreements of October 1954.

[28] e.g. Professor Thielicke, the noted Protestant theologian, was invited to address the 1957 Congress at length on the subject of 'Responsibility and Conscience in the Atomic Age'.

[29] The CDU-FDP coalition in North-Rhine Westphalia under Karl Arnold was thrown out of office, when the FDP changed sides and passed with the SPD a constructive vote of no-confidence in January 1956 against Arnold which led to the formation of an SPD-FDP coalition.

[30] There was a group of about 30 CDU/CSU deputies at this point who favoured pressing Adenauer to stand for President. They included Rainer Barzel, Heinrich Windelen, Werner Dollinger, Kurt Schmücker and Ernst Müller-Hermann (interview with Arved Deringer, CDU Bundestag deputy 1957-69, in Cologne, April 1973).

References

1. Maurice Duverger, *Political Parties* (1951), p. 308.
2. Arnold Heidenheimer, 'Der starke Regierungschef und das Parteien-

System' in *Politische Vierteljahresschrift*, Sept. 1961, pp. 242-3.

3.   *Christ und Welt*, 7 May 1959.
4.   Arnulf Baring, *Aussenpolitik in Adenauers Kanzlerdemokratie* (1971),
      Vol. I, p. 93.
5.   Heidenheimer, *op. cit.*, pp. 241-62.
6.   Heidenheimer, 'Federalism and the Party System: The Case of West
      Germany' in *American Political Science Review*, September 1958, p. 810.
7.   *Allgemeine Zeitung* (Mainz), 23 October 1950.
8.   See Klaus Dreher, *Der Weg zum Kanzler: Adenauers Griff nach der Macht*
      (1972), pp. 229-30 as well as chapter 14 on the Rhöndorf Conference.
9.   *Ibid.*, pp. 242-3.
10.   *The Times*, 6 September 1949.
11.   *Der Tagesspiegel*, 20 October 1949.
12.   *Allgemeine Zeitung*, 3 October 1949.
13.   *Ibid.*
14.   Dreher, *op. cit.*, pp. 216-7 and 221.
15.   *Ibid.*, pp. 221-2
16.   *NZZ*, 13 May 1950.
17.   Minutes of conference of *Land* party chairmen, 11 September 1950,
      Archiv CDU Hamburg.
18.   *Ibid.*
19.   *Erster Parteitag der CDU* (1950), p. 9.
20.   *Ibid.*, pp. 11-21.
21.   *Ibid.*, pp. 19-20.
22.   *Ibid.*, p. 112.
23.   *The Times*, 21 October 1950.
24.   *NZZ*, 23 October 1950.
25.   Arnold Heidenheimer, *Adenauer and the CDU* (1960), pp. 199-200.
26.   *Die Neue Zeitung* (Munich), 21 October 1950.
27.   For 1950 party statutes, see *Erster Parteitag der CDU*, pp. 174-6.
28.   *Ibid.*, pp. 174, 175.
29.   Zimmer to *Land* party chairmen, 3 November 1950, Archiv CDU
      Westfalen-Lippe 221.
30.   Zimmer, letter 7 November 1950, *ibid.*
31.   *Rheinisches Monatsblatt*, October 1951.
32.   *NZZ*, 26 October 1950.
33.   Jürgen Domes *Mehrheitsfraktion und Bundesregierung* (1964), p. 53.
34.   *Ibid.*, pp. 88-9.
35.   *Ibid.*, p. 50.
36.   *Ibid.*, pp. 89-90.
37.   Arnulf Baring, *op. cit.*, Vol. II, p. 30.
38.   Felix von Eckhardt, *Ein unordentliches Leben* (1967), p. 225.
39.   *Der Spiegel*, 4 April 1956, p. 16.
40.   Paul Bausch, *Lebenserinnerungen und Erkenntnisse eines schwäbischen
      Abgeordneten* (1970), p. 166.
41.   *Ibid.*, pp. 166-7.
42.   *Ibid.*, p. 167.
43.   *Ibid.*, p. 167.
44.   Baring, *op. cit.*, Vol. I. p. 41.
45.   *Ibid.*, Vol. II, p. 21.
46.   *Ibid.*, Vol. I. pp. 262-3.
47.   *Ibid.*, Vol. I, pp. 261-2.
48.   *Ibid.*, Vol. II, pp. 96-7.
49.   *NZZ*, 13 March 1958.

50. *Ibid.*
51. *Stuttgarter Nachrichten,* 14 March 1958.
52. See voting figures in Domes, *op. cit.,* pp. 122-3.
53. See Arnold Heidenheimer, 'Foreign Policy and Party Discipline in the CDU' in *Parliamentary Affairs,* Winter 1959-60, pp. 72-3.
54. Heinz Markmann, *Dass Abstimmungsverhalten in deutschen Parlamenten* (1955), p. 129.
55. Heidenheimer, *Foreign Policy and Party Discipline,* p. 71
56. See Gerhard Loewenberg, 'Parliamentarism in Western Germany: the functioning of the Bundestag' in *American Political Science Review,* March 1961, pp. 87-102.
57. Ernst Deuerlein, *CDU/CSU 1945-1957* (1957), p. 150.
58. Loewenberg, *op. cit.,* p. 94.
59. *Weser-Kurier* (Bremen), 13 February 1958.
60. Domes, *op. cit.,* pp. 28-30.
61. Loewenberg, *op. cit.,* p. 95.
62. Domes, *op. cit.,* pp. 128-30.
63. *Ibid.,* pp. 134-5.
64. Quoted in Heidenheimer, *Adenauer and the CDU,* p. 201.
65. Helmuth Putz, *Innerparteiliche Willensbildung: empirische Untersuchung zum bildungspolitischen Willensbildungsprozess in der CDU,* Ph.D. thesis 1973, p. 251.
66. *Ibid.,* pp. 247-8.
67. *6. Bundesparteitag der CDU* (1956), p. 23.
68. Quoted in Pütz, *op. cit.,* p. 210.
69. *6. Bundesparteitag der CDU,* p. 171.
70. Pütz, *op. cit., pp. 256-257.*
71. F. Roy Wills, *France, Germany and the New Europe, 1945-1967* (1968), pp. 125-6 and 265-72.
72. *Ibid.,* pp. 126-7.
73. Letter from Heck to Landesgeschäftsführer, 3 June 1952, Hauptstaatsarchiv Düsseldorf, RWV 26, No. 233.
74. Adenauer circular letter, undated, Archiv CDU Westfalen-Lippe 221.
75. For a study of this attitude in the case of West Berlin, see Renate Mayntz, 'Oligarchic Problems in a German Party District' in D. Marvick (ed.), *Political Decision-Makers* (1961).
76. Baring, *op. cit.,* Vol. II, pp. 208-13.
77. See Heino Kaack, *Geschichte und Struktur des deutschen Parteiensystems* (1971), pp. 210-15, for election details.
78. *5. Bundesparteitag der CDU* (1954), p. 12.
79. *NZZ,* 24 October 1951.
80. *The Times,* 18 September 1958.
81. See *Dokumente zur Christlichen Demokratie* (1969), p. 227.
82. *Der Tagesspiegel,* 8 May 1957.
83. *5. Bundesparteitag der CDU,* p. 60.
84. Minutes of the meeting of CDU Landesvorstand Hamburg, 8 May 1953. Archiv CDU Hamburg.
85. *Bremer Nachrichten,* 3 November 1950.
86. *FAZ,* 21 April 1953.
87. *Ibid.*
88. *New York Times,* 29 April 1956.
89. *The Times,* 30 April 1956.
90. *SZ,* 30 April 1956.
91. *NZZ,* 4 May 1956.

92   *NZZ*, 18 May 1956.
93.   *8. Bundesparteitag der CDU* (1958), pp. 58-70.
94.   Adenauer to all CDU members, 3 September 1956. Archiv CDU
      Westfalen-Lippe 221.
95.   Article by Stoltenberg in *Rhenischer Merkur*, 11 April 1958.
96.   *Die Abendpost*, 25 February 1959.
97.   *NZZ*, 16 May 1959.
98.   Domes, *op. cit.*, p. 99.
99.   *Der Spiegel*, 15 April 1959, p. 22.
100. *Ibid.*, p. 20.
101. Domes, *op. cit.*, p. 103, and *Der Spiegel*, 15 April 1959, p. 22.
102. Domes, *op. cit.*, p. 105.
103. *The Times*, 25 May 1959.
104. Domes, *op. cit.*, p. 116.
105. *Die Welt*, 23 April 1959.
106. Friedrich Thomas, 'Die CDU unten' in *Christ und Welt*, 2 July 1959.
107. *NZZ*, 16 May 1959.
108. *NZZ*, 6 June 1959.
109. *The Times*, 25 May 1959.
110. *Der Spiegel*, 17 June 1959, p. 18.
111. *NZZ*, 7 June 1959.
112. *Der Spiegel*, 17 June 1959, p. 15.
113. *SZ*, 20/21 June 1959.
114. *The Times*, 20 June 1959.
115. *SZ*, 22 June 1959.
116. Text of three letters in *Die Welt* (Essen), 24 June 1959.
117. *Der Spiegel*, 17 June 1959, pp. 19-20.
118. e.g. *NZZ*, 24 June 1959.
119. Domes, *op. cit.*, p. 109.
120. See report on West German press reactions in *NZZ*, 8 June 1959.
121. *Deutsche Tagespost* (Augsburg), 21 October 1959.
122. *The Times*, 24 June 1959.
123. *NZZ*, 24 June 1959.
124. CDU Kreisgeschäftsführer Wiedenbrück, 9 June 1959 to LGS
      Westfalen, BGS Bonn and Bundestag-Fraktion, Archiv Westfalen-Lippe 221.
125. Freidrich Thomas, 'Ist die Juni-Krise überstanden? ' in *Christ und Welt*, 15 October 1959.

3 THE DECLINE OF ADENAUER AND THE QUESTION OF PARTY REFORM (1959-1963)

E ven the prospect that Adenauer might resign from the Chancellorship was a major occurrence. It would have been the first change of leadership in the history of the post-war Federal Republic, which was all the more portentous in view of Adenauer's longevity in office, his dominant personality, his considerable achievements and the circumstances surrounding it. Within the decade of his rule West Germany had emerged fairly rapidly from the dislocation and chaos of the immediate post-war years to acquire a new international recognition and respect as a stable political and economic power in the western world. Adenauer was widely respected and revered by the German people for his part in bringing about such a successful development of the West German state. In this context, therefore, Adenauer's openly expressed contempt for the popular Erhard, the father of the economic miracle, came as a disturbing shock.

Yet there was no immediate prospect for a change of leadership, and this reflected on the nature of authority in the CDU/CSU at the time. For, in spite of fears of electoral repercussions from the events of April-June 1959, the regard for Adenauer within the CDU/CSU had so governed its internal relations over the previous ten years that any initiative for a leadership change against his will assumed the appearance of regicide: hence, the repeated emphasis in speeches made by CDU/CSU leaders during the early 1960s that the succession question should be settled only in co-operation with the Chancellor. They perceived that an open challenge to Adenauer with his reluctance to retire would only produce a major crisis in the party. The long and painful process of Adenauer's political decline from 1959-63 therefore continued to illustrate how much the CDU/CSU was dependent psychologically on the figure of West Germany's first Chancellor, even though it was increasingly feared in the early 1960s that he might be holding the party back from coming to terms with a changing world. Adenauer's persistent reluctance to withdraw from office itself therefore proved such an influential factor with the party. The problem for the CDU/CSU in settling the post-Adenauer succession was also not helped by the absence of satisfactory organisational channels for deliberating and processing the selection of the new Chancellor. The Bundestag *Fraktion* would ultimately have to elect him and would play an important part in his choice, but there were no formal provisions for consultation within the party at a wider level. The CDU's national executive organs had virtually no independent authority, for they could only function when Adenauer as party chairman chose to summon them and this he did not do regularly. If only because of the lack of precedent, it was unclear how the party would guide the transfer of authority. This was one reason why the question of party reform was coupled with the problem of the succession.

Seen in the broader context of political developments in West Germany, Adenauer's abortive presidential candidacy provided the occasion rather than the cause for the consideration of change in the party in the light of new circumstances. The problem of Adenauer's age had to be faced sometime, and party problems which had been sidestepped during the 1950s were emerging as requiring immediate attention. The CDU/CSU had achieved political dominance after the establishment of the Federal Republic too rapidly, exploiting skilfully as it did the advantages of being the governing party. Although the 1957 Bundestag Election result was indeed a triumph for Adenauer and his party, now that his foreign policy aims had been achieved there was a lack of momentum in West Germany's external relations. There were also in the early 1960s signs on the horizon that the exceptional economic growth of the 1950s would not continue, and that problems might arise from the high expectations conditioned by the 'economic miracle'. Finally, the political dominance of the CDU/CSU now seemed directly threatened by a reformed and rejuvenated SPD, which, following the trauma of its defeat in 1957, had chosen to reduce the emphasis given to programmatic differences between itself and the CDU/CSU in its reformist Godesberg Programme, which among other things included the acceptance of a mixed economy. The polarisation over foreign policy between the two main parties, which had helped to maintain the CDU/CSU's political dominance for much of the 1950s by allowing Adenauer to devalue the role of parliamentary opposition, was now concluded. The first significant electoral evidence of this change in the CDU/CSU's political position occurred in 1961,[1] followed by further CDU setbacks in *Land* elections during 1962-3. The party system was now consolidating itself (with only the three political parties of the CDU/CSU, SPD and FDP represented in the Bundestag from 1961) but, unlike the first stage of this process in the 1950s, it now favoured the CDU/CSU less exclusively.

The principal incentive for the discussion of party reform in the CDU[2] was consideration of its electoral position — both as a potential problem prior to the 1961 Election, and as a real problem following it. The question of party reform became inevitably linked with the leadership issue, because Adenauer's political qualities which had for so long been taken as a substitute for substantial party organisation were now showing signs of decline. The SPD, once scorned by Christian Democrats, was now enviously viewed as a model on which to base reform, with its superior organisation and the greater discipline of its voters[3], although Adenauer still managed to produce applause at CDU Congresses for his derisive comments on the Godesberg Programme. The issue of party reform did also become a vehicle for aspiring younger CDU politicians, who sought to strengthen their profile as potential leaders through the publicity they gained. Each main drive for party reform (1959-60 and 1961-3) was spearheaded by a rising younger party leader, respectively Kai-Uwe von Hassel and Josef-Hermann Dufhues, neither of whom belonged to that founding generation of CDU leaders who had been politically active earlier in the Weimar Republic. As so often happened in the later history of the CDU, a serious threat to its political position from electoral failures proved the only real catalyst for its interest in organisational change. But this first serious attempt to prepare for 'après Adenauer', like other later efforts at party reform, reverted full circle and progress came to be determined by the nature and present incumbency of the leadership. Dufhues and other party reformers found their attention necessarily diverted into solving the question of who should succeed Adenauer, when and how. In this way the question of party reform illustrated the balance of internal party relations during Adenauer's last four years as Chancellor, for the reformers found themselves torn between their concern about the party's future and their reluctance to express any antipathy towards Adenauer, while the issue was further complicated by conflicting internal party interests and the first labour pains of the birth of a future political leadership.

(a)   The First Stimulus to Reform: the Aftermath of Adenauer's Presidential Candidacy

The crisis over Adenauer's presidential candidacy in 1959 did not initiate the idea of party reform; rather it acted as a catalyst for the internal party debate about it. First, it shook confidence in

Adenauer's leadership, apparently justifying the fears about his advancing age which had accumulated in previous years. Secondly, this crisis provided an opportunity for reformist pressures, which before had appeared only sporadically, to emerge and try to determine the party's future course. Efforts to initiate reform had already been made both at the national and provincial level. In the former area, Franz Meyers, as the member of the CDU Federal Executive responsible for party organisation, had attempted from 1956-8 to introduce more co-ordination in relations between the Federal party and the *Landesverbände* and selected younger talent in his organisational preparations for the Bundestag Election of 1957, but his efforts did not go any further. Meyers' active interest in party reform declined once he took on the duties of Minister-President in North-Rhine Westphalia in 1958. At the *Land* level, the spur to party reform had come typically from electoral defeat. In Hamburg, the loss of power by the Sieveking centre-right coalition (CDU/FDP/ DP and BHE) in 1957 had opened the way for an attack on the dominant role in the CDU there of local notables led by the *Land* branch of the Young Union, which for some years had acted as a kind of fronde against the party leadership.[1] More significantly, the CSU's loss of office in Bavaria from 1954-7 occasioned important changes such as its formation of a structured party organisation.

The initiative for the discussion of reform in 1959 was taken, within a few weeks of the Adenauer-Erhard public quarrel over the former's presidential candidacy, at a conference of the CDU *Land* chairmen held in Berlin at the beginning of July. The feeling prevalent at this meeting was dissatisfaction at the way in which the party as a whole had stood by virtually helpless, while its two prominent figures had insulted each other, instead of being able to intervene to prevent the quarrel from getting out of hand. As Kai-Uwe von Hassel announced at a press conference following the conference, it was hoped to prevent the recurrence of another such crisis by drawing up organisational contingency plans.[2] One problem the *Land* chairmen deliberated was that the national executive organs of the CDU depended effectively on the party chairman for being summoned. During the whole crisis there had been not one meeting of either the Federal Executive or the Federal Committee of the CDU. Adenauer had not in fact called a session of the Federal Executive since 11 March, while the Federal Committee had not met since 28 November of the previous year.[3] It was only because the conference

of *Land* chairmen was not an officially constituted body of the CDU
that it was not dependent on Adenauer for being summoned, and
was able to gather as it did. The regional 'party barons' nevertheless
comprised the largest single element in both party organs and could
in effect exercise much influence if united on the national party
leadership. Kai-Uwe von Hassel, the young and ambitious Minister-
President of Schleswig-Holstein,[4] now emerged as the spokesman
of the reformers among the CDU *Land* chairmen.

The Berlin conference of *Land* party chairmen, which also
included the members of the CDU's Business Executive (*geschäftsführender Vorstand*),[5] produced a series of proposals which by
the early autumn became the basis for the subsequent discussion of
party reform later in 1959. These proposals included ideas for
strengthening the extra-parliamentary party leadership vis-à-vis
the chairman, for creating a multi-member 'party leadership
capable of action' and for tightening up party organisation in order
to control the eventual succession to Adenauer and prepare for the
1961 Election. They comprised the following specific suggestions:[4]

1. The CDU should replace the four equal deputy chairmen by a
   first and second deputy of the chairman. It was argued that
   none of the four deputies felt really responsible, and that the
   functions of the two new appointments should be made
   absolutely clear. The party chairman should delegate to them
   those tasks which he could not fulfil because he was over-
   burdened as Chancellor.

2. A smaller 'political executive' or 'closer executive' consisting
   of ten men should take over the 'political leadership' of the
   party. This would be a more flexible body than the complete
   Federal Executive of 65 persons, whose cumbersomeness had
   in the past allowed the political initiative in the party to be
   taken by the Bundestag *Fraktion*. It was pointed out that
   during the presidential candidacy crisis the *Fraktion* had been
   the only CDU organ in any sense 'capable of action'.

3. The highest party organs, the Federal Executive and Federal
   Committee, should meet regularly and should not have to
   wait for the party chairman to decide on a meeting.

These proposals for reform if adopted would have amounted to the first major concrete steps to give the CDU a measure of political independence from the Government. They would have required final approval from the next party congress, then not planned until the following spring. This was likely to become a tactical disadvantage for the party reformers, for the longer the discussion of the proposals was protracted the more likely it was that the urge for reform might lose momentum, particularly as memories of Adenauer's behaviour during the June crisis became less poignant. But the proposals had in any case to be examined and approved by that national organs of the CDU, ironically the bodies which were the object of reform. Solidarity behind the reformers within the Federal Executive and Committee was predictably limited, so that Adenauer was not under any united pressure to concede to the proposals. The other key factor was of course the attitude of Adenauer himself. Adenauer's initial reaction to the Berlin conference of *Land* chairmen was apparently amenable, but in fact non-committal. Heinrich Krone, the *Fraktion* Chairman, and von Hassel conferred a few days after the conference with Adenauer, who declared that he was 'agreed in principle' with the plans, but commented evasively that they would have to be looked at in more detail: 'These are very reasonable ideas; they must be formulated more precisely.'[5]

Adenauer agreed none the less to call a meeting of the Federal Committee in September to discuss the reform proposals. Both CDU organs met during this month — the Federal Executive on 16 September, and the Federal Committee on 28 September. Both sessions proved in their outcome to have a decelerating effect on the course of party reform, although neither produced as such any final decisions. Adenauer managed to steer the discussion away from the specific plans proposed by the Berlin conference by emphasising the need to 'activate party work' rather than reform the leadership structure. The party must wake up from its 'Sleeping Beauty sleep' and act more unitedly, he said, with closer co-operation between the *Landesverbände* and the Federal leadership. Although he did not directly say so, Adenauer's sceptical attitude towards the idea of appointing two more responsible deputy chairmen echoed his hostility to any challenge to his authority as party chairman.[6] The session of the Federal Executive chose to take a neutral position on the Berlin proposals, neither giving them its official backing nor rejecting them, and thereby revealed a general lack of conviction about the proposals.

Von Hassel was determined to revive the Berlin proposals at the meeting on 28 September of the Federal Committee, in spite of the

lack of support from the Federal Executive. A lively debate
followed at this meeting. Von Hassel received vocal support for
the idea of a smaller political executive from Helmut Lemke
(Minister of the Interior in Schleswig-Holstein), Erik Blumenfeld
(CDU chairman in Hamburg) and Johann Baptist Gradl (West
Berlin), but met vociferous opposition from Josef Hermann
Dufhues, the CDU chairman in Westphalia, surprisingly in view of
his later reputation as a party reformer. However, at that time Dufhues
was acting as spokesman of the CDU in North-Rhine Westphalia,
which had begun to show considerable reservations about the Berlin
proposals because these would involve a reduction in its overweighty
representation on the Federal Executive. Adenauer and Krone
tended to support the line of Dufhues. The supporters of party
reform now found their proposals of the summer reduced to an
innocuous level. The meeting agreed to drop the idea of appointing
two deputy party chairmen with strengthened powers, but agreed
to support the plan for a 'closer executive'. Adenauer had apparently
succeeded in neutralising the efforts of the reformers, because many
of their original supporters among the *Land* chairmen had since
lost their enthusiasm.

The weight of opinion at this meeting of the Federal Committee
moved decisively in Adenauer's favour when Eugen Gerstenmaier,
who had been one of Adenauer's adamant critics during the 'June
crisis', sensed the mood of the occasion and rose unexpectedly
to pay a fulsome tribute to Adenauer's ten years as Chancellor,
giving in a moved voice his 'respectful thanks for everything which
you have done for us, for Germany and for freedom in the world'.
The Chancellor could be certain of the loyalty of all Christian
Democrats. When Gerstenmaier wished him 'God's blessing further
on the way', the 150 members of the Federal Committee had
stood up. Adenauer was touched by this silent demonstration,
when in response he commented that it was a 'special grace of God
for the German people that it could since 1945 rise up again from
the deepest fall it had ever made'. Adenauer concluded the meeting
with a speech claiming it was essential for the Western world
that the CDU should win the next Election in 1961, for Khruschev
was waiting to see if a new government came to power in Bonn
which would be more agreeable to his plans.[7] Adenauer's use of
his statesman's image for internal party reasons had been accompanied
by the tactical game of waiting several weeks to allow the party
reformers their head of steam, and then acting at the appropriate

moment when it became clear that solidarity behind them was brittle. Adenauer was then able to outmanoeuvre the reformers and regain the initiative, for four reasons.

First, the reformers themselves were not so united that they were prepared to carry out their plans against formidable internal party opposition. This of course posed the question who exactly were the reforming element in the CDU. The reformers were difficult to categorise as a separate pressure group, because apart from certain *Land* party chairmen initiating it the concept of 'party reform', in fact a fashionable theme of the moment in the party, attracted some favourable though only passive interest in the CDU. More significantly, the reformers did not gain the support of one prominent national figure in the party. Solid support from the *Land* chairmen was essential if reform were to have a reasonable chance because of their powerful influence in internal party matters, but differences of interest in reform between the *Landesverbände* emerged as the weeks went by. Support for it remained strong in those states like Hamburg, Schleswig-Holstein, Lower Lower Saxony, Württemberg and Hesse, where either party organisation was weak or where the SPD dominated state politics.[8] The two regional parties in the Rhineland and Westphalia were on the other hand the best organised in the country, and felt less urgency for reform. They also had a strong position in the already established party hierarchy and chose to defend it.

Secondly, personal political ambitions proved to be a major obstacle to reform. Those with such hopes tended to favour the *status quo,* simply because reform threatened to unscramble the complicated personal network of internal party relationships. When it became clear that von Hassel was in the running for first new deputy chairman and seemed likely to benefit from his advocacy of reform, his rivals sided more strongly with the party establishment. Most resistance to his plans came from North-Rhine Westphalia, where the CDU feared that his appointment might help to predetermine the Chancellorship succession. There were even rumours of an alternative plan for a party General Secretary with Franz Meyers, Minister-President in North-Rhine Westphalia, as the most suitable candidate.[9] Adenauer exploited the reluctance of any of the current four deputy chairmen to forego their positions to accord with the plan for only two deputies. At the meeting of the Federal Executive he had even asked each member of the *geschäftsführender Vorstand* in turn whether he wished to reign![10] Party reform as interpreted by Adenauer now came to be seen as too much of a threat for the careers of prominent CDU leaders. It seemed more comfortable to leave matters as they stood, a point underlined by Adenauer who adopted his successful approach of playing the gracious host by inviting members of the Federal Executive to join him on the lawn of the Palais Schaumburg: 'I have had a cold buffet set up outside in the garden: the weather is still so fine, and a glass of wine is also to be enjoyed.'[11]

Thirdly, the reformers were basically limited by their own lack of ruthlessness in their scope for action, since not even they considered bringing about Adenauer's retirement before the 1961 Election. This gave their plans less urgency, for these were presented in terms of the post-Adenauer era whenever that transpired. The anti-Adenauer motive behind reform sprang from disillusionment over his behaviour earlier in the year rather than a conscious desire to instigate a palace revolution, but memories of the June crisis were by the autumn submerged by some revival of the Chancellor's leadership skills and by the general belief that any reform without his consent was 'unthinkable'. Uppermost in the minds of CDU leaders was the wish to see the Adenauer-Erhard controversy finally buried and a united team presented in good time for the next election. Persistent reservations in the party about Erhard's abilities as a political leader strengthened the feeling of relief that Adenauer was still actively in his place, and weakened any intention of experimenting with another Chancellor candidate at this stage.[12]

Fourthly, Adenauer presented his own plans for reform as a diversionary tactic. In this way he avoided the mistake of rejecting the idea of reform in principle, with its attendant risk of arousing unnecessary resentment in sections of the party and turning passive sympathy for reform into active support of it. His plans, which included a 'Federal list' of candidates for Bundestag elections and creating a 'Federal membership' in the CDU, appeared almost deliberately radical, although they did express the frustrations which Adenauer had experienced on earlier occasions in his dealings with the *Landesverbände*.

The only concrete result of this first stage in the reform movement was the formation of a 'closer executive' consisting of 25 members to meet at more regular intervals than the Federal Executive without having to be called by Adenauer — at least once a month — for the purpose of discussing immediate questions. It remained, however, no more than a rather weak advisory body with no policy-making role. This 'small reform of the Executive' appeared to meet the demands for more regular consultation within the party, although it did not substantially affect the power structure in the leadership which, as before, was weighted in Adenauer's favour. The plan received final approval at the party congress at Karlsruhe in April 1960, and was incorporated in the statutes.

By the time the Karlsruhe Congress took place, the reform drive had lost its momentum. The next Bundestag Election was in the offing and party delegates in their desire to demonstrate solidarity tended to forget the anger caused by the June crisis of nearly a year before. Even von Hassel, in his speech justifying the importance of the new 'closer Executive', opened by referring to the recent series of mild CDU reverses in *Land* elections and emphasising the purpose of good party organisation in preparing for the next national election.[13] Adenauer's own speech typically played on the fears of an SPD victory in 1961. This was the most difficult election campaign the CDU had to face since the War, he said, but it could still be won if the party pulled together and made every effort. He made several mocking references to the Godesberg Programme ('either the old programme was bad, or the new one is bad or both are bad'), and attacked the SPD's 'unreliability', in foreign affairs in contrast to his own experience in dealing with international statesmen. His speech was peppered with jocular remarks, such as that on the 'question of the Crown prince' ('when the moment arrives then, my friends I am convinced, there will be sufficient people around who will take over the helm with a firm and strong hand').[14] Adenauer succeeded in putting across the impression of a revived and robust campaigner, which delighted the majority of delegates judging by the reception of his speech. There was a striking absence of dissension at the Congress, even during the session dealing with the changes in the statutes.[15]

From then until September 1961 the Bundestag Election campaign became the dominant preoccupation of the party. Already, in November 1959, Adenauer had met with leading CDU politicians to discuss election preparations. A working group was set up for this purpose, which would hold such meetings every one or two weeks to decide on essential themes for the CDU campaign.[16] It was later decided that younger CDU leaders like von Hassel and Strauss should play a prominent part in the campaign to balance the youthful appeal of the 46-year-old Willy Brandt, the SPD Chancellor candidate. By the autumn of 1960 the working group to discuss election plans was meeting under the chairmanship of Kai-Uwe von Hassel.[17] The former leader of the party reformers thus found himself fully involved in the re-election of Adenauer as Chancellor.

The discussion of party reform had proved to be abortive, partly due to the lack of determination and conviction by those advocating reform, and partly due to Adenauer's reassertion of his tactical skill and demonstration of his personal and political appeal. In addition, with the threatening approach of the 1961 Election, the tradition of party solidarity in the face of the electoral enemy was powerful enough to overcome the sense of dismay that still remained from the crisis over Adenauer's presidential candidacy.

The ideas for reform presented during 1959-60 were in fact modest in their scope. They involved some restructuring of the national leadership of the CDU in order to lend its extra-parliamentary organisation some political independence, but they never went further in the direction of furthering internal party democracy at a lower level. However, since a principal motive behind party reform was a concern about the CDU's electoral future, it was to be expected that any serious setback in the 1961 Bundestag Election would re-open the question of party reform, this time as a more viable proposition because it would be directly linked with a change of leadership.

(b)   The Second Stimulus to Reform: the 1961 Bundestag Election Result

The second initiative for party reform, which was a major subject of discussion within the CDU from the autumn of 1961 until Erhard's assumption of the Chancellorship two years later, was in several respects similar to the first. Attention was once more focused on the need to strengthen party organisation in order to make the CDU more effective as a political force, although the discussion was widened to include an assessment of the party's ideology and the question of renovating the CDU's image in the light of new circumstances. The main outcome of this initiative was the creation of a new leadership position responsible for organisational matters, itself a variation on an old theme. As with the attempts at other organisational changes which followed, the discussion over this appointment brought to the surface pressures and counter-pressures within the CDU relating to internal traditions and interests. These again prevented in the end any radical implementation of party reform.

There was, however, an important difference between this and the
earlier discussion of party reform, for the combination of difficulties now faced by the CDU lent it a much greater urgency.
First, the 1961 Bundestag Election result with the CDU/CSU's
loss of its absolute majority and almost 5 per cent of the national
vote — its first loss of support in any Bundestag election since the
War — was interpreted as a serious setback, even though it could
still claim the leading role in government as the largest parliamentary
group. Secondly, it was now widely accepted in the CDU/CSU that
the 85-year old Adenauer would have to retire well in time before
the next election in 1965. The CDU/CSU had tried to counteract
public memories of Adenauer's behaviour in the 1959 crisis with the
slogan 'Adenauer, Erhard and the Team', and by concentrating its
campaign appeal on the achievements of the party rather than the
person in office; but all the same Adenauer's signs of campaign
fatigue and his inept conduct after the building of the Berlin Wall[6]
had reopened criticism of his rigid and occasionally tactless style
of leadership. Adenauer managed to delay still further the likely
appointment of Ludwig Erhard as his successor, although his
mistake in the Spiegel Affair of 1962 forced his retirement the
following year. Thirdly, party unity was further placed under pressure
by emerging differences over areas of foreign policy, especially
European affairs, which had formerly been a source of solidarity
within the CDU/CSU. All these problems featured as real or
potential threats to the political dominance of the CDU/CSU.

Although the election result of September 1961 gave the question
of party reform a prominence it had not previously enjoyed,
proposals for reform did not receive any consideration until the
end of the year. The party's attention was meanwhile riveted on
the unprecedentedly long formation of the new Adenauer Government
lasting over seven weeks into November. An attempt mounted by the
FDP, the CDU/CSU's prospective coalition partner, to force
Adenauer's immediate retirement following its anti-Adenauer (but
pro-CDU/CSU) line in the election campaign eventually collapsed
when the Chancellor skilfully exploited the fears of the Free
Democrats about a possible grand coalition and after their move
had aroused resentment in the CDU/CSU over this encroachment on
its right to determine the Chancellor.[18] Only in the middle of
December did the CDU Federal Executive settle down to discuss
the consequences of the election setback for the party's long-term
future. It then decided on four measures: Rainer Barzel,[7] a

promising young Bundestag deputy, should compile a report by the middle of March on the 'future tasks' of the party: Konrad Kraske, the CDU Business Manager, should produce an analysis of the 1961 Election; a commission should develop proposals for closer co-operation between the Federal and *Land* levels of party organisation; and greater co-operation should be fostered between the party organisation and the Bundestag *Fraktion*. [19] These were all useful plans, but it remained to be seen how far they would be implemented.

As with the attempt at reform in 1959, it was realised that the basic problem was to grant the extra-parliamentary party more individual weight vis-à-vis the CDU's Government leaders in Bonn. The solution was sought by adopting an idea which had been circulating in party circles since the later 1950s[8] to separate the political and organisational leadership of the CDU. It was recognised that Adenauer's fourth election as Chancellor late in 1961 had also for the moment foreclosed the question of the party chairmanship, but attention now turned to the possibility of creating the new leadership position of CDU Business Chairman concerned exclusively with organisation. Although this idea sprang from the CDU's highly underdeveloped state of national party organisation, it could not avoid the problems posed by the federal structure of the CDU, for as relations between the *Landesverbände* and the national leadership had shown in the 1950s the former reacted sharply to any attempt which suggested a reduction in their control over internal party matters. These relations had further underlined that any strict distinction between political and organisational power was artificial. This same problem arose in relations between national organisation leaders of the CDU and its political leaders, for in order that the former might be effective thay had to acquire sufficient political weight. In view of the CDU leadership as presently constituted, this idea therefore contained the seeds of institutional conflict.

The original plan to create the new leadership post of Business Chairman (*Geschäftsführender Vorsitzender*) of the CDU came from the party in North-Rhine Westphalia, which had previously obstructed the similar plan introduced by party reformers in 1959. The North-Rhine Westphalian CDU's motive this time was electoral, for it had suffered from one of the highest regional swings against the party in the 1961 Bundestag Election (of 6.8 per cent, well above the national average).[9] Regional party interests also played a part in this initiative, for the plan was immediately linked with the

nomination for the new post of Josef-Hermann Dufhues, whose
promotion would remove a dissatisfied rival for Franz Meyers,
Minister-President, and other CDU leaders in Düsseldorf.[10]

   The North-Rhine Westphalian plan had envisaged a strong position
for Dufhues, placing him next to Adenauer in the party hierarchy
and above the four deputy chairmen. Adenauer apparently gave
his consent at a meeting he had on 7 February with Krone,[20] who
was using his considerable influence with the Chancellor to back
party reform, but the matter did not stop there. Dufhues's nomination
touched off a bitter dispute within the party, arousing in particular
adamant opposition from many of the *Land* chairmen. Although
Dufhues himself counted as one of their number, the regional party
barons distrusted his elevation, seeing in this a possible prejudgement
of the Chancellor succession. The most intense resistance came from
the North German *Landesverbände*, who raised an old argument in
the CDU that the appointment of Dufhues, a strong Catholic who
had earned the label of 'Jesuit in Civvies', would together with the
Catholic Adenauer disturb the necessary balance of confessional
parity in the CDU leadership. The proportional concept had become
a convention in determining party promotions, but could also be
used as a cover to promote internal group interests or further
personal careers by checking those of others. The four deputy
chairmen — Gerstenmaier and von Hassel (both Protestant), and
Krone and Blank (both Catholic) — had met the requirements of
'confessional arithmetic'. Of them only Heinrich Krone, now a party
elder statesman, was prepared to take positive steps to promote
reform in the party leadership, even to the extent of offering to
retire as deputy in Dufhues's favour as one solution to the deadlock
over the powers of the new Business Chairman. Ironically, some of the
Land party leaders who now raised objections to the North-Rhine
Westphalian plan had been associated with the circle of party
reformers around Kai-Uwe von Hassel during 1959-60.

   Support for the original plan to give Dufhues a new leadership
post with organisational teeth came most strongly from the
younger and progressive elements in the CDU. The Social Committees,
concerned at their own lack of weight in the party, had proposed
after the 1961 Election dividing the party chairmanship from the
Chancellorship on the grounds that Adenauer should be relieved
of some of his burdens.[21] More vociferous in their attacks on the
nature of party leadership with its need for rejuvenation, the 'local
notables' with their restrictive attitudes and the practice of concentrating

party offices in a few hands[11]   were the leaders of the Young
Union (JU). The newly elected national chairman of the JU, Bert
Even, himself from the Rhineland *Landesverband*, demanded that the
party acknowledge the consequences of the election result and made
the blunt statement that 'with Adenauer twenty age groups will
be put into retirement'.[22]   He followed this up with public speeches
and newspaper articles urging that 'the position of Dufhues should
be strong and his power of authority far-reaching'.[23] At the end of
March a conference of the Rhineland JU in Siegburg passed a
resolution demanding strong powers fur Dufhues, including the
right to summon the Federal Executive, and deploring any chance
that his election might fail because of 'proportional thinking'.[24]
Franz Meyers was present to make a speech supporting the reform
claims of the Young Union.

The two reports commissioned by the CDU's Federal Executive
meeting in December were now ready — the Kraske analysis of the
1961 election results and their consequences appeared in February,
and the Barzel report on future tasks for the CDU in April. Both
of these added fuel to the reform debate. The message of the Kraske
study was that there was a reduction in the 'emotional antipathy'
among bourgeois voters towards the SPD, a fall in the CDU's
regular voters compared with 1957 and a genuine possibility that the
SPD could win a relative majority in 1965. The party needed
someone who could relieve the Chancellor of party work, take the
party apparatus firmly in hand and give it new life. Kraske also
raised a matter of fundamental principle concerning party ideology:
whether in the light of the more fluid electoral situation suggested
by the 1961 result the CDU should base its future development on
the assumption of a three-party system and content itself with
being a 'Christian party', or whether it should adhere to the idea of
a two-party system in spite of the result and dilute party ideology
in order to attrach liberal voters.[25] The Kraske analysis threw up
many such issues, some of which remained academic, but its relevance
as far as the appointment of Dufhues was concerned was that it
increased the pressure to produce an agreement.

The Barzel report, a 210-page 'Study on the Intellectual and
Social Picture of the Present and on the Future Tasks of the CDU',
dealt with the programmatic consequences of the election result,
but couched as it was in fine phraseology it read more like a restatement of Christian Democratic principles than a practical plan
for reformist action. Barzel claimed that party reform was not just

an organisational question but an 'intellectual task', and argued that
what the party needed was a 'declaration of principles' and a 'new
consciousness of the Christian element'. His report which caused
violent internal party debate advocated that the CDU turn away
from being a 'party of interests', that it should concentrate on
domestic and social policy rather than foreign affairs and that it
should adapt more readily to sociological changes.[26] Barzel stopped
short of the ultimate controversial issue of the leadership question.
Indeed, Adenauer himself had inspired the report in an effort to
divert criticism of his election campaign. Barzel revealed his own
standpoint by his comment during a speech to the *Land* congress
of the Rhineland CDU at Neuss early in April, that party reform
could 'not be undertaken without the Chancellor or against the
Chancellor, but only with him'.[27]

Discussion of the two reports progressed alongside further
dissension over the role of Dufhues.[28] After continuing resistance
from *Land* chairmen and successive meetings of the CDU Federal
Executive a compromise was finally worked out at another session
of the Federal Executive in the middle of May. It was decided to
appoint the Protestant von Hassel as Dufhues's deputy, to grant
Dufhues the right to summon and chair the Federal Executive and
to proceed with a plan to create a seven-man Party Praesidium to
replace the 'closer Executive', formed only two years before, as an
inner leadership circle. This would consist of Adenauer, Dufhues,
von Hassel, Krone, Erhard, Gerstenmaier and Blank.[29] The
confessional balance would thus be neatly kept between four
Catholics and three Protestants.

The Dortmund Congress of the CDU in June 1962 earned a
reputation as the party's 'reformist congress', though this was not
fully justified. It saw the election of two committed party reformers
to new leadership positions, and for the first time the question of
party reform was a principal item on a CDU Congress agenda. One
of three working groups, apart from those dealing with foreign and
economic policy, looked at 'Future Tasks of the CDU', under the
chairmanship of Kai-Uwe von Hassel. This prompted some very
verbose speeches, such as one by Gerstenmaier on freedom and
basic values, but also gave a platform to rising young party politicians
like Rainer Barzel, Gerhard Stoltenberg[12] and Helmut Kohl.[13]
The Congress was not 'reformist' in any deeper sense of initiating any
radical decisions about the future nature of the party, nor did it
encourage a freer form of internal party debate. Barzel presented

his report to a meeting of the Federal Committee and was listened
to with respect, but its importance in real terms remained strictly
academic. Adenauer's opening speech to the Congress immediately
touched on the 1961 Election ('not the result desired by us'),
but then diverted attention by referring to his Government's
achievements since 1949 (but for the CDU 'this country would no
longer belong to the free countries of the world') and to the
party's determination to win back its absolute majority at the next
Federal election (lively and continuous applause). He chided his
critics about his forthcoming retirement, making facetious jokes
about his health and God being kind to him, and refused to divulge
any date saying merely that the press would continue to have to
put up with him.[30]

In one essential respect the Dortmund Congress failed to produce
clarity. While it raised expectations that party reform would now
with Dufhues's election as Business Chairman be achieved by decisions
from above, the exact definition of his powers and functions
remained unclarified. Dufhues's success ultimately depended on his
weight and influence, but the signs were not hopeful that he would
acquire a position with real powers. Not only had his rank in the
party hierarchy been pared down at the insistence of the *Land*
chairmen, but his role would be determined above all by how much
genuine authority Adenauer was prepared to grant him. Adenauer's
readiness to concede on the substance rather than merely the
appearance of party reform was doubtful, especially in view of his
persistent wish to maintain control over essential matters because
of the ever pending succession problem. It is significant that
Dufhues in his first speech as Business Chairman to the Bundestag
Fraktion claimed that he had political leadership tasks but was
careful to mention that discussion of the Chancellor succession
should be conducted 'with all respect and in confidence' and that
it should be solved with the consent of Adenauer.[31]

It must be remembered that Dufhues's efforts at organisational
reform proceeded against the background of Adenauer's slow-motion
retirement from the Chancellorship with its corroding effects on
party morale, and that consequently it was difficult to divorce
these two developments in the CDU. The best measure of Dufhues's
achievements as Business Chairman is to summarise his aims and
then examine how far they were implemented. Broadly, these aims
amounted to giving the CDU an independent party organisation
and were the first thorough attempt at party reform in the history

of the CDU. As Dufhues said in his major speech on party reform at the Dortmund Congress:

> The party — as representative of its members and voters — can only be suited to its great tasks if it enjoys its own existence (*Eigenleben*), and is more than an auxiliary organisation of the Government or an appendage of the Bundestag *Fraktion*. It must further all the more be able to exist, when the time comes — which may God prevent in the interests of the German people — for it not to be in government.[32]

The most important of Dufhues's measures of party reform, mentioned in his Dortmund speech, memoranda and the statements he made to *Land* party organisations, were as follows:

1. *To create an effective party organisation.* This involved dealing with two principal features of the CDU: its federal structure and the nature of its activist personnel. In a memorandum on the tasks of party reform, Dufhues recognised that the party's federal structure derived from its origins and that it was impossible to change this although it must be made more 'functionable'. This was as much a psychological as an organisational problem, so what was envisaged was a 'meaningful co-ordination' between the national party and the *Landesverbände* rather than a 'schematic centralisation'. The second problem was developing a responsive professional body of party functionaries, who would replace the exclusive system of local notables. As Dufhues put it, 'they should not cling to their party offices but make way in good time for younger followers, so that these may prepare themselves adequately for assuming responsibility later'.[33] Dufhues's answer to this problem was to increase the staff of the Federal party headquarters, reduce the amateurish working conditions of local party officials, provide means of training party functionaries and establish a system of party 'confidants' (*Vertrauensleute*), who would act as information officers at the regional level on a permanent basis and not just at Federal elections.[34]

2. *To enliven party activities.* The overwhelmingly passive outlook of the party membership should be replaced by a more active participatory role. The first step should be better methods of providing members with political information for

this would 'further attachment between members and with the
party organisation'.[35] His plans included a 'study centre'
to develop ideas for party policy as a basis for discussion among
members, with a view to formulating an electoral platform for
1965. This would consult academic experts and was modelled
on the technique Brandt had adopted as SPD Chancellor
candidate in preparing himself for the 1961 Election.
Dufhues also planned to introduce new party publications to
further the information of party activists.

3. *To increase party membership.* The aim here was to lessen the
disparity between the proportion of CDU members to CDU
voters. A stronger membership was necessary to combat the
potential danger facing the CDU as a result of the greater
volatility of voters. The problems of implementing this aim
were not to be underestimated. The plan to set up a central
card-index of members in Bonn for co-ordinating a membership
policy· had to overcome the reluctance of the *Landesverbände*
to provide the Federal headquarters with detailed information,
while this whole policy was likely to offend the local notables
who in many areas practised a closed shop on the question of
membership admission. Nevertheless, Dufhues decided to
provide guidelines for membership drives, which he planned
to introduce first of all in his own party in Westphalia and
then on a national scale.

4. *To establish closer contact with voters.* As Dufhues emphasised
in his Dortmund speech, the CDU should not be simply an
'electoral instrument'. It should encourage continuous
contact with voters and not just at election time, and review
propaganda methods introducing a more personal approach.
Once again Dufhues drew on techniques used by the SPD in
1961. There should be more systematic publicity work, and
more effort to cultivate the intelligentsia.[36]

5. *To improve the state of party finances.* The CDU finances
were weak, particularly after the heavy debts to be met from
the 1961 Election. It was hoped to improve one source with
the membership drives, namely registration fees, and to
improve financial administration which was hampered by the
inadequate state of co-operation between the national party
and the *Landesverbände*. The urgency of the problem was
underlined by the fact that party reforms would not be
possible without the necessary funds, for a well-functioning

party organisation costs money.

Dufhues's plans amounted to an ambitious scheme for streamlining the CDU in many important respects in order to create a more efficient and structured party organisation. Although Dufhues's interviews showed a concern for the programmatic orientation of the party, his real interest lay in the purely organisational side of party reform. As such he was a new phenomenon among CDU national leaders, who had tended to look askance at matters of party organisation, although he was on the other hand in danger of ignoring problems of the party's image and policy outlook which were alienating voters. Dufhues did not achieve any root-and-branch reform of the party structure, although some changes of a secondary nature were implemented: membership drives were initiated and were partially successful; changes were made at the Federal headquarters with the formation of a new department for publicity work; a party spokesman was appointed; and the various publications Dufhues planned were introduced. Dufhues's ultimate intention to renovate the party fundamentally failed, although his ideas did provide guidelines for later party reformers in the later 1960s and early 1970s. The reasons for his relative failure were several.

First, Dufhues chose to challenge too many vested interests in the CDU and above all failed because of mistrust towards his plans among the *Landesverbande*. He was fully aware of this problem, and attempted to overcome the deep reservations at this level towards any possible 'centralisation' by following through an intensive programme of visiting the headquarters of each *Landesverband* from October 1962 to May 1963. Dufhues discussed his reform plans with regional party officials, went round each room asking everyone detailed questions about the work done, sometimes held press conferences and occasionally addressed party rallies.[37] These occasions were invariably dubbed 'state visits' or 'inspection visits'. Dufhues was received with courtesy and interest, although he did not really bring about a change of attitude. *Land* party leaders were receptive to the idea of better co-operation with Bonn, but when it came to practical measures affecting their control over party organisation, such as the opening of a central membership card-index, they were inclined to obstruct and procrastinate. The *Landersverbände* were required to send in their membership lists and many refused.[14] Practical co-operation with the *Landersverbände* was the crucial factor in Dufhues's plans, for without this many of his other measures had no chance of success.

Secondly, the necessary financial backing for the various projects was lacking. The Federal headquarters did not have the funds, while other internal party sources depended on more lucrative support from the regional and district branches. This was not forthcoming. Any systematic regulation of membership fees could not be adopted because of the basic belief in the CDU that a member should voluntarily contribute to the party funds. As a result, several projects were abandoned or postponed including the one for a 'study centre'. Schemes for training party personnel suffered, and had also to be cut back. Dufhues made frequent reference in public statements to the need for suitably qualified people to work for the party, but this problem was never solved satisfactorily for lack of response as well as financial reasons.

Thirdly, Dufhues did not acquire real political weight in his new position as Business Chairman of the CDU. Partly this was because his attention was not devoted fully to his party work, for he continued to maintain a flourishing law practice in Bochum. The main reason, however, lay in the fact that his appointment was not strengthened with important leadership powers. Had Adenauer been willing to retire from the chairmanship and hand it over formally to Dufhues, this might possibly have been different. Adenauer instead continued to exercise authority as CDU chairman and, although he conferred with Dufhues about his plans, he showed little real acknowledgement of Dufhues's position. Dufhues was present at meetings of the Federal Executive and appeared at sessions of the Bundestag *Fraktion*, but he generally remained unassertive and kept out of policy disputes such as over the Common Market, relations with France and the question of British entry to the EEC. After the most controversial issue of all, the Spiegel Affair of 1962, Dufhues put quiet pressure on Adenauer to re-form his Cabinet and helped to allay ill feelings inside the party. But he was never admitted to Adenauer's inner circle of policy advisers. While his neutral position on policy matters made Dufhues few enemies, it did on the other hand limit his status and authority in the party.

Fourthly, Dufhues spent in fact much of his time dealing with the problem of the succession question rather than directly with party reform. In a very real sense Adenauer's pending retirement and the choice of a new Chancellor overshadowed the question of party reform. The process of selecting Erhard was ironically Dufhues's main achievement as Business Chairman, for as one of the king-makers he sounded out opinion at the grass-roots of the party and helped to smooth the way for Erhard. Dufhues's speeches to *Land* organisations from the autumn of 1962 made frequent reference to Erhard's good qualities, and to the fact that he together with Adenauer had made post-war Germany what it was. Erhard's nomination as successor in the spring of 1963 took much of the steam out of the movement for party reform. Although the change in Chancellor was used as the occasion for a successful membership campaign, the adoption of a popular figure to lead the CDU into the next election made other plans to stimulate party activities and develop more technical approaches to winning voters seem no longer necessary. This goes far in highlighting the difficulties of reforming a party while in government.

(c)   The Transfer of the Chancellor's Mantle: Adenauer to Erhard

The choice of Ludwig Erhard as the new Chancellor in 1963 confirmed the marked dependence of the CDU/CSU on the personal and electoral popularity of its leader, all the more as it had been preceded for several years by a persistent concern about his abilities as a party politician and disquiet over his relative inexperience outside economic affairs. The nomination of Erhard by the CDU/CSU *Fraktion* in April of that year represented the victory of necessity over doubt. The CDU managers, who prepared and organised the change of leadership, had as their principal motive the desire to win the 1965 Bundestag Election. In Erhard they had a ready-made popular figure, who had played a prominent part alongside Adenauer in previous elections, while his main rivals were regarded as perhaps more skilled party politicians but could not match his level of appeal to the public. Erhard's liberal image seemed the answer to those in the CDU who were concerned about the competing attraction of the FDP for bourgeois voters. Although the succession question had been prolonged so much, Erhard had remained ultimately the only real choice.

The period 1961-3 saw a progressive decline in Adenauer's political position, although his tenacious hold over the loyalty of his colleagues explained the unwillingness of any of them, least of all Erhard, to play Brutus. There was in any case no precedent for a leadership change, while doubts about Erhard's candidacy only encouraged procrastination. These doubts allowed other CDU politicians to be considered as possible candidates, notably the new Foreign Minister Gerhard Schröder, Heinrich Krone the party elder statesman with Franz-Josef Strauss, the 47-year old CSU chairman, considered as a long-term possibility. Dufhues although mentioned was not viewed as a likely candidate. The apparent multiplicity of candidates was an argument used by Adenauer to postpone the choice of Erhard, yet there were limits to how far the 'Old One' could play out his objections. The shock of the 1961 Election result was kept fresh by the trend against the CDU in *Land* elections during 1962. Growing criticism was voiced about Adenauer's performance as Chancellor.[15]

The issue which clinched the matter and forced Adenauer to declare at last the date for his retirement was the Spiegel Affair in the autumn of 1962, which erupted after the arbitrary arrest of several leading members of the editorial staff of *Der Spiegel* following the publication of an article on Government defence policy. The ensuing public storm shook the Government, but it produced a variable attitude in the party. The first reactions there were critical towards the Government. The *Fraktion* felt alienated by Adenauer's failure to take it into his confidence,[16] while sharp attacks from the Young Union and the RCDS (the CDU's student organisation) were made on Strauss, the minister held responsible for the police action.[38] Relations between the CDU and the CSU, which remained firmly loyal to Strauss, worsened. There was a stormy meeting of the CDU Federal Executive on 12 November, at which von Brentano blamed Strauss for the CDU's setback in the Hesse *Land* election the previous Sunday and Schröder was scathing about Strauss's dishonest justification of his involvement in the arrests before the Bundestag. The critical attitude towards Strauss was reflected in the CDU press that week.[39]

If any CDU politicians considered using the scandal as an opportunity to lever Adenauer out of power, such a thought was dismissed after the bitter and concentrated attack on the Government from the SPD Opposition. This aroused a determination in CDU circles not to allow Adenauer, who had rendered such great services to Germany, to become the victim of a sordid affair. A special meeting of the *Fraktion* less than a week later demonstrated its solidarity behind Adenauer, and von Brentano officially denied any rumours of a rift between the CDU and the CSU.[40] The closing of ranks behind Adenauer was further reinforced by blatant demands from the FDP coalition partner that there should be a change in the Chancellorship if the coalition were to continue.[41] Party attention was now directed at re-forming a government under Adenauer, once Strauss was forced to resign as Defence Minister. For the first time a grand coalition was seriously considered as a possibility. Unexpectedly, the *Fraktion* authorised Adenauer to open negotiations with the SPD. Support for the idea had been increasing among CDU deputies in recent years and was now assisted by annoyance with the FDP. The talks which followed failed to increase the chances of a grand coalition, because there were at this time strong divisions in the CDU between those who were prepared to try out the new coalition formula, and others who warned the party against the 'deadly embrace' from the SPD.[42] The outcome of the crisis was after all a renewed coalition with the FDP and the announcement by von Brentano of Adenauer's forthcoming retirement in the autumn of 1963. Adenauer's senior colleague had persuaded him to fix a date, although he was unwilling to go so far as to make a 'crown prince proclamation'.

The unhappy episode of the Spiegel Affair therefore speeded up the solution of the succession question. Pressures for settling on a new Chancellor became overwhelming during the winter of 1962-3. Confidence about Adenauer's command over policy matters was wavering, for he had already been criticised for his lack of interest in social affairs, education and other domestic questions as well as for his obstinate suspicions of the young President Kennedy's flexible approach to East-West relations. It further received a stunning blow from Adenauer's signature of the controversial Franco-German Treaty of Co-operation with de Gaulle at the height of the Common Market crisis over Britain's entry to the EEC. Adenauer's precipitate action, although motivated by his desire to set an official seal on Franco-German reconciliation before his retirement, divided opinion inside the CDU/CSU because of its negative implications for the future of the EEC. The party's state of misery was compounded by its loss of 8.9 per cent in the West Berlin state election in mid-February, with a corresponding gain by the SPD, which brought forth the electoral ghost to haunt the party. The prospect of more *Land* election reverses later in the year persuaded CDU leaders to press for a final solution. The bloc of Bundestag deputies from Lower Saxony, where the state election was taking place on 19 May, met in Hanover and decided to press for a formal decision on Adenauer's retirement and the nomination of Erhard before that date.[43] Meanwhile, the *Fraktion* had taken the initiative of authorising von Brentano and Dufhues to deliberate with party circles and make a proposal for Chancellor candidate.[44]

There followed some informal consultation of opinion within the party, meetings of the Federal Executive and the collation of viewpoints from different levels of the party leadership.[45] Dufhues then presented Adenauer with a report that a vote among various CDU *Land* executives favoured both an early decision and the nomination of Erhard,[46] thus strengthening the hand of the *Fraktion*. Adenauer was now virtually powerless to resist the inevitable. It was clear that a substantial majority in the party tolerated Erhard's nomination, even if they were not fully enthusiastic about it. On 23 April, the CDU/CSU *Fraktion* elected Erhard as Adenauer's successor by 159 out of 225 votes, with 19 abstentions and 47 votes against.[47]

In the middle of November, a month after Erhard had become Chancellor, a demonstration of loyalty in his favour by party deputies and activists was held in the Beethoven Hall in Bonn. With the motto 'Forward with Erhard', the CDU sought to forget the differences and conflicts of the past. Adenauer made a speech in support of his 'Colleague Erhard', and was seen to shake hands with his successor to ecstatic applause from the audience. The occasion reached its climax in a policy speech from Erhard expressing confidence that the CDU/CSU would win the Bundestag Election in 1965. The rapturous enthusiasm with which his remark was received reflected the relief felt in the party ranks that after the painful process of choosing a new Chancellor another popular leader was fortunately ready to take his place.[48] As one foreign observer put it, 'Dr Adenauer has been part of the international scene for so long that it seems as inconceivable that he should leave it as it would be for Nelson to step down from his column in Trafalgar Square . . . like Dame Nellie Melba, Dr Adenauer has announced so many farewell appearances that is is difficult to be sure which will be his last.'[49]

This feeling of relief by the CDU was to prove short-lived, for Erhard had come to power at a time when the party was in a brittle state of disarray; indeed at a far more difficult time than if he had succeeded Adenauer in 1959 when the Chancellor succession was first raised seriously. In spite of his electoral appeal, Erhard was not the ideal leader to bind the party together and heal the adverse effects on its solidarity and morale resulting from the perennial problem of Adenauer's retirement. The struggle inside the party during these past four years had essentially not been over the choice of his successor, but rather it arose from the more complex problem of the party extricating itself from its pervasive dependence on the figure of Adenauer, which still persisted although reduced during his political decline.

Notes

[1]   The margin of difference between the vote of the CDU/CSU and the SPD declined in the 1961 Bundestag Election from 18.4 per cent in 1957 to 9.2 per cent, i.e. by half.

[2]   Organisational reform had already been initiated in the CSU from the mid-1950s for reasons of its weakened position in Bavarian politics; see below chapter 10 (c), pp. 323 ff.

[3]   CDU leaders interested in party reform made frequent defensive references to the SPD's superiority in these matters in speeches they gave in 1960.

[4]   The 46-year-old Kai-Uwe von Hassel had been one of the four deputy chairmen of the CDU since 1956. He gained his reputation during the 1950s of an active younger leader of the party from his political role in his native Schleswig-Holstein. In 1954 he succeeded his patron Friedrich Wilhelm Lübke as Minister-President in that *Land,* having briefly been a member of the Bundestag. Von Hassel later managed the CDU campaign for the Bundestag Election in 1961, and became Adenauer's Minister of Defence the following year.

[5]   This was a smaller body within the Federal Executive formed at the Stuttgart Congress of the CDU in 1956, officially to relieve Adenauer of some of his work and commitments as party chairman, but it failed to develop any political initiative.

[6]   The erection of the Berlin Wall in August 1961 gave the SPD Opposition and particularly its Chancellor candidate Willy Brandt (mayor of West Berlin) an opportunity to gain favourable publicity in the campaign. Its principal speakers broke off their election engagements and rushed to Berlin, while Adenauer continued with his meetings around the country, including one in which he caused public dismay by an attack on Brandt's illegitimate birth.

[7]   The 37-year-old Rainer Barzel had been a protégé of Karl Arnold and high-ranking civil servant in North-Rhine Westphalia. He was elected to the Bundestag in 1957, where despite his early association with progressive Christian Democrats he gained a reputation for his strident attitude towards Communist infiltration especially among left-wing intellectuals. Elected a member of the CDU Federal Executive in 1960, Barzel was appointed Minister for All-German Affairs in Adenauer's Cabinet in 1962.

[8]   This idea had first appeared with the decision at the CDU Congress in 1956 to form a Business Executive to relieve Adenauer of some of his duties as chairman. A mild version of the same idea was contained in the party reform proposals of 1959.

[9]   In the Landtag election of July 1962 in North-Rhine Westphalia, the CDU lost its absolute majority, acquired in 1958, despite the popularity of Franz Meyers as a *Landesvater.* Federal politics played a large part in the campaign, so that the CDU's loss of electoral support in this *Land* was attributed to the uncertainty created by the leadership question.

[10] Josef-Hermann Dufhues, born in 1908, had nursed strong ambitions to become Minister-President of North-Rhine Westphalia in 1958, when the CDU returned to power in Düsseldorf, but had been beaten by Meyers. He had then settled for the consolation prize of *Land* Minister of the Interior. Dufhues had been a protégé of Karl Arnold, Adenauer's old rival, and had first made his name as an effective chairman of the Young Union in the early 1950s. He was regarded as a critic of the party establishment, having successfully led the revolt against Adenauer over the statute changes at the 1956 CDU Congress (see above chapter 2 (c), pp. 94-5). He also gained the reputation of a party reformer for his work in overhauling party organisation in Westphalia, where he had become CDU chairman in 1959. Maintaining a distant relationship with Adenauer, Dufhues refused his offer to become a Federal minister in 1961. He was known for his good contacts with the younger generation of CDU politicians. (Background on Dufhues from 'Dufhues: der schwarze Wehner' in *Der Spiegel,* No. 23, 1962, pp. 24-40 and files on Dufhues in Archiv BGS.)

[11] The word *Ämterhaufung* became a term of abuse in the mouths of younger party reformers, reflecting a certain frustration with the rule of gerontocrats in the CDU.

[12] The 33-year-old Gerhard Stoltenberg had risen fast in the party,having been chairman of the Young Union (1955-61) and elected the youngest member of the Bundestag in 1957. Adenauer offered him the Defence Ministry after the Spiegel Affair in the autumn of 1962, but he declined. He later became Federal Minister of Research and Education in 1965 at the age of 37.

[13] The 32-year-old Helmut Kohl was at this time building a career in *Land* politics. Elected a member of the Rhineland-Palatinate Landtag in 1959 and chairman of the CDU group on the town council of his native town Ludwigshafen in 1960, he was now deputy chairman of the CDU *Fraktion* in the Landtag in Mainz. He became its chairman in 1963, and was elected to the CDU Federal Executive in 1964. Kohl became a member of the Dufhues Commission on organisational questions.

[14] The classic case of obstruction came from the district branch in Cloppenburg, in Oldenburg, which replied briefly: 'Our executive committee takes the view that our members do not want this Federal membership card-index; moreover we do not have the data to complete the forms and therefore will not send these back.' It was pointed out to Dufhues that his efforts were unnecessary, for in Cloppenburg '80 per cent of all voters opt for the CDU'. (*Civis*, No. 3, 1964, p. 17.)

[15] His frequent visits to his North Italian villa in Cadenabbia occasioned remarks about 'the absentee Chancellor' and jokes about his running the country from abroad, a method known as 'Bonnabbia'. As the *Neue Zürcher Zeitung* commented, on 4 March 1963, this situation offered 'the perfect Gordian knot, only an Alexander is not in sight'.

[16] See the letter to Adenauer from Heinrich von Brentano, *Fraktion* chairman, on 7 November 1962 warning him that the mood in the *Fraktion* was 'unusually bad and irritated'. Many deputies were complaining that once again they were presented with a *fait accompli*. Brentano objected that Adenauer might have spared himself some difficulties if he had taken the trouble to inform the chairman of his own *Fraktion* in good time. (Arnulf Baring, *Sehr verehrter Herr Bundeskanzler* (1974), p. 472.)

140   *Christian Democracy in Western Germany*

References

1.   *Die Zeit*, 16 January 1958.
2.   *FAZ*, 3 July 1959.
3.   *Der Spiegel*, 29 July 1959.
4.   *Christ und Welt*, 9 July 1959.
5.   *SZ*, 11 July 1959 and *Der Spiegel*, 29 July 1959.
6.   Reports on this meeting in *FAZ*, 17 September 1959; *Die Welt* (Essen), 17 September 1959, and *Telegraph* (W. Berlin), 18 September 1959.
7.   Reports on Federal Committee meeting in *Flensburger Tageblatt*, 29 September 1959; *FAZ*, 29 September 1959 and *NZZ*, 30 September 1959.
8.   Rolf Zundel, 'Wer reformiert die Partei? Tauziehen in der CDU um die Organisation' in *Die Zeit*, 25 September 1959.
9.   *Der Tagesspiegel*, 25 September 1959 and *FAZ*, 29 September 1959.
10. *Die Welt* (Essen), 17 September 1959 and *Der Spiegel*, 7 October 1959.
11. *Der Spiegel*, 7 October 1959.
12. *Ruhr-Nachrichten* (Dortmund), 26 September 1959.
13. *9. Bundesparteitag der CDU* (1960), pp. 75-89.
14. *Ibid.*, pp. 21-33.
15. *Ibid.*, pp. 91-92.
16. *Deutsche Zeitung und Wirtschaftszeitung*, 24 November 1959 and *FAZ*, 25 November 1959.
17. *SZ*, 28 October 1960.
18. P. Merkl, 'Equilibrium, Structure of Interests and Leadership: Adenauer's Survival as Chancellor' in *American Political Science Review:* 1962, pp. 634-50.
19. *Wiesbadener Kurier*, 12 December 1961.
20. *Der Spiegel*, No. 23, 1962, p. 34.
21. *SZ*, 7 February 1962.
22. *Der Spiegel*, No. 23, 1962, p. 25.
23. Bert Even, 'Die Erneuerung der CDU' in *Bonner Rundschau*, 15 March 1962.
24. *Allgemeine Zeitung*, 26 March 1962.
25. *FAZ*, 8 February 1962 and 9 February 1962; *Der Tagesspiegel*, 27 February 1962.
26. *FAZ*, 7 April 1962; *Deutsche Zeitung*, 19 April 1962; *SZ*, 10 May 1962; and *Christ und Welt*, 11 May 1962.
27. *FAZ*, 7 April, 1962.
28. Dietrich Strothmann, 'Kronprinz ohne Krone? Die Macht des künftigen CDU-Generalsekretärs Dufhues soll beschnitten werden' in *Die Zeit*, 23 March 1962.
29. *FAZ*, 11 May 1962 and *The Times*, 12 May 1962.
30. *11. Bundesparteitag der CDU* (1962), pp. 15-18.
31. *FAZ*, 14 June 1962.
32. *11. Bundesparteitag der CDU*, p. 318.
33. J.H. Dufhues, 'Aufgabe und Ziel einer Parteireform' in *Soziale Ordnung*, No. 3, 1963.
34. Dufhues, report to Federal Executive, 22 November 1962, Hauptstaatsarchiv Düsseldorf, RWV 26, No. 233b.
35. Dufhues in *Soziale Ordnung*, No. 3, 1962.
36. *Union in Deutschland*, 19 July, 1962.
37. Interview with Franz Grandel, Bezirksgeschäftsführer of the CDU in North Württemberg, in Stuttgart, August 1973.
38. *FAZ*, 20 November 1962.

39.   *The Times*, 14 November 1962.
40.   *FAZ*, 17 November 1962.
41.   *FAZ*, 19 November 1962.
42.   See discussion of the coalition negotiations in *FAZ*, 28 November
      1962; *NZZ*, 29 November 1962, and *FAZ*, 4 December 1962.
43.   *The Times*, 20 April 1963.
44.   Klaus Günther, *Der Kanzlerwechsel in der Bundesrepublik* (1970),
      p.54.
45.   *Ibid.*, pp. 44-5.
46.   *The Times*, 23 April 1963.
47.   *The Times*, 24 April 1963.
48.   *NZZ*, 14 November 1963.
49.   *Observer*, 9 December 1962.

4 THE PERIOD OF TRANSITION: THE ERHARD AND GRAND COALITION GOVERNMENTS (1963-1969)

Two difficulties faced the CDU/CSU during the 1960s: those of internal solidarity and electoral appeal. At first sight these may be attributed to the problem of a political movement adapting to the absence of an exceptional leader figure, around whose authority and policy successes it had risen to preeminence in the state; and in view of the CDU/CSU's special dependence on Adenauer there was much truth in this assumption. However, the party's crisis during this decade could only be fully explained by other factors related to the need for a change in the CDU/CSU's role in the West German party system and its inability to adapt to a new milieu. Although the party's difficulties of 1963-9 may be partly seen as a continuation of those it had faced as a result of the presidential candidacy crisis of 1959, the years which followed Adenauer's retirement from the Chancellorship in 1963 emphasised that they had not been merely temporary aberrations because he overstayed his time in office. The years 1963-9 may therefore be fittingly called a period of transition in the development of the CDU/CSU, for they witnessed its loss of political dominance and subsequently national office when the first Left-Liberal coalition was formed in the autumn of 1969.

The following factors accounted for the changing political position of the CDU/CSU. First, the institution of the Chancellor was undergoing a transformation, thereby affecting the incumbent's role as party leader. The term 'Chancellor Democracy', which had involved a structural modification of parliamentary democracy in the direction of strong executive leadership, was no longer applicable. The less autocratic political natures of Erhard and Kiesinger compared with that of Adenauer obviously meant a different interpretation of the role of Chancellor. Also, any successor to Adenauer would have been in a less favourable position to assert his supremacy in relation to his colleagues because of the greater political weight as a policy-making body acquired by the Cabinet from the early 1960s. Erhard's collegial style of leadership in the Cabinet may have been appropriate in view of its new found influence, but there were other wider reasons why his authority was not so pervasive as that of Adenauer. In spite of this reduced scope of the chief executive, public expectations of the role of Chancellor conditioned by the precedent of Adenauer in the 1950s remained high. The functions of the Chancellor were also more complicated by his need to pay more attention to internal party affairs than had been the case in the previous decade. The CDU/CSU as a party was no longer willing to play such a subordinate role to the Chancellor, as shown by the new assertiveness of the CSU within the Christian Democratic camp as well as the political authority now demanded by individual *Landesverbände* in the CDU, which were also motivated by a concern over the electoral future of the party. Party cohesion was therefore more difficult to achieve in the 1960s, and accordingly the Chancellor of the day could no longer dominate his party in the manner of Adenauer.

Secondly, the CDU/CSU's loss of political dominance in the state was also a result of profound changes in the nature of the party system. The SPD was enjoying the electoral benefits of its new reformist position Godesberg-style. The margin between the votes of the two main political parties declined during 1961-6 from 9.2 per cent to 3.4 per cent, a trend only halted by Erhard's election victory of 1965. This loss of its electoral supremacy by the CDU/CSU made increasingly possible a grand coalition, introducing the SPD to national office, an event which occurred in 1966. The FDP meanwhile broke away from its long-standing alliance with the Christian Democrats to take up a left-centre position by the later 1960s. This change, underlined by Walter Scheel's election as FDP chairman early in 1968, brought the FDP closer to the SPD, gave it a more 'modern' image and tended to emphasise the isolation of the CDU/CSU. Consequently, there was a general consolidation of the two/three-party system, a development only interrupted by the brief impact of the NPD on the Right during 1966-8.

Thirdly, the changing internal and international political environment already apparent in the early 1960s could no longer be explained as a problem for the CDU/CSU simply by the criticism that Adenauer had been out of touch with the times. The more variegated international scene (highlighted by the SPD's initiative in espousing Ostpolitik) was in contrast to the East-West confrontation of the 1950s and combined with problems of economic readjustment (such as the recession of 1966-7) and a new critical political mood, especially among the younger generation, to indicate that the

'Adenauer values', to which the CDU/CSU was still strongly
committed, were outdated. The attitudes and assumptions of the
party since the late 1940s were now seriously being called into
question.

The West German political parties were therefore having to
respond to major political, economic and social changes during
the 1960s, and of the three main parties, the CDU/CSU was the
least able to adapt for four reasons. The party's strong dependence
on Adenauer meant that its expectations of his two successors
as Chancellor were unrealistically high considering the changed
circumstances. Neither Erhard nor Kiesinger was able therefore
to act as an integrative leader in the CDU/CSU, and each was in
power too briefly to assert any commanding authority. Ironically,
the party continued to hanker after an Adenauer-type leader at
the same time as Adenauer himself, who remained party chairman
until 1966, became a divisive figure in the CDU/CSU. In addition,
the party became deeply divided over a number of policy areas,
particularly foreign and European affairs, over which there had
been greatest internal solidarity during the 1950s. Partly circumstances
such as de Gaulle's individualistic stand among the Western powers
were at the root of this trouble, but the CDU/CSU was unable to
absorb and react to major new developments due to the lack of any
real tradition of internal party debate. The fundamental differences
of opinion that occurred therefore developed into an embarrassing
slanging match between various CDU/CSU leaders. These tended
to reflect the intense personal rivalries of the immediate post-
Adenauer years, since Erhard's weak leadership indicated that he
would be no more than a stopgap Chancellor. These policy
differences within the party were submerged during the Grand
Coalition, but the CDU/CSU unity of the Adenauer era over
foreign policy was never really restored. Furthermore, the party
reacted defensively to the rise of the SPD and the latter's breakthrough in electoral support during the 1960s. In some CDU circles
this produced a feeling of pessimism about the party's electoral
future, while more generally the question was resumed about how far
the party should change its image or restructure its organisation.
The lesson of Dufhues's work had proved, however, that such
changes were difficult to implement. In the end the CDU/CSU
true to its nature as the Chancellor-orientated party once again
sought a solution for its concern over its future in a further leadership change, as was dramatically demonstrated after the North-Rhine

Westphalian *Land* election (July 1966), where the CDU setback
provoked moves to force Erhard's retirement. Finally, the CDU/CSU
was suffering from having been in power too long. It was in the
words of Theodor Eschenburg, a contemporary analyst of the party's
crisis, a 'worn-out governing party'.[1] The CDU/CSU had been
comfortably dependent on the advantages of office, which had
inhibited attempts to strengthen the party itself and also determined
that its most influential figures were in any case too busy as ministers
to devote time to party affairs. Public discussion began to revolve
around the need for the CDU/CSU to rejuvenate itself with a period
in Opposition.

(a)   Erhard: Charisma without Authority, 1963-1965

Erhard's Chancellorship began in the autumn of 1963 with a burst
of organised enthusiasm among the Christian Democrats in an effort
to boost his leadership and steer the party away from the recent
crises. In August Konrad Kraske, the CDU Business Manager, had
devised a plan to set in motion various publicity measures once
Erhard took over.[2] The plan included a declaration of solidarity
by the CDU Praesidium or Federal Committee after Erhard's
Government Declaration in the Bundestag, a short film on the new
Chancellor prepared by the party headquarters in Bonn to be distributed for showing to the *Landesverbände* and special press conferences held by *Land* party leaders on the lines of those normally
staged in preparation for Bundestag elections. The change in
Government leadership was also to be coupled with increased
efforts to stimulate party activities and general interest in the
party at the grass-roots level. The newly elected Chancellor was
required within a fortnight of assuming power to send a
printed personal 'Erhard letter' to party activists throughout the
country asking for their support. There would be arrangements for
a general 'wave of meetings' on the theme 'Forward with Erhard',
running from mid-October to mid-December, to boost the party
membership drive. Dufhues and von Brentano, the *Fraktion* chairman, would send a letter to Bundestag deputies urging them to
make themselves available as speakers during this time.

Party organisers were hoping to capitalise on Erhard's ability
as an 'electoral locomotive'. The chances of halting the party's
electoral decline since 1961 seemed hopeful now that the CDU had
started to make gains rather than losses in *Land* elections from the
spring of 1963, a new trend influenced positively by the forthcoming

change in Chancellor. In the Lower Saxony election in May Erhard,
by now Adenauer's officially declared successor, had participated
actively and the CDU vote rose by 6.9 per cent. Kraske planned to use
Erhard's appeal to help restore morale at the party grass roots.
It would be arranged for the new Chancellor to visit each *Landesverband* of the CDU after his taking office, though not until
early in the New Year because he would have to remain at first
chiefly in Bonn because of his commitment and 'also because of
the impression made on the public'.[3] An exception would be made in
the case of Baden-Württemberg because of preparations for the long
campaign for the *Land* election set for May 1964. A party report of
1963 on the outlook for the CDU in Baden-Württemberg blamed
the party's general loss of support since the 1961 Bundestag
Election on the fact that it had

> presented a picture of inner strife, disunion and indecision, not
> least in its top leadership — we can only hope with the election
> of Erhard as Chancellor successor that at least this problem,
> which is a burden to both the party and the public, is settled.[4]

It was also hoped that the Erhard Government would co-operate
with the Bundestag *Fraktion* in achieving 'a solution of the great
and pressing legislative problems with new energy and as quickly
as possible'. CDU leaders in the south-west state clearly feared the
impact of Bonn politics there despite the reasonable record of the
Kiesinger *Land* government. In the event Erhard played a prominent
role in the campaign, and the CDU's impressive rise in the vote by
6.7 per cent strengthened Erhard's position in the party. The new
Chancellor had already delighted the party faithful with a virulent
partisan speech denouncing the Social Democrats at the CDU
Congress at Hanover in March 1964. Erhard's relationship with his
party seemed solidified when he received the final distinction in
CDU circles of being attacked by the SPD for continuing Adenauer's
attitude in his speech.[5]

   Despite the sense of elation among the party faithful and Erhard's
electoral impact, his political position was in fact already potentially
insecure. What were not yet apparent at the Hanover Congress were
the disagreements between many CDU/CSU leaders about the future
course of foreign/European policy. This was one of the main
problem areas inherited from Adenauer's last years in office, in
addition to the demand for long-delayed domestic legislation (social

policy, reform of the penal code and the emergency laws), the
question of contacts with Eastern Europe and the strained relations
in the CDU/CSU-FDP coalition which all augured ill for the new
Chancellor. Erhard came to power in a precarious situation, so
that it was difficult to extend his political honeymoon period. Any
real break with the past, involving as this would casting some
discredit on the previous administration, in which he himself had
played a prominent part, was inhibited by his retention of the same
Cabinet with few changes and persistent veneration for Adenauer (who
remained CDU chairman) in the party. Erhard did not therefore
enjoy the initial relative freedom of manoeuvre desired by a new
head of government.

One other crucial factor in Erhard's position was his own nature
as a politician and his outlook on politics in general. Erhard lacked
Adenauer's firm paternalistic approach to government management, and did not show the same taste for calculated political
action. The key to Erhard the politician was his conscious desire to
appear as the 'People's Chancellor' (*Volkskanzler*), a popular figure
who appealed directly to the electorate and stood somewhat above
party horse-trading. Erhard's concept was attractive to that traditional German outlook which distrusted the partisan element in
politics, but it was not suited to the realities of the Federal
Republic where political parties provided the channels of political
activity. With public popularity as his political strength, Erhard was
in danger of constructing his Chancellorship on shifting sands.

Erhard's principal strategic mistake as Chancellor was that he
did not cultivate his party as his political base. This would have
involved treating the party not as an integral whole, but as a combination of different elements some of them in conflict with each
other. This absence of perception on Erhard's part resulting from
his lack of interest in and inclination for internal party affairs
derived from a deep distaste for party labels which had coloured his
political career.[1] He made no move to assume the party chairmanship when he became Chancellor, in any case difficult as Adenauer
wished to retain that position, and he again made it clear at the
Hanover Congress in March 1964 that he did not want to combine the
two offices.[6] The implications for party solidarity of this division
for the first time of the two leadership positions depended on the
relationship between the two incumbents, but the portents for
this were not at all good in the light of past experience. The
situation whereby both CDU and CSU chairmen were outside the

148   *Christian Democracy in Western Germany*

Erhard Government meant that Adenauer and Strauss were freer
to manoeuvre against the new Chancellor, should the opportunity
arise, because the restraints of ministerial responsibility did not
apply.

Erhard made no sustained effort to woo influential circles in the
CDU. His relations with party activists were generally distant,
although his addresses at party congresses made a strong impression
and aroused admiration, even if they lacked Adenauer's occasional
touches of impish humour which had always won applause.
Erhard did not canvass extensively within the party in order to
promote his policies, and could react lethargically and then
querulously to internal party bickerings. Erhard freely admitted
that he had 'no understanding for party political disputes in a
political situation, where world-wide problems are to be solved'.[7]
Consequently, during 1964 a disenchantment with Erhard developed
at the grass-roots in the CDU, a party nourished on a firm leadership,
which during the 1950s had controlled internal party tensions.
Regional party organisers were made aware of this by the autumn of
that year. The chairman of the *Landesverband* North Württemberg
received many critical letters from party members threatening to
resign because of the absence of a clear definition of the CDU's
aims and the lack of leadership from Erhard, one of which complained
in October:

> A Chancellor should have a relationship with power! He ought
> to be able to manage it, and know how to make use of it. He
> should be able to manoeuvre tactically. He should not go above
> Parliament! He should not rush to the television cameras whenever
> any difficulty occurs! The real decisions still take place in Parlia-
> ment.[8]

The reply from the *Land* party office stated that these criticisms were
'very harsh to some extent, but one could not say that they were wrong',
and promised to refer the complaint to higher authorities in the
party.[9] Erhard had a loyal ally in Dufhues, who remained CDU
Business Chairman until 1966, but his reputation had waned after
disappointment with his party reform plans, and in any case he
remained subordinate to Adenauer in the party hierarchy. Dufhues
together with Kraske, CDU Business Manager, carried the burden of
party administrative work, but they were reluctant to become embroiled
in the policy and personal conflicts between the party's leading

Schröder,[2] the Foreign Minister, were too divisive or isolated
figures to help the Chancellor with strengthening his position in the
party.

Erhard could not count on a hard core of influential loyalists
in the CDU. The obvious source for this would have been the
Bundestag *Fraktion*. Erhard kept in regular contact with *Fraktion*
leaders and attended its meetings, but his relations with it were not
particularly warm.[10] There was the so-called 'Erhard Brigade', a
loose group of several loyal supporters, but the new Chancellor
withdrew its parliamentary leader Kurt Schmücker[3] to become
Minister of Economics. Schmücker as deputy *Fraktion* chairman
had been envisaged as the successor to von Brentano,[11] and in this
capacity as *Fraktion* chairman would have been Erhard's anchor
of support on the floor of the Bundestag. Instead, the eventual
successor to the ailing von Brentano was the young and ambitious
Rainer Barzel, whose election as *Fraktion* chairman in December
1964 and skill at *Fraktion* management forced Erhard into a
position increasingly dependent on Barzel, who acted as intermediary between the Palais Schaumburg and the Bundestag deputies
of the CDU/CSU.[12] Barzel's swift rise to a major leadership
position in the party opened the way for a possible long-term
challenge from him to Erhard, for the Chancellor's one great
strength so far had been the absence of a serious rival.

Erhard's lack of secure authority over the CDU/CSU to buttress
his popular appeal proved all the more fatal for his tenure of the
Chancellorship, because the party itself became increasingly
disunited during 1964 over policy matters. The conflict which
followed at the leadership level was chiefly over the course of
foreign and European policy, an area in which Erhard did not possess
an instinctive political flair or interest. However, the root of this
conflict lay not so much in Erhard's qualities as leader, as in the
irreconcilability which had begun to appear between the two bases
of Adenauer's foreign policy of the 1950s, his pro-American
position and his search for a special relationship with France. New
factors such as the USA's pursuit under Kennedy and Johnson of
détente with the Soviet Union, and de Gaulle's individualistic
interpretation of European integration to accord with French
policy interests as well as his anti-American outlook forced the
leaders of West Germany's main governing party into taking sides.
The new divisions occurred during Adenauer's last year as Chancellor,

so that a premium was placed on fresh leadership from his successor. This proved virtually impossible in view of the state of internal party tensions and Erhard's lack of interest in party management.

There were four mainsprings of the ensuing conflict within the CDU/CSU between the 'Gaullists' and the 'Atlanticists'. First, fundamental policy outlook divided them. Both sides differed markedly over such issues as the question of political union in Western Europe, the enlargement of the Common Market to include Britain, policy towards Eastern Europe, the US defence presence in Europe and the relationship with France. The 'Atlanticists' generally showed a more outward-looking approach by favouring better contacts with the Eastern Bloc, placing a priority on relations with the USA and strongly supporting British membership of the EEC. It was more here a question of contrasting priorities rather than of totally exclusive attitudes, although the course of the debate suggested otherwise. The 'Gaullists' were generally sympathetic to de Gaulle's ideas on Europe, with his distrust of American hegemony in Europe, and they placed emphasis on political union based on Franco-German bipolarity. Their fears concerning East-West *détente,* however, meant they did not go along with the French President's search for flexible relations with Eastern Europe. So far as their viewpoint was ideological, it was either Francophile (as with Adenauer) or anti-Communist (as with the CSU leader von Guttenberg) or both, although in fact anti-Communism was equally found among CDU 'Atlanticists' even if it were less emotionally pronounced.

Secondly, the Gaullist-Atlanticist controversy was all the more embittered since it adversely affected the confessional alliance in the CDU/CSU. This had been reasonably satisfactory during Adenauer's ascendancy, but it had become increasingly strained because of ill-feeling among Catholics in the party at the rise of 'Protestant' influence in the leadership. The country's external relations were now controlled by the trio of Erhard as Chancellor, Schröder (Foreign) and von Hassel (Defence), all of whom were Protestants. This ill-feeling was reflected in the habit of the press of referring to 'Gaullists' and 'Atlanticists' in the CDU/CSU respectively as 'Southerners' and 'Prussians' There was some truth in this over-simplification for prominent 'Gaullists' tended to be southern Catholics and prominent 'Atlanticists' tended to be northern Protestants, while the 'Gaullists' enjoyed more sympathy in the South German CDU *Landesverbände* and the CSU and the

'Atlanticists' in the North German *Landesverbände.*[4]

A third source of conflict was Erhard's declared and uncompromising Atlanticist stance. This stemmed partly from his strong pro-American sympathies ever since his dealings with the US Occupation authorities after the War, and partly from his sceptical attitude towards European integration. It was the latter which had already alienated him so deeply from Adenauer, who particularly for this reason had opposed Erhard's succession to the Chancellorship so vigorously. Adenauer, now mistrustful of the USA and fearing that his life's work in European affairs was threatened, joined with the 'Gaullist' wing to counter Erhard's influence in European policy. Adenauer, who had devoted more time to party affairs since his retirement from office, exploited the party quarrel to inflame discontent with Erhard's position as Chancellor by open criticism of his successor.

Fourthly, personal political ambitions were involved in the controversy and the European issue was exploited by Gaullists to weaken Erhard's leadership. During 1964 it appeared increasingly likely that the Chancellor's term of office would be brief, and that the succession question would arise again. The Gaullist-Atlanticist antagonism was sharpened by the bitter rivalry between Strauss and Schröder, who were both strong claimants to Erhard's throne. This added an extra dimension to Strauss's demands for a new course in foreign policy and public clashes between the two as over the Test Ban Treaty.[13]

Although the Gaullist-Atlanticist controversy was the first major instance of a deep policy rift in the CDU/CSU, it is impossible to estimate the relative strengths of the two camps within the whole party. The controversy itself was largely confined to prominent party leaders, accounting for the dramatic interpretation of it by the press, although it did severely affect the moods of the CDU/CSU as a whole. The Young Union had been heavily involved in the 1950s in transnational co-operation with other Christian Democratic youth organisations, and had espoused the idea of a European federal state.[14] Its members felt disillusioned with the trend of events in the EEC since the early 1960s. Party activists tended to be less concerned with policy concepts out of deference to the leadership, and they were therefore embarrassed at the exposure of bitter divisions within the leadership structure because they were fearful that this might be another chapter in the Adenauer-Erhard conflict. Thus they preferred to play down the matter at the local level for the sake of party unity and public appeal.

A new problem for party solidarity was also emerging as the CSU was developing an independent profile in foreign affairs from the mid-1960s under the leadership of Strauss.[15] The CSU's concept of an independent Europe brought it into line with the 'Gaullist' wing of the CDU. Finally, personal sympathy for one party leader or another during the Gaullist-Atlanticist controversy was often coloured by their general popularity, as shown by the enthusiastic reception for Strauss at the 1964 CDU Congress in contrast to Schröder's 'cold' image among the party rank-and-file, although this was not a direct comment on the relative state of support for either camp in the controversy. Within the CDU/CSU Bundestag *Fraktion*, the 'Gaullists' appeared to be a substantial minority.[16] On the other hand, they boasted the allegiance of more prominent figures in the party with Adenauer (CDU chairman), von Brentano (*Fraktion* chairman), Strauss (CSU chairman), Guttenberg and at a later stage Gerstenmaier (Bundestag President). The chief protagonists of the 'Atlanticist' wing were Erhard and Schröder.

Erhard's primary disadvantage in this dispute was that his role in the controversy prevented him from acting as an integrative figure in the party. His association with the one faction allowed leaders of the other to operate openly against him. This was not at first apparent, since Erhard had benefited from the initial prestige that accompanies a new incumbent as Chancellor. His Government Declaration in October 1963 had emphasised the need for an outward-looking EEC, 'friendly relations with other European states, above all Britain' as well as 'cultivating and deepening of relations with France'.[17] Despite this Atlanticist tone, Erhard won a vote of confidence in his foreign policy from the CDU Federal Committee shortly before his official visit to Rome in January 1964, although he felt obliged to stress the importance of Franco-German *rapprochement.*[18]

The quarrel in the party erupted in July 1964, shortly after de Gaulle's visit to Bonn in accordance with the provisions of the Franco-German Treaty of Co-operation (January 1963). The 'Gaullists' expressed bitter disappointment at the outcome of the meeting, for the cool atmosphere between Erhard and de Gaulle had been followed by no progress on the question of political union in the EEC. The CSU Congress was due to begin in Munich a few days later. Adenauer and Strauss met in their capacity as the two party chairmen on the eve of the Congress, and issued a statement to the effect that in future both parties should closely co-ordinate their standpoints on foreign policy.[19] The CSU General Secretary, Anton Jaumann, demanded in a separate statement that the Government should reach an agreement with France as soon as possible.[20] At the CSU Congress itself Erhard, who had only just returned from a visit to Denmark, made a bold speech reminding his audience that 'the foreign policy of the Federal Republic is my policy, the policy for which I bear responsibility — I will not and cannot give up this responsibility'.[21] This assertion of his basic right as Chancellor to determine the guidelines of Government policy (*Richtlinien-kompetenz*) was a defiant response to Strauss's view that this power was 'not absolute and unlimited'.[22] Erhard summarised his own policy, which failed to satisfy the CSU delegates who applauded most of all demands from the platform by their own party speakers that a concerted effort should be made to break out of the 'stagnation' in European policy.[23] The expected clash between Strauss and Erhard did not materialise partly because of the Chancellor's conciliatory intervention with Strauss within an hour of his arrival back from Denmark.[24]

The assertiveness of the CSU vis-à-vis the Erhard Government over policy matters only encouraged further disloyalty in the CDU because of the Bavarian sister party's influence within the ranks of the latter. Most notably, Adenauer put himself on record, usually in the form of a newspaper interview, as a regular critic of Erhard's policy. In an interview with *France Soir*, reprinted in the West German press, the ex-Chancellor warned that the Government ran the risk of being beaten in the Bundestag Election the following year if it gave up the policy of still closer relations with France.[25] Erhard's authority had deteriorated so far that by September Dufhues and Barzel felt it necessary to reaffirm in public speeches that the CDU had every intention of fighting the 1965 Election with Erhard as its Chancellor candidate.[26] Adenauer, who kept an office in the Bundestag, all the same continued to promote discontent with the Chancellor. Erhard's failure to establish a rapport with de Gaulle still rankled with Adenauer, as became apparent in a further interview he gave to *Bild am Sonntag* in November. Referring to recent local election losses by the CDU, Adenauer commented tartly that, if only the Government ceased to dither in settling on a clear foreign policy, then the outlook for the CDU/CSU in the Bundestag Election would be 'not at all bad'.[27] This remark at least brought criticism of Adenauer from the *Fraktion* Executive, concerned at the effect of such remarks on the party's electoral chances.

The controversy over foreign policy, exacerbated by Adenauer's public sniping at Erhard, had an undermining effect on party morale. The whole affair involving internal party relations had been given extensive coverage in the press over the previous months. Polls were showing the SPD ahead of the CDU/CSU by the autumn of 1964, and the Social Democrats naturally made the most of this opportunity by exploiting and publicising the conflicts between Christian Democratic leaders. Letters from CDU activists to regional party offices bemoaned the damaging effect of the controversy on the membership drive:

> The lack of unity within the CDU itself, in the CDU/CSU, in the Coalition in Bonn, the conflict of interviews, denials and statements of all kinds over the past months simply went beyond what was tolerable! That was no climate for a recruitment action! The answers one receives from recruitment efforts show this very clearly, and the results of local elections only too plainly![28]

Particularly distressing to party workers was the undignified sight of their leaders fighting each other in public. Another local party leader wrote the same autumn:

> Put yourself in the position of our party friends, who on recruiting trips keep hearing: 'Oh, the CDU/CSU is a party which is tearing itself apart in destructive battles.' And what is the matter with Adenauer, who knows nothing better than to knock Chancellor Erhard off balance at every suitable and unsuitable opportunity, just like the dear good Franz-Josef Strauss.[29]

Apparently, the picture of disunity was most of all disaffecting women voters, who were one of the mainstays of CDU electoral support. According to a report earlier in the year from Aenne Vrauksiepe, chairman of the CDU women's organisation, the controversy was making a 'catastrophic' impact on women for 'solidarity in the CDU will all the more produce success [with them] because of the need among women to be led'.[30]

The prospect of the Bundestag Election in September 1965 had a unifying effect on the CDU/CSU because it feared the further

exposure of its policy disputes would affect its chances of remaining
in power. Foreign policy disputes disappeared from public view,
except for criticism by Adenauer of American policy at the Geneva
Disarmament Conference a few weeks before the election. Erhard
succeeded in turning the 'Chancellor effect' to his advantage in
the campaign, thus confounding earlier predictions of a neck-and-
neck race between the SPD and the CDU/CSU, for the latter
concentrated its appeal on the figure of Erhard. The electoral fray
was the one respect in which Erhard excelled as a party politician,
for he was still able to capitalise on his economic achievements and
so recover some of his lost authority as Chancellor. In projecting
itself as the guarantor of 'security and stability', the CDU/CSU
was in spite of its recent internal crisis able to regain some of the
vote it had lost in 1961 by the use of Erhard's popular appeal.[5] But
Erhard's electoral triumph in 1965 allowed him only a brief respite
from the internal crisis in the CDU/CSU, for vote-getting ability
was not a sufficient basis for leadership of the party unless complemented by political authority.

(b)   The Crisis of the Party and Erhard's Fall from Grace

During the weeks following the 1965 Bundestag Election, it seemed
that Erhard was using his election success to restore his lost authority,
for he selected his new Cabinet swiftly and retained his staunch ally
Gerard Schröder as Foreign Minister in spite of contrary pressures
from the CSU, Adenauer and even Federal President Lübke. Yet
within a few months, various groups in the party were already
pressing for a change in the Chancellorship halfway through the
new legislative period because of their concern that the CDU/CSU
would lose the next Bundestag election in 1969 with Erhard as
leader.[31] Before the year was over, internal criticism had once
again begun to undermine Erhard's position in the party. So
began the protracted crisis of confidence in Erhard's
leadership.

Although the CDU/CSU's expectations of firm leadership
inevitably meant that its state of dissatisfaction was focused on the
person of Erhard, the problems arising over the change of leadership in 1966 were strongly related to deeper difficulties in the party,
concerning its cohesion and electoral appeal, since the early 1960s.
The immediate occasion for the new eruption of dissatisfaction in
the CDU/CSU was the feeling in some quarters of under-representation
in the new Erhard Government, which was itself a reflection of

those difficulties. The CSU had pressed successfully for an extra seat in the Cabinet, although this did not amount to the required 'effective say in foreign policy', nor did Strauss re-enter the Cabinet because of the opposition to him from the FDP: hence the accusation by the CSU organ *Bayern Kurier* that the Chancellor suffered from 'bad nerves' and had allowed his freedom of decision to be reduced by the FDP.[32] Within the CDU the feeling of neglect of particular interests was strongest among the South-West German *Landesverbände*. Regional party leaders from the Rhineland-Palatinate, Baden-Württemberg, Hesse and the Saar had established contacts in October 1965 to oppose the growing influence of the 'archcon-servative' and 'neo-liberal' wings in the CDU and advocate a 'middle way'. Unlike the direction of Helmut Kohl, the 35-year-old *Fraktion* chairman in the Mainz Landtag, this informal group objected to the FDP's forcing its demands in the Cabinet formation in spite of its election losses in 1965, and was determined to prevent 'the liberalisation process in the CDU from continuing in its boundless way'.[33] The previous week the chairman of the Young Union in Baden-Württemberg, Heinrich Geissler, had published an official statement that the Government formation represented a 'political underdevelopment', for the Baden-Württemberg CDU had only one minister in the Cabinet (Family Minister Bruno Heck) in spite of its own electoral advances in 1965, its achievements in *Land* politics and its supply of political talent.[34]

Two other reasons for restlessness were also related to older sources of discontent in the party. The younger generation of leaders in the CDU were claiming more political influence and were pushing strongly for a rejuvenation of the party leadership.[6] Although the 37-year-old Gerhard Stoltenberg, a former chairman of the Young Union, had been appointed Education Minister in the new Erhard Government, this was not enough to satisfy their demands. Egon Klepsch, the current JU chairman, organised some 46 Bundestag deputies into a pressure group for new ideas.[35] Roughly one-third of the entire *Fraktion* were newcomers after the 1965 Election, although not all from the same generation. The younger element in the CDU possessed a different outlook from their elders, for they viewed politics more positively as a professional career, having been young enough after the War to show an early interest in becoming politicians without their desire being tarnished by active memories of the Third Reich. They also showed less interest in traditional ideological assumptions, pragmatism or pure tactics than in principles and clear lines of policy.[36]

The divisions in the CDU/CSU during the mid-1960s ignited another source of discontent by bringing to the surface confessional tensions, which had been already apparent during the Gaullist-Atlanticist controversy and which were further irritated by SPD gains among Catholics in the 1965 Election. There was also a persistent feeling among Catholics in the party that with so many leadership positions held by Protestants the CDU leadership was no longer adequately representing Catholic interests.[7] The Protestant North German wing of the CDU together with the FDP (effectively a Protestant-supported party) were seen as holding the power strings in Bonn. This concern by Catholic politicians about the loss of their influential role in the CDU as the 'majority within the majority' was related in particular to the future ideological course of the party. They feared that under Erhard the CDU was becoming a liberal-conservative *Bürgerpartei* (bourgeois party). One right-wing Catholic paper the *Neue Bildpost* claimed that the Catholic CDU electorate was being challenged by the 'Prussian Protestant Liberal National-Reactionary Fronde' in the party.[37] It was this feeling of concern that helped to account for the reversal of opinion in the Catholic press towards support for a possible Grand Coalition. The SPD was no longer seen as an outright political enemy, it having become a more acceptable alternative to Catholic voters; instead the liberal Protestant wing in the CDU was selected for attack. A Grand Coalition, increasingly advocated by several prominent Catholic politicians in the CDU/CSU, was considered the best means of expelling Erhard (who had a long record as an absolute opponent of a Grand Coalition) and reducing the influence of the liberal Protestant wing (involving also the exclusion of the FDP from the Government).

The question of a Grand Coalition with the SPD now imposed further strains on party solidarity by becoming a subject of divisive controversy within the CDU/CSU. It had long been a matter of occasional discussion in the party, and had been consistently favoured by a minority element, particularly the progressive wing located in the Social Committees who hoped thereby to enhance their own influence. Following the crucial decision by Adenauer in 1949 to form a small coalition of the Right, the issue had declined in interest during the 1950s with Adenauer's electoral victories except for its lone advocacy by such figures as Jakob Kaiser.[38] The question was reopened in the 1960s by the

'Godesberg trend' of the SPD and its new electoral success as
well as the general crisis which now affected the CDU/CSU. The
idea of a Grand Coalition had arisen only tentatively after the
1961 Election, but the formal negotiations between the two large
parties after the Spiegel Affair in 1962[a] had increased the SPD's
respectability as a potential ruling party and had apparently since
then stimulated public support for that form of coalition.[39] Those
negotiations had exposed deep differences in the CDU/CSU over an
alliance with the SPD, so that the issue was shelved by the party
leadership by early 1963 in spite of greater support for a Grand
Coalition in the *Fraktion*. It was feared that even talk of such a
possibility would harm the CDU's electoral prospects.[40]

Public discussion about a Grand Coalition had once more
revived during the 1965 Bundestag election campaign. That summer
the CDU in Lower Saxony formed a Grand Coalition with the
Land SPD contrary to Erhard's express wishes. Talks between
Adenauer and Brandt had stimulated speculation in the press,
which maintained an interest favourable to the idea during the course
of the campaign. A few weeks before election day, Adenauer
announced his support for a Grand Coalition in an article in
a CDU journal.[41] The speculation occasioned by this move died
a quick death when on election day Erhard's victory became
certain. But internal party differences over a Grand Coalition
were not stilled for long, and support for the idea increased for
further reasons. The issue became linked with mounting criticism
of Erhard at the turn of the year. Anti-Erhard motives (as with
Adenauer) were coupled with Strauss's playing with the idea of a
Grand Coalition, because the expulsion of the FDP from the
Government might open the way for his return to power, and
general irritation with the FDP as a coalition partner. One of the
projected aims of the proposed Grand Coalition was electoral
reform, which was now favoured by many in the CDU/CSU as a
means of ensuring the party's electoral stability. At the beginning
of the New Year, President Lübke added fuel to the coalition
controversy and further strained his relations with Erhard by
publicly indicating his support for a Grand Coalition as the only
way to solve the Government's major outstanding political
problems.[42] Speculation in the party once more got out of control,
so that the *Fraktion* leadership felt compelled to intervene and

a   See above chapter 3 (c), p. 136.

issue a statement that there was no intention of breaking up the coalition with the FDP.[43]

Gradually, there was a crystallisation of opinion in the CDU/CSU in favour of a Grand Coalition which was a direct challenge to Erhard's authority as Chancellor, which was already vulnerable. In addition, the question of Adenauer's successor as CDU chairman arose in 1966, and this seemed to highlight further the difficulties that Erhard had faced. Yet the party chairmanship question produced only an interim solution, for the final irony was that, although Erhard now added the post of CDU chairman to that of Chancellor, he suffered a further diminution in his authority as a result of the manner in which his election was conducted.

Just before Christmas 1965 Adenauer, who was on the verge of becoming a nonogenarian, suddenly announced in a newspaper interview his forthcoming retirement as CDU chairman, a post he had held for 15 years. At first the solution of his successor seemed straightforward for, although various rumours circulated about Adenauer's favourite (at first Kiesinger, then Paul Lücke, Federal Minister of the Interior, but never Erhard), it soon emerged that the most suitable candidate was Dufhues. As CDU Business Chairman since 1962, he had acquired much experience of party affairs, while his much praised management of the 1965 election campaign made him the favourite of virtually all prominent CDU politicians and of most *Landesverbände*. He also satisfied the desire for confessional balance for being a (strong) Catholic he would offset the Protestant Erhard in the Chancellorship, and his lack of ambition to become minister or Chancellor suited Erhard, who was further pleased with Dufhues's preference for a coalition with the FDP.[8] Finally, Dufhues seemed the perfect complement to Erhard who had little inclination for party affairs, and in fact Adenauer voiced no objections.

This apparently clear situation changed dramatically with Dufhues's unexpected announcement at the end of January 1966 that he was withdrawing his candidacy. His decision was made on health grounds, for he had recently suffered minor brain damage from a fall and was due to undergo a kidney operation, and he also made it clear that the state of the party 'places much greater demands on the office of chairman of the CDU than in the past'.[44] Various alternative names were mentioned, although the choice of a new candidate was complicated by confessional considerations for the general view persisted that the CDU chairman should be a Catholic in view of the strong complaints in the party about Protestant dominance. These names included those of some minister-presidents from *Land* politics because of a certain preference for a political leader unassociated with the party's recent history of divisiveness and controversy in Bonn politics. Franz Meyers could not, however, reasonably withdraw as Minister-President in North-Rhine Westphalia since he faced a difficult election in the summer. Kiesinger showed a reluctance at this stage to vacate his comfortable position as *Landesvater* in Baden-Württemberg for an uncertain future as CDU chairman, and he took the initiative in proposing Erhard.[45] Paul Lücke, also a Catholic, was briefly viewed as a possibility, but his refusal to give up his post in the Cabinet alienated some of his supporters.[46] There was in any case strong opposition to his candidacy from the North German *Landesverbände*, who argued that his open sympathy for a Grand Coalition would further polarise relations in the party.[47]

During the first week after Dufhues's withdrawal, Erhard showed no signs of demanding the chairmanship, although the situation developed in such a way that it became increasingly difficult to select any alternative candidate without appearing to disown the Chancellor. Erhard's preference for seeing how opinion about his candidacy developed in the *Landesverbände*, his basic lack of interest in the post and his awareness of possible confessional objections combined to make him hesitate to press his claim. His silence in fact cost him some of his initial support.[48] At this point of indecision, there was a surprise initiative by the Rhineland CDU which launched the candidacy of Rainer Barzel, the 41-year-old chairman of the Bundestag *Fraktion*.[49] Although this move suited Barzel's impatient ambitions,[9] it arose from a general discontent with Erhard's leadership coupled with the wish of the North-Rhine Westphalian CDU to maintain strong representation at the summit of the party leadership, now that Adenauer and Dufhues were both retiring and Lücke was not standing. Barzel's candidacy seemed to offer a reasonable solution, and gained approval in other *Landesverbände* including Schleswig-Holstein and Lower Saxony.[50] Sensing the mood in favour of fresh leadership, Barzel associated himself with demands for a modern party organisation geared to the 1970s.[51]

The initiative to install Barzel as party chairman finally spurred

Erhard, who saw in this move the promotion of a rival, into declaring his own candidacy in the second week of February,[52] from which time the party instinct for closing ranks behind the present leader operated in Erhard's favour. Weariness with the detailed public exposure of internal party consultations during the previous weeks became a compelling argument for a speedy solution to the protracted affair. The prospect of Barzel's chances being strengthened to succeed Erhard as Chancellor had also prompted opposition to him especially from younger CDU leaders led by Helmut Kohl,[53] for in spite of his youth Barzel was seen as a protégé of the older generation of CDU leaders and did not generally enjoy the favour of the younger element in the party which he had not attempted to cultivate. A compromise was agreed, whereby Erhard would stand unchallenged for the CDU chairmanship with Barzel being nominated as first deputy chairman.[54] Erhard's intentions of containing Barzel had not been entirely satisfied, although the latter's hopes for becoming the virtual crown prince were marred by the vote for him at the Bonn party congress in March 1966. Barzel received 385 votes out of a possible 558, with 108 votes against him and 63 abstentions.[55] Erhard to his relief did marginally better with 413 votes out of 548 (80 'no' votes and 50 abstentions).[56] The party had settled half-heartedly on its new chairman. Erhard was deprived of an overwhelming victory, while a stop-Barzel movement was clearly in evidence.

Even while the CDU chairmanship was being settled, it was generally felt in the party that Erhard would not remain long as Chancellor. The affair of the CDU chairmanship had made an adverse impression on the public, so that CDU strategists feared the party would suffer accordingly in the vital *Land* election due to take place in North-Rhine Westphalia in July. Their pessimism was deepened by opinion poll warnings of Erhard's loss of popular esteem and the gloomy electoral prospects for the CDU.[57] A detailed report compiled by the CDU headquarters in Bonn on preparations for the campaign dwelt on the problems of the party's 'very bad image' in that state, the popularity and skill of the SPD's top candidate Heinz Kühn, the 'very critical' role and likely 'negative effects' of Bonn politics on the *Land* election and the short-term perspectives of voters.[58] It was hoped to reduce the impact of these problems by concentrating on the figure of Franz Meyers, the Minister-President, but the intrusion of national political events proved unavoidable once the worsening economic situation with the crisis in the Ruhr mining industry came to the attention of the voters. This reduced confidence in the CDU's management of the economy (and with it Erhard's reputation as an economic wizard), while the publicity attached to SPD initiatives in opening contacts with East Germany in the months before the election found a sympathetic public response and put the CDU further on the defensive. Bonn politicians from the other parties played a very prominent part in the campaign, so that the CDU was compelled in turn to engage Erhard as an active campaigner. His political future was therefore clearly involved in the outcome of the election. Erhard showed some loss of nerve in reaction to hecklers, and this was the subject of critical comment in a party report produced the week before the election[59] as well as in the press.

The result in NRW was interpreted as the first major electoral débâcle in CDU history. The SPD overtook the CDU to become by far the largest party there with a vote of 49.5 per cent (gaining 6.2 per cent and 9 seats) compared with the CDU's vote of 42.8 per cent (losing 3.6 per cent and 10 seats). Overnight, Erhard's last remaining crutch as Chancellor — his vote-getting ability— was knocked spinning from under him, particularly as the result was confirmation of the SPD's new electoral attraction. The effect on CDU confidence was shattering. There followed a spate of hurried post-mortems among party leaders. Internal party analyses of the movement of voters expressed alarm at the long-term electoral prospects for the CDU. Particular concern was shown over its losses in the Ruhr and the SPD's gains among Catholics.[60] Numerous reviews of the situation by CDU supporters emphasised the party's need to adapt to new circumstances, and reproached it for behaving as if it were 'still existing in the high time of the '50s'.[61] Soon a 'personalisation' of the election defeat began to occur. There were rumours, officially denied, during August that the CSU wished to dispense with Erhard's participation in the forthcoming Bavarian Landtag election in November.[62] In the weeks that followed some CDU leaders murmured about calling a special party congress, implying the need to choose a new party leader.[63]

With his reputation as an 'electoral locomotive' now derailed, Erhard's fall was now a matter of time, although there was no apparent alternative Chancellor. Barzel's leading position in the spring as a possible contender had been dissipated by a tactless speech he made in New York in June about the future of a united Germany and the remaining presence of Soviet troops.[64] This opportunity was used by Barzel's determined opponents in the party, who were active in these intervening months in organising opposition to any future Barzel candidacy, to encourage doubts about his political judgement.[65] Erhard's position crumbled progressively, with the *coup de grâce* coming at the end of October with the resignation of the FDP minister from his Government after irreconcilable differences with the CDU/CSU over budgetary policy.

Since Erhard was clearly discredited once his Government had collapsed, the CDU/CSU had no alternative but to search for a new leader. This time their possession of the Chancellorship was not a certainty, for the SPD was threatening with the support of the FDP to introduce a constructive vote of no-confidence against Erhard in the Bundestag. This pressure for speed forced the CDU/CSU into hurried sessions of consultation about what to do, and helped to counter the fact that even at this late stage the anti-Erhard forces were still not united in the party, for leadership circles were divided among themselves because of so many rivalries. Gerstenmaier, the first of the self-appointed heirs apparent, had cancelled himself out with a newspaper interview in late September, in which he made a headstrong declaration of availability which found a cool reception.[66] A group of anti-Barzel planners had now formed themselves into the so-called Hünsruck Circle, consisting primarily of Heck, Dufhues, Kohl and Gerstenmaier.[67] Their candidate was Kurt-Georg Kiesinger, the 62-year-old Minister-President of Baden-Württemberg. Other possible candidates included Gerhard Schröder, but his appeal was seen as too restricted and, like Franz-Josef Strauss, also mentioned, he had too many enemies inside the party. Strauss satisfied himself with being the king-maker rather than the king, with the secure bet that he would return as Minister, so that the CSU gave its support to Kiesinger, who now appeared the favourite. He proffered several advantages in this situation. His withdrawal to *Land* politics since 1958 was an attraction, since the distance he had maintained from Bonn politics made him seem more neutral on policy positions than other candidates, particularly as he had not been directly involved in the malignant party conflicts over the previous years. His record as an effective vote-getter, his elegant presence as an orator and his background as an expert in foreign affairs during the 1950s added to his qualifications. Kiesinger's one obvious disadvantage was his former membership of the Nazi Party, but in their haste to nominate a Chancellor candidate the CDU/CSU chose not to view this as a serious obstacle.

The Bundestag *Fraktion* of the CDU/CSU confirmed this preference for Kiesinger by giving him 137 votes for Chancellor candidate, against 81 for Schröder and only 26 for Barzel. In view of the improbability of a renewed coalition with the FDP, the CDU/CSU concentrated on governmental negotiations with the SPD leading to the formation of the Grand Coalition early in December 1966. Unlike the SPD, which experienced internal difficulties over its decision to enter national office with the Christian Democrats, the CDU/CSU encountered few such problems. The question of a Grand Coalition, which had divided the party only a year or two before, was now left uncontested. The lack of resistance within the CDU/CSU to a Grand Coalition in 1966 arose partly out of necessity due to the absence of any viable alternative; it was facilitated by anger with the FDP's recent unreliability as a coalition partner, but also came from a feeling of relief at this means of escape from the party's damaging crisis during the Erhard years.

But the party's tendency to seek a drastic solution to its wider political difficulties through a change of leadership and government contained serious dangers, for the constellation of problems which had accumulated since the early 1960s demanded urgent attention. These problems included uncertainty over the CDU/CSU's electoral future in the light of new socio-political trends, and the impact of this external pressure on internal party solidarity; strains imposed on its cohesion by disharmony in the balance of internal party interests, affecting in particular the confessional alliance, as well as strains caused by divisions over policy; and, mounting younger-generational pressures over the future leadership of the party arising from the long overdue 'changing of the guard'. All these problems arose essentially from the need to adapt to changing political conditions, but the delay in solving them had turned them altogether into a growing affliction which had continued to corrode the CDU/CSU's authority and confidence as a governing party. The formation of the Grand Coalition would not automatically solve them.

(c)   The Impact of the Grand Coalition and the Creation of a Party General Secretary

The birth of the Grand Coalition under Kiesinger and Brandt in 1966 may be seen as an attempted solution of the CDU/CSU's long-term crisis as well as a consequence of the SPD's search for national office since Godesberg. The immediate crisis of Erhard's agonising fall from power acted as the midwife to this process, although too many people in the CDU/CSU were inclined to view the events of 1966 as the mother of the Grand Coalition. This short-term view of the governmental alliance with the SPD as a solution to the collapse of the CDU/CSU's confidence in 1966 seemed vindicated by the party's retention of the Chancellorship, the recovery of the economy from the recession that autumn and the revival of the party's electoral fortunes in *Land* elections from the spring of 1967. This was accompanied by a generally positive attitude to the new government on the part of the press and public opinion, which among other things was tempted to view it as a response to the 'nostalgia for synthesis' (Dahrendorf) and a welcome change from the confrontation of parties in the 1950s. Theo Sommer's terse comment at the time of the Grand Coalition's formation that the CDU/CSU was 'a centipede which has got out of step, and will not find its way back to a uniform pace so quickly'[68] however contained an important message for the party, for although the Grand Coalition provided immediate relief it also posed new challenges and further problems for the CDU/CSU.

An important consequence of the Grand Coalition was its effect on the CDU/CSU and therefore on the party system generally. Its formation in 1966 may have been a 'marriage of convenience', but it nevertheless forced the CDU/CSU to adapt to a new political situation. First, it was no longer the dominant governing party for it was required to share power on a virtually equal basis with the SPD in contrast to the hegemonial character of coalitions with the FDP under Adenauer and Erhard. Hence, there was a significant modification of the right of the Chancellor to determine 'general policy guidelines' (*Richtlinienkompetenz*), and therefore in the Chancellor's scope for imposing his party's policy preferences on the Cabinet. The weaker position of the CDU/CSU in the Federal Government was under-lined by the SPD's control of those policy areas (economic and foreign affairs), where through their performance the Christian Democrats had created their reputation as 'the party of the state'. This situation created new problems for the relationship between party leaders in government, especially the Chancellor, and the CDU/CSU as a whole. Although the CDU/CSU remained basically a Chancellor-orientated party, Kiesinger could not enjoy the undis-puted authority that Adenauer had enjoyed in the 1950s. He was

compelled to bow to the need for greater compromise with his
coalition partners compared with previous Chancellors because of the
political weight of the SPD, so that he played an intermediary rather
than commanding role. The CDU/CSU showed in the course of time
only a limited understanding of Kiesinger's different leadership
role, as was evident from accusations that he was not 'pugnacious'
enough. Such adaptation was difficult for the CDU/CSU because
party polemics had traditionally been vented against the SPD,
Adenauer's chosen political enemy.

Secondly, the CDU/CSU's consciousness of the SPD's attractive
profile as a new governing party and its fear that the SPD would use
its greater cohesion as a party to strengthen further its role in
government produced a revived interest in the question of party reform.
This had been essentially forgotten during the Erhard years, if only
because the more technical than political proposals suggested up to
that time seemed to offer no solution to the magnitude of the party's
crisis. Relief from the sense of desperation about Erhard's leadership
in 1966 turned attention to this question once again. The keynote
of party reform this time was the creation of the new post of a CDU
General Secretary, who would assume responsibility for giving the
party a new and lasting lease of life. The fact that the appointment
of someone to this post was settled in conjunction with Kiesinger's
election as the new CDU chairman in 1967, however, reaffirmed the
CDU's inclination as a 'Chancellor's party', for it was accompanied
by an assertion of the new Chancellor's authority on the question of the
General Secretary's powers.

The immediate reaction of the CDU/CSU as a whole to the Grand
Coalition seemed to reflect the passive acceptance of it by the
Bundestag *Fraktion*, although this had been qualified since a fair
proportion of deputies from both coalition parties had voted against
Kiesinger in his election as Chancellor in the Bundestag.[10] Christian
Democrats at different levels certainly appeared at the most only
mildly affected by any problem of clash of political principal
in co-operating with the SPD, although according to one survey
roughly 20 per cent 'convinced supporters' of the CDU/CSU
among the voters rejected the Grand Coalition.[69] The party seemed
by and large content with Kiesinger's argument that there had been no
real alternative solution to the 1966 crisis over Erhard's leadership
except a Grand Coalition, and that the best should be made of it.
All the same, the party leadership took precautionary measures to
ensure that no serious disaffection arose. Bruno Heck, Executive

Member of the CDU Praesidium, despatched a series of circulars to regional and district branches urging them to undertake the task of explaining the recent decisions in Bonn to party members by holding branch meetings during January. He added that it should be emphasised that the Grand Coalition had been formed because of the unreliability of the FDP as a coalition partner, and that it was necessary to implement important policy tasks although the new government was not envisaged as a permanent state of affairs. While the Grand Coalition demanded a 'loyal partnership', it did not mean that the CDU/CSU would surrender 'its political independence and its unmistakeable principles'.[70]

The first problem facing the party in the early months of the Grand Coalition was once more the CDU chairmanship, since Ludwig Erhard had indicated as expected his wish to stand down as chairman shortly after his departure from the Palais Schaumburg. This time the question did not reach crisis proportions partly because party circles were determined to avoid any repetition of the painful episode of a year before, but mainly because of Kiesinger's impressive start as Chancellor.

Bitter memories of the 1966 feud over the CDU chairmanship complicated the question at first. Dufhues quickly declared his interest in standing, and with his experience of party organisational matters he seemed the obvious choice, particularly as Kiesinger was apparently ready to accept him.[71] Soon, however, the early support he accumulated began to dissipate, when resentment over his abrupt withdrawal from the chairmanship contest in 1966 revived and was increased by his announcement that he would still not give up his lucrative law practice if elected.[72] There was a general feeling that after the recent governmental crisis of 1966 the party should be led by someone who would devote himself exclusively to reviving the CDU's fortunes, and that in any case Dufhues did not possess the requisite political authority.[73]

Kiesinger, choosing not to push his claims openly at this time, allowed his candidacy to 'evolve' to the point where support for him became widespread throughout the party. Several reasons convinced Kiesinger that he should stand. He later defined his task as party chairman as 'confronting the compact block of the SPD with an equally compact block of the CDU/CSU',[74] meaning that if the Chancellor were also CDU chairman this would strengthen the party's solidarity behind the Government. Kiesinger argued that the chairman of the CDU, like the chairmen of the SPD (Brandt)

and the CSU (Strauss), should be in the Cabinet. He was supported
in his viewpoint by Herbert Wehner, the SPD minister with whom
Kiesinger had developed close relations.[75] He insisted that whoever
should be chairman should show absolute loyalty to the Grand
Coalition. It was on these grounds that Kiesinger increasingly
showed coolness towards Dufhues's candidacy, for the latter
shared Erhard's antipathy towards a Grand Coalition although more
discreet about showing it. His distant attitude towards the new
government became offensive to Kiesinger when Dufhues attacked
the SPD with an article in the CDU publication *Deutsches Monatsblatt*
in January: 'We do not have a Kiesinger/Brandt Government, we
have merely a Kiesinger Government; the Social Democrats are
still Socialists, we do not have the same principles in politics.'[76]
Dufhues's advocacy of 'more profile' for the CDU threatened dissent
from the Chancellor, whose overriding concern was that the success
of the Grand Coalition (based on co-operation with the SPD)
would revive the fortunes of the party.

Kiesinger could have forced the choice in his own favour simply
because he was Chancellor, but he chose to bide his time as opinion
had not yet gelled inside the party. The old argument about the
division of the two offices of Chancellor and CDU chairman
received a new airing. Regional considerations also played a part.
The Rhineland CDU, ever mindful of its weight inside the party,
made a claim for one of its own leaders, but weakened its case
through indecision about which to choose. Having withdrawn support
from Dufhues, it settled on Meyers but when he eventually declined
to stand it tried in vain to persuade Schröder to stand.[77]

Kiesinger's opportunity to secure the chairmanship came with the
movement to establish the post of CDU General Secretary, as it could
be argued that the latter would relieve Chancellor (and chairman)
of the burden of regular party affairs. This was the plan approved at
the congress of the Rhineland CDU at Oberhausen in February 1967,
when such a motion initiated by the Young Union was passed
contrary to the wishes of the *Land* party executive.[78] This meeting
also demonstrated wide support for Kiesinger as chairman.[79] The
advocates of the division of offices had lost the initiative of argument,
for the Oberhausen resolution, which reflected sympathy for party
reform, directed discussion inside the CDU meanwhile away from the
choice of chairman to the position and powers of a General Secretary.

Following its congress resolution, the Rhineland party leaders
formally proposed the creation of this new post at the next meeting

of the CDU Federal Executive in February. This authorised the party
Praesidium to work out the necessary statute changes and consult
regional party leaders for their reaction to the proposal.[80] The
answers to Kraske's consequent letter to *Land* party managers of
3 March produced a positive view about a General Secretary
contrary to expectations that majority opinion with its traditional
dislike of 'functionaries' would reject such an idea.[81] The reply
from the *Landesverband* Hanover, for instance, expressed approval
for a General Secretary while emphasising that the man appointed
should have the 'necessary political experience and authority', such
as a former minister, and that he should be interested in the position
for its own sake rather than as a means for advancement.[82] Once
the idea of a General Secretary was agreed in principle, there followed
the inevitable discussion about the position within the established
party hierarchy.[83]

Kiesinger had been gaining ground rapidly in the chairmanship
stakes as it became increasingly evident that the future of the CDU
would depend above all on its performance in the Grand Coalition.
What swung opinion decisively in Kiesinger's direction was the series
of CDU triumphs in *Land* elections, from West Berlin (when the
CDU gained 4.1 per cent and the SPD lost 6 per cent) through
Schleswig-Holstein and the Rhineland-Palatinate in April to Lower
Saxony in June. Kiesinger campaigned actively in these elections
with the slogan 'Once again there is government in Bonn', and
received much coverage for his skill in speaking.[84] Public opinion
polls during the spring presented a more subtle picture. While they
often registered a lead of the SPD over the CDU/CSU, there was a
marked divergence between the restrained support for the CDU/CSU
as a whole and the astronomical rise in the popularity of Kiesinger
as Chancellor even among SPD and FDP supporters.[85] Although
opinion had in any case been moving towards the choice of
Kiesinger as chairman, his popular appeal clinched the matter. This
illustrated once again the strong electoral instinct of the Christian
Democrats.

Kiesinger's tactics of waiting paid dividends for he now used his
increased authority in the party to impose his own ideas for the role
of the new General Secretary. This demanded changes in the proposed
statute alterations, so that the General Secretary would not after
all enjoy an independent political position for he should be subject to
the effective appointment and dismissal by the party chairman; that he
should not be full-time, but eligible to sit as a minister in the Cabinet;

and that he should exercise his various functions such as managing the affairs of the party and calling meetings of the Praesidium and Federal Executive 'in agreement with the chairman'.[86] Kiesinger's clear aim was to ensure both loyalty to himself as chairman and loyalty to government policy through the involvement of the General Secretary in Cabinet policy-making. The question was ultimately one of personal political loyalty. Kiesinger's first choice had been Helmut Kohl, already renowned as a party manager in the Rhineland-Palatinate, but after Kohl declined Kiesinger's eventual choice was an old political confidant and fellow Swabian, Bruno Heck.[11] Heck agreed with Kiesinger in insisting on staying in the Cabinet as Minister for Family Affairs.

The issue was not finally settled until the CDU Congress at Brunswick in May 1967. Much ill feeling had followed Kiesinger's pressure for a reduced status of the General Secretary, for it was seen as an attempt to strengthen his own position at the cost of party reform. Kiesinger decided at this point to apply some political muscle. He arrived at the meeting of the Federal Committee at the beginning of the Congress to threaten in so many words that the party could not count on him unless he had his own way.[87] There followed all the same an acrimonious debate at the Congress following a motion from the Young Union and several *Landesverbände* that the General Secretary should be full-time (*hauptamtlich*) since his ministerial duties would distract him from his prime task of co-ordinating all party work.[88] The Rhineland CDU demanded that a decision on this matter should be subject to further discussion within the party. The wrath of the party reformers, whose proposals had been thwarted, was to some extent neutralised but Kiesinger's proposals were approved when the decision was finally taken.

The wide support for Kiesinger at the Congress was demonstrated in his election as chairman by 423 out of 449 votes, and by the Congress's approval of Heck's appointment. Kiesinger's speech emphasised the need to support the Grand Coalition, for its collapse would also bring a 'crisis of the state'.[89] Apart from the objections to the new proposals for the statutes, the Brunswick Congress was in every other way a reproduction of the Chancellor adulation evident on such occasions in the 1950s. The attitude of the delegates revealed, in the words of one critical political commentator, that 'the Union has accepted Kiesinger's Chancellorship as a gift from heaven',[90] for having apparently overcome its crisis of confidence in 1966 the party now looked ahead to the 1969 Bundestag Election. Kiesinger's

taste for the charismatic touch was evident in his dramatic arrival at
the Congress by helicopter, which prompted the same journalist
to refer to him as the 'Deus ex machina of the CDU'.[91] At the same
time, the giant photograph of Konrad Adenauer, who had recently
died, on the wall behind the podium at the Congress seemed to
suggest that the CDU still looked to his inspiration.

(d) The Appearance of Revival, 1967-1969; Formulation of the Berlin Programme

Kiesinger's concern that the success of his Government should not
be hindered by any lack of solidarity from his own party was
justified, as his image as Chancellor during the period 1966-9 tended
to fluctuate according to the impact and effectiveness of the Grand
Coalition.[92] But the special governmental pressures on him to play
an 'above party' role presented the risk that he might alienate
opinion in the CDU/CSU, particularly as it had become more
difficult to lead since the heady days of Adenauer's ascendancy.

   Kiesinger regarded the CDU chairmanship in a similar light to
Adenauer, as a buttress to his Chancellorship, although unlike both
his predecessors in the Palais Schaumburg he had risen to the summit
of political power through a career in the CDU together with his
eight years as *Landesvater* in Stuttgart. He was therefore less
inclined by background to distance himself from his party. While
obviously not of the stature of Adenauer, Kiesinger possessed more
tactical skill as a party politician than Erhard and he acquired a
reputation for his skills as a public performer, notably the description
of him as 'the best of all possible Chancellor actors',[93] the frivolous
quip that he was 'the more handsome Erhard' and his nickname of
'King Silver Tongue', occasioned by his facility for literary German.[12]
Any problems he had in establishing his party authority were
moderated by the absence of any serious rivals for most of his
period in office. Here Kiesinger was more fortunate than Erhard,
since any possible challengers were weakened for one reason or
other. His closest competitor for the Chancellorship, Gerhard
Schröder, remained in the Cabinet as Defence Minister but he
performed less impressively there than at the Foreign Ministry. The
icy relationship between these two since their rivalry for the Chancellorship in 1966 erupted in a bitter personal quarrel in 1967 about
defence financing, but Schröder suffered as before from his lack
of enthusiastic or broad support in the party. Barzel's miscalculated
reach for power in 1966 still devalued his chances for advancement,

although he continued to perform in exemplary fashion as *Fraktion* chairman with his special role during the Grand Coalition of intermediary between the Cabinet and CDU/CSU backbenchers. Kiesinger's main potential threat was from Franz-Josef Strauss, now back in the Cabinet (as Finance Minister) after four years' absence from ministerial office since the Spiegel Affair. Although Strauss was at first preoccupied with learning expertise in his new field of finance policy, Kiesinger's dependence on the CSU for the Chancellor nomination and Strauss's semi-independent position as CSU chairman made the former vulnerable to future pressure.

Kiesinger's primary function as Chancellor of the Grand Coalition was to act as co-ordinator between the CDU/CSU and SPD or, in the words of Conrad Ahlers, deputy Government spokesman, as a 'walking mediation committee'. While this utilised his skills at diplomacy, Kiesinger's position as CDU chairman also compelled him to ensure that his party's profile was maintained within the Government. The difficulty which this entailed of maintaining a balance between the need to emphasise the CDU/CSU's importance in policy-making and the requirement not to provoke the SPD was discussed by Kiesinger at a meeting of the CDU Federal Committee on 9 October 1967. He commented that the many problems of management and policy facing the Grand Coalition were encompassed not so much in the daily work of the Cabinet, but tended to be what he called of a 'more underground nature' for they derived from the fact that the two parties had essentially 'remained what they were before'. In his view the special problem facing the CDU/CSU was how to counter the SPD's 'making propaganda' over its policy initiatives. According to Kiesinger, the SPD had 'the interesting ministeries', but on the other hand 'we have the Federal Chancellor and that hasn't paid off badly'. At least through the Grand Coalition the CDU had won a 'breathing space' in which to revive its strength, although SPD circles were encouraging the view that the party was acting as a 'brake block' inside the Government.[94]

The SPD was becoming increasingly competent in two of the most important and powerful policy areas, foreign and especially economic affairs,[95] a development enhanced by the popularity of Willy Brandt and Karl Schiller, respectively Foreign and Economics Minister. This succeeded in putting the CDU/CSU increasingly on the defensive. Differences resulted inside the CDU/CSU over the degree to which it should assert itself in the Government, with those lulled into complacency by the CDU's *Land* election successes taking a moderate line. These successes caused in turn a new problem as too impressive a performance by the CDU was likely to provoke discontent among the Social Democrats for its gaining sole electoral credit for the Grand Coalition's record. As Brandt warned, 'arrogance on the part of the CDU would be as fatal to the success of the Grand Coalition as despondency on the part of the SPD'.[96] Kiesinger, who sought to avoid 'breaking china' with the SPD, took a middling line within his party, although there were moments when he felt compelled to show some partisan muscle, such as his remark to the Young Union Congress in November 1967 that 'despite all prognostications, the CDU is and will remain the driving force behind the Coalition', for which he was wildly applauded.[97] Sometimes, the CDU/CSU's defensiveness appeared in oversensitive reactions to SPD assertions of old partisan feelings. The programmatic document of the SPD for the 1970s, which accused the CDU of 'plunging the country into a crisis that has given an opening to neo-Nazi elements after two decades of self-satisfied use of power', produced a storm of abuse early in 1968 which severely shook the Coalition.[98]

The CDU/CSU's self-confidence, which had been restored with the revival of its electoral fortunes and Kiesinger's popularity as Chancellor, was therefore demonstrated to be remarkably brittle when faced by the SPD's determination to exhibit its ability as a governing party. While the SPD failed to gain votes in the series of *Land* elections during 1967-8,[13] it nevertheless gradually came across to the public as an active partner in the Government, especially in those areas where it was able to take the initiative, in time for the Bundestag Election in 1969. The CDU/CSU was often forced to react to SPD policy initiatives, but its own position in the Grand Coalition was also complicated by differences within itself over policy matters as well as the extent to which it should take the offensive against the SPD. The problems of the CDU/CSU leadership in the Grand Coalition will now be examined in the two major areas controlled by an SPD ministry, economic policy and foreign affairs.

In economic policy, the Government's efforts were concentrated at first on overcoming the recession which had occurred in the autumn of 1966. Schiller (Economics) and Strauss (Finance) co-operated in January 1967 in presenting a balanced budget for the forthcoming year, which introduced large expenditure cuts, and other measures were taken to revive confidence in the economy, which by the following autumn had substantially recovered from the recession. The pleasing picture of harmony between the two ministers was first disturbed by differences between them over the defence budget at the end of July. Schiller's modernisation of economic policy instruments and his introduction of 'middle-term financial planning' caused unease in the CDU/CSU, concerned at any departure from the Erhard philosophy of the social market economy. The party feared that the success of Schiller might detract from its profile created during the Erhard years of competence in economic affairs. Schiller with his unquestioned expertise seemed to be gaining the stature of Erhard, while the CDU/CSU felt sensitive about its lack of an authoritative economic spokesman to equal him. The party's position was undermined by differences within itself which had been concealed during the Erhard period of rapid economic growth. The majority conservative economic interests found themselves in conflict with the progressive Social Committees, who hoped to strengthen their influence through the party's alliance with the SPD, and with agrarian interests which had long remained critics of Erhard. Conservative interests were represented in the CDU/CSU by the Economic Council (*Wirtschaftsrat*) and the Middle-Class Circle (*Mittelstandskreis*), which was led by Kurt Schmücker, the CDU Minister of Economics until the Grand Coalition. Their dislike of Schiller's 'new economic policy' and their idolisation of Erhard exhibited itself at the Economic Conference of the CDU in January 1967, when Schmücker made a speech urging the party not to capitulate to Schiller.[99] Schmücker's stout defence of Erhard's 'great successes' provoked attacks on him from the Social Committees. The CDU/CSU's chief problem was that it had not developed any up-to-date economic concept during the Grand Coalition to take account of the different economic situation in the later 1960s.[100]

In foreign policy the conflict between the two parties arose in a similar way with Brandt the minister taking initiatives, which were viewed by many in the CDU/CSU as a departure from the principles of previous governments. The conflict became intensified because of deeply felt beliefs in the CDU, and particularly CSU, over relations with Communist states. The problem of mediation for Kiesinger was made more difficult by his own abiding interest in foreign relations and by the Adenauer tradition, whereby the Chancellor developed his own political profile primarily in this field.

Differences began to emerge once active steps were taken in German and Eastern policy. Kiesinger's Government Declaration of

13 December 1966, with its reference to the will for peace and diplomatic relations with the Eastern bloc 'wherever circumstances make this possible', had given the impression of at least verbal adjustment by the CDU/CSU to a 'new Ostpolitik'. The Chancellor's verbal gymnastics served temporarily to paper over likely cracks in the Coalition, but Brandt's insistent moves in establishing formal relations with Romania in 1967 and opening similar negotiations with other countries like Yugoslavia brought CDU/CSU resistance into the open. Tension often revealed itself in a sensitivity to public statements by ministers of the other party, such as Brandt's remark over Romania that the Government viewed the European security question 'in the light of existing realities',[101] which occasioned objections from the CDU/CSU. From the middle of 1967 Kiesinger could no longer claim with the support of his whole party that the Grand Coalition was pursuing a policy which followed the guidelines of earlier governments.

The most serious display of antagonism between the SPD and CDU/CSU occurred over German policy. This 'neuralgic point of the Union'[102] accounted for its own anxiety that any official declarations of policy initiatives towards East Germany might imply some partial recognition of the DDR. Hence, there was a lengthy dispute in the Cabinet over the form of Kiesinger's reply to a letter from Prime Minister Willi Stoph. Equally, Kiesinger's scathing remark about the DDR as a 'phenomenon' in the foreign-policy debate in October 1967 and his reference to a 'Recognition Party' (referring to a movement of growing support for recognition of the DDR such as in the mass media) were viewed as offensive by the SPD. The SPD countered with accusations of Christian Democratic 'obstructionism'. Notably, Helmut Schmidt demanded provocatively that the CDU/CSU should undergo a 'psychological process' in German policy,[103] and Wehner attacked the party for wanting to put 'political decisions of life importance in the marshalling yard'.[104] The CDU/CSU did not always act as a united bloc over the issue, although its basic inclination was negative towards the SPD's more flexible approach towards the DDR. Opinion in the party ranged from sceptical moderates like Kiesinger himself and Barzel (who emphasised the need for a quid pro quo such as a renunciation of force and an end to threats against Berlin) to fundamentalist opponents in the CSU (who talked about the 'erosion of our claims', and placed supreme importance on adhering to 'rightful positions').[105]

The reasons for this conflict between the parties in the Grand

Coalition lay partly in the different strategic approaches behind the policy attitudes of the SPD and CDU/CSU. Whereas the SPD regarded Ostpolitik as a means of recognising the *status quo* in Europe, the CDU/CSU viewed Ostpolitik as having to make concessions for the sake of *détente*, and this it was reluctant to do. The latter's standpoint was also influenced by its consideration that foreign policy was an extension of domestic policy with its aim of maintaining the form of economic society and political system fostered in the Adenauer years.[106] In addition, the anti-Communist ethos was deeply held as ever before in the ranks of the CDU/CSU. An indication of this was its appalled reaction to the Warsaw Pact invasion of Czechoslovakia in August 1968. This event strengthened the fundamentalist opponents of Ostpolitik in the CDU/CSU, and put an end to the attempt by moderate party leaders at a differential approach to the various countries of the Eastern bloc, an idea which had been influenced by the reform Communism of Dubcek. From then on, the CDU/CSU returned to its traditional stance on Ostpolitik, thus producing open conflict in the Grand Coalition which lasted until the Election of 1969.[107]

On the question of electoral reform, the positions of the parties were reversed, for the CDU/CSU had long advocated a change desiring to adopt something akin to the British majority system, while the SPD had shown little enthusiasm for reform. In both cases, party interests were the decisive factor for neither wanted to improve the other's chances of becoming the permanent governing body. Electoral reform had nevertheless been generally presented as one of the great changes to be implemented by the Grand Coalition; Kiesinger's Government Declaration late in 1966 had promised to pass a new law to take effect in time for the Bundestag Election due in 1973, and to 'examine' the possibility of a transitional law for the 1969 Election. The CDU formed an electoral commission in February 1967,[108] but nothing was undertaken by the Government as a whole until the end of 1967. By then SPD reluctance had become clear, reinforced as it was by *Land* election results. The basic division between the parties also reflected the SPD's growing interest in a *rapprochement* with the FDP, whose future existence depended on there being no change.[109] Enthusiasm had also waned in the CDU/CSU, since some of its own surveys on the likely effects of introducing a majority voting system had indicated the possibility that the CDU/CSU might thereby narrow its electorate and become a more rurally based party. Kiesinger therefore chose not to press the issue, which involved him in an argument with his Minister of the Interior, Paul Lücke, who was committed to electoral reform and resigned.

Despite these major points of conflict in basic policy outlook and party interest, there were some achievements in special areas such as the legal reforms implemented by Gustav Heinemann as Justice Minister and relations between some individual ministers from the two parties became fairly close. Inter-party co-operation was exemplified by the two *Fraktion* chairmen, Rainer Barzel and Helmut Schmidt, who developed an excellent working relationship. Nicknamed the 'ball-and-socket of the Coalition', Barzel and Schmidt acted as a 'fire-service' or 'clearing house' for differences of opinion in the *Fraktion*.[14] The role of the *Fraktion* chairman was enhanced at the policy-making level by the inclusion of both Barzel and Schmidt in the informal group of ministers from both parties known as the 'Kressbronn Circle', named after the Chancellor's residence at Lake Constance, which met regularly to iron out differences and discuss a common programme.[110] Barzel and Schmidt were instrumental, for instance, in working out a compromise on the issue of the controversial emergency laws in 1968 involving internal security matters. The great majority of the Government also had the effect of encouraging greater independence by Bundestag deputies during the Grand Coalition period. This new sense of freedom was particularly noticeable among CDU/CSU deputies, especially younger ones, who no longer felt they had to be automatic defenders of the Government, while the SPD *Fraktion* was more noted for its discipline.[15]

At the extra-parliamentary level of the CDU, there was a general concern over the party's position in the Grand Coalition. Uneasiness over the party's loss of policy-making initiative and the heightened awareness of challenge from the SPD forced leaders of the CDU to consider its future policy orientation. A sense of urgency was stimulated by new movements in the political environment with the growth of anti-establishment feeling and left-wing activity among the younger generation, the continued success of the neo-Nazi NPD in *Land* elections and the rise of progressive leadership in the FDP, marked by the election in early 1968 of Walter Scheel as its chairman, thus opening the way for its closer relations with the SPD. The need to take account of these changes[16] influenced the CDU in formulating its Action Programme (later known as the Berlin Programme) during 1967-8. The Programme amounted to the first major step which the CDU took towards becoming a more programmatic party, for although previously policy matters had rarely been discussed below the leadership level it was now recognised by Bruno Heck, the General Secretary, that this state of affairs was no longer appropriate in the later 1960s. As the personal driving force behind the elaborate consultation over the Programme which involved different levels of the CDU, he urged that 'what we need is an Action Programme that provides an answer for today and tomorrow to the questions of today and tomorrow — that is to say in the language of our times'.[111]

Although the debates over the Action Programme brought a novel measure of internal party democracy, the primary motive behind such extensive party involvement seems to have been the intention by party leaders to maintain the CDU's individual profile in the Government, although it was no more the dominant party. It was understood from the beginning that the results of the Action Programme discussion would form the basis of the CDU's election manifesto in 1969. As Franz Meyers, the North-Rhine Westphalian party leader, commented in his speech to the Oberhausen Congress of the Rhineland CDU in February 1967:

> The CDU as a party will find it still more difficult now to differentiate itself in the eyes of the broad masses from the SPD, and to make itself clearly visible in its outward confrontation with the latter . . . It is *not* the SPD, it is *not* the FDP, it is a party with its own character and distinct from other political groupings. That one must be able to recognise clearly from its Action Programme. This is no profile neurosis but the urgent and necessary development of the profile of the CDU, necessary especially in view of the *rapprochement* efforts of the SPD since Godesberg and in view of the dangers arising from the Grand Coalition.[112]

These considerations overcame any traditional arguments inside the CDU that any extensive programmatic discussion within the whole party would have a disuniting effect on its cohesion because it included so many different political tendencies. In fact, discussion of the Action Programme generated a degree of local enthusiasm unprecedented in the CDU. A wider active interest in political issues had been fermenting inside the CDU during the 1960s. It had long been encouraged by growing public involvement in politics, especially among the younger generation, and also promoted by less deferential attitudes within the party ranks over policy matters partly due to disillusionment coming from the recurrent leadership crises.

The process of consultation began as early as December 1966, immediately after the Erhard crisis, when 24 commissions on various policy aspects were formed with a view to reporting eventually to a central commission, which would formulate a first draft of the Programme[113]. Heck tapped much younger talent, especially new members of the Bundestag *Fraktion,* to lead many of these commissions. The first stage of programme discussion progressed throughout 1967. Heck envisaged that his main task as the new General Secretary was to promote this method of formulating the new party programme, which would be the first official programme of the CDU since the Hamburg Programme of 1953. He carried out a rigorous agenda of personal consultations with party leaders and members at the regional and district levels so that he became known in the press as the 'party educator' or the 'headmaster of his party'.[114] In the early autumn of 1967 the draft programme was examined by the Federal executive bodies of the CDU, and then presented formally to the public shortly before Christmas.[115] During the following months, the draft was discussed intensively within the lower echelons of the party resulting in as many as 30,000 requests for changes in the draft following some 10,000 meetings of local party activists.[116] Heck's 'Swabian obstinacy' ensured the success of this process of consultation, which helped to counter the feeling within the whole party that policy in the Grand Coalition was being made too much behind closed doors and to overcome some of the sense of frustration remaining after the 1966 crisis.

On one particular issue, the discussion became unmanageable and indeed posed some threat to party unity because it encouraged polarisation between different groups within the CDU. That issue was whether or not to extend worker participation. A conflict flared up over this question between the Social Committees and the Economic Council, the two auxiliary organisations of the CDU, with the former insisting on extension (e.g. its Offenburg Declaration, 1967). The Economic Council resented this move by the Committee's chairman, Hans Katzer, all the more as the SPD applied pressure on the CDU with its resolution at its Nuremberg Congress in the spring of 1968 in favour of a substantial increase in worker participation during the current legislative period.[117] Klaus Scheufelen, chairman of the Economic Council, warned of the consequences if the SPD *Fraktion* pressed the issue in the Bundestag, while Strauss accused the

SPD leadership of not being prepared to resist its left wing.[118] This debate between different interests within the party became more and more bitter, with Norbert Blüm, the press spokesman of the Social Committees, asserting in an article in its organ *Soziale Ordnung* that the CDU was a popular party (*Volkspartei*) and not, in his words, a 'branch colony of the Economic Council'.[119] The controversy continued right up to the Berlin Congress in November 1968, and produced a very lively debate there. The outcome was no more than a postponement of the question, and there the matter rested for the time being.

The final version of the now-called Berlin Programme involved various important departures from earlier CDU programmes, as represented by the 1953 Hamburg model. In the new programme much more space was devoted to economic and social policy at the expense of foreign policy, so demonstrating the party's awareness of social change. There was less blatant emphasis on the interests of business, and less insistence on the priority of 'Christian' values in the formulation of education policy. In foreign policy, the Berlin Programme revealed some willingness to follow the more flexible approaches established by the Grand Coalition, including the statement: 'The improvement of economic, cultural and political relations with the Soviet Union, and with the other East European nations, is an important task of German foreign policy in the coming years.' On German policy, the programme advocated all forms of contact with the DDR (described as 'the other part of German'), but no recognition.[120] The word 'Communism' was not even mentioned in the text. The Berlin Programme did not, however, amount to a CDU Godesberg, because the reformist symbolism attached by the SPD leaders themselves to their Godesberg Programme of 1959 contrasted with the insistence by the CDU in 1968 that it was not departing from its basic principles. As far as the Berlin Programme was a milestone in CDU history, it reflected more changes in the atmosphere of internal relationships in the party rather than a profound reassessment of policy approaches.

The programme formed the centre-piece of the CDU Congress in Berlin early in November 1968. The other noteworthy event here was the critical attitude shown towards the Grand Coalition. This appeared dramatically during Kiesinger's opening speech, when he remarked that the Grand Coalition could continue 'under certain conditions' after the 1969 Election. Kiesinger was hissed at this point, the first time ever a breach of deference had been shown towards a

CDU leader at a party Congress.[121] It expressed a feeling of resentment that Kiesinger had been too much concerned with his role as head of the Grand Coalition at the cost of his position as party chairman. Rainer Barzel and Helmut Kohl both made aggressive speeches which suited more the mood of the party, rejecting all 'coalition constraints' until after the election and taking the SPD to task for 'breaking its word' on electoral reform.[122] Majority opinion tended to the view that Kiesinger should have made a specific effort to raise party morale by claiming an absolute majority for the CDU/CSU in 1969.

Relations between the two parties in the Grand Coalition had by this time become more difficult to maintain because the forthcoming election campaign already affected the political atmosphere. This coloured the unsavoury dispute between Schiller and Strauss over the question of revaluing the D-Mark, producing a polarisation between Christian and Social Democratic ministers. The failure to co-operate over a common candidate for the Federal Presidency in March 1969 further deepened the rift, especially after the CSU vice-president of the Bundestag, Richard Jaeger, attacked personally the SPD candidate, Gustav Heinemann. Kiesinger's own reluctance in supporting his old rival Schroder as CDU/CSU candidate only caused ill-feeling inside his own party, which set off rumours in the press that there was a move to force his resignation. Kiesinger felt now more insecure in the leadership than ever before, a weakness which was exploited by Strauss in a broadside of innuendoes in press interviews. During the years of the Grand Coalition, Strauss had encouraged a political profile for the CSU more independent from that of the CDU, which inevitably widened the scope for disharmony between the two sister parties.[b] Kiesinger sought during the months before the Bundestag Election to reinforce his leadership position by asserting his supremacy as Chancellor in determining the lines of foreign policy, but this only multiplied tension in his relations with Foreign Minister Brandt.[123]

Both the SPD and the CDU/CSU entered the election campaign of 1969 reluctant to continue together in the Grand Coalition. It was expected that the SPD would benefit from its performance in government and make significant electoral gains, while speculation about a 'change of power' was encouraged by the success of the SPD/FDP alliance in electing Heinemann as Federal President in the spring. The CDU/CSU therefore had to aim for an absolute majority in order to be sure of retaining power, but its chances were impeded by

b   See below chapter 10 (a), pp. 308-9.

the problems of cohesion and solidarity which had afflicted it during most of the last decade. Its recovery from the traumatic change of leadership in 1966 had injected some new political awareness into the CDU and its internal tensions were now as usual stilled during the course of the election campaign, but the external challenge of the SPD's popular appeal had meanwhile increased. The party was suffering from having been in power for too long — two uninterrupted decades in total. The CDU/CSU, however, still possessed one considerable advantage in being headed by the incumbent Chancellor. It attempted to capitalise on this, with its main slogan 'It all depends on the Chancellor', even though the Chancellor had been reduced to a less commanding position in the Grand Coalition. Ironically, the CDU/CSU depended more than ever on its 'governmental bonus' at a time when its prospects of remaining in power were under the most serious attack.

Notes

[1]   Ludwig Erhard had risen to prominence from his achievements in Government office, as Federal Minister of Economics 1949-63 and Vice-Chancellor 1957-63, rather than position or activities in the party. In fact he did not formally become a member of the CDU until the early 1960s. According to one source, Erhard was accepted as a member by a CDU district organisation in north Württemberg on 1 January 1963 (*Deutsche Zeitung*, 12 March 1963), although Erhard's own verbal reply as to the date was that he did not know but it was probably before he became Chancellor. Erhard had nevertheless been a member of the CDU Praesidium since 1960. He expressed to the author his distaste for formal party membership, which he said stemmed from the general reaction against the Third Reich when party membership was the key to all important posts. 'I wanted to keep my button-hole clean', he said in reference to his attitude after the War (interview with Ludwig Erhard in Bonn, September 1973).

[2]   Gerhard Schröder, born 1910, had been Foreign Minister since 1961 and became known for his cautious 'policy of movement' towards Eastern Europe leading to the establishment of trade relations with these countries unhindered by the Hallstein Doctrine. He had been a Bundestag member since 1949, was deputy *Fraktion* chairman 1952-3 and had become Minister of the Interior in 1953. As a Protestant, his special political base in the CDU was the chairmanship of the *Evangelischer Arbeitskreis,* the party auxiliary organisation, since 1955.

[3]   Kurt Schmücker, born 1919, had started his party career as chairman of the Young Union in Oldenburg in the late 1940s. A Bundestag deputy since 1949, he became chiefly known as a representative of business interests in the CDU and was elected chairman of the CDU/CSU working group on middle-class questions in 1956. He was elected to the CDU Federal Executive in the same year.

[4]   Asked whether there was a confessional side to the controversy between the 'Gaullists' and 'Atlanticists', Erhard replied that 'this was not *openly*

the case' (interview with the author, September 1973).

[5]   For a discussion of the CDU/CSU campaign for the Bundestag Election in 1965, see below chapter 11 (b).

[6]   E.g. 'It is high time that public opinion advocated more and more a change of generation in politics', Helmut Kohl, *Zur Parteireform der CDU* in *Gesellschaftspolitische Kommentare*, 1 March 1966, p. 44.

[7]   Erhard as Chancellor, Schröder (Foreign Minister), von Hassel (Defence Minister) and Kurt Schmücker (Economic Affairs) were all Protestants and held the key positions in the Government. Gerstenmaier, who had a strong Protestant theological background, was Bundestag President. Adenauer and Dufhues, the two most prominent Catholic politicians in the CDU, were both outside the Government. So too were Strauss and Guttenberg from the CSU. The two well-known CDU Catholic politicians in the Cabinet were Bruno Heck (Family and Youth) and Paul Lücke (Interior). Four FDP ministers were balanced against five from the CSU (a predominantly Catholic party). Needless to say, confessional motives were not uppermost in Erhard's selection of ministers, but Catholic interests chose to see the matter from their own angle; e.g. the headline of the Catholic paper *Neue Bildpost*: 'The C of the CDU must remain credible, the claim above all of Catholic voters that their principles have in no way been represented with the requisite emphasis since the Erhard era' (quoted in *Die Zeit*, 18 February 1966).

[8]   These comments are based on a discussion with Konrad Kraske, former CDU Business Manager and General Secretary, in an interview in Bonn, September 1974.

[9]   Although relatively young, Barzel had risen dramatically over the past two years to a position of eminence in the CDU. He used his new position as *Fraktion* chairman since 1964 to develop his reputation as a deft political manager and elegant parliamentary speaker and on which to build his political base. Criticism of Erhard's form of decision-making and the Chancellor's regular Monday morning consultations with Barzel over Government business allowed Barzel both to maintain a political independence vis-à-vis Erhard and yet seem an important influence on policy. His main weakness was his reputation of being too ambitious.

[10] Kiesinger was elected in December 1966 by 356 votes out of 495. Of the 112 deputies who voted against him, at the most 50 could have come from the FDP Opposition. Considering there were 26 abstentions, nearly ninety deputies from the SPD and CDU/CSU did not support him. There were, however, more objections to the Grand Coalition in the ranks of the SPD than of the CDU/CSU.

[11] Bruno Heck, born in 1917, had been Business Manager *(Bundesgeschäftsführer)* of the CDU from 1952-8, during which time he successfully organised two Bundestag election campaigns having studied electoral methods in the USA. Before then he had been active in *Land* party affairs in south Württemberg, having joined the CDU in 1946. Heck was elected Bundestag deputy in 1957, and was Federal Minister for Family Affairs from 1962-8. He had a specialist interest in educational policy. He had maintained an independent attitude in his relationship with Adenauer, suggesting privately to the latter in 1956 that he should step down as party chairman in favour of a new man. (Interview with Bruno Heck in Bonn, September 1973.)

[12] Kiesinger's 'relaxed' style of government management had already been evident in Baden-Württemberg, where he had invariably spent Mondays at his home in Tübingen and developed his political ideas on long 'working walks' with colleagues and assistants in the forest. He had a penchant for

184   *Christian Democracy in Western Germany*

the French philosophers, particularly de Tocqueville. He was once aptly described as having 'a contemplative relationship with politics' (*Die Zeit*, 5 July 1968). Kiesinger's style of work occasioned criticism of his conduct of office. It was said he confined himself to 'speaking, travelling and representing', and was widely regarded as a 'lazy' Minister-President (author's interviews with journalists in Stuttgart, August 1973). He nevertheless enjoyed strong public popularity in his home state, as shown by the CDU's gain of 6.8 per cent in the *Land* election of 1964 in Baden-Württemberg which was attributed in part to Kieseinger.

[13]   The last of these *Land* elections took place in Baden-Württemberg in April 1968, nearly one-and-a-half years before the next major test of electoral opinion in the Bundestag Election of September 1969. In this *Land*, where the SPD was also in a grand coalition with the CDU as senior partner, the former lost 8.2 per cent of its vote of 1964. The SPD suffered electorally far more than the CDU during 1967-8, because many of its former voters protested against its inclusion in a CDU-led government in Bonn. The CDU was able on the other hand to benefit from the restoration of stability in the Federal Government.

[14]   On the co-operation between Rainer Barzel and Helmut Schmidt, see the excellent article by Rolf Zundel, 'Die Koalitionszwillinge, Bonn's wichtigste Instanz: die Fraktionschefs Barzel und Schmidt' in *Die Zeit*, 29 November 1968.

[15]   For a discussion of this change, see the useful article by Heinz Rausch, 'Parliamentary Consciousness and Parliamentary Behaviour during the Grand Coalition' in *International Journal of Politics*, Winter 1971-2, pp. 299-338.

[16]   E.g. see the handbook issued in 1968 by the publicity department of the CDU headquarters in Bonn, *Gestörte Wahlversammlungen: Der Umgang mit der sogenannten ausserparlamentarischen Opposition*, which began with the comments: 'The traditional election rally is dead . . . in its place has come the election meeting with discussion . . . also ordinary citizens participating in election meetings come now with questions which they wish to put to prominent or less prominent speakers.'

References

1.   Theodor Eschenburg, 'Röntgenbild einer Parteikrise: wie die Unionsparteien ihre Herrschaft verspielt haben' in *Die Zeit*, 18 November 1966.
2.   Konrad Kraske, *Politisch publizistische Massnahmen im Anschluss an die Wahl des neuen Bundeskanzlers*, 28 August 1963, Archiv CDU Westfalen-Lippe 221.
3.   *Ibid*.
4.   CDU report on the outlook for the Baden-Württemberg election, 1963, Archiv CDU Nordbaden.
5.   *NZZ*, 21 March 1964.
6.   *The Times*, 18 March 1964.
7.   Interview with Erhard, *Die Welt am Sonntag*, 14 August 1966.
8.   Otto Grandi to Dr Klaus Scheufelen, 6 October 1964, Archiv CDU Nord-Württemberg.
9.   Grandel to Otto Grandi, 9 October 1964, *ibid*.
10.   *Der Spiegel*, 29 April 1964, p. 30; Klaus Gunther, *Der Kanzlerwechsel in der Bundesrepublik* (1970), p. 139.
11.   *Christ und Welt*, 12 November 1965.
12.   See profile of Erhard in *Der Spiegel*, 8 September 1965, pp. 26-35.
13.   *Der Spiegel*, 15 July 1964, article on 'Gaullism' in Bonn.

14. *25 Jahre Junge Union Deutschlands* (1972), pp. 139-45.
15. Erich Eisner, *Das europaische Konzept von Franz-Josef Strauss* (1975), pp. 29-32.
16. According to *Der Spiegel*, 15 July 1964, the 'Gaullists' had about 100 supporters. There were altogether 251 CDU/CSU deputies in the Bundestag.
17. *The Times*, 19 October 1963.
18. *NZZ*, 27 January 1964.
19. *The Times*, 9 July 1964.
20. *NZZ*, 10 July 1964.
21. *The Times*, 13 July 1964.
22. *Der Spiegel*, 15 July 1964.
23. *Guardian*, 11 July 1964 and 13 July 1964.
24. *Der Spiegel*, 15 July 1964.
25. *Guardian*, 11 July 1964.
26. 'Bonn witnesses end of Erhard honeymoon' in *The Times*, 21 September 1964.
27. *Der Spiegel*, 11 November 1964.
28. Alfons Hermann, Oberkochen, to CDU LV Nord-Württemberg, 18 November 1964, Archiv CDU Nord-Württemberg.
29. Gerhard Schick to CDU LV Nord-Württemberg, 18 October 1964, *ibid.*
30. *Besprechung mit den Vorsitzenden der Vereinigungen*, 21 April 1964, Archiv BGS.
31. *Die Zeit*, 18 February 1966.
32. *Bayern Kurier*, 20 October 1965.
33. Dieter Lau, 'Oppositionswind aus Südwest' in *SZ*, 30 October 1965.
34. *Südwest-Union-Dienst*, 22 October 1965.
35. *FAZ*, 15 November 1965
36. Klaus Dreher, 'Die Dreissigjährigen mit den Ellenbogen' in *SZ*, 21 March 1966.
37. Heinz Kornetzki, 'Ludwig Erhards schlechte Kirchenpresse' in *Die Zeit*, 18 February 1966.
38. Heribert Knorr, 'Die Grosse Koalition in der parlamentarischen Diskussion der Bundesrepublik, 1949-1965' in *Aus Politik und Zeitgeschichte*, 17 August 1974, pp. 28-30.
39. *Ibid.*, pp. 40-41.
40. *FAZ*, 20 February 1963 and 21 February 1963.
41. Konrad Adenauer, 'Moglichkeiten einer Koalition – Erfahrungen mit vier Regierungen' in *Die Politische Meinung*, September 1965, pp. 13-17.
42. *Der Spiegel*, 10 January 1966, pp. 15-16.
43. *FAZ*, 11 January 1966 and *Die Zeit*, 14 January 1966.
44. *CDU Presse-Mitteilungen*, 31 January 1966.
45. *FAZ*, 3 February 1966.
46. *FAZ*, 4 February 1966.
47. *FAZ*, 3 February 1966 and 8 February 1966.
48. *NZZ*, 11 February 1966.
49. *FAZ*, 8 February 1966 and 9 February 1966.
50. *FAZ*, 9 February 1966.
51. *New York Herald Tribune*, 12/13 February 1966.
52. *FAZ*, 10 February 1966.
53. *Der Spiegel*, 21 March 1966, pp. 41-2.
54. *FAZ*, 17 February 1966.
55. *14. Bundesparteitag der CDU* (1966), p. 208.

186   *Christian Democracy in Western Germany*

56. *Ibid.*, p. 207.
57. See *FAZ*, 11 February 1966; Elisabeth Noelle and E. P. Neumann (eds.), *Jahrbuch der öffentlichen Meinung, 1965-67*, p. 198; and E. Noelle-Neumann, 'Die Kunst, dem Volk aufs Maul zu schauen: die Rolle der Demoskopie in der Bundesrepublik' in *Die Zeit*, 23 February 1968.
58. CDU-BGS, Abt. Offentlichkeitsarbeit, *Einige Uberlegungen zue Wahlkampf-und Werbekonzeption für den Landtagswahlkampf NRW im Juli 1966*, Archiv CDU Rheinland, Vorbereitung Landtagswahl 1966.
59. *Der Spiegel*, 18 July 1966, p. 22.
60. e.g. CDU-BGS, *Zum Ausgang der Landtagswahlen 1966 in NRW*, Archiv CDU Rheinland, Vorbereitung Landtagswahl 1966.
61. e.g. Anton Böhm, 'Mehr Mut zum Neuen: die Union vor der Selbstprüfung' in *Die Politische Meinung*, July/August 1966.
62. *Die Welt*, 5 August 1966.
63. *FR*, 12 September 1966 and *NZZ*, 1 October 1966.
64. Klaus Dreher, *Rainer Barzel* (1972), p. 100.
65. Robert Strobel, 'Die Union nach der Affäre Barzel' in *Stuttgarter Nachrichten*, 28 June 1966.
66. *Rheinischer Merkur*, 30 September 1966.
67. Klaus Günther, *op. cit.*, p. 43 and Klaus Derher, *op. cit.*, pp. 103-4.
68. *Die Zeit*, 25 November 1966.
69. Quoted in Rudolf Wildenmann, 'Regierungspartei von morgen – oder was sonst?' in R. Löwenthal and H.P. Schwarz, *25 Jahre Bundesrepublik Deutschland* (1974), p. 355.
70. Bruno Heck to regional and district branches of CDU, 5 December 1966 and 12 January 1967, Archiv CDU Westfalen-Lippe 222 IV and Archiv CDU Nord-Württemberg.
71. *Der Spiegel*, 22 May 1967, p. 36.
72. *FAZ*, 29 December 1966.
73. See profile of Dufhues by Rolf Zundel, 'Parteistratege – aber kein Volksführer' in *Die Zeit*, 13 January 1967.
74. *Der Spiegel*, 20 March 1967, p. 31.
75. *Ibid*, 22 May 1967, p. 38.
76. *Deutsches Monatsblatt*, January 1967.
77. *FAZ*, 29 December 1966 and *NZZ* 7 January 1967.
78. *FAZ*, 13 February 1967 and *Die Zeit*, 17 February 1967.
79. *SZ*, 13 February 1967.
80. *FAZ*, 14 February 1967.
81. *FAZ*, 11 February 1967.
82. Arnold Fratzscher, Landesgeschäftsführer CDU Hanover, 11 March 1967 to Dr Kraske, Archiv CDU Niedersachsen.
83. e.g. article by Franz Meyers, 'Braucht die CDU einen "General"? ein Diskussionsbeitrag zum Bundesparteitag in Braunschweig' in *Die Zeit*, 21 April 1967.
84. See analysis of Kiesinger's election tours in *Der Spiegel*, 17 April 1967, pp. 40-42.
85. *Der Spiegel*, 22 May 1967. See also Werner Kaltefleiter *et. al.*, 'Im Wechspelspiel der Koalitionen, eine Analyse der Bundestagswahl 1969' in *Verfassung und Verfassungsworklichkeit*, Jahrbuch 1970, Pt. I, p. 33.
86. *Der Spiegel*, 22 May 1967, p. 40.
87. *Die Zeit*, 26 May 1967.
88. *FAZ*, 24 May 1967 and *NZZ*, 25 May 1967.
89. *FAZ*, 24 May 1967.
90. Rolf Zundel in *Die Zeit*, 26 May 1967.

91. *Ibid.*
92. Kaltefleiter, *op. cit.*, p. 34.
93. Rudolf Augstein in *Der Spiegel*, 7 July 1969, p. 16.
94. Report on meeting of CDU Federal Committee, 9 October 1967, Archiv CDU Nordbaden.
95. See Kaltefleiter, *op. cit.*, p. 55, on voter's changing attitudes towards the two parties.
96. *SZ*, 6 June 1967.
97. *Welt am Sonntag*, 19 November 1967.
98. *Die Zeit*, 19 January 1968.
99. *Die Zeit*, 3 February 1967 and *Der Spiegel*, 22 May 1967, pp. 38-9.
100. Kurt Simon, 'In Bonn ist eine Stelle frei — bei der CDU steht Erhards Thron noch immer leer' in *Die Zeit*, 17 January 1969.
101 *Die Zeit*, 25 August 1967.
102. Rolf Zundel in *Die Zeit*, 9 February 1968.
103. *Die Zeit*, 20 October 1967.
104. *Die Zeit*, 22 March 1968.
105. Theo Sommer, 'Knabbern an Tabus' in *Die Zeit*, 22 March 1968.
106. For a discussion of this point, see Henning Storz, *Aussenpolitik als Gesellschaftspolitik: die aussenpolitische Konzeption der CDU mit besonderer Berücksichtigung der Zeit der Grossen Koalition, 1966-1969*, Ph.D. thesis, 1973.
107. *Ibid.*, pp. 253-4.
108. *FAZ*, 14 February 1967.
109. See David P. Conradt, 'Electoral Law Politics in West Germany' in *Political Studies*, September 1970, pp. 341-56.
110. *Die Zeit*, 5 July 1968 and Gerhard Lehmbruch, 'The Ambiguous Coalition in West Germany' in *Government and Opposition*, Vol. 3, pp. 193-4.
111. Article by Heck, 'Wir brauchen eine leistungsfahige Union' in *Deutsches Monatsblatt*, June 1967.
112. *Union in Bewährung, 17. Landesparteitag der CDU des Rheinlandes*, Oberhausen (1967), pp. 11-12.
113. Kaltefleiter, *op. cit.*, p. 36.
114. See profile of Heck by Rolf Zundel, 'Brunel Heck, der neue CDU-Generalsekretär — Schulmeister seiner Partei?' in *Die Zeit*, 2 June 1967.
115. *FAZ*, 16 December 1967.
116. *FAZ*, 9 August 1968 and Kaltefleiter, *op. cit.*, p. 36.
117. *Die Zeit*, 29 March 1968.
118. *Ibid.*
119. *FAZ*, 25 July 1968.
120. See analysis of Berlin Programme by Rolf Zundel, 'Die CDU mausert sich' in *Die Zeit*, 22 December 1967.
121. *NZZ*, 6 November 1968.
122. *SZ*, 6 January 1968.
123. See Brandt's complaints about his role as Foreign Minister in interview with *Der Spiegel*, 15 September 1969, p. 52.

5 THE CDU/CSU OUT OF POWER: THE RELUCTANT OPPOSITION (1969-1972)

(a) The Loss of Office and the Problem of Legitimacy

The move to the role of Opposition proved to be the decisive turning-point for renewal in the political and organisational development of the CDU/CSU. Such renewal was long overdue in the CDU/CSU after two decades in power, and although various attempts at such change had been made during the 1960s they had all fallen well short of any radical reform, particularly as its implementation had been hindered by the political activities of the party being so focused on the role of the chief executive in Bonn. Political and organisational rejuvenation was slow to develop in the CDU/CSU, and it was not really initiated until the 1972 Bundestag Election had confirmed the 'change of power' which had occurred three years before. Even though the loss of Chancellorship in 1969 had brought a profound change in the status of the CDU/CSU, it continued nevertheless during its first period in Opposition to ack like 'a governing party in the waiting-room' for, as Rainer Barzel himself commented retrospectively, the CDU/CSU 'did not unpack its bags' as Opposition party during 1969-72.[1]

The reason for the CDU/CSU's reluctant adaptation to Opposition must be sought first of all in the problems of legitimacy, which had inhibited the Opposition role in the Federal Republic from the beginning. These problems derived historically from the influence of Hegelian ideas of the 'neutral' state on nineteenth century German politics, which encouraged an association between the governing political elite and the state, a picture reinforced by the 'negative' experience of parliamentary government during the Weimar Republic. Consequently, political opposition tended to be regarded as opposition to the state.[1] The evolution of a relatively stable democratic system in post-war West Germany had not witnessed a radical departure from this pattern, for Government leaders (notably Adenauer in the 1950s) had encouraged the undervaluation of the Opposition role[2] while the mass media and the public, with their concentration of attention on the activities of Chancellor and Government, had done nothing to counter this attitude. The move towards co-operative opposition by the SPD in the 1960s, culminating in the Grand Coalition, has been rightly interpreted as their 'resignation in the face of the German past'.[3] but now the sudden break initiated by the SPD's speedy formation of the Left-Liberal coalition with the FDP in 1969 raised the question of Opposition legitimacy in a new context. Voter movements in the 1969 Bundestag Election were such that the CDU/CSU disputed that the new Government ('coalition of losers') had an electoral mandate,[2] while Barzel as leader of the largest *Fraktion* claimed a 'special right' of co-responsibility in the leadership of the state.[4] Early interest in the possibilities presented by a large parliamentary Opposition soon gave way however, with the reappearance of intransigent Opposition similar to that of the early 1950s, to the traditional undervaluation of the Opposition role. The interpretation of many voters of the CDU/CSU's constructive vote of no-confidence against the Brandt Government in 1972 as an attack against the state demonstrated that tendency clearly.[5]

The CDU/CSU's immediate reaction to its loss of power in the autumn of 1969 was one of almost total disorientation. The instinctive attitude of several of its leaders, including some moderate younger ones like Helmut Kohl, was to question normatively the 'change of power'. They argued that this amounted to a 'falsification' of the voters' wishes because of the assumed convention that the largest parliamentary party should appoint the Chancellor, while phrases like 'the great betrayal', 'stolen victory' and 'putsch against the voters' were used in interviews given by CDU/CSU leaders or in editorial comment by newspapers supporting the party.[6] The basic aversion to the recent events in Bonn was expressed most blatantly by Franz-Josef Strauss, when he described the *Machtwechsel* as 'not a simple change of government according to the rules of parliamentary democracy, for it aims at introducing a fundamental and long-term reorientation in German politics both internally and externally'.[7] A widespread tendency among Christian Democratic leaders was therefore to view the formation of the Left-Liberal coalition as a challenge to the values of the political system which had developed under their leadership after the War.

The CDU/CSU leadership seemed to believe it had a natural right to govern, but its sharp reaction to being thrust into the role of Opposition reflected at a deeper level alarm and uncertainty about the party's long-term electoral prospects magnified by its unsolved internal problems which had accumulated during the 1960s. As Ernst Benda, former CDU Minister of the Interior, put it succinctly, 'the change in power relations poses for the CDU as a party questions of an existential importance'.[8] Interviews with some younger CDU leaders in the months following the 'change of power', notably with Helmut Kohl, showed how much they were pessimistic about the electoral fortunes of the party in the light of new trends in the 1969 Bundestag Election.[9] Other such younger leaders were similarly galvanised by these problems and emphasised the need for 'a new face' by modernising the party's image to attract the technocratic and educated 'new middle classes'.[10] Their uncertainty was compounded by the fear in the CDU/CSU that the SPD would undoubtedly exploit its new position as governing party in elections.[3] Possession of the Chancellorship had for too long been the basis of the CDU/CSU's 'way of life', so that the sudden loss of this advantage produced a feeling of profound deprivation. The loss of office also posed new problems of party solidarity, for common responsibility in government had, in spite of the history of party disunity in the 1960s, acted as some unifying force between the CDU and CSU,[a] not to mention as a factor of cohesion within the CDU, and had helped to mollify internal divisions. All these problems hindered the CDU/CSU's ready adaptation to the new and unwelcome role of Opposition.

The question crucial to the future development of the CDU/CSU as a political party was how long it would take to recover from its state of political shell-shock to embark on a course of self-reassessment. This itself required as a precondition that the party come to terms with the Opposition role, but following the 'change of power' it became clear that there was disunity among CDU/CSU leaders about the best long-term approach to this new situation and its accompanying problems. One pragmatic voice in the autumn of 1969 was that of Bruno Heck, CDU General Secretary, who warned at the CDU Congress at Mainz in November that 'the Government creates the facts and largely determines the themes', and that 'Opposition parties are as a rule compelled to adapt in the long-term to the Government parties' decisions over great policy matters',[11] but otherwise there were few signs then that the party was yet willing to engage in any post-mortem or general analysis of the situation so soon after the election. Barzel, one of the few party leaders to react soberly to the 'change of power', also warned that 'we have hard times before us' because 'the way ahead lies through thistles and thorns',[12] but a more popular vein of thought was expressed by Kiesinger (re-elected CDU chairman at this Congress) who proclaimed that any 'illusions' by the Government about relations with

a   See below chapter 10(a), esp. pp. 309-10.

the East would 'soon be destroyed' and that he could speak with authority because 'I have experience'.[13] This view that the CDU/CSU, rich with its long experience in government,[4] was politically more worldly wise than the new Government under Brandt helped the party initially in bearing the painful loss of power.

The CDU/CSU's confusion over its strategic objectives as the Opposition increased rather than diminished as time progressed. Barzel, who had shown early signs of favouring constructive opposition, later seemed forced by reason of internal party pressures to follow an intransigent path, particularly as this appeared to represent majority feeling in the party once the Ostpolitik issue (where bipartisanship between the Government and Opposition parties was low) became dominant. Barzel's first speech as the new CDU chairman to the Bundestag in November 1971, dwelling on the necessity of 'internal political peace' and posing pragmatic alternatives in taxation and social policy,[14] was recognised as an effort to revive the line of constructive opposition, but Barzel failed to impose this as a lasting position because his own leadership of the party remained weak. Kiesinger took an increasingly intransigent line by concentrating actively on using *Land* elections to 'catapult' the FDP out of the state parliaments and so demonstrate the voters' disapproval of the Brandt/Scheel Government. This strategy, so tempting in view of the Government's unstable majority in the Bundestag, served to boost party morale with the CDU/CSU's repeated successes in *Land* elections, but at the same time risked overlooking those factors which limited them as a guide to national electoral trends.[15] The commonly held belief in the party that the 'change of power' in 1969 was somehow an 'accident' (*Betriebsunfall*), which had to be rectified, inhibited one of the main practices of constructive opposition — the habit of holding regular consultations with the Government over policy matters — especially over controversial issues like Ostpolitik.

The polarisation over Ostpolitik in particular was apparent in the early months of the new coalition,[16] and lasted virtually the whole of the legislative period. This arose from the drama occasioned by the *Machtwechsel* and the internal situation in the political parties as well as the nature of the issue itself, and helped to produce a reversal of roles between the main parties with SPD leaders now choosing to undervalue the role of Opposition.[5] Polarisation reinforced the tendencies towards intransigent opposition in the CDU/CSU, but this presented in its turn problems of public appeal.

The impression of a negative stand by the CDU/CSU on Government
policy in general was generated by the Ostpolitik controversy
and tended to obliterate the considerable amount of bipartisan
co-operation over detailed legislative work between Government
and Opposition parties in the Bundestag.[6] The negative image
acquired by the CDU/CSU explained partly why it mobilised protest
votes in *Land* elections without any rise in its 'competence image'
on crucial issues.[17] The Government parties were able to use the
advantages of office to establish a superior image of competence
in foreign affairs, being able to count on a certain national
solidarity and exploiting their monopoly of the production of news.
In the other major field — economic affairs — the CDU/CSU was
still unable to present an authoritative counter spokesman to Karl
Schiller.[7]

There were other reasons why the CDU/CSU was unable to take
advantage of its Opposition role, apart from the impact of polarisation,
notably the influence of the balance of political interests within the
party and the opportunity offered by intransigent opposition for an
easy way of keeping party morale afloat. There was a concern that
party solidarity might be endangered by any radical change; this
fear arose as a reaction to enthusiastic calls for party reform by
younger party leaders in the autumn of 1969. The demand by
Manfred Wörner, the 35-year-old deputy chairman of the Bundestag
Fraktion, that 'signals must be given' at the Mainz Congress for
modernising the CDU[18] raised old fears among local party leaders
of renewed divisions in the leadership.[8] Similarly, this problem
arose with the party programme commission which began its
deliberations in the spring of 1970 under the chairmanship of
Helmut Kohl to revise the Berlin Programme. Its original proposals
involved a new departure from earlier CDU programmatic formulations
with its emphasis on social and other domestic reforms, which
indicated a common agreement with much Government thinking,
and its low priority accorded foreign policy.[19] They expressed a
reformist outlook, but the ensuing internal party controversy over
these proposals, arising from the antagonisms of industrial and
business interests, led to major compromises in the final version
presented at the Dusseldorf Congress in January 1971. It was felt
at the time that any reform debate of a programmatic kind would
endanger party unity.

Ultimately, the shortened legislative period allowed little freedom
of time for initiating major party reform, although there were some

organisational improvements at the Bonn party headquarters[b] and
party membership began to increase dramatically, particularly as a
by-product of polarisation.[c] There was hope of further reform in the
autumn of 1971 with the election of Konrad Kraske and Walther Leisler
Kiep, respectively as General Secretary and Treasurer of the CDU, but
little time remained before the Opposition became absorbed in the
political crisis of spring 1972 and the early Bundestag Election which
followed closely afterwards. Both for reasons of political circumstances
and the balance of internal party interests, the CDU had no real
opportunity for self-regeneration during its first period in Opposition,
1969-72. There were two further factors, which must now be
discussed, also operating against change: the leadership question
dominated much of the party's attention during this period; and
the focus of party activity after the loss of the Chancellorship became
the CDU/CSU *Fraktion* in the Bundestag — so that interest waned
in the condition of the party as a whole. ·

(b)   The Rise of Rainer Barzel

Political parties frequently react to the loss of national office with
a change of leadership. There may be two possible solutions: when
the outgoing leader is identified with the discredit attached to
the party in office and its consequent loss of power (the scapegoat
thesis), or when a change of leadership is regarded as a necessary
prerequisite for party renewal of a programmatic kind, with the new
leader presenting a more appealing interpretation of the party's
future course (the alternative programme thesis). It was to be
expected that the first case would apply to the new CDU/CSU
Opposition, because of its low degree of programmatic development
up to 1969 — which itself was a fundamental reason why the party
did not easily seek an outlet through programmatic renewal during
1969-72. The *Kanzlerpartei* was now minus *Kanzler,* but paradoxically
this helped to explain why the party did not follow its traditional
habit of replacing one leader by another, for any new figure could not
of course acquire the political authority which had derived from the
office of Federal Chancellor. Consequently, the leadership question
was not essentially solved in terms of providing a new integrative
force for the CDU/CSU, and it remained a continuous source of

b   On the organisational changes in the CDU during 1969-72, see below
    chapter 7 (c), pp. 263-4.
c   See below chapter 8 (b), pp. 281, 284 ff.

internal party dissatisfaction during most of this period. It proved indeed to be, in the already quoted words of Ernst Benda, a problem of 'existential importance', in view of the party's dependence for twenty years on the figure of the Chancellor.

The 'change of power' in October 1969 implied that the CDU/CSU would have to emancipate itself from the Chancellor figure, but the CDU Congress at Mainz (17/18 November) occurred too soon afterwards for any leadership change to be formalised there. Kiesinger was re-elected party chairman – he was described by one respectable conservative newspaper as 'being preserved as the party monument'[20] – although a desire for some personnel change was evident in the elections to the party Praesidium.[9] Kiesinger retained a certain aura as former Chancellor in spite of criticism that he had not made sufficient effort to counter the Brandt/Scheel coalition initiative on election night, but it was likely that his prestige would gradually wane, as indeed proved the case. One advantage in retaining his services as chairman was that it would supposedly give the CDU time to readjust and work out its priorities in settling the problem of its future leadership. Whenever this occurred the CDU still had to face the quandary that any leader it chose would have to try to compete with Brandt's increasing prestige as Chancellor: hence, the attraction of a reverse 'change of power' before the next Bundestag Election due in 1973, not an unrealistic proposition considering the instability of the Government's majority in the Bundestag (reduced to six from twelve in the summer of 1970 with the defection of three FDP deputies to the Opposition). CDU/CSU leaders guessed correctly that any electoral confrontation with Chancellor Brandt would place them at a considerable disadvantage, and this was a principal motive in their attempt at a constructive vote of no-confidence against Brandt in April 1972.[10]

The CDU/CSU leader who benefited most directly from the 'change of power' was Rainer Barzel, *Fraktion* leader in the Bundestag since 1964, who did not lose his position in 1969, but on the contrary, took full advantage of the opportunity presented by the enhanced position of the *Fraktion*. His rise to the party leadership, culminating in his election as CDU chairman in 1971 and selection as CDU/CSU Chancellor candidate in 1972, seemed a logical consequence of the fact that, with the loss of the Chancellorship, the *Fraktion* finally broke with the pattern whereby it had played an auxiliary role in relation to successive Federal Governments, and it became 'the active core of the party'.[21] Barzel made himself virtually indispensable

to his party with his gifts as a tactician and his position in the limelight
as parliamentary leader. Under Barzel's careful and efficient direction,
the *Fraktion* adapted more easily to its new role in the first painful
months of Opposition than the party as a whole, mainly because
it channelled its energies through an assertive role in legislative
activity. In October 1969 Barzel reorganised the *Fraktion* by
enlarging its Executive to include many former ministers as well
as aspiring younger leaders who now looked to Barzel for promotion.[22]
This was achieved in such a way that Barzel's position was strengthened,
for *Fraktion* leadership posts were now in more hands and so less
concentrated than before,[11] while at the same time the auxiliary
staff of the *Fraktion* was increased and a new disciplinary code was
introduced to ensure regular attendance and an effective response
from backbenchers.[23] In so reinforcing his power base in the
Fraktion, which in turn had acquired increased political weight,
Barzel became effective leader of the CDU/CSU Opposition in the
early months after the party's loss of power.

   Barzel's political standing was nevertheless greater in the *Fraktion*
than in the party as a whole.[24] This was hardly surprising since
Barzel had risen to prominence in the CDU/CSU by concentrating his
skills and energies on his leadership of the parliamentary party,
but it also pointed to Barzel's one crucial weakness as a politician: his
public image. His image problem derived from his reputation as a
technocrat-style politician, respected for his disciplined application
(*Leistungsfähigkeit*) and tactical ability, but lacking in that
recognised quality of 'trust' so necessary for establishing his
credibility as a future national leader.[25] Barzel's image among
party supporters improved during 1971, as it became clear that he
would become the next CDU chairman, although he was still
viewed with less favour by the public at large.[26] The trauma for
the CDU/CSU of the failure of the constructive vote of no-confidence
against Brandt in April 1972, when Barzel was nominated as the
Opposition's candidate, also reinforced the negative public impact
of his political personality and consequently during the crucial
months before the 1972 Election polls underlined Barzel's defective
popular appeal.[27] He was clearly no charismatic personality.

   Barzel's rise as Opposition leader meant that, in choosing him as
its Chancellor candidate, the CDU/CSU was breaking with its
tradition of placing overriding importance on its leader's electoral
appeal. Underlying Barzel's own political weakness was of course the
problem for the party that it was selecting someone who would not

automatically acquire the authority of the Chancellor's role, in view of the pattern whereby Opposition Chancellor candidates had always trailed the incumbent Chancellors in popularity. However, within the CDU/CSU Barzel had another main advantage apart from his leadership of the *Fraktion,* which was the weakness or division of his possible rivals. Ex-Chancellor Kiesinger as the most senior in status of the CDU leaders never challenged Barzel for the *Fraktion* leadership and seemed temperamentally unsuited for its managerial requirements, having enjoyed the official trappings of the Chancellorship yet showing little interest in party politics.[28] Gerhard Schröder, a long-time claimant for the position of Chancellor, was reluctant to exploit his greater appeal among floating voters than Barzel and cultivated a non-partisan silence in the Bundestag. He lacked in any case strong support in the *Fraktion.*[29] Among younger CDU leaders, Stoltenberg featured for a while as having potential *Kanzlerformat* and proven electoral skill, but his departure from Bonn for the minister-presidency of Schleswig-Holstein in spring 1971 removed him from further discussion.

The main protagonist to emerge against Barzel was Helmut Kohl, who had recently arrived as a member of the party leadership,[12] Having established a reputation as an effective party reformer of his own *Landesverband* in the Rhineland-Palatinate, Kohl was strong in those areas where Barzel was weak, in his popularity among party functionaries. He sought to promote his standing by a series of press interviews during 1969-71, which emphasised the CDU's need to become a 'modern party' in order to meet the new electoral challenges of the 1970s. Kohl announced his candidacy for the CDU chairmanship late in 1970, declaring he was interested in that position alone and would devote himself to party affairs. As an avowed party reformer, Kohl attracted support among progressive elements of the CDU and in the Young Union, and was able to maintain their sympathy as an imaginative chairman of the party programme commission (1970-1). However, Kohl played his hand unskilfully at the Düsseldorf Congress in January 1971, when he openly backed down over the commission's proposals on the highly controversial issue of worker participation, so alienating sympathy for him in the Social Committees. Barzel's much more refined performance at this Congress set the scene for the leadership contest the following October at the Saarbrücken Congress, when Barzel beat Kohl decisively by 344 votes to 174. This was the first open contest for the CDU chairmanship in the party's history. The discussion which preceded it saw a revival of the institutional question whether the CDU chairmanship should be separate from the Chancellor candidacy, because of the alternative presented by Kohl, but the dice were heavily loaded in Barzel's favour as he had collected majority support in the various *Landesverbände* during the months preceding the election.[30] One obvious drawback for Kohl at this time was his lack of profile in foreign politics, which had become the central area of political debate in the Federal Republic due to the Government's pursuance of Ostpolitik.

In electing Barzel as its chairman in 1971, the CDU was confirming the dominant role acquired by the Bundestag *Fraktion* in the party since the 'change of power'. It was also indicating the priority it placed on resuming national office over improving the condition of the party in view of Barzel's supreme intention of replacing Brandt as Chancellor. Nevertheless, his election as chairman did not substantially improve his authority in the party, for continued misgivings at its lower levels about his leadership and his ability to win the next Bundestag election prevented him from ever becoming sovereign master of his party. Consequently, the CDU chairmanship lost much of the integrating force it had previously provided, a process which had already developed because of the unimpressive performance in the first Opposition years of Kiesinger (chairman until 1971). Barzel's main aim in claiming the party chairmanship in addition to the *Fraktion* leadership was to prevent the emergence of any strong rival and strengthen his position vis-à-vis Strauss, so making virtually certain that he would also become Chancellor candidate. His preoccupation with parliamentary business in Bonn did, however, restrict the time he could devote to party affairs, although, unlike his three predecessors as CDU chairman, he put in regular appearances at the party headquarters and initiated more regular meetings of the party Federal executive organs.[13] Barzel's inability to establish his political authority as party leader was reflected in the tendency of several other CDU/CSU figures to speak out in a disunited fashion on policy matters during the first Opposition period, which served to diminish the sense of party solidarity. As Rudiger Göb, CDU Business Manager (1970-71), commented critically at the time:

> The Opposition is like an automobile that is being driven by several motorists at one time: one is doing the steering, another has his foot on the accelerator, a third is pumping the brakes and yet another is operating the indicator. If this car is first past the

chequered flag in 1973, it will be mainly as a result of luck.[31]

The greatest strain on the party's solidarity was the growing rift between the CDU and the CSU. Differences over Opposition strategy and policy between the two parties were manifest at the personal level in the relationship between Barzel and Strauss. As *Fraktion* leader the former was required to work out a common position and compromise with the CSU, whereas although Strauss chose not to challenge Barzel's managerial leadership in the Bundestag, he nevertheless cultivated an independent position as an Opposition policy spokesman and as leader of the CSU. Strauss's hardly concealed contempt for Barzel's qualifications as Chancellor candidate was accompanied by the sense of alienation in the CSU at the prejudgement of this question by Barzel's election as CDU chairman and by the feeling there that Strauss was the more powerful political personality. The CSU's calculated hesitation in confirming Barzel as Chancellor candidate undermined further his authority in the first months of 1972, so that Barzel was tempted to see a solution to his accumulating internal party problems in a short cut back to power. The political crisis of April/May 1972, with the attempted constructive vote of no-confidence against Chancellor Brandt and the controversial ratification of the treaties with the Soviet Union and Poland, must be considered in the context of the CDU/CSU's overall position on Ostpolitik since 1969 in order to appreciate these problems for the party's leadership and its position at the outset of the Bundestag Election campaign which followed.

(c)   The Ostpolitik Debate and the Question of Party Unity

The issue of Ostpolitik was the supreme instance where the CDU/CSU's inability to accept fully the role of Opposition, which, combined with the weakened authority of its leadership, propelled the party in a direction which both lost the party credibility among the West German public and undermined its internal solidarity. This occurred even though there was growing public support for the policy of Brandt and Scheel in settling relations with the Eastern bloc, of which the principal stages were the treaties with Moscow and Warsaw signed in 1970, the Berlin Agreement of 1971 and the General Treaty with the DDR of 1972. There were two principal reasons why the Opposition found itself in this dilemma.

First, Ostpolitik was the area where the new Left-Liberal coalition most obviously and dramatically demonstrated its initiative in 'creating new realities' in policy-making. The new Opposition found this all the more difficult to accept because of the alacrity with which the Government embarked on its initiatives towards the East. This soon outmoded the CDU/CSU's emphasis on the importance of continuity of Ostpolitik with the policy of previous governments.[14] It was in any case likely that conflict would arise between the main parties in view of their tension over Ostpolitik during the Grand Coalition,[d] while the SPD and FDP had indicated new initiatives when they preempted the issue during the 1969 election campaign.[32] As the SPD's first period of Opposition during the early 1950s had shown, foreign policy was not a prudent field in which to confront the Government since the latter had a monopoly of policy information and acted as the representative of national security. Barzel attempted to bridge the gap between the CDU/CSU's basic antipathy towards Ostpolitik and his desire to maintain the party's legitimacy as a governing force by insisting on the CDU/CSU's claim for co-responsibility in policy-making, as shown by his demand that the Government should consult the Opposition regularly over important matters: hence, Barzel's significant remark on the eve of his visit to Moscow in December that 'there is now an invitation to the leader of the Opposition from the Soviet Government', and that 'basically, our whole debate revolves around the consequences of an Ostpolitik that we have not created, and that the Federal Government has undertaken alone against our good counsel'.[33] A similar vein of thought had prompted Barzel's assertion to the CDU Congress at Düsseldorf in January 1971 that he had brought back more improvements from his recent Polish visit than had Brandt.[34] The main fault of this approach was that the Opposition's successive objections to each treaty in turn were easily overtaken by the speed of events. Tactics were not a sufficient substitute for the Opposition's lack of a convincing alternative approach on Ostpolitik, so that it was forced to react in an *ad hoc* fashion to Government initiatives.

Secondly, the CDU/CSU had traditionally shown a strong inclination towards foreign politics since the early years of Adenauer's leadership, as witnessed by the priority accorded the theme of 'security' in its election campaigns.[e] Adenauer's enforcement of party solidarity over Westpolitik had forged a clear association between strong leadership and a united stand on foreign policy, and indeed the

d   See above chapter 4 (d), p. 171.
e   See below chapter 11 (b), p. 340.

opposite had occurred with the Erhard crisis and divisions over European policy in the mid-1960s.[f] These patterns of party behaviour helped to elucidate the CDU/CSU's reaction to the Ostpolitik of the early 1970s. The party's fundamental anti-Communism, which had been well-rooted in its international outlook since the late 1940s, with its mistrust of Soviet intentions made it difficult for the CDU/CSU to break with the firm and cautious German policy it had followed in government over two decades. The emotionalised attitude towards Ostpolitik at all levels of the CDU/CSU, particularly at the grass-roots,[15] influenced more and more the Opposition's stand on this issue. It was evident too in the tendency of many CDU/CSU leaders to adopt moralistic positions, notably Kiesinger's emotive statement at the time the Moscow Treaty was being negotiated, answering the claim that Brandt was continuing his policies: 'I wanted to negotiate, but I did not want to go to Moscow to take orders.'[35] Understandably, the Opposition reacted violently to Brandt's provocative quoting of Adenauer in support of his Ostpolitik, claiming continuity with the latter's search in the mid-1950s for a settlement with the Soviet Union.[36]

The negative impression created by the CDU/CSU's evolving position on Ostpolitik accentuated its problems of public appeal. In particular, it was in danger of becoming entangled in a political cul-de-sac (called the *Neinsager-Ecke*), from which it could only emerge with loss of face. This impression was not always justified as positive stands were also taken, notably by the CDU Federal Executive in recommending the ratification of the Moscow and Warsaw Treaties in May 1972 and the decision by the *Fraktion* to allow the Transport Treaty with the DDR to pass the Bundestag uncontested the following September, although in both cases these moves were insufficient to erase the negative image acquired by the party. Some Opposition leaders were fully aware of the dangers presented by the CDU/CSU's position on Ostpolitik. Heinrich Köppler, chairman of the Rhineland CDU, pressed for a reduction in the discussion of the issue in 1970 because of its popularity with the voters, but complained that 'the Social Democrats keep bringing the matter up, and besides the voters ask us about it'.[37] As late as January 1972, Kraske sent a confidential memorandum to executive managers in the *Landesverbände*, expressing the hope that the party could free itself from the dominance of the Ostpolitik

f   See above chapter 4 (c), pp. 150-53.

issue and concentrate on other matters more favourable to the CDU/CSU:

> The CDU has neither the motive nor the intention of postponing the ratification process of the Eastern treaties. It must, on the contrary, be interested in seeing the arguments over the treaties concluded by the summer, so that, in the event of the acceptance of the treaties, the time remaining until the election can be used to design a new strategy (the main points: European unification, inter-German relations, and the alleviation of human problems). In spite of the topicality of foreign political questions, domestic policy must become our chosen field, and must largely determine the exchanges with our opponents at the latest from the summer of 1972.[38]

These comments by Köppler and Kraske illustrated how CDU/CSU leaders were incapable of controlling the impact of events on the party. This arose because of the problems of adapting to the Opposition role and at the same time keeping the party united, but also because they themselves were divided in their reactions to Ostpolitik. They failed consequently to make their position appear plausible, even to their own supporters, because of the lack of a clear direction from above, so that the emotionalised attitude of the grass-roots was able to influence the stands taken by individual party leaders, particularly as the party leadership question remained unsolved for so long.[39] This in turn furthered uncertainty at the lower levels of the party alarmed at the hydra-headed attitude of its leaders. The Opposition's failure to produce a ready statement on the final negotiation of the Moscow Treaty in August 1970 was a case in point. For several weeks the party executive remained officially silent until an agreed formula was produced. Several leaders had meanwhile issued their own individual statements, with some expressing an outright rejection of the Treaty and others warning against too hasty a condemnation.[40]

The main problem for the CDU/CSU Opposition was that, while the weight of opinion within it was tilted decisively towards a negative position, there was a significant variation in the scale of attitudes adopted by party leaders. The inevitable simplification of controversial political issues, as presented to the public by the mass media, glossed over this aspect, although the public was certainly aware generally of divisions within the Opposition. Sometimes it was difficult to tell how far these fluctuations of opinion were based on conviction, and to what degree they were influenced by the need to placate internal party pressures. Barzel, whose own position on Ostpolitik was relatively flexible, used fundamentalist language when the occasion suited it, such as in his addresses to CSU Congresses. Taking into account changes of stand by individual CDU/CSU leaders during this first Opposition period, it is nevertheless possible to categorise the variations of attitude within the CDU/CSU.

First, the absolute or principled opponents of Ostpolitik dwelt on the need to combat Communism, accused the Government of 'appeasement' and warned about the dangers of 'Socialism' within the Federal Republic itself. For them Ostpolitik also had a domestic dimension. The core of this group was provided by the CSU, but it enjoyed fairly wide support too from the CDU — among leaders like Dregger, indeed Kiesinger for a while, and at the grass-roots of the party, especially where such support was coupled with a general sympathy for the ideas of Strauss. Secondly, the conservative or 'flexible' opponents of Ostpolitik stressed the importance of continuity with CDU/CSU policy in Government during the 1960s and complained that Brandt was moving too fast. They included figures like Schröder, although a fine dividing-line between these first two groups was often difficult to draw, as in the case of Kiesinger. The third and fourth groups represented a minority. They included 'rational' or conditional critics of Ostpolitik like Richard von Weizsäcker, who indicated a sympathy with Brandt's policy in principle but protested he had not negotiated realistically; and, the small positive element, notably Walther Leisler Kiep, who favoured Ostpolitik in principle and more or less approved of Brandt's actual process of negotiating.[16]

The lack of solidarity within the CDU/CSU Opposition evidenced by the Ostpolitik debate was fully exposed to the public's gaze and scrutiny in May 1972 during the ratification of the Moscow and Warsaw Treaties. Barzel had agreed on a common formula with the Government to facilitate their passage but was forced to renege it after renewed pressure from intransigent opponents within the *Fraktion*, specifically the CSU, so that the only form of unity possible was that of abstention on the treaties. This event demonstrated vividly that Barzel's authority in his own power base, the Bundestag *Fraktion*, was no longer to be taken for granted. The sense of betrayal felt by the different rival groups over Ostpolitik within the Opposition was such that the effects of this trauma remained long afterwards.[17] This was not a propitious start for the CDU/CSU's campaign for the Bundestag the following autumn; indeed the reappearance of the Ostpolitik issue in the final crucial week of the election with the announcement of the General Treaty with the DDR served to remind the public of the party's divisions here. The CDU/CSU's loss of credibility over Ostpolitik was underlined in particular by some loss of sympathy in this respect among its own voters.[18]

In general, the events of 1972 as well as the CDU/CSU's performance in Opposition during 1969-72 showed how much the three problems facing it of adapting to the Opposition role, settling the leadership question out of office and responding to the Government's initiatives, especially in the area of Ostpolitik, were strongly interlinked. The CDU/CSU had failed essentially to take full account of the new political circumstances of the early 1970s. The weight of its traditional outlook, the balance of political forces within it and the strains imposed on its cohesion and solidarity by its lack of preparedness for the role of Opposition dictated that its adaptation to change, at least in the short time available during 1969-72, was virtually impossible. It remained for the shock of its election defeat in November 1972 to cut the Gordian knot of this political dilemma.

Notes

See Dieter Grosser, 'Die Sehnsucht nach Harmonie: historische und verfassungsstrukturelle Vorbelastungen der Opposition in Deutschland', in Heinrich Oberreuter (ed.), *Parlamentarische Opposition, ein internationaler Vergleich* (1975), pp. 206-29. On the problems of Opposition in Germany, see also Waldemar Besson, 'Regierung und Opposition in der deutschen Politik', in *Politische Vierteljahresschrift*, 1962, p. 225 ff., and Michael Hereth, *Die parlamentarische Opposition in der Bundesrepublik Deutschland* (1969).

[2] While the SPD had made significant gains, the FDP had overall lost heavily. The CDU/CSU had managed to balance many of its losses by gains from other parties, especially the FDP. As a result, the CDU/CSU remained the largest *Fraktion* in the Bundestag, with 242 seats against 224 for the SPD and 30 for the FDP.

[3] E.g. Kiesinger's remark at the CDU Congress in October 1971 that not only was the SPD superior to the CDU in organisation, but 'we ought not to underestimate the great advantage acquired by the SPD that it will enter the election campaign for the first time with a Chancellor' (*19. Bundesparteitag der CDU* (1971), p. 26).

[4] Apart from two ex-Chancellors (Kiesinger and Erhard), there also sat on the Opposition front-bench 18 former ministers and four ex-parliamentary state secretaries. This occasioned references to the

CDU/CSU as providing 'Opposition in Ministerformat'.

[5]   E.g. Herbert Wehner's remark in an interview with *Der Spiegel* (26 January 1970) that 'I do not need the Opposition', as well as Brandt's assertive remark in his Government Statement that the *Machtwechsel* represented the 'beginning of democracy', implying the lack of it under CDU/CSU governments.

[6]   The CDU/CSU Opposition voted for 93 per cent of the laws which passed the Bundestag during this legislative period, 1969-72. It rejected only 14 laws and abstained on nine (Hans-Joachim Veen, *Die CDU/CSU Opposition im parlamentarischen Entscheidungsprozess* (1973), pp. 106-7).

[7]   There were initially signs that Gerhard Stoltenberg might have filled this role, but his departure in spring 1971 to become Minister-President in Schleswig-Holstein deprived the *Fraktion* of probably its most competent shadow to the Government in this field. Barzel's nominee for the economics portfolio in his shadow team for 1972, Karl-Heinz Narjes, failed to establish an authoritative image.

[8]   E.g. the letter to Wörner from the chairman of the CDU district branch in Ravensburg, who agreed that the party must adapt to new circumstances but was alarmed that the way in which reform demands were being made would 'harm the image of the party rather than benefit it, for they offer the voter the picture of a party torn and consumed in power struggles'. He reminded Wörner that many people had not forgotten the party's crisis of 1966 (letter of 4 December 1969, Archiv CDU Nord-Württemberg).

[9]   Many younger leaders received high votes in the election of the five deputy CDU chairmen, with Stoltenberg topping the poll followed by Kohl. Schröder, who had topped this poll two years before, now came in last place. In the election for party chairman, there were 386 votes for Kiesinger (out of a total of 471) with 51 'no' votes and 33 abstentions (*17. Bundesparteitag der CDU* (1969), p. 209).

[10]   See Kraske's memorandum to local party leaders of 25 April 1972, explaining the decision to apply the constructive vote of no-confidence: 'We believe that a change of government at this point of time would have more advantages than disadvantages in view of the Bundestag Election 1973' (Archiv CDU Nord-Württemberg).

[11]   Barzel had no first deputy chairman in the *Fraktion*, but as many as seven deputy leaders of equal standing. Important decisions were taken by an inner group called the 'Council of Eleven' (*Elferrat*), in fact consisting of 21 members, including Barzel, Kiesinger, Strauss, Heck, the chairmen of the *Fraktion*'s working groups and the parliamentary business managers (see the interesting article by Rolf Zundel, 'Politik und Machtstrukturen der CDU/CSU Fraktion' in *Die Zeit*, 29 May 1970, as well as 'CDU in der Opposition', in *Der Spiegel*, 17 November 1969, pp. 27-34, for a discussion of Barzel's leadership of the Fraktion).

[12]   Helmut Kohl became Minister-President of the Rhineland-Palatinate in May 1969, and was elected a deputy chairman of the CDU at the Mainz Congress in November 1969.

[13]   Barzel's less lofty role as CDU chairman compared with Adenauer, Erhard and Kiesinger may be seen as a consequence of the Opposition role, for this position could no longer be coupled with that of Chancellor. Like his own successor as CDU chairman, Helmut Kohl, Barzel was constantly seen walking in and out of the party's *Bundesgeschäftsstelle*.

While Barzel's chosen colleagues, like Konrad Kraske (CDU General Secretary) and Ottfried Hennig (CDU Business Manager and former personal assistant to Barzel), moved into the BGS to replace the team of Bruno Heck in autumn 1971, they failed to overcome their isolated position there chiefly because of the reserved feeling towards Barzel in the party organisation as a whole, and a stronger sympathy in the headquarters and among party functionaries generally for Helmut Kohl, still seen as Barzel's main rival (based on interviews with Konrad Kraske, September 1974, and with Thomas Jansen, personal assistant to Barzel, September 1973).

[14] E.g. see Bruno Heck's circular letter to CDU members of 4 October 1969, in which he stated: 'We will exhaust all possibilities under our constitution of ensuring the stability and continuity of German policy' (Archiv CDU Nord-Württemberg).

[15] The strong antipathy to Ostpolitik impressed itself on the author in his many interviews with party activists at the regional and local level during 1972-3, before and after Brandt's election victory of 1972. A principled objection to Ostpolitik seemed to have been built into the party's 'belief system'.

[16] For a fuller discussion of these variations of attitude, see Geoffrey Pridham, 'The Ostpolitik and the Opposition', in Roger Tilford (ed.), *The Ostpolitik and Political Change in Germany* (1975), esp. pp. 49-52. See also Christian Hacke, *Die Ost- und Deutschlandpolitik der CDU/CSU* (1975), pp. 61-79, for a detailed discussion of the different phases of the Opposition's position on Ostpolitik and how these related to leadership rivalries.

[17] For a detailed and interesting discussion of the behaviour of the CDU/ CSU *Fraktion* over the ratification of the treaties in May 1972, see the long article by Jürgen Busche, 'Das Trauma des 17 Mai', in *FAZ*, 10 May 1973.

[18] On this see L. Eltermann, H. Jung and W. Kaltefleiter, 'Drei Fragen zur Bundestagswahl 1972' in *Aus Politik und Zeitgeschichte*, 17 November 1973, showing that half the CDU/CSU voters in 1972 had a positive view of Ostpolitik.

References

1. *FAZ*, 13 December 1972.
2. Michael Hereth, *Die Parlamentarische Opposition in der Bundesrepublik Deutschland* (1969), pp. 131-3.
3. *Ibid.*, p. 156.
4. Hans-Joachim Veen, *Die CDU/CSU Opposition im Parlamentarischen Entscheidungsprozess* (1973), pp. 48-9.
5. Dieter Grosser, 'Die Sehnsucht nach Harmonie: historische und verfassungsstrukturelle Vorbelastungen der Opposition in Deutschland', in Heinrich Oberreuter (ed.), *Parlamentarische Opposition: ein internationaler Vergleich* (1975), p. 206.
6. *Der Spiegel*, 20 October 1969 and *The Times*, 10 October 1969.
7. Quoted in *Die Zeit*, 17 April 1970.
8. Ernst Benda, 'Golgerungen für die Partei und die Parteivereinigungen' in G. Gölter and E. Pieroth (eds.), *Die Union in der Opposition* (1970), p. 131.

206   *Christian Democracy in Western Germany*

9.   E.g. *Der Spiegel*, 3 November 1969, p. 36.
10.   See interview with Manfred Wörner in *Der Spiegel*, 13 October 1969, p. 38-41, and Dietrich Rollmann (ed.), *Die CDU in der Opposition, eine Selbstdarstellung* (1970), pp. 1501-1.
11.   *17. Bundesparteitag der CDU* (1969), p. 36.
12.   *Ibid.*, p. 121.
13.   *Ibid.*, p. 24.
14.   *Das Parlament*, 6 November 1971, p. 9.
15.   For a discussion of this problem with reference to *Land* elections in 1970-2, see Geoffrey Pridham, 'A Nationalization Process? Federal Politics and State Elections in West Germany' in *Government and Opposition*, Autumn 1973, pp. 455-72.
16.   See Rolf Zundel, 'Das Ende aller Eintracht' in *Die Zeit*, 3 April 1970.
17.   See Werner Kaltefleiter, *Zwischen Konsens und Krise: eine Analyse der Bundestagswahl 1972* (1973), pp. 35-7.
18.   Interview with *Der Spiegel*, 13 October 1969, p. 38.
19.   See the summary in *Die Zeit*, 3 July 1970.
20.   *FAZ*, 19 November 1969.
21.   See Rolf Zundel, 'Politik und Machtstrukturen der CDU/CSU Fraktion' in *Die Zeit*, 29 May 1970.
22.   *Die Zeit*, 31 October 1969.
23.   *Der Spiegel*, 17 November 1969, p. 30.
24.   See article on Barzel as *Fraktion* leader in *Die Zeit*, 18 September 1970.
25.   *Der Spiegel*, 17 November 1969, pp. 27 ff., and Klaus Dreher, *Rainer Barzel* (1972), p. 159.
26.   Christian Hacke, *Die Ost- und Deutschlandpolitik der CDU/CSU* (1975), p. 68, 141 and 142 for opinion poll evidence on Barzel's public image.
27.   *Der Spiegel*, 20 March 1972, p. 28, and report in *SZ*, 6 October 1972, as well as the evidence of internal party polls discussed in interviews with local party activists, summer 1973.
28.   For an appraisal of Kiesinger's role in Opposition, see Carl-Christian Kaiser, 'Altkanzler Kurt-Georg Kiesingers bitterer Weg in die Machtlosigkeit' in *Die Zeit*, 29 May 1970.
29.   *Die Zeit*, 12 March 1971.
30.   For an analysis of support for the two candidates among the CDU *Landesverbände*, see Carl-Christian Kaiser, 'Wer schiebt wen auf den Vorstandsstuhl? in *Die Zeit*, 1 October 1971.
31.   Rüdiger Göb, 'Vom Auftrag der Partei zur Lösung ihrer Strukturprobleme' in *Sonde*, 3/71, p. 13.
32.   See Klaus von Beyme, 'The Ostpolitik in the West German 1969 Elections' in *Government and Opposition*, Vol. 5, No. 2, pp. 193-217.
33.   Interview with *Die Zeit*, 10 December 1971.
34.   *The Times*, 27 January 1971.
35.   *The Times*, 18 June 1970.
36.   *The Times*, 5 June 1970.
37.   *Der Spiegel*, 6 April 1970, p. 28.
38.   Konrad Kraske to CDU Landesgeschäftsführer, 10 January 1972, Archiv CDU Westfalen-Lippe, 222 VII.
39.   Christian Hacke, *op. cit.*, pp. 68-9.
40.   *SZ*, 27 August 1970.

6 THE CDU/CSU ADJUSTS ITSELF: THE RENOVATED OPPOSITION (1972-1976)

(a) Opposition in a Different Setting

The unprecedented sense of demoralisation which afflicted the CDU/ CSU after its decisive electoral defeat in 1972 arose from a sense of finality that the party had reached a stage, at which it could no longer avoid facing the problems concerning its popular appeal and state of internal relations which had accumulated since the early 1960s. The feeling of deep pessimism that so long as Brandt remained as Chancellor the CDU/CSU would have no chance of regaining power pervaded the party down to its grass-roots.[1] This gloom of the Christian Democrats was reinforced by many contemporary studies of the party's position which showed that it was electorally in a 'structural minority situation', and that it was in danger of setting into a 'shrinking process'.[1] There was a general feeling that the CDU/CSU had lost touch with modern political trends, and this was poignantly emphasised when Brandt claimed soon after his re-election as Chancellor that the parties of the Left-Liberal coalition represented the 'new centre' of West German politics.[2] The nature of the electoral system and of coalition politics seemed to add to the dismal prospects of a return to power for the CDU/CSU, since there was no precedent for ready alternation in office between the main Government and Opposition parties. The long and complicated process of the one 'change of power', which had occurred after a transition period of the Grand Coalition and involved the evolution of new policy positions by the SPD and FDP, underlined this rigidity in the West German party system, and suggested that any second 'change of power' would only occur after a similar period of adaptation by the parties concerned.[3]

The period of Opposition for the CDU/CSU during 1972-6 differed substantially from that of 1969-72. Externally, the electorate had confirmed the 'change of power' of 1969 and the Government's Ostpolitik. This direct challenge to the CDU/CSU's traditional policy outlook meant that it was forced at last to come to terms with its Opposition role, particularly as the absence this time of any prospect of an early return to power meant that the party now had time for self-reappraisal. At the same time, the transfer of the focus of political debate to domestic issues from 1973 facilitated this change, because the CDU/CSU could free itself from its quandary over Ostpolitik.

Internally, the demand for fundamental renewal which affected all levels of the party following the 1972 election result meant that the three interconnecting factors of accepting the Opposition role, the persistent leadership problems and attitudes towards Ostpolitik could be dealt with more easily. Since Ostpolitik was now virtually accepted as a fact of political life, and was therefore less immediately problem-atical for the CDU/CSU, it was able to attack the leadership question (automatically raised once more by the 1972 Election) with swift surgery early in the new Bundestag period, allowing the party consequently more time for concentrating on the remaining factor. The chances for the party drawing lessons from its first period of Opposition were enhanced by the solution adopted for the leadership problem, with the division of offices between the Bundestag *Fraktion* leader (Karl Carstens) and the CDU chairman (Helmut Kohl), both elected in the late spring of 1973. The failure of Barzel's approach, with the clear subordination of the party to the *Fraktion*, made it inevitable that the former would now receive greater attention than ever before. With the change in the balance of political weight from *Fraktion* to party, and the commitment of the new CDU leadership of Kohl and Biedenkopf (as CDU General Secretary) to party renewal, the basis for a different Opposition role from that of 1969-72 was formed.

The new political environment in which the CDU/CSU Opposition now operated meant that its attention was directed far more than during 1969-72 to its own position than the Government, whose legitimacy could no longer be viably questioned. The signs of a reversal to constructive opposition were indicated by the new tone adopted by party leaders. Barzel had advocated 'an untroubled yes to Opposition',[4] while in his speech to the Westphalian *Land* party congress in January 1973 he announced a changed strategy for the Bundestag *Fraktion*, whereby it would not automatically provide an answer to every Government proposal but concentrate on essential areas of policy and build towards the 'better alternative' for 1976.[5] Schröder similarly condemned a 'total Opposition' in a speech at Düsseldorf, although this was coupled with a warning that the Government should be ready for thorough and confidential discussions of a 'genuine consultative character' with the Opposition.[6] Kohl followed this through with warnings against 'Opposition at any price' and periodic offers of co-operation with the Government, notably in overcoming the country's economic and financial difficulties in the summer of 1975.[7]

The changed approach to the Opposition role by the CDU/CSU was not, however, without serious consequences for its unity and solidarity. Although the traumatic shock of 1972 substantially increased those voices in the leadership favouring party renewal, there were nevertheless major differences over Opposition strategy. These surfaced predictably between the CDU and CSU, for the latter was far less affected by the crisis of demoralisation following the 1972 Election. The CSU had gained electoral support unlike the CDU (with the exception of its gain in Hesse), while its self-confidence was generally buttressed by the personal nature of its leadership structure and its more pronounced conservative ideological stand-point than that of the CDU.[a] While the CDU pursued a reformist course under Kohl/Biedenkopf, the CSU remained adamant in its pursuit of intransigent opposition to Government policy.[2] The harshest manifestation of uncompromising opposition politics came in November 1974 with Strauss's speech at Sonthofen to a gathering of CSU activists, which took issue with CDU leaders who advocated co-operation with the Government because of the critical state of the country.[3] While not typical of Opposition thinking as a whole, the Sonthofen speech all the same highlighted differences of approach between the CSU leader and his party and the new CDU leadership. Although polarisation between Government and Opposition over policy issues was generally reduced during 1972-6, these remnants of principled opposition on the part of some CDU/CSU leaders[4] served, together with renewed attempts by Government leaders to cast doubts on the Opposition's legitimacy,[5] as a brake on the party's full adaptation to the role of Opposition.

These differences both between the CDU and CSU and within the CDU over the Opposition's approach naturally affected discussion within the CDU/CSU concerning its strategy for ensuring a return to power in 1976. While intransigent opposition was geared to the all-or-nothing aim of winning an absolute majority, the new CDU leadership of Kohl/Biedenkopf presented the alternative strategy of the 'coalition flirtation' process, creating the option of an eventual alliance in government with the FDP. This strategy, which was basic to the CDU's policy of renewal from 1973, depended on reducing

a See below chapter 10 (a), passim.

polarisation[6]   and took into consideration the difficulty under the West German electoral system of any one party acquiring an absolute majority.[7]   It gained credibility because of Kohl's own long fostered contacts with FDP leaders, but in the course of time this strategy faced difficulties because of the impact of political events. While 1973 had been a quiet year electorally, 1974 saw the commencement of a series of Landtag elections in which the CDU/CSU scored some dramatic gains at a cost to both Government parties.[8]   This produced a more aggressive CDU/CSU line towards the FDP, for one element arising in Biedenkopf's electoral strategy was that the Opposition should offer 'a genuine alternative' for liberal voters.[8] This could in the long term facilitate a common policy outlook with the FDP and possibly force the latter to reconsider its alliance with the SPD, but the immediate exigencies of everyday politics required the FDP to pay attention to its commitment to the Left-Liberal coalition. Brandt's political decline from late 1973 gave the Opposition new hope, but the change of Chancellor from Brandt to Schmidt in May 1974 once more pushed the CDU/CSU into a defensive position. It gave the Government a new lease of life at a critical time, particularly as Schmidt's assumption of office was accompanied by widespread changes in Cabinet personnel. The change of Chancellor compelled the Opposition to reconsider its strategy because Schmidt's conservative image and policy preferences deprived the CDU/CSU of many of its trump cards,[9] while the impression he created of strong leadership exposed a principal weakness of the Opposition for it had not yet settled on a Chancellor candidate.

The most important structural change which occurred in the CDU/CSU during 1972-6 was the increased political weight of the party as a whole vis-à-vis its Bundestag *Fraktion*, which was accompanied by a more pluralistic form of Opposition leadership.[10] During the first Opposition period, the Bundesrat (where the CDU/CSU had a majority of one) had begun to emerge as more of an alternative party political forum to the Bundestag with the tendency of the party's *Land* representatives to take uniform policy positions. Now that the CDU/CSU was likely to remain out of national office for at least four years, its leaders made increased use of the advantage under the West German federal system, whereby an Opposition party may still remain in government at the regional level and thus appoint *Land* representatives to the Bundesrat. Several CDU/CSU leaders, like Helmut Kohl (Minister-President of the Rhineland-Palatinate),

Gerhard Stoltenberg (Minister-President of Schleswig-Holstein), Hans
Filbinger (Minister-President of Baden-Württemberg) and later Ernst
Albrecht (who became Minister-President in Lower Saxony early
in 1976), acquired greater prominence in Bonn through their
development of the Bundesrat as an organ to vet, check or even
assert co-responsibility over Government policy measures. The most
publicised example of this activity came towards the end of the
legislative period, when the CDU/CSU Opposition led by Kohl
used its increased majority in the Bundesrat[11] to claim a say in
the ratification of the Polish treaties in 1976 and use the occasion to
demonstrate an affinity with the FDP leadership.

The enhanced role of the (extra-parliamentary) party was
evident in the successful efforts of the new CDU leadership from 1973
to improve party organisation and promote membership,[b] both of
which played an important part in reviving party morale. Their
attempt to further programmatic discussion in the CDU proved far
more difficult for, despite the first step in this direction with the
formulation of the Berlin Programme during 1967-8,[c] the party still
lacked the habits of internal debate which might have channelled
such a discussion in a disciplined way. Even after several years in
Opposition, the CDU had not yet overcome the fact that party
solidarity had for so long been built on support for its own Government policies while it was in office. Consequently, there was the
danger that programmatic discussion might provoke serious divisions
between the various interest groups contained within the CDU.
Thus, a meaningful discussion over policy direction would be a
principal test of how far the party could emancipate itself from
its former role in Government. For this reason, it is important to
examine the change of leadership which occurred early in the second
Opposition period, for unlike earlier occasions in the CDU's history
this was marked less exclusively by personal-political factors.

(b)   The Change of Leadership, 1973: Kohl and Biedenkopf

The change of leadership which occurred following Barzel's twin
resignations from the posts of *Fraktion* leader and CDU chairman in
May 1973 provided the first important stage in the party's development
of a politically independent profile in relation to its parliamentary

b   Party organisation and membership during 1972-6 are discussed separately
    below in chapters 7 (c) and 8 (b) respectively.
c   See above chapter 4 (d), pp. 177-80.

212 Christian Democracy in Western Germany

leadership. The separation of the two leadership positions resulted in the election of Karl Carstens as *Fraktion* leader and Helmut Kohl as CDU chairman and so created the opportunity for such a development, as did the fact that the issue over the successor for the CDU chairmanship was treated for the first time in the party's history as separate from that of the Chancellor candidacy. In both cases, there was a strong desire in the party to make a clean break with the recent past through a change of leadership personnel, particularly as Barzel and his entourage were associated with the unfortunate events of 1972, from the failed constructive vote of no-confidence in April to the electoral débâcle of November. Having only just been elected a Bundestag deputy, Carstens was viewed as a 'new face' by the *Fraktion* rank-and-file despite his long association with Schröder as secretary of state in the Foreign and Defence Ministries.[12] The election of Helmut Kohl, and Kurt Biedenkopf as CDU General Secretary, in June 1973 represented more obviously the rise of a new leadership generation in the party, for in spite of his relative youth Barzel was regarded as a member of the older generation of party leaders, having held the *Fraktion* leadership for nine years.[13] Biedenkopf was even more than Kohl a brand new face in the CDU leadership, for he had never before held a place in the party hierarchy.[14] Neither man had become a Bundestag deputy, so that they retained a freedom from the pressures of everyday parliamentary business to develop new approaches for the party.

Barzel's fall was predictable after the 1972 Election, for his claim to all three leadership positions of CDU chairman and Chancellor candidate, as well as *Fraktion* leader, involved a fateful political gamble, for his future career was thereby linked to the outcome of that election. Barzel's original political base of the Bundestag *Fraktion* was all the more weakened because its newly elected members proved more unmanageable to lead, containing as it did some 80 new deputies, none of whom felt obliged to Barzel for their election.[9] The decisive election result, condemning the CDU/CSU to long-term Opposition, encouraged a sense of independence in the *Fraktion* ranks and affected discipline vis-à-vis the *Fraktion* leadership.[15] Barzel's methods of tight control over *Fraktion* activities for the sake of effective Opposition to the Government were no longer suitable, so that his inability to cope with new political developments in the *Fraktion* affected his overall political authority. Barzel's position was also weakened by the presentation of a convincing alternative to him in the person of Kohl. Since his defeat by Barzel for the CDU chairmanship in 1971, Kohl had worked solidly visiting party managers in the *Landesverbände* and had made himself better known through more regular appearances in Bonn.[10] Barzel's election defeat immediately brought Kohl to the fore again as a leadership possibility, particularly as his promise of exclusive devotion to party affairs, supported by his name as a party reformer in the Rhineland-Palatinate, now seemed far more relevant to the needs of the CDU.

The process of Barzel's fall began with the challenge to him through the dispute between the CSU and the CDU about continuing the common *Fraktion* in the Bundestag during the weeks which followed the election.[d] This move promoted by Strauss aimed at embarrassing Barzel, even though Strauss had (with deliberate hesitation) proclaimed him 'Number One' in the CDU/CSU before the television cameras on election night. Barzel was, however, re-elected *Fraktion* chairman when the dispute was closed, though only for one year.[11] Once the New Year began, the attack on Barzel exposed his most vulnerable political point, the belief that he was an electoral liability. Internal party analyses of the election trends (notably that conducted by the North-Rhine Westphalian CDU)[12] portrayed a bleak picture for the future; just as the research institute of the Konrad Adenauer Foundation emphasised the 'loss of image' by the party at a time of social change.[13] The conclusion of the authoritative Allensbach Institute that Barzel had lost the party 3-4 per cent of the vote received publicity during a post-mortem meeting of the CDU Federal Executive at the end of January.[14] It was at this meeting that Kohl announced his candidacy for the CDU chairmanship. Once this choice was offered, Barzel's standing among the different *Landesverbände* declined progressively during the months which followed.[15] The most important breakthrough here for Kohl was the disintegration of support for Barzel in his own home base of North-Rhine Westphalia, which was influential in persuading him to resign the chairmanship following his dramatic resignation as *Fraktion* leader.[16] Kohl's timing of his announcement at this point that he would appoint Kurt Biedenkopf CDU General Secretary helped to push the tide further against Barzel, for Biedenkopf's own regional base was North-Rhine Westphalia.[16] Any hope that Barzel may have entertained that his resignation from the *Fraktion* leadership could revive his chances for re-election as CDU chairman were brusquely dashed at a crucial meeting of the Federal

d   See below chapter 10 (a), p. 311.

Executive in mid-May. This meeting demonstrated the thinness of solidarity behind Barzel, and irresistible pressure for a quick solution to the leadership crisis brought forward the date of the chairmanship election from the autumn to June.[17] Barzel's consequent withdrawal from the chairmanship election left no time for any rival to emerge against Kohl in the few weeks left before the special CDU Congress in Bonn.

Kohl was therefore the beneficiary of a demand for 'renewal' in the CDU, which showed itself in the decisive vote for him as chairman. He won the support of 520 of the 601 delegates, while Biedenkopf similarly gained 529 votes. There was a general sense of relief at Barzel's going. He had attempted to ride the wave of 'renewal' in the party after the 1972 Election by a series of reformist speeches advocating the need to 'go out and meet the people', but his effort to improve contact with the grass-roots came too late for his reputation as a parliamentary tactician was difficult to change. His closer alliance with the Social Committees after the Election and his reformist statements had only alienated the CSU and the CDU Right and were consequently seen as divisive. During the last weeks before Barzel's resignation his rivalry with Kohl had so embittered internal party relations and affected morale that work in the CDU headquarters had come virtually to a halt.[18] His first resignation had therefore made inevitable the second one.

The Barzel leadership crisis seemed at the time like a repetition of earlier painful episodes in the CDU's history. Barzel himself had warned against the personalisation of the party's wider crisis in his speech to the Federal Executive on 12 May: 'He who believes that all is solved by only a personal decision is not only programming the next crisis, but initiating it.'[19] There were, however, several reasons why the party was less likely to follow precedent. The urge to re-establish the party's identity was too strong to be ignored, so that expectations settled not so much on Kohl and Biedenkopf in person as on what they promised to achieve. Kohl was not, like Barzel, using the chairmanship merely as a springboard to the Chancellor candidacy, for he had been elected on the understanding that the latter question would be left open until 1975. This meant that his chances of becoming Chancellor candidate depended on his success as CDU chairman.

The Kohl/Biedenkopf team emphasised through their relative youth (they were both 43) the change of generation in the CDU leadership. Kohl's lack of association with the politics of Bonn — the advantageous side of his image as a 'provincial' — and Biedenkopf's new face in politics underlined that this was a new start for the party. Despite his inexperience at the Federal level, Kohl was in fact a political professional of fairly long standing in the Rhineland-Palatinate. The decisive question was how far his political skills were capable of leading the CDU out of the depths into which it had fallen. Two obvious tasks needed attention: the state of personal relations in the party was such that a healing remedy was an essential prescription, before which the long-term problem of reviving party morale could not be attempted. Kohl's skills in cultivating personal relationships in politics, together with his recognised ability to choose able advisers, made him a shrewd choice with regard to the first requirement.[20] The second task was far more difficult. It was clear from the beginning that Kohl's chief concern as CDU chairman was to act as integrator of his party. In an interview he gave to *Der Spiegel* shortly before his election, Kohl described his contribution as 'reviving and stabilising the self-awareness' of the party, and defined internal party integration as follows:

> Integrating does not mean sweeping conflicts or problems under the table. It means rather promoting conditions which make it possible for conflicts to be cleanly and fairly carried through, that in a party no hostile relations develop, that in the course of objective conflicts one can say clearly and decisively: that this will be carried through, then it must be voted on and then the will of the majority will prevail, during which one must always remember that the majority can be wrong and the minority right.[21]

Kohl's leadership was criticised at first for his not taking a strong enough line, as he tended to await the crystallisation of opinion in the party for too long.[22] The risk of his placing so much emphasis on integration that he lost his image as a party reformer was a subject of comment,[23] but Kohl apparently saw the need of a party chairman, particularly a new one, to keep open his lines of contact to all groups in the party. This included above all making continuous efforts to improve the basis of co-operation with the CSU and Strauss in particular, in which respect Barzel had failed so obviously. To this end, Kohl assumed a special responsibility for contacts with the CSU and sought patiently to cultivate a good working relationship with Franz Josef Strauss. Kohl remained noticeably silent on all issues during his first hundred days as new CDU chairman, which included the summer lull, and only towards the end of September 1973 did he reveal something of his intentions with his appointment of Walther Leisler Kiep as foreign policy spokesman of the CDU Praesidium.[17]

Kohl embarked on his career as party chairman with much goodwill, although his inheritance from Barzel was highly problematical. Much depended on his own political mettle, for it remained to be seen how far he would be able to establish a new form of leadership in style and substance which would serve to unite the party. As Heinrich Köppler, chairman of the Rhineland CDU, had noted at the time of Kohl's election, what the party needed were 'resolutions by the leadership which were commonly held' and 'close interlinking between Federal and *Länder* interests'.[24] In other words, the party should break with its recent history of highly personalised disputes within the leadership by allowing wider consultation over policy matters, so that differing viewpoints could be absorbed in the formulation of party policy positions. In this sense, demands that the CDU really wanted 'a second Adenauer'[25] were misguided, for collegial rather than authoritarian leadership was more suited to the CDU of the 1970s, although such speculations were correct in their stress on the need for the undisputed personal authority of its chairman.

Despite his solid personal qualities as a politician, Kohl lacked several of the obvious leadership skills. His absence of charisma and his mundane oratorical style were not fully compensated by his towering physical stature (hence his nickname, 'the black giant') and his robust political manner.[26] He nevertheless had several bases of support, such as his staff at the Minister-President's office in Mainz, and to a lesser extent the Rhineland-Palatinate representation office in Bonn, as well as his personal staff in the CDU chairman's office at party headquarters in Bonn, which included several young assistants in their earlier 30s like Wolfgang Bergsdorf and Helmuth Pütz. Kohl therefore spent part of the week in Mainz, and the rest in Bonn. To some extent Biedenkopf offset Kohl's political weaknesses, for the former was soon recognised as a key figure in the CDU, especially because of his ability to stimulate a lively interest within the party over its own activities, communicate new approaches on policy matters and harness academic talent for these purposes.[27] Biedenkopf conceived of his role as CDU General Secretary as substantially more political than any of his predecessors. He envisaged his task as not merely reforming party organisation, but also directing the process of discussion in the party: 'I will not formulate policy, but I will see to it that policy is formulated.'[28] According to Biedenkopf, the party's problem was that 'we have too many individual policies and too little coherent discussion' and he felt it was important that the CDU should learn to 'discuss in a disciplined manner'.

Under Kohl and Biedenkopf the CDU as a whole began to develop a new self-assurance and attracted a new public interest, especially as the Bundestag *Fraktion* continued to act with a lack of solidarity and, in contrast to the 1969-72 period, was less obviously the locus of party policy formulation. A revival of party morale, as now happened with the CDU, did not automatically create internal solidarity within the Opposition, for there remained in particular the unsolved question of relations with the CSU, not to mention remaining divisions over policy matters in the CDU itself. The real test of the political authority of the new CDU leadership was yet to come over the question of the Chancellor candidacy for the 1976 Bundestag Election. The CSU had played little direct part in the choice of CDU chairman in 1973. While the election of Kohl and Biedenkopf had offered the CDU a fresh start, it is important before examining their success in promoting programmatic discussion in the party to turn to the matter of the Chancellor candidacy. This would provide significant evidence on whether the CDU/CSU as a whole could draw further lessons from its Opposition role and solve this leadership question in a manner conducive to party integration.

(c) The Conflict over the Chancellor Candidacy, 1974-1975

The question of the Chancellor candidacy, which absorbed the CDU/ CSU's attention for more than one-and-a-half years until Kohl's final nomination in the early summer of 1975, was a far more difficult problem than the change in the CDU chairmanship because it involved a series of wider factors: the potential electoral appeal of the various possible contenders, especially in relation to the SPD Chancellor; their political weight and acceptability within the whole Opposition, including the CSU; and the availability of individual candidates. On the three previous occasions since Adenauer, the selection of CDU/CSU Chancellor candidate had been predetermined by the overriding claims of the incumbent Chancellor or (as in the case of Barzel) by the predominance of the influence of the *Fraktion*. During the second Opposition period, the situation was a more open one with the tendency towards a pluralistic leadership and the greater weight acquired by the (extra-parliamentary) CDU. This meant that there developed for the first time a real contest for the Chancellor candidacy nomination, involving wider consultation in the CDU/CSU. Even so, it must be discussed whether this contest amounted merely to a power struggle between party leaders (as the press inevitably portrayed it), or whether it also accorded with new demands for internal party democracy (especially in the CDU) and included discussion of alternative policy strategies. The selection of a Chancellor candidate was even less of an easy task because of the progressively divergent paths followed by the CDU and CSU, with the former's reformist course and the latter's more pronounced claims for its own political independence.

Since the likely Chancellor candidates were with one exception (Strauss) largely untried in Federal electoral terms, the first criterion had to be applied with reference to potential rather than proven electoral appeal.[18] Hence, the series of Landtag elections during 1974-5, which also dominated party activities at the same time as the evolution of the Chancellor candidacy, played an influential part. It was generally understood that the selection of the candidate would be finally made once the Landtag elections in the spring of 1975 were over. The CDU/ CSU therefore wished to make sure of its electoral strength regionally before committing itself, but in personal terms this procedure implied subjecting the possible candidates to an electoral popularity contest in their own *Länder:* Kohl in the Rhineland-Palatinate (March 1975); Stoltenberg in Schleswig-Holstein (April 1975); not to mention Strauss, whose national electoral strengths and weaknesses were already well-known, in Bavaria (October 1974). The Landtag elections did at least affect the timing of the selection, for it was argued that the early decision on a candidate, who later suffered an electoral setback in one of the *Länder,* would place the CDU/CSU in an impossible position for 1976.[29] Individual Landtag election results did affect attitudes towards the candidates in question, though they did not always prove decisive. The impressive victory of the CSU in Bavaria (with an increased absolute majority) and the significant rise in the vote for Dregger's CDU in Hesse on the same day in October 1974 strengthened support for a Strauss candidacy, but, as Strauss himself was later to remark provocatively to foreign journalists; 'If performance in state elections were the only criterion, I would be the only choice.'[30] The Bavarian result was inevitably presented by the Strauss camp as a measuring-rod for Kohl and Stoltenberg the following spring. Kohl's clear but not outstanding victory in the Rhineland-Palatinate meant that his chances were not substantially affected either way, while Stoltenberg's loss of support in Schleswig-Holstein seemed finally to erase his chances, which were in any case not strong. Opinion polls had played a subsidiary influence in gauging the potential popularity of the various candidates, though they were not particularly decisive. During 1974, they showed little difference between them all, while some revealed a certain lead in electoral appeal by Stoltenberg. By early 1975, polls moved in Kohl's favour and underlined as his main strength his credibility among voters.[31]

The electoral-appeal factor was not the exclusive determinant in the selection of Chancellor candidate. The importance of the Landtag elections was over emphasised for tactical reasons by some of the candidates, particularly those opposed to Kohl, who thought their chances would be improved by delaying the question until the further exposure of the Government's financial and economic difficulties strengthened the demand for an expert in this field, like Strauss or Stoltenberg. Further factors, however, countered such tactics, notably persistent pressure from the grass-roots in the CDU to settle the matter. By the autumn of 1974 this pressure could not be ignored, for Bundestag deputies tended to be asked in members' meetings when the Chancellor candidate would 'finally come'.[32] This reflected a feeling of defensiveness in the party since Schmidt's accession to the Chancellorship in the spring, for this had directed attention away from Brandt's declining authority to the absence of an obvious opponent to the new and vibrant Chancellor.

One decisive matter affecting the outcome of the contest over the Chancellor candidacy was the relationship between different elements within the CDU/CSU, and how far each of the possible candidates was acceptable to them. This meant, in other words, their respective ability to harness the various and sometimes conflicting internal party groups for electoral purposes. Kohl had a leading advantage over his rivals because of his position as CDU chairman, since this placed him in a stronger position than Stoltenberg, and also Carstens, to cultivate these different groups. Once Kohl's candidacy was launched in 1974, it became increasingly difficult to refuse him without affecting morale in the CDU. The acid test of Kohl's candidacy was his performance as CDU chairman, for his claim to the nomination would be based largely on his success in renovating the party, which was the essential precondition for an election victory in 1976.

The major risk faced by Kohl was that his record as party integrator would fall too short of expectations for his candidacy to be regarded as viable. His chief danger lay in relations between the two Opposition parties. Kohl's own contacts with the CSU had not previously been so close as those of other CDU leaders, but since his election as CDU chairman he had been assiduous in cultivating Strauss through regular telephone consultations and even hikes with him in the Bavarian mountains.[33] The conflict point between him and Strauss arose with the latter's own availability as Chancellor candidate. Strauss had the stronger political temperament of the two, and the more evident leadership qualities, if only because he was more experienced than Kohl. For this reason his attempts to undermine Kohl[19] had a powerful effect, even if they also alienated opinion in the CDU and helped eventually to discredit Strauss's own chances. Strauss's crucial weakness was his lack of acceptability among broad sections of the CDU, even though he excelled at mobilising grass-roots feeling in the party. Strauss's incapacity to integrate the CDU/CSU because of his divisive personality, together with the antipathy he aroused among the electorate at large, basically undermined his candidacy, rather than simply the fact he was leader of the smaller of the two Opposition parties.

Kohl's main tactical strength was that he emerged as the only real rival to Strauss, so that Kohl's preference for allowing situations to develop paid off. Kohl's advantages concerning the CDU/CSU's possible return to power were his appeal to floating voters, essential for obtaining an absolute majority, and his good links with the FDP; but his selection as Chancellor candidate was by no means a foregone conclusion at the outset. Doubts persisted for some time in sections of the CDU, especially in North Germany, that Kohl's 'provincial' image would fail to mobilise the party.[34] The change of Chancellor in 1974 encouraged these doubts, particularly as Kohl's relative lack of expertise in economic and financial affairs seemed to offer a weak alternative to Schmidt. There was pressure on Stoltenberg to declare himself, for, not only did he cut a better figure in this respect, but he was also more experienced on the national stage. Stoltenberg's candidacy eventually had little chance, partly because of his half-heartedness in pushing his case and partly because he lacked the kind of wide support Kohl was already finding in the CDU.[35]

The fourth possible candidate was Karl Carstens, chairman of the CDU/CSU Bundestag *Fraktion* since 1973. He was a respected figure in conservative circles and was very presentable on television, but his chances as candidate sank due to his disappointing performance as *Fraktion* leader, the main complaint being that he not so much directed politically as merely 'administered' the *Fraktion*.[36] Carstens had developed a style of leadership contrary to that of his predecessor, Barzel, for the former allowed much more internal consultation in the *Fraktion* as a whole over policy matters with the emphasis on discussion rather than decisions.[37] This was, however, necessary because CDU backbenchers were showing a greater independence than ever before, as a result of which a planning group was formed in 1973 to assist backbench involvement in policy-making.[38] Added to this was the political status of the CSU group of deputies as a *Fraktion* within the *Fraktion*.[e] With this diffuse situation, effective leadership of the Bundestag *Fraktion* became more difficult. It was also not helped by the presence of too many claimant spokesmen on individual policy areas, or in the principal case of economic affairs the absence of a competent spokesman.[20] It could therefore be said that Carstens' political profile in the CDU/CSU suffered from the reduced status of the *Fraktion,* just as that of Helmut Kohl benefited from the greater self-awareness of the CDU as a political party.

By the end of 1974 the contest for Chancellor candidate had effectively narrowed down to Kohl and Strauss. While Strauss probably assessed realistically his chances as being restricted by strong opposition to his candidacy at all levels of the CDU, there was nevertheless intensive pressure from his own party and solid conservative groups in the CDU for him to stand. Strauss's minimal aim was to strengthen his 'say' in the Opposition's policy, especially for the election, and secure a strongly influential future role in Government, but he was sufficiently tempted by the prospect of his own candidacy to offer Kohl his strongest rivalry.[21] What finally destroyed Strauss's remaining chances and left the field open for Kohl was his highly controversial speech at Sonthofen, which reinforced old feelings about Strauss as an unpredictable 'man of order'.[f] Kohl was not, however, confirmed as Chancellor candidate without further party in-fighting, which further soured relations between the CDU and CSU and encouraged general speculation for a time that the conflict over the Chancellor candidacy was undermining the Opposition's chances in the 1976 Election.[22] This was sensed in the CDU, for Kohl's re-election as party chairman by the outstanding vote of 696 out of 707 delegates at the Mannheim Congress in June 1975 was an effort to strengthen solidarity behind Kohl from fear that his conflict with Strauss might reflect adversely on his leadership qualities.[39] The month before the CDU Federal Executive had voted unanimously for Kohl's nomination,[40] and so the matter was formally settled as the CSU reluctantly supported Kohl in the interests of the common cause, though with the unflattering dissenting statement that it still regarded Strauss as 'the suitable candidate'.[41]

The conflict over the Chancellor candidacy illustrated in a dramatic

e   For further discussion of this point, see below chapter 10 (a), pp. 305-6.
f   See above chapter 6 (a), p. 209.

way the difficulties faced by Helmut Kohl in playing the role of party
integrator, particularly as the two Christian Democratic parties had
grown farther apart during the years of Opposition. This same problem
was manifested in another form in the autumn of 1975, when
complications arose over the selection of party leaders for the ten-man
'team' to supervise election strategy. Although this 'team' was
justified as a form of collegial leadership, disagreements occurred over
the need to placate different groups in the CDU/CSU and the old habit
in the party of regarding personalities as representing political tendencies
within the CDU/CSU reappeared.[23]

Kohl's nomination as Chancellor candidate had come about as a
result of a process of elimination, during which he had demonstrated a
greater ability than his predecessor Barzel in handling relations with the
CSU. Kohl's strength was the solidarity for him within the CDU, which
had become his firm power base, whereas Barzel's basis of support had
been the Bundestag *Fraktion* (which of course included the CSU) and
not the extra-parliamentary CDU. This difference in the location of
political support indicated in turn the special significance of the contest
for Chancellor candidacy in 1974-5, for it involved wider consultation
than on any previous occasion. While it saw a repetition of the
embarrassing personalisation of issues within the CDU/CSU leadership,
the matter was decided this time within the party more widely than at
the parliamentary level.

(d)   Reorientation and Revival

The CDU/CSU had in the past sought to effect change within the bounds
of continuity along traditionally determined lines. Such change had
always been of a restricted nature, for as a Government-orientated or
dependent political party it had attempted to adapt to new political
circumstances primarily through a change of leadership. This tradition
of solving its political problems by a personal change at the top had
characterised the CDU/CSU since the ascendancy of Adenauer, and was
especially evident in the way in which the party recognised the need for
electoral cosmetics.[g] The tradition was not carried into the first
Opposition years after 1969, for the person chosen to lead the party
back to power lacked strong voter appeal. The decisive electoral defeat
of 1972 finally persuaded the CDU in particular to change its method
of adapting the party to new political circumstances. The shock of 1972

---

g   See below chapter 11 (b) for a discussion of the CDU/CSU's dependence on
popular appeal of the Chancellor in Bundestag elections.

so pervaded the CDU that recognition of the need for a thorough re-assessment of its traditional methods of adaptation proved irresistible. It was realised that the exclusive reliance on a popular leader-figure was no longer possible in the role of Opposition. In 1973 the CDU elected with Kohl and Biedenkopf for the first time leaders who were committed seriously to programmatic revival.

There was another wider problem associated with the need for party renovation. Since Adenauer's rise to the leadership at the end of the 1940s during the height of the Cold War, the CSU/CSU had developed into a markedly pragmatic political force, for its various ideological motives did not provide a cohesive basis for political activity.[h] The early assumption of government responsibility by the CDU/CSU had solidified this development, but in the course of its long years in national office the party's self-identity had become weakened, and from the early 1960s it progressively lost its sense of orientation. The increasing challenge by the SPD during the 1960s to the political dominance of the CDU/CSU, which had acted as a unifying force of the centre and right, was crowned by the result of 1972, so that a re-examination of its ideological motivation by the party was now imperative. Concerned at the CDU/CSU's image acquired during 1972 of becoming a sectional party for the interests of employers (*Unternehmer-Partei*),[i] even the old leadership under Barzel had recognised the need for programmatic revitalisation and laid the groundwork for the Hamburg Congress of November 1973 which marked its official beginning.[42] [24] The CDU was at last recognising that the era of the 'pragmatic' 1950s had long since become history, and that in the West Germany of the 1970s a special importance was placed on programmatic positions in politics. In doing so, the CDU pinpointed an essential difference between itself and the CSU as a political party, for the latter had developed a much lower degree of internal party democracy and revealed a high dependence on its charismatic leader.[j] Indeed, the programmatic revival which characterised the CDU from 1973 hardly affected the CSU.[25] There was a further internal party reason for the trend towards programmatic discussion. By the mid-1970s, the CDU had become in a quantitative sense a membership-party with its extraordinary rise in membership from 1972.[k] This radical change inevitably affected internal party relations, for not

h   See above chapter 1 (c), pp. 40-52.
i   See below chapter 11 (c) on 1972 Election.
j   See below chapter 10 (b).
k   See below chapter 8 (b).

only had the vast majority of members joined since the beginning of the Opposition period but they had different expectations from older members. A survey of 1975 of CDU members who had joined since 1970 showed that their chief reason for doing so was interest in policy matters or 'political-programmatic'.[43] A higher level of internal party democracy was therefore a necessary consequence of the CDU's growth as a membership-party, and indeed such democracy was the principal characteristic of a membership-party. In responding to all these changes the CDU was attempting to meet the challenge of its Opposition role. This would provide the crucial test of its adaption to the loss of power.

The leading figure in the CDU's efforts at programmatic reorientation and revival was undoubtedly Kurt Biedenkopf, the new General Secretary of the CDU. Biedenkopf provided in this way the essential complement to Kohl's aim of political integration in the party emanating with the new generation of CDU leadership. Biedenkopf's ideas were emphasised in his first speeches in office, and were developed in a series of addresses and interviews in the years which followed.[26] The essence of Biedenkopf's approach was that the CDU should break with its past habit of thinking merely in terms of 'stereo-typed ideas'.[44] In order to return to Government, the CDU had to regain 'substance of principle' and show that it was capable of offering 'a political prescription for the future, that it presented an objective at which to aim and demanded the co-operation of the citizens'.[45] With the loss of office in 1969, it had become clear that the party had not been successful in developing 'its own "political philosophy" in the sixties'.[46] As Kohl himself noted in his acceptance speech as new CDU chairman in June 1973, 'the changes in society, the growing-up of a new and younger generation, the consequences of the Bundestag elections for our policy — all this must be well considered'.[47] A frequent leitmotiv in this approach was the need to respond to the demands of the younger generation and to establish a dialogue with intellectuals.[48] It was especially in relation to the latter that the party had, according to Biedenkopf, been most on the defensive since the 1960s.[49] Partly with this in mind, Biedenkopf encouraged a specialist interest in the skills of political speech in concert with the development of political concepts.[27] He drew attention to the importance of this in his speech to the CDU Congress in November 1973, when he said that speech involved not just 'a means of communication . . . but also an important means of the strategy', for it was a question of 'possessing the concepts' so that the CDU had something to say.[50]

There was a variety of motives behind Biedenkopf's policy as General

Secretary, although these amounted to different aspects of the same overall strategy. Biedenkopf had said in his speech at the Catholic Academy in Bavaria in December 1973 that the problem with the CDU/CSU was not so much the lack of programme as the lack of 'programmatic leadership'. In other words, he was saying that the party should give new life to its ideological motivations though adjust them to the conditions of the 1970s: hence the adamant denial by CDU politicians that the party needed a 'Godesberg' along the lines of the SPD in 1959.[51] The emphasis was placed on creating an 'alternative' to the values represented by the Government parties, particularly the SPD (hence the new slogan, 'Alternative '76'). The intention of Biedenkopf was to bring the CDU out of its defensive corner, and re-establish its self-identity. This line was evident in both Biedenkopf's speech to the Catholic Academy and in Kohl's speech to the Mannheim Congress in June 1975 when he asserted:

> The CDU is today *the* liberal, *the* social, *the* conservative party in the Federal Republic of Germany — based on firm principles but not ideologically constricted, it is prepared for acting decisively with clear alternatives in German policy.[52]

In conjunction with the revival of party self-confidence went a strategy of mobilisation against the SPD as the embodiment of 'socialism'. A crucial factor in the raising of a party's morale is the unqualified location of the political enemy and identification of it in simplified conceptual terms. Biedenkopf's aggressive and all-embracing designation of the SPD as 'socialist' enthused party activists at a time when the left-wing of the SPD was exerting stronger influence.

Biedenkopf's approach, however, arose not only from internal party motives. Like the whole of his strategy, it was electorally orientated. As Biedenkopf announced when he assumed the General Secretaryship, the election campaign for 1976 would 'begin tomorrow'. The long-term projection to the next Bundestag Election (as Kohl put it in his speech of June 1973, 'steering to 1976') coloured the speeches of both CDU leaders during these three years. The Mannheim Declaration, a further stage in the party's programmatic development, was introduced in the summer of 1975 as the basis for the election manifesto of 1976, while Biedenkopf declared in an interview on the CDU/CSU's election strategy, in September 1975, that the party hoped to 'win a considerable section of floating voters with this policy'.[53] The electoral arm of this programmatic strategy in fact stretched further, aiming to attract support from FDP voters on the basis that the CDU stood for true 'liberal' policies.

The question arises of how 'new' the CDU had really become. One critic of Biedenkopf's strategy disputes this on the grounds that what he really changed was the party's antiquated image.[54] Biedenkopf certainly combined a new style and presentation with the skilful use of marketing methods and a revival of traditional Christian Democratic ideology. Biedenkopf also followed party tradition in that his policy of programmatic reform was above all electorally motivated. There could be some confusion between the aim of refurbishing the party image and that of delineating its programmatic stand, but in fact both aims served the same purpose for Biedenkopf argued that the Christian Democrats could only win the next election if they also looked beyond it, and indeed the revival of party morale was crucial to the conduct of the election campaign. If only for electoral purposes the image of an opportunistic party had to be erased, for the CDU had to stand for something in order to attract new voters. Hence, Kohl introduced the Mannheim Declaration as a 'strategy paper', rather than a programme, which would serve both as 'argumentation help' for the increasing number of party members at the next election and as a means of reaching a broad cross-section of voters.[55] Similarly, the 'New Social Question' (*Neue Soziale Frage*), the centrepiece of the Mannheim Declaration which argued that the state must protect the unorganised sections of society against powerful groups and associations, aimed at providing the party with an outlet from the formerly defensive postion it had held in the field of social policy.[28] Biedenkopf's programmatic strategy therefore amounted to a method of internal and external mobilisation for the CDU. The 'thinking' image which Biedenkopf projected for the CDU always had an implicit political purpose, even on such occasions as the podium discussion he held with the noted philosophers Herbert Marcuse and Alexander Mitzcherlich in September 1976 during the Bundestag election campaign.[56] This strategy assumed an acceptance of the Opposition role, for according to Biedenkopf: 'From the position of Opposition one can formulate concrete policies only conditionally, for here the Government is always at an advantage; therefore an Opposition must in the main offer principled alternatives.'[57]

There were, however, many internal party problems facing Biedenkopf's strategy. These stemmed principally from the CDU/CSU's heterogeneous character and the lack of harmony between many of its internal groups. Just as Biedenkopf hoped to free the party's programmatic stand from too close an association with individual interest pressures, he had also to beware of so offending internal party groups

that his strategy came unstuck. A major pointer to the changing
character of the CDU would be how far it could now engage in programmatic discussion without this leading to serious internal conflict.
The problem was illustrated in a small way by Biedenkopf's reassertion
of the value of the Ahlen Programme (of 1947)^l in 1975, which
caused an uproar in the CSU;[58] while his presentation of the 'New
Social Question' occasioned protests from the party's eminence
grise, Ludwig Erhard, forcing Kohl to intervene and conciliate the
father of the social market economy.[59] According to Erhard,
Biedenkopf's 'political reorientation of the CDU' had provoked
'weighty irritations'.[60]

Much depended on the internal balance of forces within the
party, as was shown by the dispute at the Hamburg Congress in
November 1973 over worker participation. This had been a very
divisive issue both during the discussions over the Berlin Programme
and during the first Opposition period.^m Largely under pressure from
the Social Committees, which were hoping for a more influential role
following the shock of 1972, the question was raised as the centre-
piece of discussion of domestic issues in 1973.[61] The dispute
provoked the hostility of the party's Economic Council and other
conservative groups, not to mention the unconcealed scorn of the CSU
for the Social Committees.[62] A serious split was eventually prevented
after strong intervention by Biedenkopf and Kohl, who formulated a
compromise draft on behalf of the Federal Executive which received
the approval of the Congress.[29] This was conducted in such a way as
not to alienate the Social Committees too far in spite of their
evident disappointment, while it also avoided a serious setback for
the new leadership which would have occurred if their compromise
formula had been rejected or if there had been a serious outbreak
of disunity.[63]

A crucial factor in the movement for programmatic revival in
the CDU was Kohl's own role as conciliator of different internal
party interests. This often proved a difficult task in the first years of
his leadership, when he had yet to show his political fibre, so that
his reluctance for the sake of party unity to be too specific about party
policies opened him to charges of hesitation. He was all the same a
determined supporter of 'discussion' within the party at all levels,
a feature which achieved momentum because of the active interest

l   See above chapter 1 (a), pp. 25,31.
m   See above chapter 4 (d), pp. 179-80 and 5 (b), p. 196.

in policy matters among the many new members in the CDU.[n]
Biedenkopf's systematic visits to party district branches from the
time of his election as General Secretary also helped to promote
this new tendency.[64] Kohl was also instrumental in his encouragement
of programmatically-minded leaders in the CDU, notably in the case
of Richard von Weizsäcker,[30]   who chaired the Basic Policy
Commission (*Grundsatzkommission*), which started work on formulating a new long-term policy outlook for the party in the spring of
1974.[31]   The Commission set out to 'submit to the Federal
Executive and the party proposals as to how the CDU can achieve its
aims and meet the political challenges of the time'.[65] The draft
version of the Basic Policy Programme presented in the spring of
1976 included an emphasis on social solidarity as a Christian
principle and was particularly noted for its restatement of the
concept of freedom as a fundamental value: 'Freedom based on
responsibility is the central element of Christian Democratic policy.'[66]
The latter theme had already been taken up by Helmut Kohl in his
first speech as CDU chairman in June 1973, when he had called
the CDU the 'party of dynamic freedom'. The concept of freedom,
which was one of the original ideological motives of Christian
Democracy in West Germany,[o] later became the central theme of the
CDU/CSU's main slogan in the 1976 Election: 'Freedom instead of/or
Socialism'.

The most dangerous threat to the party's renovation and
solidarity came predictably in the field of Ostpolitik, especially as
this involved potential policy clashes with the CSU. While the era of
Ostpolitik was largely over by 1973, there were enough remaining
questions, like the Nuclear Proliferation Treaty, the treaty with
Czechoslovakia and the European Security Conference, to remind
the public of the Opposition's previous negative and divisive
attitude. It proved impossible to break with past positions, if only
because of strong fundamentalist pressure from the CSU in particular
on these questions.[67] Kohl's original conciliatory line, that the party
would henceforth work on the basis of the Ostpolitik treaties
concluded, became difficult to implement. Even though the public
showed a more sober attitude towards Ostpolitik from 1973-4, the
Opposition was unable to harness this new mood, so that even though
Kohl was himself a moderate critic of Ostpolitik he was forced by the

n   See below chapter 8 (b), especially pp. 285-6 for an elaboration of this point.
o   See above chapter 1 (a), pp. 29-30.

state of internal party relationships to reserve his position.[68] While Ostpolitik most expressed the party's divisiveness, it also distracted attention from the CDU's efforts to build its renovated image in the field of domestic policy. Only with the issue early in 1976 of the Polish treaties on financial arrangements between the two countries was Kohl able with considerable persistence to regain some credibility in this field. With Poland's willingness to make a small concession and with the help of the new CDU Minister-President in Lower Saxony, Ernst Albrecht,[32] the Opposition allowed approval of the treaties in the Bundesrat while at the same time demonstrating a like-mindedness with the FDP and causing some confusion and disunity in the CSU.[69]

Having avoided a repetition of its earlier traumas over Ostpolitik, the Opposition embarked on its Bundestag election campaign in 1976 fortified by a revived party morale and condition of preparedness in contrast to its state of disarray and uncertainty at the time of the 1972 Election.[33] Its election result, the best since Adenauer's triumph of 1957, reflected its recovery from the doldrums of the first Opposition period, for unlike the years 1969-72 the party had chosen with the change of CDU leadership in 1973 to come to terms with the loss of national office. In short, the CDU had at last attempted to meet the challenge increasingly made since the early 1960s that it should 'become a political party'. This had been possible because the party had realised that its future electoral fortunes would depend basically on its success in reforming itself, and therefore its shorter-term electoral strategy for 1976 dovetailed with its overall strategy for revival. This process was also facilitated by changed political circumstances in the Federal Republic, for growing disillusionment with the SPD/FDP coalition in Bonn, a new conservative mood among the public and the transfer of political debate to the domestic field all provided the Christian Democrats with an opportunity for presenting a convincing alternative to the Left-Liberal government.

At the same time, this reorientation did not encompass the whole of the Opposition. While the CDU evidenced a political self-confidence not seen since the 1950s and had made significant progress with its development of a better organisation and a much larger and more participatory membership than ever before, the CSU did not undergo such a process of change because in its case electoral pressures were less strong and the continuity of its leadership under Strauss ensured against party reform. The state of party integration within the CDU had

improved considerably by 1976, but this also involved less solidarity
in its relations with its Bavarian sister party. The greater difficulties
in the CDU/CSU alliance appeared soon after the 1976 Election in a
dispute over the Opposition's future strategy towards the FDP[70] and
was highlighted in the temporary rupture of the common Bundestag
Fraktion during November-December 1976.[p] In the light of this
problem, several questions remained open about the Opposition's
future role, while furthermore Kohl's election as leader of the CDU/
CSU Bundestag *Fraktion* in addition to his retention of the CDU
chairmanship and Biedenkopf's resignation as CDU General Secretary
in 1977 brought about a new change in the personal structure of the
CDU leadership.[71]

Whatever the outcome of the CDU/CSU's continued course as an
Opposition party, and naturally this relates to the question of its
return to national office, the achievements of the Kohl/Biedenkopf
collegial leadership of the CDU during 1973-7 were an important
milestone in the history of the party.[72] Primarily, the CDU had
overcome its crisis of identity which had derived from its political
decline since the ascendancy of Adenauer. The most significant aspect
of the party's adaptation from the role of Government to that of
Opposition was its ability to 'recharge' its ideological batteries as a
Christian Democratic movement to take account of new moods in
West German politics in the 1970s. While certain ideological themes
had remained apparent during the CDU/CSU's long years as a
'pragmatic' governing party – notably, anti-Communism, the social-
market economy and European integration – these were redeveloped
or, as with other leitmotivs in Christian Democracy, given new force.
Just as the Mannheim Declaration of 1975 began with a reference to
the work of Adenauer and Erhard, so the CDU/CSU played an active
part in promoting the integration of Christian Democratic parties at the
European level with a view to direct elections to the European
Parliament. This occurred in concert with a new emphasis on the
concept of freedom, the formulation of an alternative to democratic
socialism and even a revival of the principles of Christian socialism.
The result of this reorientation of the CDU was not so much that it
changed from a pragmatic to a consciously ideological party, as
that it sought a middle way by becoming programmatic in its
political activity to an extent not witnessed since its early years after
the Second World War. As Kurt Biedenkopf had envisaged the role

p   See below chapter 10 (a), pp. 313-14.

of the party in his speech to the Catholic Academy in Bavaria in 1973:

> The policy of the Union is the policy of a *Volkspartei*. The task of a *Volkspartei* is not to translate theories into reality, but to secure majorities capable of governing. As a constitutionally viable organ for forming the political will, it fulfills in this way an integration function indispensable for the functioning of the state . . . In view of its theoretical commitments in politics, a *Volkspartei* is set certain limits in individual questions. Translating its basic positions into practice allows as a rule various possibilities for forming arrangements. In a *Volkspartei* these possibilities can be disputed without the principles concerned being called into question . . . For this reason it is essential that a *Volkspartei* restores a functionable balance between theoretical obligations and a necessary openness towards alternatives . . . If it is important for a *Volkspartei* to find a suitable balance between commitment to theory and pragmatic openness, it faces at the same time the danger of avoiding necessary fundamental political obligations through a flight into pragmatism. The CDU has not remained exempt from this danger. At least in the recent past it has suffered basically more from a lack of programmatically-orientated leadership than from the lack of programmes.[73]

Notes

[1]   The view of the younger party reformers in '*Sonde*', the publication of the CDU/CSU student organisation, that Brandt was the 'embodiment of the Landesvater' and could beat any Chancellor of the Opposition (*Die Zeit*, 5 January 1973) was held fairly widely among regional and local party organisers, according to the impressions gained by the author during interviews in the late summer of 1973.

[2]   E.g. Strauss's demand late in 1972 that a renewal of the CDU/CSU *Fraktion* in the Bundestag was only possible, when the CDU agreed to a rejection of the General Treaty with the DDR. At Strauss's prompting, the CSU Bavarian *Land* cabinet applied to the Constitutional Court for a ruling against this treaty.

[3]   The text of Strauss's highly controversial speech was published later by *Der Spiegel* (10 March 1975, pp. 34-41), causing a public uproar because it implied that any means of exposing the Government's failures were justified for the sake of bringing about its fall before the 1976 Election.

[4]   E.g. also Carstens' much publicised statement early in 1974 that the CDU/CSU was the 'only political force' opposing subversion of the

'democratic order based on freedom' and that the Government had an underdeveloped sense of 'constitutional loyalty' (*Deutschland Union-Dienst*), 2 January 1974).

[5]   Notably Brandt's remark at the SPD Congress in November 1975 that the CDU/CSU Opposition was a 'security risk for the Federal Republic in foreign as in domestic policy, economic as well as social' (*Rheinischer Merkur*, 21 November 1975).

[6]   See the interview with Walther Leisler Kiep, whom Kohl appointed as foreign-policy spokesman for the CDU Praesidium in 1973, with *Die Zeit*, 1 December 1972, when he commented: 'By reducing polarisation in foreign policy and restoring a common basis for all parties, we will make it easy for the FDP in future to enter a coalition with the CDU in a few *Länder* and perhaps later also at the Federal level.' Kiep was viewed as a strong representative of the 'liberal' approach in the CDU, and in 1976 became a minister in the new CDU *Land* cabinet under Ernst Albrecht in Lower Saxony with a view to a later coalition with the FDP there. This coalition was formed early in 1977.

[7]   This had occurred only once when the CDU/CSU won an absolute majority in 1957.

[8]   The CDU/CSU's most impressive gains during 1974 were 7.8 per cent in Hamburg, 7.6 per cent in Hesse and 5.7 per cent in Bavaria, while its support in the 1975 *Land* elections also increased though less dramatically. (For a comprehensive discussion of *Land* elections during 1974-5, see the special number of the *Zeitschrift für Parlamentsfragen*, December 1975).

[9]   Schmidt was viewed from the CDU/CSU Opposition as representing many Christian Democratic policy positions, so that with the new Chancellor the Opposition had 'few points of attack' for the time being until mistakes occurred or unemployment rose (interview with Jürgen Heidborn, personal assistant to Richard von Weisäcker, Bonn, September 1974).

[10]   For an interesting discussion of this change, see the article by Carl-Christian Kaiser 'Die Speerspitze ist stumpf geworden: Machtverschieb-ung in der CDU – nicht die Fraktion, die Partei gibt den Ton an' in *Die Zeit*, 11 October 1974.

[11]   The Opposition's majority in the Bundesrat rose to eleven early in 1976, after the election of a minority CDU government in Lower Saxony under Ernst Albrecht, which replaced the previous coalition of SPD/FDP.

[12]   Karl Carstens, born 1914, had been a CDU member since the late 1950s and was secretary of state under Schröder, who was successively Foreign and Defence Minister in the 1960s, until later he became state secretary in the Chancellor's Office under Kiesinger from 1967. A north German from Bremen, he was persuaded by his colleagues from Schleswig-Holstein, Stoltenberg and von Hassel, to stand for the Bundestag in 1972. Carstens made an impressive maiden speech early in 1973 on Ostpolitik, which created a sense of euphoria among CDU/CSU deputies leading to his defeat of Schröder and von Weizsäcker for the *Fraktion* leadership in May 1973 (see profiles of Carstens in *Die Zeit*, 23 February 1973 and *FAZ*, 12 May 1973).

[13]   The lack of generation change in the CDU/CSU leadership during the first Opposition period was emphasised by the party's 'quadriga' of leaders presented to the electorate in 1972 with Barzel, Strauss, Schröder and Katzer, all of whom had been prominent figures in the party in different ways through the 1960s.

[14]   The career of Kurt Biedenkopf, who like Kohl was born in 1930, had
        previously included a university chair of economic law, the rectorship
        of Bochum University and a senior managerial position in the chemical
        firm of Henkel. He had been a member of the CDU organisation's
        committee on economic affairs, and was a renowned expert on worker
        participation, on which he had been consulted in the formulation of the
        Berlin Programme during 1967-8. He had first made a political
        appearance with his selection by Heinrich Köppler for his team in the
        Land election campaign in North-Rhine Westphalia in 1970.

[15]   The leadership of the *Fraktion* was complicated also by the fact that
        many more CDU/CSU deputies than before had been elected in 1972 on
        the party list rather than with a direct mandate. This meant that internal
        party interest groups were represented more prominently in the *Fraktion*,
        making it less cohesive as a body (interview with Thomas Jansen,
        personal assistant to Rainer Barzel, in Bonn, September 1973).

[16]   Barzel resigned the *Fraktion* chairmanship in May 1973 over the issue
        of West German entry to the United Nations, which was linked with
        acceptance of the General Treaty with the DDR. Barzel associated his
        own prestige with this issue, but the CDU/CSU *Fraktion* voted 101-93
        against UNO entry. The CSU voted as a bloc among the 'no' votes,
        while two-thirds of the CDU deputies voted in favour of entry. The 'no'
        votes were motivated by a mixture of personal (anti-Barzel) and policy
        reasons (see *FAZ*, 10 May 1973 and *Die Zeit*, 18 May 1973).
        According to Franzheinrich Krey, business manager of the Rhineland
        CDU, Barzel's resignation as *Fraktion* leader led to an immediate
        collapse of support in the Rhineland party for his remaining as CDU
        chairman (interview with Krey in Cologne, August 1973). In the case of
        the Westphalian CDU, Barzel's regional base, the *Landesverband* leader-
        ship had wanted both candidates for the CDU chairmanship to appear
        at a meeting for a discussion of their policy intentions. Barzel had
        somewhat arrogantly replied that everyone knew him already as a
        Westphalian, and refused the invitation (interview with Günter Rinsche,
        CDU Mayor of Hamm, in Hamm, August 1973).

[17]   Walther Leisler Kiep, who was still CDU Treasurer, was regarded as
        an 'outsider' in the party especially as he had almost alone advocated
        a positive attitude towards Ostpolitik during the first Opposition period.
        Kiep's appointment was regarded both as a 'signal' to the FDP because
        of his moderate views on foreign policy and his general 'liberal' image,
        and as an attempt by Kohl to integrate different viewpoints in the
        party leadership. Because his sudden appointment of Kiep caused
        consternation among conservative CDU and also CSU members of the
        Bundestag *Fraktion*, Kohl felt compelled to play down the significance
        of the appointment, emphasising Carstens' predominance in representing
        the party on foreign policy. He nevertheless added that minority views
        should also have some weight in the Praesidium (*Die Zeit*, 28 September
        1973).

[18]   There were four candidates considered seriously: Helmut Kohl,
        Franz Josef Strauss, Gerhard Stoltenberg and Karl Carstens. Biedenkopf
        was never a strong possibility, although mention of his name reflected
        the high regard in the CDU for his performance as General Secretary.
        He was in any case at this stage ultimately dependent politically on Kohl,
        who had appointed him.

[19]   For instance, his remarks in interviews with *Der Spiegel* and *Stern* that 'Herr
        Kohl is an extraordinarily successful minister-president, but he himself

must recognise where his limitations lie', and his 'Churchillian' comment that there was an absence of 'great personalities of contemporary history'.

[20]   Based on interviews with Wolfgang Bergsdorf and Helmuth Pütz, CDU chairman's office in the party headquarters, Bonn, in September 1974 and July 1976.

[21]   These comments are based on interviews with Lothar Späth, CDU *Fraktion* chairman in the Landtag of Baden-Württemberg, in Stuttgart, August 1976, and with Dieter Kiehl, spokesman of the CSU, in Munich, September 1976. Strauss's visit to see Mao Tse-tung in Peking in January 1975 and his election appearances in North-Rhine Westphalia from the end of 1974 were designed to promote his public impact. There was the additional psychological problem for Strauss that Kohl's nomination as Chancellor candidate would underline in a supreme way the rise of the younger generation of party leaders (Kohl was nearly 15 years younger than Strauss).

[22]   Strauss's challenge to Kohl was taken to the extreme lengths of occasional pessimistic hints about the CDU/CSU's chances for 1976. The final move to settle on Kohl was taken by Biedenkopf, who publicly recommended Kohl at the end of April 1975 just before the *Land* election in North-Rhine Westphalia, for there had been pressure from the CDU there to settle the matter because of the uncertainty created among the party's voters. Biedenkopf later explained his initiative to the CDU Federal Executive on the grounds that the large majority of CDU members wanted Kohl as their choice. Biedenkopf's move had been made without consulting the CSU, so that the CDU General Secretary's relations with the Bavarian party fell to an all-time low until Kohl succeeded in smoothing over ruffled feathers (reports in *FAZ*, 28 April 1975, 29 April 1975 and 13 May 1975).

[23]   See the article by Rolf Zundel, 'Die Spitzenmannschaft der Union' in *Die Zeit*, 22 August 1975.

[24]   Barzel had in fact introduced the idea of concentrating on matters of social policy well before the 1972 Bundestag Election. Early in 1973, several months before his resignation, there had been a special meeting of the Bundestag *Fraktion* in West Berlin which set up ten commissions, four of them concerned with the themes of the later Hamburg Congress: co-determination, land reform, employment training and employee share in capital growth (interview with Jürgen Heidborn, personal assistant to Richard von Weizsäcker, in Bonn, September 1974).

[25]   Cf. Strauss's statement at the time of the CDU Congress at Hamburg 1973 that the CDU/CSU must remain 'the party of Adenauer and Erhard' indicated he felt that their political 'values' should continue to remain as the basis of the party's way of life (*FR*, 22 November 1973).

[26]   For instance, see Biedenkopf's speech to the *Land* Congress of the CDU Baden-Württemberg in June 1973 (CDU Baden-Württemberg, *Erneuern und Bewahren* (1973), pp. 23-36); his article on the strategy for Opposition in *Die Zeit*, 16 March 1973; on worker participation in *Die Zeit*, 1March 1974; his speech on the dangers to democracy in a free society to the CDU Economic Council, FAZ, 29 March 1974; and especially his address to the Catholic Academy in Bavaria in December 1973 on the fundamentals of Christian Democracy (reprinted as *Die Politik der Unionsparteien – die freiheitliche Alternative zum Sozialismus* (1974)).

[27]   For this purpose, a special planning group was formed in the CDU headquarters in 1973. Its purpose was to study systematically speeches by political leaders, including those of Willy Brandt and the late John F. Kennedy, advise Kohl on speech-making techniques and devise ideas for slogans (*Die Welt*, 30 January 1974 and *Der Spiegel*, 5 August 1974).

[28] The name particularly associated with the concept of the 'New Social
      Question' was that of Heinrich Geissler, a progressive Christian Democrat
      who had been minister for social affairs in the *Land* government of the
      Rhineland-Palatinate since 1967 and was a close colleague of Helmut Kohl
      (see Geissler's book, *Die Neue Soziale Frage*, published in 1976, for an
      analysis of this concept). Geissler may be considered one of the CDU's
      new 'programmatic' leaders. He succeeded Biedenkopf as CDU General
      Secretary in 1977 (see profile of Heinrich Geissler by Carl-Christian Kaiser,
      'Ein Advokat der "Neuen Sozialen Frage" ' in *Die Zeit*, 4 February 1977).

[29] Biedenkopf had played a key role in the internal party discussion over
      worker participation in industry during the months before the Hamburg Con-
      gress. As well as being a specialist on the subject, he had acted with tactical
      skill. Some 2-3 months before the Congress, he had made proposals, which
      were attacked by a coalition of the Social Committees and the Young Union.
      There followed much heated discussion so that about a month before the
      Congress those involved had begun to 'have enough' of the issue. It was
      at this point that Biedenkopf stepped in again with new proposals, which
      included some ideas from the progressive wing of the party. Biedenkopf
      then managed to push through this new formula. (Interview with Jürgen
      Heidborn, personal assistant to Richard von Weizsäcker, in Bonn,
      September 1974.)

[30] Richard von Weizsäcker, born 1920, was regarded as the CDU's chief
      ideologist. He came from a distinguished intellectual family, and was a
      former president of the Protestant Church Assembly. First elected to the
      Bundestag in 1969, von Weizsäcker only became prominent in the CDU
      during the Opposition years but then he rose fast. A close party colleague
      of Helmut Kohl, he was the Opposition's candidate for Federal President
      in 1974 against Walter Scheel. He also stood unsuccessfully for the *Fraktion*
      chairmanship in 1973.

[31] Like other programmatic features of the CDU, it was intended that the work
      of the *Grundsatzkommission* should be electorally orientated. It was
      planned from the beginning that the draft version should appear late 1975
      or early 1976 and provide 'the basis of principles for the election programme'
      of 1976. Of its principal themes, foreign policy formed only one and was
      given less priority than domestic issues (interview with Jürgen Heidborn,
      personal assistant to Richard von Weizsäcker, in Bonn, September 1974).

[32] Ernst Albrecht, born 1930, was regarded as an obvious 'new face' in the
      CDU and a representative of the party's willingness to coalesce with the
      FDP. He was for some time a high official in the EEC in Brussels, before
      entering politics in Lower Saxony early in the 1970s as the CDU's economic
      spokesman there. He became the party's candidate for minister-president
      after the CDU's close defeat in the *Land* election of 1974. His upset
      victory against the SPD/FDP coalition in Hanover with the election of a new
      minister-president in January 1976 caused a sensation. As head of a minority
      government Albrecht was the first CDU minister-president in Lower Saxony
      since the War. In January 1977, he formed a coalition with the FDP.

[33] For a discussion of the CDU/CSU Bundestag election campaigns in 1972
      and 1976, see below Chapter 11(c). For a report on the state of the CDU
      during the 1976 campaign, see *Der Spiegel*, 23 August 1976, pp. 17-23,
      including the comment from this publication normally critical of the party
      that 'as party leader Kohl has achieved a success which the CDU has not
      experienced since the time of Konrad Adenauer'.

236   *Christian Democracy in Western Germany*

References

1.   E.g. Rudolf Wildenmann, 'CDU/CSU: Regierungspartei von morgen – oder was sonst?' in R. Löwenthal and H.P. Schwarz, *Die Zweite Republik* (1974), pp. 345, 361.
2.   *Die Zeit*, 2 February 1973.
3.   E.g. see cover story on CDU/CSU, 'Opposition auf 20 Jahre?' in *Der Spiegel*, 27 November 1972, pp. 25-33.
4.   *Die Zeit*, 5 January 1973.
5.   *Union in Deutschland*, 17 January 1973.
6.   *SZ*, 7 May 1973.
7.   *FAZ*, 22 August 1975.
8.   *FAZ*, 9 March 1974.
9.   *Die Zeit*, 15 December 1972.
10.   See portraits of Kohl in *FAZ*, 30 December 1972 and 9 June 1973.
11.   *The Times*, 12 December 1972.
12.   *FAZ*, 1 December 1972.
13.   *FAZ*, 29 January 1973.
14.   *Ibid.*
15.   See reports on support for Barzel and Kohl among the *Landesverbände* in *FAZ*, 30 January 1973; *Frankfurter Rundschau*, 15 February 1973; and *Hannoversche Allgemeine*, 14 March 1973.
16.   'Barzel kann nicht mehr auf die CDU von Rhein und Ruhr bauen' in *FAZ*, 16 May 1973.
17.   See *SZ*, 14 May 1973 and Eduard Neumaier, 'Führungswirrnis in der CDU: eine Anatomie der Unions-Krise' in *Die Zeit*, 18 May 1973.
18.   *Deutsche Zeitung*, 4 May 1973.
19.   See the reprint of this speech in Rainer Barzel, *Zur Sache* (1973), p. 7.
20.   See profile of Kohl in 'Ein Schaffer mit einer Nase fur politische Talente' in *FAZ*, 9 June 1973.
21.   *Der Spiegel*, 4 June 1973, p. 36.
22.   See the discussion of Kohl's leadership in *FAZ*, 9 February 1974 and *Die Zeit*, 27 June 1975.
23.   Profile of Kohl by Eduard Neumaier in *Die Zeit*, 15 June 1973.
24.   *FAZ*, 2 June 1973.
25.   E.g. Rolf Zundel, 'Gesucht: ein Zweiter Adenauer' in *Die Zeit*, 18 May 1973.
26.   See portrait of Kohl in *FAZ*, 9 June 1973.
27.   Profile of Biedenkopf in *FR*, 25 May 1974.
28.   Profile of Biedenkopf in H.O. Eglau 'Aussenseiter mit Ehrgeiz und Elan' in *Die Zeit*, 22 June 1973.
29.   *FAZ*, 22 June 1974.
30.   *The Times*, 11 June 1974.
31.   E.g. *FAZ*, 21 April 1974.
32.   *FAZ*, 5 October 1974.
33.   *Hannoversche Allgemeine*, 27 October 1975.
34.   See *Stuttgart Nachrichten*, 7 February 1975 and *FAZ*, 10 May 1975.
35.   See discussion of Stoltenberg's candidacy in Hans-Joachim Noack, 'Kohl gegen Strauss – der Rest ist Verwirrspiel' in *Frankfurter Rundschau*, 29 November 1974.
36.   See the discussion of Carstens' role as *Fraktion* leader in *FAZ*, 14 December 1974; *SZ*, 18 December 1974; and *Die Zeit*, 11 October 1974.
37.   *SZ*, 20 September 1973.
38.   *Ibid.*

39. See *Rheinische Post*, 24 June 1975 and *Die Zeit*, 21 November 1975.
40. *FAZ*, 13 May 1975.
41. *NZZ*, 21 June 1975.
42. *FR*, 6 November 1973.
43. Eghard Mörbitz, 'Die Union hat ihr "Godesberg" noch vor sich' in *FR*, 16 October 1975.
44. CDU Baden-Württemberg, *Erneuern und Bewahren* (1973), p. 27.
45. Kurt Biedenkopf, 'Eine Strategie für die Opposition' in *Die Zeit*, 16 March 1973.
46. *Ibid.*
47. Helmut Kohl, *Aufbruch in die Zukunft* (1973), p. 6.
48. See Helmut Kohl, 'Für einen produktiven Konflikt: die Intellektuellen und die CDU' in *Die Zeit*, 4 May 1973.
49. Article in *Die Zeit*, 16 March 1973.
50. *22. Bundesparteitag der CDU* (1973), pp. 61-2.
51. E.g. see interview with Richard von Weizsäcker, chairman of the CDU's Basic Policy Commission, in *Deutsches Allgemeines Sonntagsblatt*, 23 August 1973.
52. *23. Bundesparteitag der CDU* (1975), p. 41.
53. *Der Spiegel*, 29 September 1975, p. 41.
54. See Hermann Scheer, 'Der Mythos des Privaten: Kurt H. Biedenkopfs Funktion für die "neue" CDU' in Martin Greiffenhagen (ed.), *Der Neue Konservatismus der siebziger Jahre* (1974), pp. 171-85.
55. *FAZ*, 6 June 1975.
56. *Der Spiegel*, 6 September 1976, p. 199.
57. Quoted in *Stern*, 2 September 1976, p. 72.
58. *FAZ*, 7 October 1975.
59. *NZZ*, 9 October 1975 and *FAZ*, 11 October 1975.
60. *Der Spiegel*, 42/1975, p. 27.
61. *Die Zeit*, 16 November 1973.
62. *FR*, 6 November 1973.
63. *Die Zeit*, 23 November 1973.
64. *Die Welt*, 29 January 1974.
65. See 'Weizsäckers Konzept für die CDU' in *FR*, 5 September 1973.
66. See the useful summary of the Basic Policy Programme in Inter Nationes, *Sonderdienst SO.8-74(e)*, as well as discussion of the Programme in *NZZ*, 1 May 1976; *FAZ*, 4 May 1976 and *Die Zeit*, 7 May 1976.
67. See Eduard Neumaier, 'Die Union am Sandkasten' in *Die Zeit*, 28 September 1973.
68. See Christian Hacke, 'Die ost-und deutschlandpolitische Argumentation der CDU/CSU seit 1973' in *Aus Politik und Zeitgeschichte*, 23 August 1975, pp. 3-22.
69. See C-C. Kaiser, 'Strategen, Taktiker und Glückskinder' in *Die Zeit*, 19 March 1976.
70. *Die Zeit*, 8 October 1976.
71. See *FR*, 21 January 1977 for a discussion of the change in CDU General Secretary.
72. See the résumé of Biedenkopf's work as General Secretary in *Die Zeit*, 28 January 1977.
73. Kurt Biedenkopf, *Die Politik der Unionsparteien – die freiheitliche Alternative zum Sozialismus* (1973), text of speech, p. 4.

PART TWO: THE COMPOSITION AND STRUCTURE OF THE CDU/CSU

7 PARTY ORGANISATION OF THE CDU

The CDU could for a long time be categorised as a loose-associational
form of political party rather than one with a highly structured
organisation. For much of its history since the Second World War the
CDU's national extra-parliamentary structure evidenced the minimum
of an organisational network and was accorded little political weight,
so that with some justification the CDU was frequently labelled during
the 1950s and even 1960s as an 'electoral association' *(Wählerverein)*,
whose primary function was to maintain the Christian Democratic
ruling elite in Bonn. During its long period in national office (1949-69),
there was no pressing need for the CDU to develop highly articulated
structural features because political success was apparently independent
of the organisational efficiency of the party. Furthermore, while
national governmental responsibility provided the overriding source
of party solidarity, the CDU nevertheless suffered from serious internal
problems of political integration and cohesion. These tensions derived
principally from the federal nature of the CDU's internal organisation,
first evident in the early years when the party developed upwards
from its local and regional levels.[a] This polycentric character of the
party's channels of internal co-ordination was taken a stage further in
the case of Bavaria with the existence there since the end of the War of
a second Christian Democratic party, the CSU, which boasted a
separate organisational development from that of the CDU.[b] There
was an additional special feature of the CDU/CSU with the presence
of various auxiliary organisations representing internal party interest
groups, whose autonomous status meant that they were not required
to be subordinate to the national party leadership.[c]

In short, the CDU was distinguished by structural articulation more
in relation to its subcoalitional elements than with its national
organisation. It was therefore in a literal sense a coalition within itself.
Yet the CDU evolved organisationally from the time the first national
co-ordination body, the *Arbeitsgemeinschaft de CDU und CSU*, was
formed in 1947.[d] This very loose association was replaced in 1950

a   See above chapter 1 (c) passim.
b   See below chapter 10 (c).
c   See below chapter 9 on the role of party auxiliary organisations.
d   See above chapter 1 (c), p. 44.

with the formal creation of a national party structure for the CDU,[e] after which various efforts were made to enlarge national organisation although not seriously until the early 1960s. The key determinant in its organisational development was the political success or failure of the CDU, for the more the political environment became less favourable (during the 1960s) so pressure for internal change mounted. There were, however, other factors countering such change, notably the strength of vested interests within the party deriving in particular from its federal structure, the low degree of its political integration which inhibited the co-ordination necessary for the implementation of organisational change and, above all, the CDU's retention of national office and especially the Chancellorship, which meant that at the national level of the party structure the balance of political weight was maintained decisively in favour of the leadership. Basic changes in the CDU's organisational character only came after its loss of national office, for it could then no longer rely on the available machinery of government (which had acted as a substitute for party organisation in providing advisory personnel and channels of policy information). The unprecedented rise in party membership which occurred during the second Opposition period made it in any case necessary for the party organisation to adapt.[f] The central factor in the CDU's organisational development has consequently been its role in Government or Opposition, all the more so as the party assumed national responsibility in office before it had any chance to create an elaborate organisation.

The discussion of the CDU's organisational character will focus on the effect on it of the party's political fortunes and examine closely its evolving internal structure to estimate how far the CDU has changed in its nature as a political party. These questions will be approached from three different angles: the general structure of the CDU and its balance of organisational weight; the state of its mass organisation and growth of bureaucracy; and, the impact of the Opposition role on the party's organisational character.

(a) General Structure of the Party and its Balance of Organisational Weight

Three principal structural features marked the CDU from the beginning of its development. First, a deep ideological antipathy towards the

e See above chapter 2 (a), pp. 65-8.

f See below chapter 8 (b) for a discussion of this particular question.

concept of 'the party machine' together with the lack of any
organisational tradition combined to hinder the development of an
effective substructure for the CDU's political activities. Secondly, the
federal political system of West Germany imprinted itself on the party
structure so that the highest form of effective structural control was
through the CDU's powerful regional organisations (*Landesverbände*).
Thirdly, early governmental responsibility reinforced the role of
election campaigns as the supreme function of party organisation,
especially at the national level, and also accounted for the pronounced
imbalance between the CDU's national parliamentary organ (the
Bundestag *Fraktion*) and its extra-parliamentary national organisation.
In all three respects, the CDU differed significantly from the other main
political party, the SPD, especially in the first and third features, for
the latter both had a long organisational tradition and was for a long
time the national parliamentary Opposition in the Federal Republic.
It is with these first and third structural features that the most change
has occurred with the CDU, while its federal structure has continued
as a basic distinctive feature of the CDU.

The presence of a strong anti-bureaucratic attitude among the
party's leadership elite and its activist element since the War was
explained both by the reaction to Nazism and by the political rivalry
which soon developed with the Social Democrats. Adenauer's remark
at the 1956 party congress that 'power and party machine, those are
things which remind us exceptionally strongly of the years which we
have behind us'[1] is typical of the tendency in the CDU to equate the
term 'party machine' with totalitarianism. It was an association deeply
held because it derived from one of the CDU's strongest ideological
convictions, its attachment to the concept of 'freedom'. As Bruno Heck
illustrated in his speech to the same Congress, the Christian Democratic
idea of 'freedom', however, could often express an antagonism
towards post-war (Communist) totalitarianism and the organised
methods of control practised by socialist movements in general:

> We want neither functionaries nor apparatchiks, who see to it
> that the party organs are constructed according to the will of a
> small group in order to compel certain decisions. Our party has
> too high an opinion of freedom, for a few sergeant majors to be
> able to give orders for the votes at party congresses.[2]

This pronounced antipathy in the CDU towards a party bureaucracy had
been present in the avoidance of the term 'party' and preference for

'union', in the choice of name for the CDU after the war.[g] Any attempt
to create a party machine would have exacerbated the CDU's
problems of cohesion, since the common unifying factor among its
members was an attachment to the values of Christian Democracy and
an allegiance to the Adenauer Government in Bonn rather than something more tangible.

This outlook was prevalent too at the activist level, where allegiance
was shown less specifically to the 'party cause', than to the cause of
Christian Democracy or the policies of the CDU.[1] The rejection of
elaborate organisational methods and a strong adherence to the
principle of voluntariness lay at the root of party activities at the
grass-roots level.[2] Because party organisation was regarded at best as
an unpleasant necessity, the idea of promoting careers for party
officials as a matter of policy was regarded with suspicion and efforts
to promote party membership were not widespread, so that altogether
the Federal party headquarters found its scope for enlarging its
activities restricted by a reluctance among activists to take 'orders'
from above.[3] Admittedly, the concept of 'freedom' as a factor in
internal party organisational relations was also a convenient cover for
the maintenance of vested interests at lower levels of the CDU hierarchy.
Kurt Biedenkopf later had this tendency in mind, when he commented
in his speech to the Baden-Württemberg CDU in June 1973 on the
problems of forming an effective political consensus within the party,
while continuing to adhere to the freedom concept:

> This task: the strengthening of our organisations so that it can openly
> settle conflicts, make decisions and following that come to uniform
> political arrangements is particularly difficult the more a party sees
> itself as based on freedom (*je freiheitlicher sich eine Partei versteht*).
> Once associations are involved as well as auxiliary organisations, sub-
> groups, interests and persons, the greater is the variety of viewpoints,
> the more numerous is the possession of partial interests and beliefs,
> and consequently all the more considerable is resistance to the
> unification of different opinions and positions for the purpose of
> combined political action. We face therefore a difficult task, if we
> want to maintain our party structure based on freedom (*unsere
> freiheitliche Struktur als Partei*), and nevertheless act vigorously . . .
> The vigorous pursuit of political positions is a problem of centralisa-
> tion. The preservation of the initiative of many is a problem of

g   See above chapter 1 (a), pp. 23-4.

openness, of the federal structure. All in all, it is a question of finding the right balance, as I once put it, between order and creative chaos. We face this task. It is also the task I have to deal with. It is the task of the renewal of our party as an organisation.[3]

This problem, which Biedenkopf described so clearly, had been previously faced by successive party reformers through the 1960s, who, while they deplored the inhibiting effect of this attitude on the development of a professional body of party activists, all the same found it necessary to respect it as representing an ideological value. While the particular abhorrence of party organisation declined gradually during the CDU's first twenty years of development and finally disappeared with the rise of a new generation of activists and the impact of the loss of national office, the wider adherence to the concept of 'freedom' nevertheless remained and served to moderate the trend towards bureaucratisation in the party's more recent years.

The principal structural reason preventing the easy growth of central control in the CDU was of course the party's deeply rooted federal character. This was explained historically by the sequence of organisational development of the party in the Occupation years with the creation of its local and regional units before a national party organisation. During these years the CDU was, in the words of Gerhard Schulz, 'a mosaic of organisationally unconnected regional associations'.[4] The party's structure developed concurrently with that of the new West German state, the federal character of which had been predetermined by the introduction of the *Länder* before there was agreement several years later on a national government. With the absence of any national organisational background, the new CDU had been required to co-ordinate its early activities within the bounds of the Occupation zones and the *Land* borders.[h] This evolution of a decentralised party structure was accompanied and endorsed by a belief in the principle of federalism, which was held most fervently among the south German *Landesverbände* and in particular in the Bavarian CSU,[i] and gradually it became buttressed by the strength of vested regional interests within the CDU. Following the Goslar Congress in 1950; Federal executive organs had been instituted with the *Bundesvorstand* (Federal Executive) and the *Bundesausschuss* (Federal Committee), but they were accorded the minimum of controlling

h See above chapter 1 (c), pp. 48-9.
i See above chapter 1 (a), p. 32.

authority and were in any case dominated by representatives from the
Landesverbände.[j] As Robert Tillmanns remarked in his report on behalf
of the Federal Executive to the Hamburg Congress in 1953:

> The Federal Executive places the greatest importance on the fact
> that the *Landesverbände*, whose independent tasks and own
> responsible work are a foundation of our union, carry out together
> with the Federal headquarters the common work. We want a
> healthy hierarchy in our party, and a genuine partnership instead of
> central organisation.[5]

Organisational power in the CDU remained substantially in the hands
of its *Landesverbände,* whose political position in the party was secured
through the federal system by their role in *Land* government and
politics.[k] Their organisational weight was demonstrated by their control
over the district branches and also finance, as well as their dominant
representation in the national party organs. It was illustrated moreover
by the fact that the vast majority of salaried party officials in the CDU
operated at the regional level,[4] and that the selection of candidates
for both Bundestag and *Land* elections was a privilege of the
Landesverbände. They also controlled the district branches
(Kreisverbände), so that the Federal party headquarters could not
usually bypass the authority of the *Landesverbände* to make contact
with the latter. Party reformers had to take note of this strong federal
character of the party organisation and recognise it as the principal
limitation to any structural changes. As Dufhues noted around 1963:

> The federal structure of the CDU arose from its founding history
> and from its basic political attitude. It is a fact that has to be taken
> into account in relation to all considerations. A centralisation of the
> party must always be restricted to particular situations or to
> particular fields. It will hardly be possible to change the internal
> structure of the party in its fundamentals.[6]

Dufhues commented that he viewed his task of reform as making the
CDU 'capable of functioning' on the basis of the federal principle
through 'meaningful co-ordination, not schematic centralisation'.[l]

j   See above, chapter 2 (a), pp. 67-8.
k   See above chapter 2 (c) for a discussion of this situation during the 1950s.
l   See above chapter 3 (a) on Dufhues's relations with the *Landesverbände.*

There were nevertheless differences between the various *Landesverbände* with regard to their outlook on a national party organisation. As the attachment to federalism as a principle for the organisation of the state as well as for ordering internal party relations was strongest in south Germany,[5] the CDU *Landesverbände* here showed most resistance to attempts to promote better central co-ordination of party activities, while the *Landesverbände* of northern Germany proved the most co-operative in relations with the Federal party headquarters.[6] It was also no coincidence that party reformers (such as Kai-Uwe von Hassel, Franz Meyers and Josef Hermann Dufhues) by and large came from the north, where the idea of a structured party organisation was more readily accepted than in the south, and that they encountered in their home *Länder* a more positive response to their reform plans.

Traditional regional loyalty and jealousy also affected relations between CDU *Landesverbände,* particularly where the regional level of party organisation did not follow the confines of the *Land* administrations: notably, with the existence of the two *Landesverbände* of the Rhineland and Westphalia-Lippe in North-Rhine Westphalia; the three *Landesverbände* of Hanover, Brunswick and Oldenburg in Lower Saxony;[7] and, the four *Landesverbände* of North and South Baden, North Württemberg and Württemberg-Hohenzollern in Baden-Württemberg.[8] Historical antagonisms such as between Badeners and Württembergers and between Westphalians and Rhinelanders[9] came to the fore when for reasons of political necessity efforts were made to simplify party structure within the *Länder,* involving a reduction in the status of the sub-*Land* organisational units. When a common praesidium for the North-Rhine Westphalian CDU was formed in 1966, party regulations stressed that this would be 'an organ of co-ordination' but that 'the competences of the *Landesverbände* remained untouched'.[7] Similar efforts were made in the other two cases from the late 1960s, with varying degrees of success. In 1968 the creation of an organisation for the Lower Saxony CDU, with its own headquarters in Hanover and a *Land* party chairman, followed only after long obstruction from certain regional 'party barons' who feared a weakening of their power bases. A greater degree of integration was achieved in Baden-Württemberg, where the four old *Landesverbände* were reduced in status to county branches (*Bezirksverbände*), and a *Land* party organisation for the whole of Baden-Württemberg with its own General Secretary was established in 1971. Even here though the new *Landesgeschäftsstelle* in Stuttgart has performed more of a co-ordinating than a centralising function.[10] Greater pressure for structural cohesion in relations between the national party organisation and the *Landesverbände* and between themselves only came after the party's loss of power in Bonn.

While there developed two layers of party organisation, with a marked bias towards the regional level, a significant interflow of leadership personnel between both layers has been apparent. *Land* party leaders have frequently become Federal politicians *(Bundespolitiker)*, and vice versa. The importance of the *Landesverbände* in organisational terms has determined that politicians primarily active in Bonn neglect their regional bases often at a cost to their own careers.[11] This political link between the Federal and *Land* levels acted as a force for political integration in the CDU, reflecting as it did the operation of the federal system in West Germany. The party was therefore structurally a creature of the post-war political system of the Federal Republic, as both had developed at the same time.

The third major influence on party structure was the impact of early governmental responsibility. This derived from the CDU's control of the Federal Government under the popular figure of Adenauer, which brought the party great advantages of publicity and patronage and produced the compelling argument within the leadership circles that the minimum of party organisation only was necessary. From this arose the contemporary view of the CDU as a *Wählerverein*. The publicist Rüdiger Altmann commented on the weak state of party organisation after a decade in Government: 'It is merely for election campaigns that the party machine and membership wake up, and then they are hardly inferior to the SPD as far as activity in general is concerned, above all for Bundestag election campaigns.'[8] Foreign journalists came to the same conclusion.[12]

How far was this indifference to organisational problems typical of attitudes within the party as a whole? Was the label *Wählerverein* in fact justified? There is much evidence to show that the apathy towards party organisation typical of national leaders throughout the 1950s and much of the 1960s, whose only interest in party reform was sparked off by adverse political events, was not always shared by party leaders and officials at the regional and local levels. In Heidelberg, for instance, the local branch showed repeated concern during election campaigns, even as early as the 1950s, that party organisation there should be extended after voting day was over, but nothing occurred because of the widespread exhaustion as a result of the campaigns and the general assumption that energies were best spent on preparing for

the next one.[9] The feeling that party voluntary workers who carried out
the mundane and detailed work of campaign arrangements (known as
Wasserträger, or 'water carriers') should be used for other more
continuous purposes grew stronger as the 1960s progressed. The CDU
Land chairman of North Baden, Franz Gurk, emphasised in his speech
at the *Land* party congress in Pforzheim in February 1966 that:

> District party executives and business managers should not allow the
> situation to continue whereby there are local branches which are
> not active between election campaigns. Also those communities, in
> which our party has no organised group, should not be forgotten. In
> co-operation with the Bundestag deputies, the Landtag deputies and
> municipal representatives, consideration must be given as to how work
> at the district level and in the localities of the district can be made
> more lively. Our party must be like this outside election campaign
> times, so that every man should remain actively in his place.[10]

Interest in orientating party organisation towards more than just
electoral activities increased at the regional level with the rise of second
and third generation party leaders, who began to exert pressure on their
seniors. They sought in particular to enhance their promotion prospects
by acquiring a reputation as effective party organisers and by seeking
influence in party affairs. The classic example of this procedure during
the 1960s was Helmut Kohl's reorganisation of the CDU in the
Rhineland-Palatinate,[11] which was a crucial factor in his replacing the
old party leadership under Peter Altmeier, Minister-President there ever
since 1947. Nevertheless, there had been a certain divorce of attitude
from the beginning between grass-roots activists in many areas and
national party leaders. An instance of this was the protest sent to
Adenauer by a conference of district party managers in Karlsruhe as
early as November 1951, complaining that 'in our party the importance
of a good organisation is unfortunately not yet recognised'. It deplored
especially the absence of personal contact between regional and
district business managers and the national executive organs of the
CDU.[12] The narrowing of the gap between the outlook of national
leaders and grass-roots organisers only really occurred during the
Opposition period in the 1970s, particularly after the shock of the
1972 Bundestag Election.

It could be concluded therefore that the CDU was not so much an
'electoral association' in the literal sense, but more a party with a
minimum of organisational articulation and that its activities were

primarily electorally orientated. Some developments did occur in the course of time, but these were primarily motivated by electoral considerations. A minor instance of a deviation from this electoral orientation occurred at the 1956 CDU Congress with an alteration in the CDU statutes concerning the selection of delegates for party congresses. Up to that time, the *Landesverbände* had been allowed to send one delegate per every 25,000 voters won in their region at the preceding Bundestag election. Henceforth, they would be entitled to one delegate for every 75,000 voters and one for every 1,000 party members in their area. Nevertheless, the CDU was for a long time to remain a political party which was chiefly voter or office-orientated, rather than one which was bureaucratic in its form of activities.

The other principal effect of early governmental responsibility on the structure of the CDU was the imbalance of political weight between the parliamentary organ of the party and its extra-parliamentary national organisation. A national extra-parliamentary organisation was not created until a year after the CDU had been in office in the Federal Government, by which time the CDU/CSU *Fraktion*, following its predecessors in the Economic and Parliamentary Councils, had already established itself as the party's foremost (and until 1950 sole) Federal organ. The *Bundesvorstand* and *Bundesausschuss,* then formed to manage party affairs between congresses, developed as little more than loose organs of contact between leaders of the *Landesverbände* and auxiliary organisations and national party figures. They could hardly be described at this stage as organs with a directive function, as underlined by Adenauer's scant interest in their activities.[13] The national headquarters of the CDU *(Bundesgeschäftsstelle),* which was slow in establishing itself, also enjoyed virtually no political weight for its functions were primarily administrative. The Bundestag *Fraktion* remained the dominant national organ in the party, because it was closest to the centre of national political power, though it was in turn dominated by the ministerial elite and in particular by the Chancellor.

The main limitation to the monopoly of political weight in the party by its parliamentary elite in Bonn (ministers and backbenchers taken together) was of course the role of *Land* party leaders. As described, the quantitative balance of organisational weight was tilted markedly towards the regional associations, and this also gave them political influence. The national extra-parliamentary party organisation therefore suffered both from the political supremacy of the CDU's Bundestag elite and from the organisational supremacy of the

Landesverbände. A similar imbalance was present also at the regional level of politics between the parliamentary organs (Lantag *Fraktionen*) of the CDU and its extra-parliamentary organisation, depending on political circumstances. The deciding factor here was whether the CDU was in government or opposition in *Land* politics, for in the former case the pressures on it to strengthen its extra-parliamentary organisation were not immediate. The party's leadership personnel were invariably absorbed in government positions so that, with the strong personal linkage between party and government élites, the party's extra-parliamentary organisation was usually overshadowed by the role played by party leaders in office.[14]

It therefore followed that any major change in the balance of structural weight within the CDU was most likely to occur with a substantial shift of political authority in the party. This would happen as a result of political circumstances adversely affecting the party's fortunes. Since electoral setbacks had alone not been sufficient to set in motion such a structural change because of the strongly entrenched position of internal party interests and the limitations of the CDU's internal political integration, an alternation in Government/ Opposition roles at the national level was the necessary precondition for the development of a more structured national party organisation. Dufhues's aim of giving the extra-parliamentary organisation some 'independent life' (his speech at the Dortmund Congress, 1962) had been illusory because this precondition did not then exist, although his intentions were motivated by the party's loss of votes in the 1961 Bundestag Election. There had been some cautious extension of party organisation during the first two decades of the CDU's existence as a national party, if only because time and new political circumstances dictated adaptation, but it remained for the shock of the loss of national office to initiate eventually any significant change in the attitudes towards reorganisation of the CDU and recognition of the need for reform.

(b) State of Organisation and Growth of Bureaucracy

The problem of the extra-parliamentary organisation of the CDU has been discussed with respect to its relative weight within the party as a whole; it is important, however, to examine it more closely internally in order to determine how much the CDU developed during the 1950s and 1960s as an organised political party. The questions relevant to this discussion are: to what extent could one at all speak of a 'party machine' apart from that activated for election campaigns?; if the CDU could be described as a coalition of institutions as well as of interests, how much integration was there between them?; and, what degree of organisational articulation was present in the CDU such as in the form of bureaucratic elements and the methodical definition and demarcation of functions? In short, how far were Christian Democrats prepared to institutionalise their internal party relationships in spite of ideological reservations about the values of party organisation? This question will be discussed with reference to three aspects of party organisation: the role of central party headquarters; the part played by activists within the party; and problems of finance and publicity.

The basic purpose of a central party headquarters should be to act as the formal channel for regular communication between the national leadership élite and the party as a whole. This implied a co-ordinating, if not a directive function. On these grounds, the *Bundesgeschäftsstelle der CDU* (BGS), which finally came into operation in 1952, was far from adequate for it was a victim of the imbalance of forces within the party structure. The 1950 statutes of the CDU specified that the *Landesverbände* should be responsible for financing the BGS,[13] underlining as this did their organisational power, but this provision proved to be a dead letter. The delay in opening its office and deciding on its tasks, following the decision on its creation at the Goslar Congress, suggested the reluctance in the party to grant the BGS more than minimal administrative functions. Its location in 16 different houses around Bonn did, in the words of Dufhues at the 1964 Congress, 'impede co-operation and make for unusually high and unnecessary costs'.[14] The physical impression offered by its main office in the Nassestrasse (where it was housed from 1952-71) was one of improvisation:

> The rooms, many of which are stuffed with material up to the ceiling, are too confined. The teleprinter is to be found in a bathroom, and the archives are overflowing. The largest party of the Federal Republic in electoral votes has available a machine, which in terms of wealth of invention operates in an improvised rather than functional or rational way. [15]

The head of the BGS, known as the *Bundesgeschäftsführer* or Federal Business Manager (Bruno Heck 1952-8, and Konrad Kraske from 1958 through the 1960s), was considered as having only an administrative role to play. Only with the appointment of a General Secretary from 1967 did the party headquarters begin to assume a more central political presence.[m]

What was the view of the CDU Bonn headquarters from the grass-roots? This was positive as long as the BGS's purpose was purely one of co-ordination rather than direction. A certain impatience with the tardiness in setting it up had been voiced in some cases at local levels of the CDU, although this was not generally true of the party for there was much variation of attitude. The Cologne and Düsseldorf branches sent official protests to the Congress in October 1951 urging progress with 'creating a really capable Federal headquarters, which should above all devote itself to political enlightenment and the extension of party organisation throughout the Federal territory', and that 'the uniformity and thrust of the party is suffering considerably from the lack of a central management'.[16] Although it was to be expected that branches in the Rhineland would for traditional reasons be more organisationally conscious than most, many *Landesverbände* felt the need for some modicum of co-ordination and this view increased as the 1950s progressed. A progressive view was contained in a memorandum produced after a conference of *Land* party business managers at West Berlin in January 1962 by a party official from Schleswig-Holstein[15] on 'What the *Landesverbände* expect from the Work of the *Bundesgeschäftsstelle*'.[17] It listed the tasks of the BGS as threefold: facilitating the formation of a 'common political will' in the CDU; assisting in co-ordinating the *Landesverbände* with the Federal party 'without the BGS "leading" in a centralised manner'; and, trying to 'make the CDU visible as a Federal party and Government party'. This expressed the feeling that the BGS should play a crucial part in the communication and information process within the party, and a special plea was made for closer relations between it and the Bundestag *Fraktion* and for its more regular personal contacts with the *Landesverbände*.[16]

It was indeed Dufhues's intention to meet these requests. In his 1963 report on the state of the party, he had emphasised that not sufficient use was made of the headquarters, although it had performed a reasonable task in distributing information and publicity material. While 'the confidence of the *Landesverbände* in the work of the BGS' had grown in recent years, he nevertheless warned that it would

m See above chapter 4 (d).

run aground if it 'ever tried to be the highest authority of command of the party (*oberste Kommandobehörde der Partei*)'.[18] The problem with upgrading the role of the headquarters was not only the suspicions of many of the *Landesverbände* about its assuming any directive functions, but also the lack of suitable personnel and the crippling absence of financial resources.[19] Plans had been discussed since the late 1950s for buying land to build a larger more modern headquarters, which should house all departments together, but this was constantly shelved specifically for the lack of funds.[20] Dufhues succeeded in initiating a few changes. An official CDU spokesman was appointed in 1962, and he enlarged and improved the publicity departments of the BGS. Since the early 1950s it had furthermore consisted of departments for administrative, legal and budgetary questions as well as departments for different policy matters.[21] During the following decade these departments had been gradually extended through the creation of new sub-divisions.[22] The BGS remained structurally the same until the major reorganisation of 1970 after the loss of power in Bonn. The basic problem with the CDU headquarters was that, in addition to institutional rivalry, it suffered from the lack of support of national party leaders.

The role of party activists can be measured by determining how far their status within the party was honorary or professional; how much their functions were formally defined; and how much regular work the activists did outside election campaigns. The first two aspects would reflect the degree of bureaucratisation in the CDU during its governmental period, while the third would indicate the strength of its commitment solely to winning elections.

A salient characteristic of the activist element during the Adenauer years was its dominance by local notables *(Honoratioren)*.[17] Indeed, it would be justifiable to refer to the grass-roots level of the CDU during the 1950s as a party of notables. The specific traits of such a party are: an organisational network which is personal rather than bureaucratic in its relationships; an exclusive or restrictive attitude to party activities marked by a desire to confine business to the privileged local elite, and by a low interest in promoting party membership; a certain 'unpolitical' attitude which expresses itself in a contempt for organisational values and a noticeable hostility towards partisan politics as such. The CDU approximated to this model, although naturally there were some considerable variations at the regional level, such as between the structured party in the Rhineland and the persistence of the control of local party power by notables in the Hanse cities of Hamburg and Bremen. Press reports commented regularly during this time on the 'closed shop' practised by notables over the selection of election candidates and the admission of new members, the perfunctory character of local party meetings and the obstruction of membership drives (as for instance in Hesse) by 'old-established members' who maintained local party membership as a 'circle of cronies' *(Stamm-tischzirkel).*[23]

A common tendency from the early days of the party was the concentration of local party positions in a few hands, a tendency known as *Ämterhäufung.* Even in 1949 Hans Schreiber (party business manager for the Rhineland *Landesverband*, 1945-61) criticised this in his review of party organisation then:

> Our organisation still suffers from various 'teething troubles'. It is high time that the loathsome, and in many places, perilous accummulation of offices should be eliminated. Responsibility must be distributed in a well-considered manner among as many suitable colleagues as possible. Duds must be replaced as soon as possible. Wrong ideas, whereby the office of *Fraktion* leader is politically less important than that of political representative of the community concerned, district or *Land* (local mayor, district president or Landtag president), should be erased.[24]

Schreiber launched one of the earliest attacks on this exclusive practice in the CDU, which inhibited the development of party officials as a professional body. In his area, the network of district party business managers (CDU-*Kreisgeschäftsführer*) was the most developed at that time, though generally they were small in number and their working conditions were unsatisfactory. It took some time before the formalisation of the system of *Kreisgeschäftsführer* replaced fully the informal network of local notables. As late as 1963, only half the district branches of the CDU generally had such an official. Of these, two-thirds earned less than DM 1,000 a month for their labours, while their business was often conducted from their private homes.[25] District managers were usually given wide scope for initiative, but it also meant that efficiency depended less on the Bonn party headquarters than on local circumstances and the energy of the district manager in question.[26]

Concern about the condition of grass-roots organisation began to be expressed at the national level even during the Adenauer period.

Bruno Heck remarked in his report to the 1956 Congress that, while the CDU did not want to become a 'party of functionaries', it all the same needed an effective body of full-time activists: 'The Executive Committee is clear that a modern party with the extra-ordinarily professional expectations of our population cannot get by without a certain number of full-time personnel.'[27] Other national leaders, who showed an interest in matters of organisation, few though they were in number, shared the same concern. Franz Meyers mentioned in his report to the 1958 Congress a recent review of party officials underlining the dangers of maintaining ageing personnel, showing how much these personnel stuck together and discouraged outsiders and warning that the CDU was backward in 'detailed party work'.[28] As always, this concern had its electoral motives. Kai-Uwe von Hassel, speaking on the same subject to the Congress two years later, emphasised: 'Good organisation means as a matter of course better electoral results and greater stability in the elections which follow.'[29]

The first party leader to insist on the systematic professionalisation of activists was Dufhues, who proposed increasing their salaries, officially defining their functions and training them in their work. As Dufhues noted, the district branch in the CDU with its control over party membership and over local branches, and its essential role as the channel of contact from below with the *Landesverband* office, was the principal formal unit of grass-roots organisation. Yet, he pointed out, there was virtually no methodical effort to facilitate their work. According to Renate Mayntz in her study of the West Berlin CDU, there was no official training of party officials either at the district or *Land* level, which had serious consequences for party activities there.[30] The picture was usually similar, judging from the evidence available on the other *Landesverbände* during the 1950s. A growing uneasiness about the need to provide for a future generation of party activists combined with electoral pressures and an impatience with the old system among younger elements in the CDU to stimulate more open criticism during the 1960s of the stranglehold of notables at the local level of the party.

The extent of the change which followed was extremely varied and depended primarily on local factors, although changing attitudes in the course of time, along with electoral reverses, were probably the most common agents eroding this system. The most systematic case of professionalisation occurred in the *Landesverband* of the Rhineland-Palatinate from the mid-1960s. Whereas in 1963 the

district and local branches there were still chiefly run by notables —
there were full-time business managers in only 12 of the 51 district
branches[31] — the shock of the loss of its absolute majority in the
Landtag election of that year, followed by Helmut Kohl's election as
Land party chairman in 1966, opened the way for change in the CDU.
Kohl, who owed his election partly to his untiring cultivation of the
party grass-roots, now pushed ahead and promoted younger talent
in place of notables.[32] Skilled personnel were enticed by better pay,[18]
a statutory definition of the duties of district managers was introduced[33] and the Rhineland-Palatinate became the first *Landesverband*
to adopt an insurance system for unsalaried activists.[34] At the same
time, the party succeeded in changing its image from one of traditional
clericalism to modernity illustrated by a more open-minded approach
to education policy and its versatile and vivacious election campaign
methods, which paid dividends in the Landtag election of 1967.[35]
The Hamburg CDU, in contrast, still complained as late as 1970 of
the lack of suitable personnel and the unreliable methods of
communication between the *Landesverband* office and the district
branches, especially with regard to the provision of information.[36]
The Rhineland-Palatinate *Landesverband* was an exceptional case
even after the CDU had entered Opposition, as is suggested by the
report on the state of party district offices submitted to the
conference of *Landesverband* business managers in June 1972
by the party Organisation Commission.[37] This deplored the
state of the party at the district level:

> There is lacking not only an elaborate definition of the aims of
> work, and therefore of the functions at the separate levels of the
> party, but likewise there is lacking sufficient effective mechanisms
> of co-ordination. Above all, the district party offices are absolutely
> insufficiently equipped personally and materially. There are strong
> differences between the individual district branches in working
> aims and methods, in personnel and equipment, so that the degree
> of effectiveness varies strongly from district branch to district
> branch. This must above all have disadvantageous consequences
> for performance in the election campaign.[38]

Thus, in general, the state of the CDU's activist element hardly
measured up to the requirements of a mass-organised political party
at the time it lost national office.

A brief examination of problems of finance and publicity reinforces the picture already portrayed of the CDU's organisational deficiencies. Several peculiarities marked its activities during the 1950s and 1960s, and indeed still applied during the Opposition period, although in a modified form: a heavy dependence on agents outside the party organisation, notably sponsors' associations and the Government machine; a low degree of discipline in the payment of their dues among party members; the absence of financial backing for extending party organisation in any substantial way; and, finally, the effect of the party's loose internal structure and especially its federal character on the control of finance. All these features again suggested a weak state of co-ordination in internal party relationships.

The first two aspects especially distinguished the CDU from the SPD, which was during the period under discussion far more developed as a mass-organised party. The role of outside sponsors, notably industrial and commercial interests, as a crucial support of the party's financial life had arisen during the post-war years when these interests affiliated themselves to the Christian Democrats, regarding them as the main political defence against the growth of socialist ideas. This became noticeable at election time, when sponsors' associations raised the level of their contributions substantially, which prompted Varain in his study of the CDU in Schleswig-Holstein to label this 'external party financing group' along with members and voters as the 'third element in the framework of the party'.[39] This situation remained constant until the decision of the Constitutional Court in 1958 declaring tax concessions for donations to political parties unconstitutional. The decision affected the CDU most of all, because it was the party by far the most dependent on this source of income. With the consequent diminishing support from outside finance, the CDU along with the other parties turned to state finance increasingly from 1959, when the Bundestag decided to finance parties out of public funds.[40] This source was challenged by a further decision of the Court in 1966 which declared against state financing for general party activities, although allowed it for reimbursing election costs. This decision resulted in the Party Law of 1967, which also specified that parties should publish a yearly statement of accounts.

While this form of state finance eventually replaced outside sponsors as the largest single source of income, the CDU budget was under pressure from other quarters. Its primary purpose had always been to oil the party's publicity machine, although the CDU had depended heavily on the free publicity from the Government information services while in office. From the mid-1960s, particularly once the

CDU had entered the Grand Coalition with the SPD, it was forced to seek more its own means of publicity. It no longer had virtually absolute control over the official information services. In 1968 the CDU created the *Union-Betriebs GmbH* to encourage modern publicity management within the party.[41] Already in 1962 Dufhues had taken a first step in systematising party publicity by appointing an official CDU spokesman. All these measures, and indeed organisational reforms in general, depended ultimately on the availability of sufficient finance.

The obvious major alternative source was internal in the form of systematic membership payments combined with larger membership numbers. While the CDU succeeded once it entered Opposition in raising its membership total dramatically,[n] any change in the method of paying membership dues was inhibited by the deeply held belief within the party that this was essentially a voluntary matter. It had a vague connection with the party's attachment to the idea of 'freedom'. By the late 1960s a certain frustration with this problem was underlined by von Hassel in his report of March 1968 on party organisation to the Schleswig-Holstein CDU:

> One of the decisive political problems is the fact that the SPD is financially strong thanks above all to the exemplary discipline of its members, but the CDU is unfortunately poor as a consequence of insufficient discipline with subscriptions.[42]

CDU members had always been more backward in their payments than SPD members, as was shown by Uwe Schleth's research on CDU finances at the time of the 1961 Bundestag Election.[19] By the earlier 1960s, the party leadership was attempting to deal with the problem albeit in a very kidgloved manner. In March 1964, the CDU's Federal Committee produced an official tariff as a 'guide' for members to work out their monthly contributions on the basis of personal income. This was sent to party members with an accompanying letter from Adenauer as party chairman. It did not, however, directly challenge the voluntary principle.[20] This reflected the underlying attitudes and beliefs which helped to determine the CDU's character as a political party.

Control of finance, as another indicator of where authority lay in party organisation, was not centralised in the CDU. The *Landesverbände* but also the district branches, who administered membership

n   See below Chapter 8(b).

subscriptions, had control over a much larger share of the party's total income than did the national party organisation, which at least initially was almost totally dependent financially on the former. By the Opposition period, the national party controlled still only about one-third of the CDU's total income for ultimately the CDU's financial administration was a consequence of its internal federal structure.

This review of the part played by the CDU's national headquarters, its activists and methods of finance has shown that the party had achieved only a modest level of internal institutionalisation by the late 1960s. Organisational articulation did develop during the 1960s for reasons of political and electoral pressure, and because party leaders showed a greater awareness of the need for good organisation. It awaited nevertheless the shock of Opposition from 1969 to force the CDU to give a clear priority to organisational matters.

(c)   Impact of Opposition and Changes in Party Organisation

Once again it was a major political development, calling into question the party's future prospects, that generated interest in organisational reform of the CDU. The concern over Adenauer's political decline and later the growing electoral challenge from the SPD had promoted such an interest, although the impact of these political pressures as a counter-weight to internal party forces opposed to organisational change had been weakened by the CDU's continuing political advantage in controlling the Chancellorship. Now this advantage disappeared literally overnight in 1969, so opening up the possibility for an alteration in the balance of internal party forces which might favour long-term party reform. For the first time in the CDU's history, party organisation became a central feature of strategic planning within the leadership élite.

The full reckoning was not to come, however, until after the 1972 Bundestag Election, which confirmed decisively the party's role in Opposition, for the political situation during 1969-72 with uncertainty over the future of the Brandt/Scheel Government gave the CDU hope of returning to power as soon as possible. Throughout the first Opposition period, the CDU/CSU Bundestag *Fraktion*'s role was enhanced as underlined by the unified leadership (CDU chairmanship as well as CDU/CSU Chancellor candidacy) in the person of its own leader, Rainer Barzel.[o] The *Fraktion* became the focus of political activity within the party, so that the strong imbalance between the

o   See above Chapter 5(b).

CDU's parliamentary organs and its extra-parliamentary organisation was hardly altered during these first years after the loss of power, thus illustrating how organisational reform depended for its momentum not simply on external political pressures but also on the effect of these pressures on the internal party balance of forces. The question of this institutional balance within the party will be looked at first of all, before discussing organisational changes involving the role and functions of the extra-parliamentary party during the Opposition period.

One of the first reactions to the speedy formation of the SPD/FDP coalition in Bonn was a series of appeals by various party leaders for wholesale changes in the party machine. The CDU was now forced back on its own resources, having lost the use of official publicity and other advantages of power as well as the enjoyment of all the trappings of office. The chairman of the Hesse *Landesverband,* Alfred Dregger, urged the CDU in a speech at Wiesbaden to take advantage of the change of power in Bonn to build up an effective party organisation at all levels.[43] Ernst Benda, the ex-Minister of the Interior called for a 'reform of head and limbs' in the CDU, while Gerhard Stoltenberg emphasised the need for more teamwork and better publicity to accompany stronger party organisation.[44] The most explicit plans came from the younger generation in the CDU. At the Hamm congress of the Young Union in November 1969, its newly elected chairman. Jürgen Echternach, concentrated his speech on the organisational consequences of the party's role in Opposition:

> The CDU should not take its opposition role as an undeserved blow of fortune and show whining self-pity, but must seize the change in roles as an opportunity . . . The CDU must finally become a party capably of activity. At present it appears predominantly as a disorganised, loosely united reservoir of heterogeneous associations and autonomous regional branches . . . the Federal party and its organisations must become the centre of political decision-making in the CDU . . . that means tightening up the organisation and modernising the party machine.[45]

The party's university association, the Ring of Christian Democratic Students (RCDS), published a critical review of the party entitled '34 Theses on the Reform of the CDU' in December 1969, calling for more effective co-operation and better communication between the national party and its regional and district branches, more inner party democracy and the reorganisation and enlargement of the national headquarters.[46]

A number of important organisational changes did occur or begin to develop in the first Opposition period, notably a reorganisation of the *Bundesgeschäftsstelle* in Bonn,[p] an increase in party membership,[q] more regular meetings of the Federal party organs and monthly conferences of the business managers of the *Landesverbände*.[47] These changes pointed to a growing self-awareness of the CDU as a mass-organised political party, but they were not accompanied before 1972-3 by any significant shift of political weight towards the extra-parliamentary party. The principal reason for this was, as already noted, the new predominance acquired by the Bundestag *Fraktion* after the loss of power. To this end the *Fraktion* was reorganised in the autumn of 1969.[r] Since the party no longer had the benefit of official information sources, the *Fraktion* developed its own planning staff and body of research assistants, for prior to 1969 it had only a few auxiliary staff.[48]

A further complicating factor arising from the CDU's new role in Opposition was the growth of open institutional rivalry between the extra-parliamentary organisation and the Bundestag *Fraktion*. Both sought to extend their degree of organisational articulation, while demands for radical party reform, coupled with much greater pressure for inner party democracy, strengthened the claims of the national party organisation to have a decisive say in party policy.[49] Hence, there were repeated complaints that the party as a whole was being under-valued, such as Kurt Biedenkopf's express concern that the CDU was in danger of becoming a '*Fraktion* party' rather than a 'Chancellor party'.[50] Biedenkopf reiterated his belief that the national party organisation and the Bundestag *Fraktion* had separate but equally important tasks to perform in Opposition in his outline of a strategy for the CDU shortly before he became its General Secretary in 1973:

> The organisational strategy must be so constituted that the party can claim and accomplish its leadership role in the field of programme and principles. At the same time the organisation must further, and not impede, the integrative force of the people's party (*Volkspartei*).

p   See below pp. 263-4.
q   See below chapter 8 (b).
r   See above chapter 5 (b), p. 195.

That is to say: the organisation of the party must be independent
from the organisation of the *Fraktion*. Co-operation must accord with
the necessary division of labour between practical opposition work
in the parliament, and the fundamental renewal of the party. The
personal separation of the *Fraktion* chairmanship and the party
chairmanship is therefore indispensable.[51]

Although some of Biedenkopf's demands were not new in CDU organisational history, this institutional rivalry was now raised to a higher
political level than ever before. It was implicit in Kohl's challenge to
Barzel for the CDU chairmanship in 1971, for Kohl made it clear that if
elected he would give prior attention to strengthening the national party
organisation. Just as Barzel's victory in 1971 symbolised the predominance of the Bundestag *Fraktion* within the party, so Kohl's
eventual election as CDU chairman in June 1973 marked the beginning
of a shift of authority towards the extra-parliamentary organisation.
Neither Kohl nor Biedenkopf were even members of the *Fraktion*. The
Fraktion leadership now under Karl Carstens played a lower-key role,[s]
while more emphasis was placed on the party's parliamentary role in the
Bundesrat where it had a majority over the Government. Biedenkopf
asserted himself as General Secretary more politically than his
predecessors, and equally the *Bundesgeschäftsstelle* claimed a stronger
presence in policy formulation.[52]

Inevitably, there is often in democratic political parties a marked
imbalance in favour of the parliamentary element over the national
party organisation. This has at least been true of West German parties,
except that with the CDU this imbalance has been extreme because
of its long period in office since its early years. What was happening
now in Opposition was not so much a swing to the other extreme as
an attempt to right the balance. This effort to strengthen the extra-
parliamentary organisation of the CDU will now be examined more
specifically.

First, the role of the *Bundesgeschäftsstelle* was gradually upgraded
to a more political level. The first change came with the reorganisation of the BGS in June 1970, involving its work being
now shared by seven departments (internal administration, personnel
planning, organisation, policy, publicity, information and press,
radio and television) with a further subdivision into working
groups, and resulting in a clearer delineation of the responsibilities

s   See above chapter 5 (c), pp. 220-1.

of each official.[53] The following year the long-awaited move to a
new headquarters was accomplished. The twelve-storey Konrad
Adenauer House was opened in the Friedrich Ebert Allee, accom-
modating for the first time all sections of the BGS together.

The new CDU Business Manager, Rüdiger Göb, a former higher
civil servant in the Ministry of the Interior and a management expert,
sought to make the BGS into 'the Government machine of the
Opposition'.[54] In a series of interviews at the time of his appointment
early in 1970, Göb emphasised that the organisational machine of
an Opposition party had 'other and more difficult tasks' than
that of a governing party. He listed as his main aims systematic
planning of party tasks, co-ordination of the 'many forces inside
the party' for the purpose of common action and the creation of a
larger and effective information system. These in short amounted
to what Göb called 'the organisational integration of the whole
party'.[55] While some steps were taken towards personnel planning,
Göb's overall ambitions for the CDU proved impossible to implement,
and he resigned at the end of 1971. His aims would have involved
the BGS as the centre of a strictly co-ordinated and professionalised
party machine, but Göb complicated matters by arguing provocatively
that there was too much confusion between political and administrative roles and that therefore the position of General Secretary
should be abolished. His use of technical language helped to alienate
traditional party officials, but the main reason for his failure was
simply that the role of Opposition was not taken that seriously
during his period of office. However, Göb's point that the CDU
needed to depend more on the BGS for specialist advice in the
absence of the Government machine was recognised fully after
the change of party leadership in 1973. Kurt Biedenkopf saw the
BGS as more than simply the administrative centre of the party. In
his speech to the Hamburg Congress in November 1973, he noted:

> The Konrad Adenauer House in Bonn is the place from
> which the party will be led. It must at the same time become
> the turnplate and junction of inner party discussion, and so
> develop the integrative force without which a great people's
> party is not viable.[56]

Biedenkopf's success in upgrading the BGS to a political level of
activity can best be measured in the light of his own performance as
General Secretary.

Secondly, the General Secretary under Biedenkopf (1973-7) developed more of a political presence not only as head of the party organisation, which will be considered here, but also as policy formulator.[21] Biedenkopf's different conception of the General Secretaryship from that of his predecessors was evident from the many statements he made at the time of his appointment. He defined his three aims as organisational, furthering internal party discussion and preparing the party for forthcoming elections. Above all, he emphasised that his work place was not only in Bonn, but also in the *Landesverbände* and auxiliary organisations for the purpose of promoting the effective co-ordination of party organisationl activity.[57] Biedenkopf's strategy was very clearly electorally motivated, for he maintained that the next Bundestag Election in 1976 could only be won if the CDU were revived from the grass-roots upwards.[58] This meant among other things activating the party's interest and role in local politics, where it had traditionally been weak. On the purely organisational side, Biedenkopf achieved much in making the presence and role of the BGS more acceptable at all levels of the party, and made progress in restructuring the party machine, having already reorganised departments at the BGS soon after he was appointed and chosen new and younger personnel to head them.[59] Through better co-ordination between the BGS and the *Landesverbände* a well-organised CDU speakers' service was developed, party spokesmen on radio and TV were better prepared and the network of salaried district party offices was enlarged and made more efficient, so that already by late 1974 the SPD was beginning to show a concern about the better organisation of the CDU.[60] Furthermore, as will now be seen, steps were taken to make the position of party officials more professional.

Thirdly, the role of CDU activists was placed on a new basis with systematic efforts to define their career pattern. Bruno Heck (General Secretary until 1971) was instrumental in encouraging the training of party officials, an idea which came to fruition with the initiation of party training courses from 1973. Biedenkopf showed a special concern when he was appointed for the problems of activists, and declared that he would always have 'an open door' for them. He lent full support to the training of officials, a new development in the CDU from the early 1970s which was facilitated by a more active party membership.[22] Personnel planning became the new 'in' word in party organisation, and was illustrated by the creation of a personnel data bank at the BGS in 1972 and the general work of the

personnel planning department there.[61] Various plans were drawn up
for the training of activists,[62] while at the local level different
models for party activity were invented, such as the Essen model for
the work of district branches,[63]   so that generally speaking the role
of local notables at the grass-roots has been phased out. An important
new feature in the party organisational structure has been the introduction from 1975 of servicing centres (*Dienstleistungszentren*), which
act as distribution agencies for party information and generally
promote the communication system in the CDU.[23] In recent
years there has developed a new emphasis on the managerial and
technical aspects of party organisation.[24] The degree of success
with this professionalisation of party activists has varied from area to
area, although generally co-ordination between the national,
regional and district levels of the party organisation has improved
greatly.

Fourthly, the state of organisation in the CDU cannot be
considered without final reference to party finance. When the CDU
first entered Opposition the situation became critical because it
not only incurred heavy debts from the 1969 Bundestag Election,
but it also generally proved less attractive to support from business
and industry since it was no longer the party of government. The
burden was further increased by the cost of extending the BGS and
housing it in its new building, although this was helped by letting
five of the 12 floors of the Konrad Adenauer House as office
accommodation. Party finances were then put in a more efficient
order by Walther Leisler Kiep, who became CDU Treasurer in 1971.
The greatest change in the source of finances has come from the
steep rise in the amount of income from membership dues, as a
direct result of the successful membership recruitment campaign
during Opposition. According to the figures for CDU income in
1974, membership dues accounted for DM 25.8 m out of a total
of DM 88.6 m, which represented an enormous increase over
previous years (DM 7.7 m in 1969 and DM 12.6 in 1971).[64]

The CDU has consequently assumed in Opposition many characteristics of a modern organised political party, with far better co-
ordination between the different levels of the party structure and
a greater consciousness of the importance of efficient organisation.
It is possible even to speak of an *Apparatbewusstsein* (an awareness
of the values of the party machine) with a virtual disappearance of
the traditional antipathy towards bureaucracy within the CDU. It
has become much more of a mass-organised party, with the extra-

parliamentary organisation having greater political weight, a growing professional attitude to party activities and the increasingly active involvement of the membership in party affairs. The improved structural integration of the national party organisation has meant that the CDU can no longer be termed an 'electoral association', although as before the rhythm of party activities is geared electorally because of the frequency of election campaigns, regional and local as well as national, in the Federal Republic. In one basic respect, the party structure has not changed radically. While the *Landesverbände* are no longer the exclusive filter for the party communication system and their position is no longer regarded with such reverence, they still remain the fundamental units in the party structure. Co-ordination rather than centralisation has therefore been the keynote of party organisational reform, which was successfully implemented for the first time in the CDU's history because of the 'historic necessity' imposed by the role of Opposition.

Notes

[1] Cf. Kurt Biedenkopf's remark in his speech to the *Land* party congress of the Baden-Württemberg CDU in June 1973 that 'the CDU was in the past 20 years less a party of organisation than a party of results'. (*Erneuern und Bewahren*, Landesparteitag CDU Baden-Württemberg (1973), p. 24.)

[2] See for instance Renate Mayntz's study of the West Berlin CDU in the 1950s. Although it was felt that the principle of voluntariness mitigated against efficiency particularly in view of the reluctance of members to engage themselves in party activities, the abhorrence of any aspect of control in party management was widespread. In one case, a member of a district executive was charged with organising the distribution of special propaganda leaflets. This had to be done on a certain day, at a given place and time, so he requested each local branch by letter to send a stated number of helpers. Most local chairmen tried to comply, but some failed because they relied on volunteers. One refused the request because 'it sounded like an order', and there was a hinted comparison with 'Nazi methods'. A heated discussion followed where most party officials tended to agree with the member of the executive under attack. Few came out openly, however, in his support, because they felt his behaviour conflicted with the principle of voluntariness to which they also subscribed. (R. Mayntz, 'Oligarchic Problems in a German Party District', in D. Marvick, *Political Decision-Makers* (1961), p. 171.)

[3] E.g. the comment of Konrad Kraske on his work as CDU Business Manager from 1958 that party activists in the CDU were 'not functionaries who received their orders, but independent-thinking self-reliant people' (interview with the author in Bonn, September 1974).

[4]   According to Heidenheimer, there were altogether some 500 salaried
        party officials in the CDU by the mid-1950s, of whom only 100 were
        employed in various party offices around Bonn (including the head-
        quarters) with the remainder employed by the *Landesverbande*
        (half of them in the two largest – Rhineland and Westphalia). (See
        A. Heidenheimer, 'German Party Finance: the CDU' in *American
        Political Science Review*, June 1957, pp. 370-71.) The CDU Federal
        headquarters employed about 60 officials during the 1950s; it
        suffered in particular from money problems during this time
        (interview with Bruno Heck, CDU Business Manager 1952-58, in
        Bonn, September 1973).

[5]   This was particularly noticeable in the CDU in south-west Germany;
        e.g. the letter of the *Land* business manager of the CDU in Wurttemberg-
        Hohenzollern to members of the *Land* party executive, 26.4.54, in
        which he criticised the 'slack organisational structure' of the *Landes-
        verband* as a reason for the below-average voter turnout in that region,
        but in order not to be misunderstood he felt compelled to assert
        that 'it is not our intention to create a centralistic functionaries' party
        out of our federalistic Union, for that would not at all accord with the
        will of the majority of our voters' (BGS Archiv, A 32d, Teil X). For a
        more recent expression of the attachment to federalism, see the
        report of the Basic Policy Commission of the Baden-Württemberg CDU,
        Gedanken zur Gesellschaftspolitik unf zum Föderalismus, produced in
        the early 1970s.

[6]   E.g. the comment of Konrad Kraske, former Business Manager of
        the CDU, that the *Landesverbände* of Schleswig-Holstein and West
        Berlin had been the most 'federally loyal' in his experience and that
        the reason lay in the Prussian tradition with its preference for
        centralism. In the case of Schleswig-Holstein, relations with the
        Landesverband had been facilitated by the influence of the party
        reformer Kai-Uwe von Hassel, who believed in the values of a structured
        political party (interview with Kraske in Bonn, September 1974).
        Kraske himself came from Berlin.

[7]   There had in fact been a General Secretary for the CDU in Lower
        Saxony from the party's early years. This post was responsible for
        co-ordinating political positions between the three *Landesverbände*
        in co-operation with the Landtag *Fraktion* in Hanover, but the
        Landesverbände each remained in control of its own party organisation
        (interview with Arnold Fratzscher, General Secretary for the CDU
        in Lower Saxony, 1946-66, in Hanover, September 1973).

[8]   In the case of Baden-Württemberg, the regional structure of party
        organisation had been formed long before the establishment of a new
        Land for the whole of south-west Germany in 1953.

[9]   In the organisational history of the CDU, Westphalians have usually
        feared dominance by the Rhineland branch.

[10]   The first General Secretary of the Baden-Württemberg CDU was
        Wolfgang Schall (1971-3), a former brigadier-general, whose efforts
        at centralisation failed. The new *Land* party headquarters has
        nevertheless been reasonably effective in co-ordinating political
        activities among the four sub-regional units, particularly with the
        organisation of election campaigns (interview with Paul Krauskopf,
        official at the Baden-Württemberg CDU headquarters, in Stuttgart,
        August 1973).

[11]   A prominent example was Rainer Barzel, chairman of the Bundestag

Fraktion, 1964-73, even though he cultivated his constituency in Paderborn.

[12] Richard Davy, assistant *Times* correspondent in Bonn 1957-9, remarked that he remembered going to the CDU national headquarters during the 1957 Bundestag election campaign for handouts, programmes, briefings about tactics and press conferences, but did not recall going there again after the election (interview with the author, London, May 1974). Cf. the comment by Konrad Kraske, assistant CDU Business Manager 1954-8 and Business Manager from 1958, that the main task of the Federal party headquarters until 1969 was to 'get majorities for the Government' (interview in Bonn, September 1974).

[13] See for instance the report presented by Bruno Heck to the Federal Executive of the CDU in October 1966, critical of the lack of authority of the Federal party organs. He said among other things that 'up to now the leadership of the CDU was characterised by the fact that certain individual leader personalities stamped their mark on it; that brought great success, and in the first decade filled the gaps missing in the experience of party matters, but the whole will of the party was not therefore sufficiently expressed; today that is no longer possible, for the party leadership as a whole must have a continuous effect on the clear formation of a will inside the party; for this it requires a certain authority, and one cannot forget that in the construction of the CDU the Federal leadership was not given this authority adequately; the Federal Executive and the Praesidium have few powers in serious decisions, so that one can ignore their votes easily without having to fear any detriment to oneself' (Heck's report was published in full in the press, see 'Selbstkritik der CDU: "Die Führungsorgane führen zuwenig" ' in *SZ*, 8 October 1966).

[14] The variety of the CDU's experience at the *Land* level of politics tends to support this thesis. This has varied from alternation between government and opposition roles in North-Rhine Westphalia, continuous office in the Rhineland-Palatinate, Schleswig-Holstein (since 1950) and Baden-Württemberg (since 1953) to continuous opposition in Hesse and the two Hanseatic city states of Bremen and Hamburg (except for 1953-7). An alternation in roles tends to reinforce attempts to structure party organisation, because the shock of the loss of power may lead to changes where there is a reasonable prospect of a return to office. Where the CDU has remained continuously in opposition because of its minority situation, party organisation may stagnate because of a sense of hopelessness (e.g. in Hamburg). Although continuous governmental office usually erases a pressing need for party reorganisation, an electoral setback may stimulate such change while still remaining in office − e.g. with the Rhineland-Palatinate CDU after its loss of votes in the 1963 *Land* election. Any estimation of the impact of the government/opposition role on party organisation at the *Land* level must of course take account of other factors, such as the shock of a national political reverse, tensions within the *Land* leadership and regional attitudes towards the concept of party organisation.

[15] The CDU in Schleswig-Holstein was known as favouring a structured political party more than most *Landesverbände,* so that the views in this memorandum were not necessarily representative of all of them.

[16] At the same time, the memorandum was careful to point out that the BGS could only establish personal contacts with the district branches 'at the wish of the authorised *Landesverband'.*

[17]　Local notables included in the case of the CDU traditional local families in villages, district presidents (*Landräte*), some professional middle-class people and (especially Roman Catholic) priests. They remained for some time prominent in CDU electoral strongholds, where there were no obvious pressures to remove their control.

[18]　According to Willy Wagner, CDU *Kreisgeschäftsführer* for the city of Mainz, party district managers in the Rhineland-Palatinate now received a full salary. As a result, the notables had been 'shelved', and only played a 'passive role' in party organisation. The emphasis was on younger activists and above all 'dynamism'. This had attracted more intellectuals into the party in Mainz, particularly from the university, and encouraged much more internal party policy discussion. A typical example of this new development was the formation of numerous working groups of members in the city, each of these dealing with specialist policy fields for the purpose of formulating the *Mainzer Programm* in time for the 1974 municipal elections. (Interview with Willy Wagner, Mainz, August 1973.)

[19]　According to Schleth, 94 per cent SPD members paid up, while only 50 per cent did in the CDU case. There was much variation, for Schleth investigated 20 representative CDU district branches. While their general rate of payment was 75 per cent, the individual branches fluctuated between 49 per cent and 93 per cent (Uwe Schleth, 'Die Finanzen der CDU' in E. Scheuch and R. Wildenmann, *Zur Soziologie der Wahl* (1968), pp. 235-6).

[20]　The problem of basic attitudes within the CDU was illustrated at this time by the case of the local party branch in Dorfmerkingen in North Württemberg. The local chairman wrote a letter of protest to the *Landesverband* chairman in Stuttgart, complaining that the direct letter to party members asking for a rise in subscriptions was a mistake, particularly as it did not take into account local conditions. In this village of 680 the chairman had been active in boosting membership to 50, although many of the poorer peasants found it hard to pay subscriptions: 'Only with an appeal to their Christian consciousness of responsibility did we move several to join the CDU; this decision meant for some a financial sacrifice in fact, and now that these people are firmly anchored in the CDU there comes the demand from Bonn for raising subscriptions.' He also added that they had made a further sacrifice in joining, 'for they are criticised and ridiculed by others and are accused of bringing party squabbling into the so far "peaceful" village life'. (Letter from Hans Gebhard, Dorfmerkingen, to Klaus Scheufelen, Stuttgart, 25 November 1964, Archiv CDU Nord-Württemberg.)

[21]　Biedenkopf's role as a policy formulator as well as his involvement in party leadership affairs is discussed above in chapter 6 (d).

[22]　E.g. this has made it necessary for the district branches to make detailed and systematic monthly reports to the *Landesverbände* offices on such matters as membership policy, party meetings (with full details), finance, the activities of the SPD and future party events in their areas (interview with Karl Enderes, district branch manager of the Sieburg CDU, in Siegburg, August 1976).

[23]　The idea for these servicing centres came from the BGS, and a resolution of the 1975 CDU Congress led to their introduction from August of that year. They were chiefly motivated by the need to improve internal party communications because of the great increase in party membership, particularly with a view to the organisation of the Bundestag Election campaign in 1976. They were particularly important in areas where party

organisation had usually been under-developed, and by May 1976 37 had been set up around the country. They worked in co-operation with the *Landesverbände* (e.g. there were 7 such centres in Westphalia-Lippe in the summer of 1976), and their advantage of speedy communication with the BGS was further improved by the institution of a teleprinter network (interview with Reinhard Weiss, head of the organisation department *Landesverband* Westfalen-Lippe, in Dortmund, August 1976; see also, report on the *Dienstleistungszentren* in *Bericht der Bundesgeschäftstekke* presented to the 1976 CDU Congress, pp. 19-20).

[24]   Some of the changes implemented under Biedenkopf were envisaged during the first Opposition period, when an Organisation Commission was established in 1971 under Konrad Kraske, General Secretary 1971-3 (see the report on the work of this Commission in *Bericht der Bundesgeschäfts-stelle* presented to the CDU Congress in June 1973, pp. 13-18).

References

1.   *6. Bundesparteitag der CDU* (1956), p. 26.
2.   *Ibid.*, p. 107.
3.   *Erneuern und Bewahren,* Landesparteitag CDU Baden-Württemberg (1973), p. 26.
4.   Gerhard Schulz, 'Die Organisationsstruktur der CDU' in *Zeitschrift für Politik,* H.2, 1956, p. 148.
5.   *Dokumente zur Christlichen Demokratie* (1969), p. 222.
6.   J.H. Dufhues, *Bundespartei – Landesparteien – Kreisparteien,* undated memo., Archiv BGS.
7.   *Politisches Jahrbuch der CDU und CSU 1968,* Pt. 2, p. 150.
8.   Rüdiger Altmann, *Das Erbe Adenauers* (1960), p. 92.
9.   See study of the Heidelberg CDU in B. Vogel and P. Haungs, *Wahlkampf und Wählertradition, eine Studie zur Bundestagswahl von 1961* (1965), p. 230.
10. Speech by Dr Franz Gurk at Landesparteitag 1966, *Tätigkeits- und Geschäftsbericht LV Nordbaden,* p. 7, Archiv LV Nordbaden.
11. See *Der Spiegel,* 3 July 1967, p. 32.
12. Quoted in letter from CDU Kreisverband Olpe to Otto Laipold, Landesgeschäftsstelle CDU Westfalen-Lippe, 29 November 1951, Archiv CDU Westfalen-Lippe 221.
13. *Statut der CDU 1950,* article 14 in *Erster Parteitag der CDU* (1950), p. 176.
14. *12. Bundesparteitag der CDU* (1964), p. 41.
15. Klaus Dreher, 'Drei Bonner Parteizentralen' in *SZ,* 5 January 1968.
16. Resolutions for the 1951 Congress, report of party headquarters, 10 October 1951, Archiv BGS.
17. H.U. Pusch, *Was erwarten die Landesverbände von der Arbeit der BGS,* Niederschrift über die 1. Landesgeschäftsführerkonferenz, January 1962, Archiv CDU Westfalen-Lippe 227 II.
18. Dufhues, *Bundespartei – Landesparteien – Kreisparteien,* Archov BGS, p. 3.
19. See report by Dufhues to Bundesvorstand, 22 November 1962, Hauptstaatsarchiv Düsseldorf, RWV 26, No. 233b.
20. See *General Anzeiger* (Bonn), 14 August 1958 and *Deutsches Monatsblatt,* January 1971.
21. See report of Bundesvorstand to Hamburg Congress 1953 in *Dokumente*

zur Christlichen Demokratie (1969), p. 222.

22. See *Organisationsplan der BGS*, February 1962, Archiv CDU Westfalen-Lippe 222 II.

23. E.g. 'Die hessische CDU wartet auf Dufhues: CDU-Landesverband will mit Honoratiorenwesen Schluss machen' in *Deutsche Zeitung*, 16 February 1963, and Günther Gillessen, 'Bliebt die Unionspartei in der Reform stecken? Von der Wähler- zur Mitgliederpartei' in *FAZ*, 31 August 1963.

24. Hans Schreiber, 'Zum Thema Partei-Organisation' in *Deutschland Union-Dienst*, 1 March 1949.

25. *Deutsche Zeitung*, 4 May 1963.

26. *Civis*, 1964, No. 3, p. 17.

27. *6. Bundesparteitag der CDU* (1956), p. 106.

28. *8. Bundesparteitag der CDU* (1958), pp. 59-62.

29. *9. Bundesparteitag der CDU* (1960), p. 76.

30. Renate Mayntz, 'Oligarchic Problems in a German Party District' in D. Marvick, *Political Decision-Makers* (1961), pp. 167-8.

31. *Die Rheinpfalz* (Neustadt), 6 July 1963 and *Deutsche Zeitung*, 16 July 1963.

32. *Die Welt*, 16 January 1967.

33. See *Dienstanweisung für die Geschäftsstellen der CDU im Lande Rheinland-Pfalz*, Archiv CDU Niedersachsen.

34. See minutes of Landesgeschäftsführerkonferenz, 8 December 1971, Archiv CDU Niedersachsen.

35. See *Die Zeit*, 12 July 1968; *Der Spiegel*, 3 July 1967, p. 32; and *Die Zeit*, 19 May 1967.

36. Report on the district branches, CDU Hamburg, 8 June 1970, Archiv CDU Hamburg.

37. *Besetzung und Ausrüstung der Kreisgeschäftsstellen, Vorlage der Organisationskommission zur Landesgeschäftsführerkonferenz am 12/13 Juni 1972*, Archiv CDU Niedersachsen.

38. *Ibid.*

39. H.J. Varain, *Parteien und Verbände, eine Studie über ihren Aufbau, ihre Verflechtung und ihr Wirken in Schleswig-Holstein, 1945-1958* (1964), p. 201.

40. For details, see Tony Burkett, *Parties and Elections in West Germany* (1975), pp. 136-8.

41. For a review of these changes in party publicity, see article on CDU finance in *Die Zeit*, 1 October 1971.

42. Kai-Uwe von Hassel, report on party organisation to CDU Schleswig-Holstein, March 1968, Archiv CDU Hamburg, p. 32.

43. *Frankfurter Neue Presse*, 9 October 1969.

44. *The Times*, 16 October 1969.

45. Quoted in Kaack, *Geschichte und Struktur des deutschen Parteiensystems* (1971), p. 539.

46. *Sonde*, No. 4, 1969.

47. *Die Zeit*, 11 February 1972.

48. *FAZ*, 7 January 1970.

49. For a discussion of this problem, see H.L. Baumanns and W. Bergsdorf, 'CDU im dritten Jahrzehnt' in *Aus Politik und Zeitgeschichte*, 2 October 1971, pp. 13-14.

50. *Der Spiegel*, 11 October 1971, pp. 31 ff.

51. Kurt Biedenkopf, 'Eine Strategie für die Opposition: Zurück zu den Grundsätzen — mehr Spielraum für die Partei' in *Die Zeit*, 16 March 1973.

52. See Carl-Christian Kaiser, 'Machtverschiebung in der CDU: nicht die Fraktion, die Partei gibt den Ton an' in *Die Zeit*, 11 October 1974.

53. For details of the reorganisation, see Helmuth Pütz, *Die Christlich-Demokratische Union* (1971), pp. 58-61.

54. Interview in *Politisch-Soziale Korrespondenz*, No. 4, 15 February 1970.

55. See interviews in *FR*, 24 March 1970; *Welt der Arbeit*, 15 May 1970 and *Die Entscheidung*, April 1970.

56. *22. Bundesparteitag der CDU* (1973), p. 54.

57. Article in *Der Agrarbrief*, 29 June 1973.

58. *Union in Deutschland*, 22 November 1973.

59. *Ibid.*, 23 August 1973.

60. See Hans Kepper, 'SPD besorgt über wachsende Schlagkraft des CDU-Apparats' in *FR*, 16 October 1974. This published details of a confidential paper produced by the SPD executive on the subject.

61. *Bericht der BGS*, June 1973, pp. 46-7.

62. E.g. *Vorschlag für ein Aus- und Fortbildungsprogramm für die hauptamtlichen Mitarbeiter der Partei*, 28 February 1973. Archiv BGS 2/201.

63. *Union in Deutschland*, 17 April 1973.

64. See *FR*, 28 November 1975 and *FAZ*, 22 January 1973.

8 PARTY MEMBERSHIP OF THE CDU

(a) Composition of Membership

It has been a theme central to the Christian Democratic way of life to present the CDU as a *Volkspartei* ('popular party'), that is one which appeals substantially across the various social classes and economic interests while at the same time representing them individually. As Kurt Georg Kiesinger, then a prominent Bundestag deputy, proudly insisted at the Hamburg Congress in 1953:

> The Christian Democratic Union is the most complicated and most differentiated of all political parties in Germany. It has an astonishing range confessionally, sociologically, topographically and occupationally . . . We are the only genuine great *Volkspartei* in this country.[1]

There can of course be no pure *Volkspartei* in a democratic state, where there is a genuine competition among different political parties seeking to represent different interests, but the fundamental criterion for measuring a particular party's degree of approximation to the ideal *Volkspartei* is how it relates externally (in its voter appeal) and internally (in the composition of its membership) to the social structure of the population. As the former aspect is treated elsewhere,[a] this chapter section will concentrate on the social composition of the CDU membership.

One essential feature of this question is to determine how much change has occurred during the party's first 30 years of existence. There has been some correlation here with the changing political fortunes of the CDU, for in the mid-1960s during the party's decline as a dominant force it was noted by Günther Gillessen of the *Frankfurter Allgemeine* on the basis of a detailed study of the CDU's membership that it was 'too old and too small, too Catholic and too rural', and that it would have to broaden its scope in order to maintain its political dominance.[2] Even during the party's heyday in the 1950s, Renate Mayntz suggested there was a similar bias in the composition of its membership for the dominant social groups among party activists

a See below chapter 11 (a) on the voter appeal of the CDU.

274

tended to recruit primarily from their own kind.[3] This was not surprising in view of the restrictive attitude towards new membership on the part of local notables with their controlling influence then at the grass-roots of the party organisation.[b] Similarly, at a later stage, the question of change in membership composition must take into account the considerable increase in CDU membership from 1972-3.

One complicating factor in scrutinising the composition of CDU membership derives from the nature of internal party relations, for during the 1950s and earlier 1960s the district branches, who admitted new members, and also the *Landesverbände,* were reluctant to impart to the national organisation detailed information about party membership.[1] This only began to change once the CDU established a central membership card-index at the party headquarters in Bonn from the mid-1960s. This reluctance to provide such information was finally overcome during the Opposition years, when the entire party was galvanised into supporting organisational change.

The social composition of CDU membership will now be discussed by looking in turn at each relevant category, taking into account any significant changes during the period as well as variations evident at the regional and local level:

(1) Occupation

A clear occupational bias has always existed in the CDU membership with a marked over-representation of the self-employed, and a very strong under-representation of blue-collar workers compared with the West German population. The latter feature has most distinguished it from the SPD, which has included a proportion of working-class members much more in accordance with their share of the population (about one-half). Figures for the early CDU (1947-55) suggested a proportion of workers in the range 11-15 per cent[4] on the basis of evidence from different *Landesverbände,* although there was a strong variation between North-Rhine Westphalia, where the CDU enjoyed its strongest support among (especially Catholic) workers (25 per cent in Westphalia, 21.2 per cent in the Rhineland), and other regions with figures declining to 5.5 per cent in the rural state of Schleswig-Holstein.[5] This overall proportion has generally remained constant since then, even during Opposition (e.g. 11.26 per cent in 1972). There has been a similar constancy in the case of the self-employed (about 30 per cent of the membership), compared with their share of the population of about 12 per cent (figures for 1962-9).[6] Roughly

b   See above chapter 7 (b), pp. 254-5.

proportionate to the population has been the share in the membership of white-collar workers (as with the SPD), although in both parties civil servants have been somewhat over-represented. While farmers (*Bauern*) have been far more strongly represented in the CDU (33 per cent) than in the SPD generally speaking, their actual proportion of the membership has varied considerably from area to area, according to both demographic structure and the relationship between their interest associations and the CDU at the *Land* level, as Heidenheimer found in his research on the party during the 1950s.[7] In short, therefore, the CDU membership is predominantly middle-class in contrast to that of the SPD, as is shown by the figures in Table 1.

Table 1: Occupational Structure of Party Membership, late 1968

	CDU	SPD	Population Structure
Self-employed	31%	6%	11%
White-collar workers	27%	23%	28%
Civil servants	18%	10%	5%
Workers	13%	37%	47%
Pensioners	12%	24%	16%

Source: Survey of the Institute for Political Science, Free University Berlin, and the Infas Institute, Bad Godesberg, published in *Der Spiegel,* 11 May 1970, p.54.

(2) Confession

How successful has the CDU's attempt since the Second World War to establish a 'confessional bridge' between Catholics and Protestants been in terms of membership?[c] Generally, Catholics have always been over-represented with a proportion of roughly two-thirds to one-third Protestants, which does not accord well with the average of the population (50-55 per cent Protestant, 45-40 per cent Catholic since the War). There have again been considerable variations at the regional and local levels following the lines of demographic structure, although an additional factor, as Heidenheimer noticed in the 1950s, was a pronounced indifference among Protestants since the founding years based on their difficulty at first in identifying with the CDU.[8] This explained the even greater predominance of Catholics among the activist membership, and also the lower proportion of CDU members to CDU voters in strong Protestant areas compared with areas of mixed

c   See above chapter 1 (a), pp. 26-8 and 1 (c), pp. 40-3.

confession and strong Catholic areas.[9] This disparity became even more
marked during the course of the 1950s, when the proportion of
Protestant members did not keep pace with the considerable rise in
Protestant CDU voters (as part of the general rise in CDU voters). It
was very noticeable in rural areas, where Catholic priests for instance
quite often joined the party but Protestant priests did only rarely.[10]
As shown by the next table, Catholics have been over-represented at
every regional level of the party compared with the population, even in
strong Protestant areas except for Schleswig-Holstein. During Opposition, the proportion of Protestants has increased marginally with the
dramatic overall rise in CDU membership: they accounted for 40 per
cent of new members during 1975, compared with 31 per cent of the
whole membership in 1974.[11]

Table 2: Confessional Structure of CDU Membership, December 1969,[12]
According to Regional Organisations, Compared with Population

Landesverband (LV)	Protestant		Catholic	
	LV %	Pop. %	LV %	Pop. %
Saar	7.09	24.6	92.30	73.4
South Baden	7.68	31.2	90.75	66.1
Rhineland-Palatinate	9.77	41.5	87.85	56.2
Württemberg-Hohenzollern	10.35	45.2	83.24	51.5
Rhineland	13.73	37.5	84.65	57.5
North Baden	14.56	48.4	77.53	47.4
Westphalia	16.00	50.2	79.93	46.0
Hesse	25.50	63.2	70.28	32.1
North Württemberg	26.36	60.2	70.55	34.0
Oldenburg	27.26	67.8	58.13	27.7
Hanover	46.38	78.5	50.29	17.9
Bremen	56.05	84.7	40.13	9.9
West Berlin	56.46	72.1	39.58	11.4
Brunswick	59.78	75.9	35.61	16.4
Hamburg	66.67	75.4	28.47	7.4
Schleswig-Holstein	82.25	87.4	6.63	5.6
Total CDU Membership	23.00	56.2	73.72	38.4

N.B. this table does not include figures for the small section of the population,
which is neither Catholic nor Protestant.

Protestants have gradually overcome their indifference towards membership of the CDU in the period since the War. It may be said in conclusion that the CDU has been relatively successful in building a 'confessional bridge', though this has been a feature more pronounced among its voters[d] than its members. This nevertheless represents an important departure from its pre-Nazi predecessor, the Centre Party.

(3) Age

As with its voters, the CDU's members have shown a marked over-representation of the older age groups throughout most of the party's 30-year history. This bias had its origins in the early years for the War had decimated the younger generation, and this was shown by the detailed membership reports of the Rhineland CDU for the late 1940s and by Varain's research on the early CDU in Schleswig-Holstein.[13] This tendency was encouraged by the initial predominance in many areas of pre-1933 party activists, and by the restrictive membership policy of local notables, except in isolated cases like Heidelberg where there was an activist circle of young people or student leaders.[14] The age structure began to alter mildly in the 1960s with the challenge to the organisational monopoly of the notables at the local level. Such a case was the Rhineland-Palatinate CDU, which showed an increase in the proportion of the younger age groups from the mid-1960s.[15] This general shift in age structure is illustrated by Table 3 for 1966 and 1969.

Table 3: Age Structure of CDU Membership[16]

	Born before 1920	1921-1940	1941 onwards
Population			
Dec. 1966	50.7%	37.9%	11.3%
Dec. 1969	46.6	38.9	14.5
CDU Members			
Dec. 1966	59.18	35.25	5.06
Dec. 1969	47.02	41.70	8.33

The proportion of younger members has increased substantially since Opposition began. By 1974 the proportion of those born from 1941 (under 33) had risen to 22 per cent, while 40 per cent of the new

d   See below chapter 11 (a), pp. 334-5.

members who joined during 1975 came from the same age group.[17]
This has been the greatest structural change in CDU membership in
recent years, and is directly related to the CDU's evolution as a
membership-party with far more internal party policy discussion[2]
as well as special efforts to woo young party members.

(4) Regional and Local

The size and composition of CDU membership has varied considerably
between the party's different regional organisations (*Landesverbände*).
This has been a factor in estimating their individual organisational and
political weight in the party. Such variation has been accounted for by
different traditions of organisational efficiency as a factor in promoting
membership, differences in the social structure and size of population
between the regions and the impact of historical political traditions in
each area as a factor in receptiveness to CDU membership. So, in spite
of the membership rise in the 1970s, the order of strength of
membership size among the *Landesverbände* has remained broadly
speaking the same as it was in the later 1960s.

Table 4: Size of CDU Membership by Landesverbände (figures for
May 1976)

Rhineland	122,901
Westphalia-Lippe	115,877
Baden-Württemberg	72,650
Rhineland-Palatinate	67,854
Hanover	63,571
Hesse	56,876
Schleswig-Holstein	31,982
Saar	28,755
West Berlin	13,722
Oldenburg	12,709
Hamburg	11,369
Brunswick	9,570
Bremen	3,339
Total:	611,175

Source: Figures provided by the Documentation Department of the CDU
Bundesgeschäftsstelle, Bonn. Note that the three *Landesverbände* of the Lower
Saxony CDU (Hanover, Oldenburg and Brunswick), as well as the two in
North-Rhine Westphalia (Rhineland and Westphalia-Lippe) have, unlike the
original four in Baden-Württemberg, retained their separate status.

The Rhineland CDU has, followed closely by the Westphalian CDU, retained its superiority in membership numbers throughout the party's history. Any such regional categorisation does not of course take account of considerable local variations in the size and structure of CDU membership, which can also help to colour the party's image as seen from the grass-roots.[3]

(5)   Miscellaneous

Certain tendencies are also evident in the structure of CDU membership in relation to other categories. There has been a considerable predominance of men over women, although this is also repeated in the other political parties. It is particularly interesting in the case of the CDU because a significant majority of the CDU voters has been women.[e] This did not change at all during the 1960s (e.g. 13 per cent of the CDU membership was women in 1969), but there has been a slow increase in their proportion during Opposition: 17 per cent of the total membership in 1974, with 26 per cent of new members during 1975 leading to 19 per cent of the total in 1976.[18] The proportion of women has been even weaker in rural areas, even though the CDU membership has generally been more rural-orientated in contrast to the SPD's predominance of membership in the cities.[19]

The CDU may be considered in the light of its membership structure during the past thirty years as a *Volkspartei,* but one with certain serious limitations. Its claim to be such a form of political party has been strengthened by new developments during the Opposition period, although the broadening of its age structure, and to a much lesser extent its sex and confessional structure, has not been accompanied by any relative rise in membership among blue-collar workers within its occupational structure (only 10 per cent in 1974). This is the CDU's most serious drawback as a *Volkspartei* in terms of the social composition of its membership, for it has remained in spite of the dramatic increase in its membership total a predominantly middle-class party in this respect.

(b)   Towards a Membership Party

A very significant change in the internal character of the CDU during the 1970s has been the dramatic rise in its membership total, accompanied by considerable advances in internal party democracy. The latter has developed since the late 1960s, and has been manifest

e   See above chapter 11 (a), pp. 336-7.

through greater policy discussion at different levels of the party with less automatic acceptance of policy statements from the leadership above. It has been a consequence of both a more critical attitude on the party of new members, as well as of the changed political environment in West Germany in the 1970s. The rise in membership was largely a result of the internal impact of the party's new role in Opposition, coupled with a profound antagonism of the CDU membership towards the Left-Liberal coalition in Bonn. The CDU's basic change in adopting an open-door membership policy with successful results in boosting numbers therefore divides fairly clearly its Opposition period from the long years it served as governing party; the party's electoral triumphs in the 1950s did not affect the stagnation of membership, while the first serious efforts to boost membership, in the 1960s, had brought only modest results.

A useful starting-point for evaluating CDU membership is its size in proportion to the party's electorate. Here there was a stark contrast during the 1950s and 1960s between the CDU and the SPD, thus underlining their differences respectively as 'voters' party' and 'members' party'. While the CDU had greater voting appeal than the SPD, the proportion of the former's voters who were also party members was considerably smaller than the latter's: by 1960, one CDU voter out of 52 was also a party member, compared with one out of 16 for the SPD.[20] The gap decreased slowly during the 1960s (e.g. one out of 40 for the CDU in 1967-9), but there was no dramatic change.

The underlying reason for this caution about joining the CDU, particularly evident among middle-class voters who were the principal source of support for the CDU, was their general aversion to the idea of joining a political party as such. As early membership reports of the Rhineland CDU after the War noted, this emotional attitude had its roots in the cauterising experience of the Third Reich which discredited the word 'party', as well as in memories of the bitterness of party politics during the Weimar Republic.[21] f As Bruno Heck emphasised in an article he wrote on the subject in 1956 (as did also Dufhues in the 1960s), this antipathy, amounting to a psychological barrier, could only be overcome in the course of time by much patient effort and a continuous education process in the values of democratic institutions.[22] Similarly, Franz Meyers commented at the 1958 CDU Congress that this problem facing the CDU derived from a 'consumer' attitude among CDU voters (i.e. recognition of CDU achievements did

f   See also above chapter 1 (c), pp. 45-6.

not readily lead to party enrolment) as well as the great distance for them between party politics and personal life.[23]

There were secondary reasons for the lack of membership appeal among CDU voters during the first two decades. The CDU made no sustained organisational effort to enlarge party membership until the mid-1960s, before which time it was lulled into complacency by its electoral dominance but was also inhibited by the restrictionist behaviour of the older generation of party activists, especially the local notables. Party life was often unexciting and unattractive at the grass-roots level, except when an election campaign was in progress. The power of the district branches over membership enrolment proved to be the major obstacle to any concerted drive for membership instigated from Bonn, as Dufhues clearly had to recognise in the mid-1960s. Memoranda from the BGS and *Landesverband* offices containing suggestions for a membership campaign were often careful to stress that the 'freedom of decision' by the district branches remained essentially untouched.[24]

The jealous maintenance of this power was best illustrated by the reactions to the persistent attempt by the BGS to establish a central membership card-index in Bonn over several years. The renowned case of the district branch in Cloppenburg, Lower Saxony, which replied in the following hostile fashion to this idea, was fairly typical of attitudes at this level of the party:

> Our executive committee takes the view that our members do not want this Federal membership card-index. Moreover, we do not have the data to complete the forms, and therefore will not send these back.[25]

In March 1963 a conference of *Landesverbände* chairmen finally gave approval to a central card-index, but it still took some years before it was fully operative. Peter Müllenbach, head of the department for organisation and recruitment at the BGS, who was responsible for establishing the card-index, still felt it necessary to allow a 'voluntariness' in the way district and regional offices could answer his questionnaires on membership details.[26] A year later, only one-third of the district branches had responded, so that Müllenbach now felt compelled to urge the *Landesverbände* to put further pressure on the district branches. Even so, variation in their readiness to co-operate continued to delay the operation of the index.[27] At the 1966 Congress Dufhues could announce at last that the card-index was 90 per cent complete. By the 1970s a computer had been installed at the BGS to operate the index, and in 1971 membership cards began to be centrally issued, thus relieving the district branches of this task.[28]

It is useful at this point to look more closely at the membership campaign launched by Dufhues in the mid-1960s, for it represented the acceptance of the need for a conscious membership policy. The chief motivation was electoral with the growing challenge from the SPD, the belief that the electorate was becoming more volatile and unpredictable and the need to budget for the party's future, especially with a view to the increasing cost of manning election campaigns. The first recruitment campaign was introduced in Dufhues's own *Landesverband* in Westphalia, and was timed to coincide with Erhard's succession to the Chancellorship. It resulted in a few thousand new members, and was intended as the first of a series of such actions elsewhere during 1963-4.[4]

The general membership campaign for 1963-4 was only moderately successful.[5] Characteristic of all CDU membership campaigns during this time was the explicit emphasis on the personal approach in the matter by party members, even though some systematic method had to be adopted for any chance of success. The official CDU 'Manual for Membership Recruitment' issued in the mid-1960s did, however, specify the different stages for these actions, define groups of 'target persons' and even include model letters to be sent and model invitations to CDU meetings.[29] Another general recruitment action was organised in 1965 to coincide with the Bundestag election campaign. The CDU staged a mobile exhibition called 'Come with us to the Year 2000' in different parts of the country. The exhibition featured posters depicting party leaders as well as spacemen ('Man unlocks the Universe'), a colourful decor of flowers and local town flags and the presence on opening day of local party dignitaries.[30]

All these efforts in the mid-1960s encountered an apathy among CDU members, except possibly in North-Rhine Westphalia. The case of the *Landesverband* North Württemberg illustrated this problem. Its chairman, Klaus Scheufelen, wrote to party members late in 1964 about the disappointing response during the recruitment action. Replies from some of them dwelt on the public's ignorance of party programmes, the fact that local organisation 'slept' and the negative effect of the national party leadership disputes. Some had tried to initiate recruitment campaigns but these had proved more difficult than envisaged, particularly as CDU members were generally less cohesive as a body than those of the SPD.[31] The position with the CDU's

membership policy at the beginning of its term in Opposition was
neatly summed up by Bruno Heck at the Mainz Congress in 1969, when
he remarked that several *Landesverbände* treated recruitment
campaigns 'without any seriousness and without any special impetus'.[32]

The general lethargy in the CDU over membership changed
dramatically following its move to the Opposition and the
establishment of the SPD/FDP Government under Brandt. The shock
of the loss of power in Bonn had a mobilising effect on the CDU
rank-and-file, which was maintained through the early 1970s by the
revival of polarisation in West German politics especially over
Ostpolitik. The result was a rise in membership among the major
political parties. With the CDU, there was by the summer of 1970 an
average net increase of 3,000 new members per month, even though
the party had not yet taken steps to introduce a systematic national
membership drive.[33] A recruitment action in West Berlin at the end of
1969 had produced an enthusiastic response, above all among young
people, at a special public gathering for new members addressed
by Barzel.[34] A gut reaction to Brandt's policies was apparently the
uppermost cause of the new urge to join the CDU. This was something
on which the party could easily capitalise, for, as Heck had advised
a conference of *Land* party managers in November 1969, the role of
Opposition was particularly suited to attracting new people.[35] This
idea of exploiting a mood of protest determined the style of CDU
membership propaganda in the months which followed. For
instance, a full-page CDU advertisement in the *Stuttgarter Zeitung*
argued that 'the CDU needs you' because it represented 'clear
alternatives to socialist policy'.[36] Kiesinger wrote to party members in
his constituency in the Black Forest introducing a recruitment drive
there in the spring of 1970 as a means of helping to dissolve the new
government in Bonn.[37] A further typical example of this approach
was the membership pamphlet produced by the district branch in
Krefeld, which attempted to exploit ill-feeling against the change of
power in Bonn by declaring that the CDU/CSU ('the strongest political
force in our country') had been 'forced' into Opposition by the SPD
and FDP with their 'flimsy' majority.[38]

The concern about Ostpolitik and the policies of the Brandt
Government spilled over into a fear among potential CDU members of
the domestic impact through a 'radicalisation' of society in the Federal
Republic. Their interest in political involvement reflected something
deeper too — a decline since the 1950s of the antipathy towards
party political involvement. The district party chairman in Darmstadt

expressed this new attitude clearly in 1972: 'Many citizens have recognised in the meantime that in politics one should not only place hope in others, but one must apply oneself.'[39] Biedenkopf identified the same potential for the CDU the following year, when he said at the Hamburg Congress that the party must exploit the 'readiness of citizens to assume responsibility, to participate in the formation of their environment'.[40] This new tendency had already generally been seen in the mushrooming of 'citizens' initiatives' over matters of public concern during the early 1970s.

Table 5: CDU Membership Total

April 1954	215,000
January 1956	245,000
June 1963	250,000
December 1964	280,000
December 1966	280,000
December 1968	280,000
October 1969	300,000
May 1970	315,000
September 1971	350,000
January 1972	350,000
October 1972	380,000
December 1973	450,000
August 1974	500,000
June 1975	580,000
May 1976	610,000
March 1977	653,000

N.B. Figures for the early years are difficult to estimate. As with the other parties there was a swift enrolment in membership after the War (CDU: 400,000 in 1947), due presumably to the relief felt at the collapse of the Nazi dictatorship. Membership totals then fell dramatically, immediately after the currency reform in 1948. There was a steady decline in CDU membership until 1952 (200,000).
(These round figures are compiled from various sources, chiefly material from the CDU.)

The link between party political polarisation and the flow of new membership was indicated by the impact of dramatic events in Bonn on the rate of recruitment. An obvious case was the political crisis in the spring of 1972 with the collapse of the Government's majority in the Bundestag, the constructive vote of no-confidence initiated by the CDU/CSU Opposition and the ratification controversy over the Ostpolitik treaties. These events led to a considerable increase in the rate of enrolment among all three parties.[6] Various *Landesverbände* of the CDU reported that reaction to the no-confidence motion had brought an immediate influx of new members.[41] The following year the CDU in Baden-Württemberg recorded that the greater readiness to join the party had been occasioned by 'the loss of government responsibility in Bonn' and the outcome of the Bundestag Election in November 1972.[42] There was another great influx of new members during 1973-4, once the leadership crisis after the Bundestag Election had been solved quickly with the transfer of the CDU chairmanship from Barzel to Kohl. In August 1974 Kohl celebrated the enrolment of the 500,000th member of the CDU with a reception for him in Berlin. By March 1976 the total membership had reached 600,000, of whom two-thirds had joined the CDU since early 1970. According to a survey published in late 1975 by the research institute of the Konrad Adenauer Foundation, two-thirds of the new members in the party were prepared to take an active part in election campaigns and to express through the mass media their political opinions in public.[7]

Finally, the CDU membership drive owed some of its phenomenal success to a properly co-ordinated organisational strategy. There was now far less reluctance at the district branch level to accept guidance from the BGS. The new version of the CDU's Membership Recruitment Manual issued in 1972 detailed very exactly the tasks to be performed by the district branches. In 1970 a special section had been set up in the publicity department of the Bonn headquarters to co-ordinate recruitment activities throughout the party.[43] The BGS played a major supporting role in supplying extensive glossy literature for the membership campaign, in devising various recruitment models and organising seminars from 1974 for training 'contact men'. The idea of prizes for the most successful recruiters was reintroduced.[8] The most favoured of the recruitment models was the so-called 'contacter model', involving a systematic approach on a personal basis.[44] Various other models were initiated by district branches, notably the Essen model which provided for a 'day of the open door' for new members. Particular emphasis was placed on the need to integrate the flood of new members through regular contact following enrolment, such as letters of welcome from the district branch and invitations to party events.[9] The keynote of the new strategy was given by the

1972 manual on recruitment: 'Membership recruitment is a permanent task of the whole party.'[45]

The dramatic rise in CDU membership from 300,000 at the beginning of the Opposition period to over 600,000 with the approach of the Bundestag Election in 1976 brought a change in the party's internal character. It was all the more significant, as it was related to a transformation in its internal relationships with greater participation by the membership and also reflected a marked decrease in public reluctance to declare affiliation with the CDU. It had narrowed the differences between itself and the SPD, for, just as the SPD had become more of a 'voters' party' over the previous decade, the CDU had become more of a 'members' party'. This process gained momentum once the CDU's role in Opposition was confirmed in the Bundestag Election of 1972, so that by the Bundestag Election campaign of 1976 the CDU membership was ready to an unprecedented degree for active involvement on behalf of the party.[g]

Notes

[1] E.g. see the complaint of Franz Meyers in his report on party organisation to the CDU Congress in 1958: 'To my particular regret I cannot give exact figures. Membership movements in the district and regional branches are notified rather too variably and sporadically. Also, it cannot be ruled out that the notification of membership is not carried out here and there with the necessary seriousness. Furthermore, the Union has a much too high — as I would put it — desire for migration. Members who change their domicile, even within a large city, frequently get lost to the party' (*8. Bundesparteitag der CDU* (1958), pp. 59-60).

[2] E.g. see the report of the research institute of the Konrad Adenauer Foundation published late 1975: 'Through this [rise in] party political activity, it becomes clear that it is precisely the young members of the CDU who do not want to restrain themselves in political discussions . . . this great readiness for party political activities, is, among the newly registered members of the CDU, different according to age groups; especially the young CDU members up to 30 years are very involved' (*Union in Deutschland*, 6 November 1975).

[3] See, for instance, the detailed study on CDU membership in Baden-Württemberg published in the *Stuttgarter Zeitung*, 19 March 1970. This examined the structure of membership locality by locality and came to the conclusion that in South Württemberg at least 'the image of the party is largely determined by the local leadership forces', which often differed in social and age composition. Different local traditions, the efficiency or otherwise of local party organisation and the degree of enthusiasm in membership drives also affected the local structure of CDU membership, so that there were wide disparities between the four

g   See below chapter 11 (c), p. 344.

administrative areas within the state. While this study was correct in pointing out the local aspect of party structure, it nevertheless underplayed the importance of national factors in determining the party image.

[4]   Various prizes were offered to the most energetic party members, including a trip for two on the luxury steamer 'Hanseatic' to the Canary Islands and North Africa (1st prize), or various trips to cities in Europe. The most successful district branches were tempted with the prospect of a free Volkswagen Export (1st prize), loudspeaker equipment (3rd prize) or a filing cabinet. Party members who managed to persuade 50 or more to join the CDU would be invited to the 1965 Congress and welcomed at the reception of the Praesidium. (Bundesgeschäftsführer to Kreisverbände, *Gewinne für die Mitgliederwerbeaktion 1963-1964*, 21 October 1963, Archiv CDU Rheinland, BGS 1963-67).

[5]   33,213 new members were enrolled in the CDU from November 1963 to July 1964, making a total of 270,000. The most successful *Landesverbände* were the two strongest ones of the Rhineland and Westphalia *(Weser-Kurier*, 13 August 1964).

[6]   E.g. Willy Wagner, district party manager for Mainz, said that he had joined the CDU in June 1972 in reaction to the 'mob' demonstrations in favour of Brandt at the time of the no-confidence motion and the SPD 'intolerance' towards the CDU afterwards. He was also motivated by a concern that the 'lefties' would 'bust up what our fathers built up after the War [under Adenauer]' (interview with the author, in Mainz, August 1973).

[7]   This survey by the Konrad Adenauer Foundation also claimed that the most important reason for new members joining the CDU was the party programme, especially as three-quarters of them formed their opinion of the CDU in the light of its position on national rather than local affairs (new members were given a copy of the party's [revised] Berlin Programme). Roughly half these new members engaged in frequent political discussion with family, friends and colleagues compared with about 10 per cent for the public as a whole, and almost half the new members set about winning further new members for the party. It was not surprising to find that this high degree of political mobilisation was reflected in the fact that three-quarters of CDU members saw in citizens' and electoral 'initiatives' a viable field of political activity, and in this respect were no less involved than members of other political parties (survey published in *Union in Deutschland*, 6 November 1975).

[8]   These ranged from trips to Beirut (a 1st prize), a visit to NATO headquarters in Brussels and a visit to the Bundestag in Bonn including discussions with 'prominent politicians of our Bundestag *Fraktion*' to receiving Adenauer memorial medals in fine silver and personally signed copies of books by prominent CDU politicians. The author noticed during a visit to the headquarters of the Rhineland CDU in Cologne in 1973 a cellar stacked high with copies of Adenauer's memoirs, and was given to understand that these were to be presents for party members successful in the recruitment campaign.

[9]   Ideas along these lines were initiated by the CDU district branch for the Rhein-Sieg-Kreis and were recommended by the party headquarters in Bonn (see *Union in Deutschland*, 20 June 1974, pp. 14-15). According to Karl Enderes, the district branch manager, a letter of welcome was sent to a new member on the same day as he joined expressing a wish to see him present at the next local party meeting. At the same time, an address plate for the new member was added to the branch office's machine for

the distribution of material. As was the general practice with other district branches, details on new members (as well as on those leaving the party) were sent twice a month to the electronically-run central membership card-index at the Bonn headquarters, which replied by sending to the branch a membership card and a filing card for its own index. The membership card was forwarded by the district branch to the new member with a further letter urging him to persuade a friend or relative to join the party and enclosing an application form. Once a month the headquarters despatched statistical details on its membership to each district branch, in addition to such reports to the *Landesverbände* on membership changes in their district branches. From January 1976, a faster computer had been installed in the headquarters for dealing with the rush of members (interview with Karl Enderes, district branch manager CDU Rhein-Sieg-Kreis since 1972, in Siegburg, August 1976).

References

1. Quoted in Helmuth Pütz, *Die Christlich-Demokratische Union* (1971), pp. 42-3.
2. Günther Gillessen, 'Zu alt und zu klein, zu katholisch und zu ländlich: Messbares über die CDU' in *FAZ*, 28 December 1965.
3. Renate Mayntz, *Soziologie der Organisation* (1963), p. 119 ff.
4. See Arnold Heidenheimer, 'La Structure Confessionelle, Sociale et Régionale de la CDU' in *Revue Française de Science Politique*, 1957, pp. 638-9.
5. Gerhard Schulz, 'Die CDU: Merkmale ihres Aufbaus' in *Parteien in der Bundesrepublik* (1955), p. 111.
6. *Statistik: Die Mitgliedschaft der CDU nach den Unterlagen der zentralen Mitgliederkartei* (1970), p. 6, Archiv BGS.
7. Arnold Heidenheimer, 'Schattierungen im Röntgenbild der Christlichen Demokraten' in *Die Neue Gesellschaft*, 1958, p. 177.
8. Heidenheimer, *Schattierungen*, p. 176.
9. *Ibid.*, p. 175.
10. See Heidenheimer's study of the CDU in rural Hesse in his article in *Revue Française de Science Politique*, 1957, pp. 633-4.
11. *Deutsches Monatsblatt*, September 1974, and *CDU-Pressemitteilung*, 5 March 1976.
12. *Statistik, op. cit.*, p. 15.
13. See CDU des Rheinlandes, *Die Zusammensetzung unseres Mitgliederbestandes*, 12 January 1950, Archiv BGS, A 32d, Teil XI; H.J. Varain, *Parteien und Verbände* (1964), pp. 44-5.
14. See B. Vogel and P. Haungs, *Wahlkampf und Wählertradition* (1965), pp. 231-2.
15. E.g. analysis of CDU Kreisverband Trier-Land in *Trierische Landeszeitung*, 12 August 1964.
16. *Statistik, op. cit.*, p. 4.
17. *Deutsches Monatsblatt*, September 1974, and *CDU-Pressemitteilung*, 5 March 1976.
18. *CDU-Pressemitteilung*, 24 March 1976.
19. See H. Kaack, *Geschichte und Struktur des deutschen Parteiensystems*, pp. 490-1.
20. Bernhard Beger, 'Das schmale Fundament: der CDU fehlen die Mitglieder' in *Die Politische Meinung*, 1960, H. 55, p. 4.

21.   See Aloys Schardt, 'Mitgliederpartei oder Wählerpartei? Das Verhältnis der CDU zum "vorparteilichen Raum"' in *Rheinischer Merkur,* 18 August 1961.

22.   See Bruno Heck, 'Mitglieder- oder Wählerpartei?' in *Deutsches Monatsblatt,* 13 September 1956; and, J.H. Dufhues, *Bundespartei - Landesparteien - Kreisparteien,* undated memo., Archiv BGS.

23.   See Franz Meyers, report of the Bundesvorstand, *8. Bundesparteitag der CDU* (1958), pp. 60-1.

24.   E.g. CDU LV Hannover, *Rundschreiben Nr. 1/64 an die Kreisverbände des LVs Hannover der CDU, betr. Aufnahme von neuen Mitgliedern und Mitgliederwerbung,* 19 March 1964, Archiv CDU Niedersachsen.

25.   Quoted in *Civis,* No. 3, 1964, p. 17.

26.   Peter Müllenbach, *Aufbau der zentralen Mitgliederkartei,* memo. to LV business managers, 22 October 1963, Archiv CDU Rheinland, BGS 1963-1967.

27.   See Müllenbach's correspondence with the LVe 1963-5, copies in Archiv CDU Nord-Württemberg.

28.   *Bericht der BGS, Anlage zum Bericht des Generalsekretärs,* January 1971, p. 47.

29.   *CDU-Leitfaden zur Mitgliederwerbung,* Hauptstaatsarchiv Düsseldorf, RWV 26 No. 233c.

30.   Müllenbach circular to Kreisverbände, 20 July 1965, Archiv CDU Nord-Württemberg. See also brochure, *Mobile Ausstellung der CDU, Komm mit in das Jahr 2000,* pub. by BGS.

31.   See correspondence of Klaus Scheufelen and Franz Grandel, Landesgeschäftsführer, with Kreisverbände, Autumn 1964, Archiv CDU Nord-Württemberg.

32.   *17. Bundesparteitag der CDU* (1969), p. 33.

33.   *Handelsblatt,* 31 July 1970.

34.   Gerold Rummler, memo. to Bruno Heck, 8 December 1969, on recruitment action LV Berlin, Archiv CDU Nord-Wurttemberg.

35.   Kurzprotokoll Konferenz der Landesgeschäftsführer, 6 November 1969, Archiv CDU Niedersachsen.

36.   *Stuttgarter Zeitung,* 20 November 1969.

37.   Letter from Kurt-Georg Kiesinger, Easter 1970, Archiv BGS.

38.   CDU-Kreisverband Krefeld, *Werden Sie Mitglied der CDU jetzt!*

39.   Gerhard Pfeffermann, interview with *Darmstadt 72,* H.2, May 1972, Archiv CDU Hesse.

40.   *22. Bundesparteitag der CDU* (1973), pp. 56-7.

41.   *FAZ,* 27 April 1972.

42.   CDU LV Baden-Württemberg, *Geschäftsbericht des Landesverbandes 1971-1973* (1973), p. 31.

43.   *Handelsblatt,* 31 July 1970.

44.   See *Union in Deutschland,* 4 July 1974.

45.   *CDU-Leitfaden für die Mitgliederwerbung* (1972), p. 4.

9 AUXILIARY ORGANISATIONS OF THE CDU/CSU

(a) General Importance

The auxiliary organisations or *Vereinigungen,* which are common to both the CDU and the CSU, may be seen in the grand sense as the institutionalisation of internal party pluralism. The *Vereinigungsprinzip* or principle behind their existence has been presented as a special feature of the CDU/CSU's claim to be a *Volkspartei,* for they represent in an organised form different interests and viewpoints within the party including those of minorities. The CDU statutes specify seven such organisations for: the young generation *(Junge Union);* women *(Frauenvereinigung);* workers *(Sozialausschüsse der Christlich-Demokratischen Arbeitnehmerschaft);* municipal politics *(Kommunalpolitische Vereinigung);* 'middle-class interests' *(Mittelstandsvereinigung);* business and industry *(Wirtschaftsrat);* and refugees *(Union der Vertriebenen und Flüchtlinge).* There are further auxiliary organisations which do not have the official status of party *Vereinigungen,* namely the *Evangelischer Arbeitskreis* representing the Protestant viewpoint and the student organisation, the *Ring Christlich-Demokratischer Studenten* (RCDS). A new organisation for school pupils called the *Schüler-Union* was also founded in 1972.

In theory, these organisations play a dual role in the CDU/CSU both in strengthening its appeal to different groups within society and in representing their interests within the party. As the CDU statutes declare, they are 'organisational amalgams with the aim of representing and propagating the beliefs of the CDU in its fields of activity, as well as looking after the special concerns of the groups they represent in the policy of the CDU'. A similar provision is included in the CSU statutes, although they are described there as *Arbeitsgemeinschaften* or 'working associations'.[1] The auxiliary organisations are therefore intended to have an integrative function through the articulation of interests, recruitment and other forms of political socialisation. Their relationship with the parent party is constitutionally a loose one, certainly much more so than has been the case with the 'working associations' of the SPD, even though they are represented in the party's national organs. They have their own individual statutes, leadership personnel, regional structure, membership (which does not entail automatic membership of the CDU/CSU) and administration of finance. They also have the right to issue their own policy statements, and they publish their own periodicals. Some of the auxiliary organisations have tended to be emphatic in their assertion of autonomy coupled with a tendency to underplay their function as internal party interest groups. The official announcement by the party of the formation of the *Wirtschaftsrat* (Economic Council) in 1963 stated: 'It is not a lobby in the CDU nor a protection for group interests, but a circle for open discussion'.[1] Similarly, the statutes of the Young Union insist that it is an 'independent association of the young generation' in the CDU, while the *Evangelischer Arbeitskreis* went so far as not seeking official status as a *Vereinigung* to allow for 'greater freedom of movement' within the party.[2]

The real importance of this autonomy has varied between the different auxiliary organisations, and this can only be measured by examining each in turn. A discussion of their role must therefore examine their contribution to internal party integration by aggregating group interests within the CDU/CSU, for their very existence suggests a reinforcement of the loose structure of the CDU/CSU. It must also evaluate their real possibilities for influence over policy-making, if they play more than just a subordinate role in promoting the Christian Democratic cause.

With a view to their major function of representing different interests and viewpoints within the party, the most effective in influence has been the *Wirtschaftsrat,* the employers' organisation, which has identified with the principles of the social market economy and through its services in securing outside financial support for the party has enjoyed considerable influence within it.[3] Its alliance at times with other auxiliary organisations, notably the *Mittelstandsvereinigung* (representing entrepreneurial interests), has strengthened its role in helping to formulate party policy positions in a conservative direction, for example with the conflicts over the stand on worker participation in 1968 and 1970-1.[a] By contrast, the progressive Social Committees, whose heyday of policy influence was during the later 1940s as represented by the party's progressive Ahlen Programme,[b] have since then been unable to counter the party's basically conservative orientation in economic policy in spite of their size of membership and elaborate organisation. Their position is now more an ideological one of representing the 'social conscience' of the

a   See above chapter 4 (d), pp. 179-80 and 5 (b), p. 196.
b   See above chapter 1 (a), p. 31.

party. Equally, the raison d'etre of the *Evangelischer Arbeitskreis* (EAK) is to safeguard Protestant interests within the CDU/CSU. It was founded in 1952 to counter the apparent passivity of Protestants generally in the CDU/CSU and as a reaction to the public controversy over Adenauer's rearmament policy, which alarmed Protestant Church leaders and those CDU politicians in close contact with them.[4] The EAK cannot, however, be rated as a pressure group in any powerful sense, seeing that any forthright assertion of Protestant interests in the CDU/CSU would be inhibited by its reluctance in the interests of internal party harmony to exacerbate confessional relations and its sensitivity to accusations that it might be a 'Protestant lobby' in the CDU/CSU.[5]

Seen from another angle, the auxiliary organisations can nevertheless provide a political base for some politicians within the CDU/CSU. Just as the EAK was such a base for Hermann Ehlers (President of the Bundestag) in the earlier 1950s, so too it has helped to cushion Gerhard Schröder (its chairman since 1955) from the twists of political fortune. In spite of their general weakness of influence, the Social Committees have acted as a similar base for Hans Katzer, their chairman since 1963 and previously business manager from 1950. The most striking example of an auxiliary organisation providing an entree for a party career in the CDU/CSU has been the Young Union, whose reputation has long been that of a careerist association.

The external function of the auxiliary organisations is primarily electoral.[2] Both the Social Committees and the EAK have stressed the importance of maintaining and enlarging the scope of the CDU/CSU's appeal to working-class and Protestant voters respectively. The latter organisation, for instance, played an active part in the Bundestag Election campaign of 1953 when the CDU succeeded in averting a challenge to its Protestant electorate from the SPD and the Heinemann party (GVP) over the rearmament issue, and even in increasing its vote substantially in Protestant areas.[6] More recently, electoral pressures on the CDU have enhanced this role of individual *Vereinigungen*. The Young Union's new habit since Opposition of taking an independent programmatic stand vis-à-vis the parent party has arisen from a concern about the CDU's lack of attraction for young voters, especially after the lowering of the voting age to 18 in 1970. Even the fairly dormant *Frauenvereinigung* assumed a new importance once women voters became less reliable supporters of the CDU/CSU from the 1969 Election, following which the organisation concentrated on discussing a new strategy for countering this tendency in the future.[7] This took the form of electoral publicity specially geared to women voters. Generally, the auxiliary organisations have traditionally performed an important subsidiary role in election campaigns by way of representing the multifaceted approach of the party, as well as carrying out detailed publicity activities.[8]

In conclusion, the auxiliary organisations perform a parallel, in some cases peripheral, function in the CDU/CSU. They are in no way comparable to the *correnti* or institutionalised factions of the Italian Christian Democratic party (DC), because in general they have not played a central role in party policy formulation.[3] Nevertheless, the close interrelationship between the auxiliary organisations and the parent party is underlined by the fact that 70 per cent of their members are also members of the CDU, and of the non-party members in the organisations the vast majority are located in the youth organisation, the Young Union. To appreciate the role of the auxiliary organisations more thoroughly, it is useful to examine the two largest which are also different in character — the Young Union and the Social Committees.

(b) The Young Union (JU)

The Young Union has been variously described or criticised as the 'motor of the party' or its 'rearguard rather than vanguard', but the most common labels have been the 'trampoline for young careerists in the CDU' and its being a 'springboard for political careers'. In spite of its new line of developing its own programmatic position since Opposition began in 1969, the careerist image has remained dominant and indeed has continued to be underlined by the high proportion of JU leaders who simultaneously win elective positions in the party.[4] This poses the question how far the JU, which is by far the strongest auxiliary organisation in terms of membership,[5] has developed an important position in the internal party balance of power or whether it has generally allowed its strong careerist aspirations to check any assertive tendency towards the party leadership during the generation since its founding in 1946. Any changes which it has undergone during the Opposition period must be set in the context of its longer-term development.

The Young Union has never been a youth organisation of the CDU/CSU in the literal sense, but rather has provided a reservoir of future and even present leadership talent. Its upper age limit for membership of 40 years (reduced to 35 in 1969) has been an obvious indication of this distinction. Many of its leadership personnel made considerable progress in advancing their party careers while still holding office in the JU. Josef Hermann Dufhues, a prominent CDU politician in the 1960s, was actually just over 40 when he was elected the JU's national chairman during 1949-50. Gerhard Stoltenberg, often quoted as the archetypal Young Union professional, remained as JU chairman for another four years after he was elected as the youngest CDU/CSU member of the Bundestag in 1957, and by the mid-1960s he had already become a Federal minister (at the age of 37).[6] As time progressed and a new generation of CDU/CSU leaders emerged from the 1960s onwards, the prominence of JU personnel became even more evident, particularly at the *Landesverband* level, as seen for example in the composition of Kohl's *Land* cabinet in the Rhineland-Palatinate (from 1969) as well as in recent elections to regional party chairmanships.[9]

This interlinkage of leadership personnel between the Young Union and the CDU/CSU called into question whether the JU's organisational autonomy involved much political importance. The JU has officially enjoyed a greater measure of independence from the parent party than the Young Socialists. Unlike the SPD youth organisation, the JU has admitted a large minority of non-CDU/CSU members to its ranks, although this has admittedly been a convenient means of enticing further members into the parent party. The fundamental difference between the two youth organisations has been that the Jusos have traditionally assumed a strong programmatic and even ideological position involving conflict with the party leadership, and the Young Union has not. During the 1950s and 1960s, the JU was characterised by its 'era of passive opportunism',[10] tending to adopt the norms of the CDU/CSU and showing no inclination to criticise Government policy. Reverence for Adenauer was, however, accompanied in time by a growing concern about the future of party organisation.[11] This clearly reflected the younger CDU/CSU politicians' uneasiness about the party's prospects of remaining in power.

Changes in the relationship of the JU with the party did not occur until Opposition. The loss of national office and the confirmation of the 'change in power' in the 1972 Election, particularly with the strong preference of young voters for the coalition parties, forced the Young Union to take a more independent programmatic stand from the national leadership of the CDU/CSU. This was notably the case with its more 'progressive' attitude over Ostpolitik, but also in its stress on the need to pay more attention to social problems. The change of approach was heralded a few weeks after the loss of national power by the party, at the Young Union's congress at Hamm in November 1969. The highpoint was the speech by the new chairman, Jürgen Echternach, declaring the JU to be a pressure-group for party reform. The so-called 'spirit of Hamm' failed to produce any lasting changes, and became forgotten in the polarised atmosphere that surrounded the years of the first Brandt Government. Only when the CDU/CSU was compelled to come to terms with its Opposition role after the 1972 election did the JU have a real chance of influencing party policy.[7] Under the chairmanship of the 24-year-old Matthias Wissmann (elected in 1973), the Young Union advocated volubly a more conceptual approach to social policy which was presented in its strategy paper on 'A Third Way to a Humane Society' (between the Marxist-socialist and the Liberal-capitalist). It formed a closer alliance with the Social Committees over worker participation, and was influential in the formulation of the CDU's policy attitude, the 'New Social Question', at the Mannheim party congress in 1975. The keynote of the JU's new strategy in relation to the party was Wissmann's statement at its 1973 congress that solidarity did not mean simple adherence to majority decisions but, for an organisation like the Young Union, it involved the need to stimulate new ideas.[12] All the same, Wissmann's programmatic line was not without challenge from its conservative fundamentalist wing, noticeably at the JU congress in November 1975 when only two-thirds of the delegates voted for his re-election.[13]

The fact that not all the younger generation associated with the CDU/CSU thought along similar programmatic lines to the new JU leadership was demonstrated by the critical attitude of the conservative *Schüler-Union* (SU) towards Wissmann's reform policy. This new auxiliary organisation, founded under the auspices of the JU itself in 1972, aimed to reverse the trend among young voters by the time of the 1976 Bundestag Election.[14] Its appeal to the 'playground vote' seemed to rise with its astonishing success, and it acquired as many as 25,000 members by the end of 1974.[15] The SU benefited from a 'non-political' reaction among young people against the left-wing inclinations of many young teachers and the education policies of certain SPD *Land* governments like Hesse, where the SU was already the largest school-pupils' organisation.[16] Like the Christian Democratic students' organisation (RCDS), the *Schüler-Union* concentrated its attack on education policy, deploring the 'politicisation' of teaching and condemning 'left-wing Fascists'. Although it differed from the JU's interest in social questions and found itself more in sympathy with the fundamentalist conservatism of the CDU/CSU, the SU has been dependent on the Young Union financially as well as on support from industry.[17]

The Young Union has asserted itself more as an internal party pressure-group as a result of the changed role of the CDU/CSU from Government to Opposition, and of new social and political pressures to which it has been more responsive than the party itself. Its new programmatic image is evidence of this. The JU has nevertheless been exceptional among the various auxiliary organisations of the CDU/CSU in that it has boasted a large membership and has been well-organised. This has given its programmatic line more impact. Moreover, its influence has continued to come from the fact that the JU is still basically a careerist organisation, owing to its purpose in providing future leadership personnel, for it has been motivated in its changes by a fear about the party's electoral fortunes and the danger of losing the middle ground of politics. The other main auxiliary organisation which is programmatically-orientated, the Social Committees, has lacked those advantages of strong organisation and careerist motivation and has consequently enjoyed relatively little influence on party policy.

(c)   The Social Committees

The Social Committees of the Christian Democratic Working Class, commonly known as the 'left-wing' of the CDU/CSU, or more flippantly as the 'social fig-leaf of the Union', are hardly comparable to the kind of organised pressure-group perhaps expected of the ideological wing of a mass political party. In spite of their fairly sizeable membership strength (rising to about 100,000 by 1975), they have suffered from the problem often faced by progressive wings in conservative parties. As one of the Social Committees' prominent members once said, *'für die Roten sind wir die Schwarzen, und für die Schwarzen die Roten'*,[18] which referred to their difficulty of identity within a party system which could become easily polarised and indeed often has been. This problem has been particularly acute in the case of the Social Committees because of the conservative orientation of the CDU/CSU since the late 1940s, with its adoption of Erhard's economic philosophy and the conservative values implicit in Adenauer's policies.[c] Consequently, the party's adoption at different times of more progressive policies has generally been for reasons other than the influence of the Social Committees. Their lack of programmatic

c   See above chapters 1 (a), pp. 31-2 and 1 (c), p. 52.

'punch' has been manifest on several occasions during internal party debates on the issue of worker participation at successive CDU congresses, as at Berlin 1968, Düsseldorf 1971 and Hamburg 1973, though in the last case the Social Committees were far more assertive than before.[19]

The Social Committees' main importance has been to represent a progressive viewpoint in the West German brand of Christian Democracy, composed as it is of different political traditions and ideological tendencies. Founded in 1947 by former Christian trade unionists like Johannes Albers (its first chairman) and Karl Arnold, the Social Committees represented the tradition of social Catholicism[d] which found its stronghold in the Rhineland, from where the greatest concentration of its members has always come. They have generally advocated moderate social change, though clearly from within the scope of the Christian Democracy, for what has fundamentally distinguished them from the SPD in general has been their view of social problems not in socio-economic but in 'personal' terms, illustrated by the slogan of their 1974 congress: 'Human beings are more important than Conditions.'[20] Norbert Blüm, the left-wing Catholic who became business manager of the Social Committees in 1968, gave as his reasons for not joining the SPD the appeal of 'liberalism' in the CDU, the dislike of the SPD's character as a 'column on the march' and its 'Utopian' attitude to power.[21] In spite of their distinct commitment to the CDU/CSU, the Social Committees' sense of powerlessness in the party has been continuous and visible in the tendency to look 'back to Ahlen', the only time when they were programmatically prominent in the party. Their scope for influence has been even more restricted in the CSU, which has been dominated by fundamentalist conservative views.[22] Has not their main problem been that the Social Committees have played too ideological a role in a political party, which for most of its history has been pragmatic and power-orientated?

A clue to this question is provided by Norbert Blüm's treatise on the party, *Reaktion oder Reform – Wohin geht die CDU?*,[23] written in the aftermath of defeat over worker participation at the 1971 Congress. This emphasised above all the importance of the CDU's programmatic character and criticised the party's socio-political approach as being geared to electoral tactics. Blüm has been frequently attacked inside the CDU for placing ethnical positions above power politics, while his

d   See above chapter 1 (a), pp. 30-1.

progressive stands have often provoked attacks on him from the conservative wing of the party, notably the *Wirtschaftsrat,* and in person from Franz-Josef Strauss. The Social Committees have acted more as a pressure-group for social Catholic ideas than as a class-conscious advocate of workers' interests within the party, believing as they do in the need for 'partnership' on the basis of 'Christian responsibility'. Their main political justification has been to maintain the CDU's appeal to Roman Catholic workers. For this reason the possibility was voiced after the 1972 Bundestag Election of an increased role for the Social Committees in view of the party's decline in working-class voters.[24] This has failed to materialise, although the Social Committees have acquired more prominence in policy discussion under Kohl and Biedenkopf, and the Ahlen Programme has been given a new acknowledgement as a programmatic signpost in the party's history.[25] The Social Committees have asserted themselves through a coalition with other auxiliary organisations, notably with the Young Union at the CDU Congresses at Hamburg 1973 and Mannheim 1975. The main reason for a revived interest in their role has come, however, from the party's need since 1972 to strengthen its position in the centre of politics and from the policy of the leadership from 1973 in seeking to improve the integration of different internal party elements in the CDU.

The example of the Social Committees, as well as that of the Young Union, illustrates two general characteristics of the Christian Democratic auxiliary organisations: that no generalisation can be made about the nature of their relationship with the parent party; and that usually their importance for the party in representing their respective interests to the electorate has been greater than their internal role in party policy-making. In the latter respect, the conservative economic organisations have been the most influential, although clearly the party rather than the organisation in question has been the dominant factor. Generally, the internal function of the auxiliary organisations has been that of representing interests rather than exerting a powerful influence on policy, as featured in the convention of appointing a woman minister (notably to the Family Affairs portfolio) or a figure (like Hans Katzer) from the Social Committees as Labour Minister in CDU/CSU Federal governments. Only the Young Union has been able to boast of a political umbilical cord attaching it visibly to the centre of power in the party. The auxiliary organisations of the CDU/CSU therefore provide as institutionalised sub-groups a further dimension to the tradition of a loose internal party structure. They have featured as a

useful though restricted platform for party politicians,[8] for their
limited influence within the whole party has been shown by the fact
that too close an association with one auxiliary organisation (except
the JU) can be inhibiting for the prospects of an aspiring national
party leader. It is in their external function of acting as a channel of
communication with interest groups outside the party and of
projecting its multifaceted image to the electorate that the auxiliary
organisations have contributed most to the CDU/CSU's viability as a
Volkspartei.

Notes

[1]   For a special discussion of the auxiliary organisations in relation to the
       CSU, see Alf Mintzel, *Die CSU: Anatomie einer konservativen Partei*
       (1975), Chapters V4 (Pt. I) and VI (Pt. II).
[2]   E.g. this is illustrated by the fact that certain positions on *Land* party lists
       are virtually reserved for certain representatives of auxiliary
       organisations, notably in the Rhineland where they are strongly
       organised.
[3]   For a comparison of the CDU/CSU and the Italian DC in this respect, see
       Geoffrey Pridham, 'Christian Democracy in Italy and West Germany: a
       comparative analysis' in M. Kolinsky and W. Paterson (ed.), *Social and
       Political Movements in Western Europe* (1976), pp. 163-71.
[4]   A relatively high proportion of JU leaders and members have usually
       been elected to the Bundestag and Landtage, with a very high proportion
       to district and local councils. According to the Young Union diary for
       1973, they included 22 Bundestag deputies, 75 Landtag deputies and
       roughly 5,000 district and local councillors. More than 64 were local
       mayors and more than 42 district branch chairmen of the CDU and
       CSU (*Junge Union 73*, p. 126). In the case of Bundestag deputies, the
       total was of course in practice limited by the age limit of JU
       membership.
[5]   120,000 members in 1970, 160,000 in 1973 and 214,000 by the end
       of 1975. As with the CDU/CSU generally, there has been a vast increase
       in JU membership during the Opposition years. This has been
       particularly significant in the light of the party's aim after the 1972
       Election to concentrate on winning young voters as well as members.
[6]   Two of Stoltenberg's successors have also risen in the party hierarchy.
       Jurgen Echternach, JU chairman 1969-73, became successively leader of
       the CDU *Fraktion* in the Hamburg *Land* parliament and then chairman
       of the Hamburg CDU by the mid-1970s. The young Matthias Wissmann,
       JU chairman from 1973, was elected to the Bundestag in 1976 at the
       age of 27.
[7]   The Young Union produced its first Basic Policy Programme
       (Grundsatzprogramm) at its congress at Fulda in October 1972, shortly
       before the 1972 Election. Echternach introduced this programme by
       saying that 'in contrast to the firmly entrenched principles of right and
       left ideologues, the Young Union is open to new ideas' and that the
       programme would 'contribute to forming the image of the "New Union",

which is being created by us younger ones . . . our function as the Young Union is that of the "critical mover" of policy, for we have in recent years made "fire under the chair" for the Union parties, as their leaders freely confess' (see his preface to the Young Union diary for 1973, pp. IV-V; also pp. 226-54 for the text of the Basic Policy Programme, titled 'For a Humane Society').

[8] This is underlined by the fact that, although the majority of members of auxiliary organisations have also belonged to the party (see above Chapter 9(a), p. 294), only a minority of CDU members have tended to join an auxiliary organisation, in fact less than a third. In 1975, the different organisations accounted for the following proportions of the total membership of the CDU: Young Union 7.72 per cent, *Frauenvereinigung* 17.78 per cent, *Mittelstandsvereinigung* 2.75 per cent and the Social Committees 3.64 per cent (*Statistischer Bericht der zentralen Mitgliederkartei,* February 1975).

References

1. *Deutschland Union-Dienst,* 11 December 1963.
2. See Peter Egen, *Die Entstehung des Evangelischen Arbeitskreises der CDU/CSU,* Ph.D. thesis 1971, p. 184.
3. See study by Jürgen Dittberner, 'Der Wirtschaftsrat der CDU e.V.' in J. Dittberner and R. Ebbighausen, *Parteiensystem in der Legitimationskrise* (1973), pp. 200-18.
4. Egen, *op. cit.*, pp. 181-7.
5. E.g. see articles on role of EAK in *NZZ*, 8 June 1961 and *Deutsche Zeitung*, 3 April 1962.
6. Egen, *op. cit.*, pp. 157-76, 187-90.
7. See report of BGS for January 1971 CDU Congress, pp. 29-30.
8. E.g. see reports on the election activities of the various auxiliary organisations in Baden-Württemberg for 1971-3 in *Geschäftsbericht des LVs CDU Baden-Württemberg 1971-1973* (1973), pp. 47-8, 51, 53-4.
9. See analysis of leadership personnel in CDU *Landesverbände* in Peter Radunski, 'Zum Generationswechsel in Parteien: die Junge Union als Sprungbrett für politischen Karrieren in der CDU' in *Reale Utopien*, Schriftenreihe, Bd. 6 (1970), pp. 152-6.
10. Ulrich Grasser, *Die CDU und die Junge Union* in Dittberner and Ebbighausen, *op. cit.*, p. 328.
11. See Wolfgang Horlach, 'Des Kanzlers junge Mannschaft hat Sorgen' in *Stuttgarter Zeitung,* 15 July 1958; and, Günther Gaus, 'Die Junge Union ist Adenauers getreue Mannschaft' in *SZ*, 9 December 1961.
12. *Die Zeit,* 26 October 1973.
13. *Die Zeit,* 28 November 1975.
14. Hans Lerchbacher, 'Ein Generationskonflikt zwischen Jungen und ganz Jungen' in *FR*, 12 August 1974.
15. *SZ*, 16 December 1974.
16. *Die Zeit,* 22 March 1974; see also report on attitudes of young voters in *Der Spiegel,* 5 April 1976, pp. 46-60.
17. *Die Zeit,* 22 March 1974, and *Hannoversche Allgemeine,* 13 August 1974.
18. *SZ*, 6 July 1971.
19. For a case-study of the Social Committees' role in the party's position on worker participation, see G. and J. Kramer, 'Der Einfluss der Sozialausschüsse der Christlich-Demokratischen Arbeitnehmerschaft auf

die CDU' in *Aus Politik und Zeitgeschichte,* 13 November 1976, esp. pp. 32-46.

20.   *FAZ,* 26 September 1974.

21.   See profile of Norbert Blüm in *FAZ,* 15 June 1973.

22.   See Alf Mintzel, *Die CSU, Anatomie einer konservativen Partei* (1975), pp. 210-12 and Chapter VI.

23.   Norbert Blüm, *Reaktion oder Reform? Wohin geht die CDU?* (1972).

24.   See Rolf Ebbighausen and Wilhelm Kaltenborn, 'Wie links ist die CDU? Zur Rolle der Sozialausschüsse' in *Die Zeit,* 28 September 1973.

25.   E.g. Biedenkopf's speech to the Catholic Academy in Bavaria in 1973, and the official CDU celebration of the 30th anniversary of the Ahlen Programme in February 1977.

10 THE CHRISTIAN SOCIAL UNION (CSU)

(a)   Political Character of the Party and Relationship with the CDU

The special feature of Christian Democracy in West Germany is that it has been expressed by two separately organised but politically linked parties, one of which is regionally based in Bavaria and the other operative throughout the rest of the Federal Republic. Although both parties profess a general attachment to the principles of Christian Democracy, the CSU in Bavaria is an autonomous political party with its own chairman and leadership structure, headquarters, membership, congresses and organisational history. The one major exception to its independent role in politics has been its parliamentary and political alliance with the CDU at the Federal level. In parliamentary terms, this has taken the form of their common *Fraktion* in the Bundestag from the first legislative period in 1949, with the body of CSU deputies (the *Landesgruppe*) constituting an autonomous and influential sub-group within the *Fraktion*. At the extra-parliamentary level, their political co-operation has involved the practice of not engaging as rivals in electoral activity and membership recruitment, no encroachment into the other's territory except in a supportive role and the agreement on a common Chancellor candidate and parallel campaigns for every Bundestag election form 1953 to 1976.

The two key variables in this relationship between the CDU and the CSU have therefore been the organisational and the political, with the former expressing the nature of their co-operation and the latter its intensity. The dominant variable has clearly been the political one, for, while organisational co-operation has more or less remained constant, it has none the less been placed under increasing strain because of a qualitative change in the political relationship. The principal determinant affecting the nature of this political co-operation has been that of mutual dependence — the degree to which the CDU's need for CSU support to form a parliamentary majority in Bonn harmonises with the CSU's desire to exert its influence in Federal politics more effectively through its alliance with the CDU. The manner in which their political interests have coincided within this framework of co-operation has varied according to three distinct stages of development in the history of the two Christian Democratic parties, summarised roughly as the three decades of the 1950s, the 1960s and the 1970s. Adenauer's political success in the first decade made for close co-operation. A change in the relationship came in the 1960s with the decline of the CDU's political effectiveness in national politics, while the 'change of power' in 1969 brought as a consequence even greater political assertiveness by the CSU vis-à-vis the CDU.

The relationship between the CDU and the CSU has therefore been centred on the question of Christian Democracy as the governing or dominant political force in West Germany, which is further confirmation that the Government/Opposition role has been the overriding determinant affecting the character of the CDU/CSU within the party system. Since the political character of the CSU at the Federal level has derived much of its identity, especially earlier, from its relationship with the CDU as has its independence within this alliance gained from the strength of its own political base in Bavaria, the discussion of the two parties' relationship will both follow the three phases of its development and generally answer the following questions: what were the reasons for maintaining the alliance and what have been the individual factors affecting its intensity; what has been the nature of the programmatic or ideological element in this relationship; and, what has motivated the change in the balance of political interests between the two parties manifested by the increasingly independent profile presented by the CSU?

The autonomy of the CSU, and its alliance rather than integration with the CDU, had historical roots in Bavarian regionalism, as the existence of a separate Catholic party in the Weimar period (the Bavarian People's Party — BVP) alongside the Centre Party had shown.[1] The reappearance of strong federalist pressures in Bavaria after the Second World War, reinforced by reactions to the Nazi dictatorship, laid the basis for the CSU's demarcation of its own role from Christian Democratic tendencies elsewhere in West Germany.[a] Developments in the newly emerging party system in the immediate post-war years determined the particular form of relationship between the two parties. The fluid and uncertain situation within the CDU itself, with its failure at that time to provide a national party organisation against resistance from some of its own regional party leaders,[b] reflected similar though much less pronounced centrifugal tendencies. On the Bavarian side, the relationship with the CDU became intertwined at this stage with the internal struggle inside the CSU during the later

a   See above chapter 1 (a), p. 24 and 1 (b), p. 36.
b   See above chapter 1 (c).

1940s over whether the new party should continue the BVP tradition and assume a Catholic-conservative-regionalist orientation, or attempt to create a new political basis geared to confessional co-operation between Catholics and Protestants in line with Christian Democratic initiatives elsewhere. This issue acquired bitter overtones since the CSU chairman, Josef Müller, an advocate of the second course, became involved with other leaders in internal party feuding over this matter. The Catholic-conservative course, promoted by ex-BVP leaders like Fritz Schäffer and Alois Hundhammer, was assisted by a number of developments. Not only did the organisational weight of the CSU, concentrated in Catholic Southern Bavaria, tilt the balance of opinion inside the party against Müller's line of a merger with the projected 'Reich party' of the CDU[2] − a line now openly attacked as 'Prussian' by his internal party opponents − but the rise of a new regionalist force, the Bavarian party (BP), also advanced support for an independent CSU since the popular impact of the BP ultimately forced the CSU along a strong federalist path in order to safeguard its political base.[1] Hans Ehard, the new CSU leader elected in 1949, confirmed the clear course now pursued by his party, when he insisted that, although the CSU wanted to maintain 'close contact' with the CDU, it was founded as 'an independent *Land* party' and that to become part of a 'centralistic' Reich party would be contrary to 'its natural law of development'.[3]

This 'close contact' with the CDU was already institutionalised through the common *Fraktion* formed by both parties in the Frankfurt Economic Council from 1947, an agreement motivated by common opposition to the SPD, although regarded with hostility by the Schäffer/Hundhammer wing of the CSU.[4] The practice of such a parliamentary alliance was repeated in the Parliamentary Council of 1948-9, and continued when the first Bundestag met in the autumn of 1949. From the beginning, the decision to progress with a common *Fraktion* at the Federal level was viewed from the CSU as the more effective alternative method, rather than going it alone, for securing Bavarian interests, especially with regard to the federal structure of the political system. As Franz-Josef Strauss, then already a leading CSU figure in the Bundestag, later remarked:

> The Land group [*Landesgruppe* − in the CDU/CSU Bundestag *Fraktion*] was from the very start unanimously determined to present its own political organisation, but nevertheless to form part of a *Fraktion* association with the CDU . . . We were clear that

through our autonomy as a *Land* group we had to display the
backbone of federalism in the Bundestag, and as a component of the
common *Fraktion* of the CDU/CSU act as an essential representative
of the Union tendency.[5]

The usefulness to the CSU of its role as a strong pressure-group within
the Christian Democratic alliance had been demonstrated shortly before
in 1948-9 over the Bundesrat issue, when CDU support allowed the
CSU to press successfully for a strengthened upper parliamentary
chamber as an expression of federalist interests.[6] The common *Fraktion*
in the Bundestag was finally concluded for the sake of securing
Adenauer the Chancellorship against SPD opposition, and because
of the CSU's desire for ministerial positions. It was recognised that
there was a common ideological ground between the two Christian
Democratic parties which would cement their parliamentary alliance.[7]

From its alliance with the CDU at the Federal level there
developed the CSU's dual function of acting on the one hand as an
autonomous *Land* political party (rather than merely a *Landesverband*
of the CDU) in its Bavarian context — a position accentuated by the
CSU's role as the continuous ruling party of Bavaria (except for
1954-7) — and on the other hand as the most important institutionalised
pressure group within that alliance. In the latter respect the CSU's
political weight has benefited from its strong sense of cohesion at the
Federal level, deriving ultimately from the common bond of regional
solidarity. The CSU's position as an autonomous political party has
been emphasised organisationally at the parliamentary level by the
existence from 1949 of the special *Landesgruppe* of the CSU deputies
within the common CDU/CSU *Fraktion* in the Bundestag. The
Landesgruppe has had its own leadership structure with its chairman
(who has also been first deputy chairman of the common *Fraktion*),
business manager, executive and staff.[2] There has been a CSU
representative at every level of the *Fraktion* hierarchy, and moreover
any *Fraktion* initiatives have had to carry the name of the *Landesgruppe*
chairman as well as that of the *Fraktion* chairman.[8] The individual
political character of the *Landesgruppe* has been reinforced by the
continuity of its leadership personnel — its chairmanship has, for
instance, been held since 1953 by Richard Stücklen (1953-7 and 1966-
76), Hermann Höcherl (1957-61) and Franz-Josef Strauss (1962-6),[9]
with Friedrich Zimmermann succeeding Stücklen in 1976.

The compatibility of the CSU's two roles has depended above all on
the degree to which the political interests of both political parties

overlapped. During the period of Adenauer's ascendancy in the 1950s political harmony between the CDU and CSU was at its highest point for several reasons. First, and most importantly, the CSU was as much dependent on Adenauer's political success as was his own CDU.[3] As Strauss himself commented before the CSU executive in 1955:

> We depend naturally in Bonn on the arrangement of the CDU/CSU, and on the success of the Bonn Government. If we had a weaker Chancellor than Adenauer, we could without further ado exert a more powerful trial of strength. But the name and, in spite of all setbacks, the success of Adenauer is . . . so great that the CSU, even if it has at its head the strong-minded Schäffer,[4] cannot afford opposition to the Chancellor. For the Chancellor would suffer from this, and we even more.[10]

Secondly, the CSU clearly benefited in Bavarian politics from its association with the CDU, especially as during the mid-1950s it had not yet established its dominance as the state party of Bavaria, and was undergoing a challenge to its political position there, having been expelled in 1954 from the *Land* government by a coalition led by the SPD. The result was a crisis of confidence in its leadership ranks and a move towards party reform.[c] The CSU managed to overcome this crisis partly through the advantages it acquired from its role in Federal politics, as was shown decisively by its winning 47 of the then 48 direct seats in Bavaria in the wake of Adenauer's triumph in the Bundestag Election of 1957.[11] Thirdly, there was an effective separation between the CSU leadership in Bonn and in Munich, both in personnel terms and in political activities. While the Munich party leadership concentrated on *Land* politics and its role as ministers in the Bavarian government, with the post of CSU chairman usually combined at this time with that of Minister-President, the Bonn party leaders focused on Federal politics, with leaders like Strauss, Stücklen, Höcherl and Dollinger alternating between the chairmanship of the *Landesgruppe* and ministerial posts in Adenauer's cabinets. The principal form of assertiveness by the CSU vis-à-vis Adenauer and the CDU was in its claim to representation (usually 3 or 4 posts) in the Federal Government.[5] The CSU could exploit the leverage supplied by the need for its contribution to Adenauer's majority in the Bundestag.

By the early 1960s, the relationship between the CDU and CSU was

c   See below chapter 10 (c).

beginning to undergo a qualitative change. Adenauer's own decline and eventual retirement was followed by a general decline in the political and electoral position of the CDU – only halted temporarily by Erhard's election victory in 1965 – which was accentuated by repeated leadership crises in the larger party, and these developments forced the CSU to reconsider the nature of the relationship. Furthermore, the CSU had by now solidified its political base in Bavaria,[6] and it consequently felt freer to claim a decisive role in national politics. A unified political approach was additionally facilitated by Franz-Josef Strauss's election as CSU chairman in 1961, which helped to close the division through this personal link between the party's *Land* leadership and its Federal leadership. In simple terms, the differences emerging between the political interests of both Christian Democratic parties showed that the 'double tracks' of the CSU's dual function – the one autonomous, the other in alliance with the CDU – no longer ran parallel.

The transformation of the CDU/CSU alliance became apparent in several ways, which acquired increasing prominence during the course of the 1960s even before the role of Opposition in the 1970s precipitated a further qualitative change in the relationship. This long process involved a move from an autonomous position for the CSU within the Christian Democratic alliance to an independent one. The CSU developed its own profile over policy issues as a self-confessed conservative force, acting, in the words of Strauss, as the 'consolidator' or 'hard core' within the alliance. This assertiveness vis-à-vis the CDU, which had previously been restricted to constitutional (i.e. federalist) matters, became evident over a number of social questions like co-determination in industry and education policy, but it was most pronounced in the field of foreign and particularly German policy.[d] The reasons for this development lay chiefly in Strauss's own interest in this field, the greater national as opposed to Bavarian orientation of the CSU's policy outlook and the firm belief held among CSU leadership circles that their party was the real guarantor of Adenauer's policy principles. This conviction that the CSU's purpose was to defend the 'inheritance' of Adenauer manifested itself principally over European and German policy, where the CSU adhered to Adenauer's concept of German reunification through European integration, involving the 'Europeanisation' of the German question through a 'policy of strength' – a view propagated by Strauss's own book published in 1965, *The Grand Design: a European Solution to*

d   E.g. see above chapter 4 (d), pp. 174-6.

German Reunification.[12] This continuity in the CSU's position, a fact proudly underlined by various party leaders, derived much of its strength from the tradition peculiar to the CSU that Bavaria's ideological role was as the 'bulwark' of Western civilisation in Germany. This 'missionary' aspect of the CSU's policy profile acquired increasing emphasis from the mid-1960s and explained such slogans as 'Germany needs Bavaria' (at the 1971 CSU congress).[7]

While the new nationally orientated CSU leadership under Strauss used European policy to enhance the CSU's own profile within the alliance with the CDU, reflecting in turn the growing rivalry of the two party leaderships in national affairs, there was also an ideological impetus behind the CSU's position which gave it considerable force. The CSU projected itself as the foreign policy 'corrective' to the CDU, and in so doing sought not only to apply pressure on the CDU leadership directly but also to mobilise support for its viewpoint among right-wing elements within the CDU. The disharmony which followed from this altered balance in the CDU/CSU relationship affected solidarity within the alliance, all the more so as the CSU's high degree of cohesion over foreign policy allowed it to exploit differences within the CDU because of the latter's vulnerability in this respect, as became only too apparent during the Gaullist-Atlanticist controversy under Erhard's Chancellorship.[e] While the new CDU leadership under Kiesinger attempted to overcome their party's crisis through the Grand Coalition, the more flexible position in East-West relations entailed by governmental co-operation with the SPD resulted in the CSU's re-emphasising its divergent policy position. Strauss's Bad Reichenhall speech in September 1968, coupling opposition to the nuclear proliferation treaty with a threat that the CSU might go 'Federal',[13] underlined the extent to which the party alliance had now changed. From the time of Erhard's Chancellorship, when Strauss had been an outcast from the Federal Government following the Spiegel Affair, the CSU leader had seriously pondered the possibility of the CSU's becoming a national rather than just regionally-based party with the primary purpose of increasing the chances of the two Christian Democratic parties acquiring an overall majority in Bonn.[14]

The move to Opposition for the CDU/CSU in 1969 gave a great stimulus to the independent line pursued by the CSU and thereby threatened solidarity within the Christian Democratic alliance more seriously than ever before, especially as the two parties were no longer

e   See above chapter 4 (a), pp. 150-3.

bound together by the common corset of governmental responsibility. Just as Opposition parties generally in parliamentary systems may frequently be compelled to adapt their ideological traditions to new political conditions, so the increasing political disharmony between the CDU and CSU now acquired a greater ideological character. The CSU, unlike the CDU, responded to the 'change of power' in Bonn not with any sense of self-criticism, but with added insistence on the importance of its policy concepts. The abortive discussion of party reform which arose in the CDU after the 1969 Election was regarded dismissively by the CSU leadership,[8] and not until the Opposition's debacle in the 1972 Election were there even whispers of the need for party regeneration (chiefly from the Bavarian Young Union), but these were soon stifled.[15] The main political driving force operating against such change proved to be the CSU's persistent ability to attract voters in Bavaria, culminating in its unprecedented vote of 62.1 per cent in the Bavarian Landtag election of 1974 and 60 per cent in the Bundestag Election of 1976. While the 1974 CSU campaign, for instance, was fought with a pronounced emphasis on the party as representative of Bavarian cultural values and capitalised on the record of the *Land* government under Alfons Goppel, the result, like that of the two previous Bundestag elections, was interpreted as a triumph for Strauss and this served to strengthen his hand in Bonn as a force in Opposition politics. The 1972 Bundestag result in Bavaria, where the CSU succeeded in increasing its vote, contrary to the trend of the CDU elsewhere except with the 'hard-line' CDU in Hesse, was exploited by Strauss and other Federal leaders of the CSU to justify their advocacy of 'total confrontation' to the Left-Liberal Coalition.

The 'change of power' in Bonn and the ensuing polarisation, especially over Ostpolitik, consequently buttressed the national political orientation of the CSU leadership under Strauss. While CSU congresses had become less *Land* political in character since Strauss's election to the chairmanship early in the 1960s, they now acquired a pronounced concern over Federal issues from 1970.[16] Equally, Strauss's customary oration at the Ash Wednesday gathering of party activists at Vilshofen (since 1974 in Passau) was usually marked by its tirade against the 'socialist' leaders, Brandt and Schmidt.[17] The main effect of Opposition politics on the CSU leadership's policy outlook was therefore to reinforce traditional attitudes. Just as Richard Jaeger, one of the CSU's foreign policy spokesmen in the Bundestag, spoke of Bavaria's need to be the 'citadel of right and free democracy' to

counter the socialist danger, so Richard Stücklen commented in
predictable terms at the CSU congress in October 1971:

> Konrad Adenauer's historic deed was that he allied free Germany,
> and the open German question, firmly with the free West. Brandt
> has with his partition treaties of Moscow and Warsaw detached the
> German question from the guardianship and careful obligation of
> the West ... We — the CSU — warn emphatically against the
> continuation of this policy ... for to the extent that free Germany
> under Brandt and Scheel leaves Adenauer's security system behind,
> it will become the prisoner of the system intended for the
> Brezhnev-Europe.[18]

The CSU's fundamentalist line on national policy matters seemed to
acquire a renewed impulse from the outcome of the 1972 Election, on
the morrow of which Strauss blatantly urged that Bavaria should become
the 'bastion against the strivings after political co-ordination along the
Bonn model' in view of the Brandt Government's 'socialisation
intentions'.[19] Differences over German policy and CSU concern over
the general course of Opposition policy were the central motives behind
Strauss's serious threat to end the common Bundestag *Fraktion* in
November 1972. The assertion by the *Bayern-Kurier* that the
independence of the CSU was 'historically and politically self-evident'
underlined too how much the separate identity of the CSU as a
political party was at the root of the ensuing crisis which lasted several
weeks following the 1972 Election. The shock occasioned by Strauss's
move produced a broadly negative public reaction, including opposition to it from the vast majority of both CDU and CSU voters,[20]
and an unexpectedly strong reaction against it from several district
branches of the CSU supported by the Young Union in Bavaria.[21] This
helped to make the Bonn CSU leadership change its mind, so that the
common *Fraktion* was renewed early in December, but only after the
CSU's claim not to be 'majoritised' in the *Fraktion* and its demand for
a clear 'alternative' to the 'socialistic course' of the Bonn Government
were recognised.[22] While the CSU thus gained formally a greater
measure of freedom to develop its own policy positions, an element of
disengagement was evident in the parliamentary alliance between the
two parties, for the renewal agreement specified the end of the CSU's
double voting right over leadership positions below that of *Fraktion*
chairman.[9]

This first serious attempt by the Bonn leadership of the CSU to

divorce itself from the parliamentary alliance with the CDU showed
how far the orientations of the two parties had diverged since 1969.
The personal aspects of the relationship had become mixed with
ideological differences, as featured notably in CSU bitterness over
Barzel's stand on Ostpolitik,[f] so that the already strained relations
between the national leaders of both parties, noticeable since their
divisions over the Moscow and Warsaw Treaties in the spring of 1972,
came close to breaking point at the end of 1972. The Bonn leadership
of the CSU was no longer willing to accept without question the
consequences of being the junior partner in the Christian Democratic
alliance. This evolution of the CSU's independent course arose
primarily from its enhanced profile as a national-conservative force.
Its changing approach was given a personal dimension by Strauss's
problem of having to play second string to any CDU leader, even
though since Opposition began none of the larger party's figures
could match Strauss with his weighty political personality and long
experience of national affairs.

The greater divergence between the political interests of the two
parties during the Opposition period was reflected too in the frequency
with which the question of the CSU's going 'federal' was discussed.
This was seen as ultimately the logical consequence of a final rupture
in the parliamentary alliance. The idea was the personal brainchild of
Strauss, and was rumoured particularly at points of high tension
between the two parties, notably over the choice of Chancellor
candidate and differences of policy outlook. It was used as a tactical
means of exerting pressure on CDU leaders, but again it derived from
CSU frustrations over restrictions on its independence within the
relationship with the CDU. The idea was predictably fraught with
dangers, for doubts were voiced by opinion research that the CSU
with its strong Bavarian roots could enjoy strong nationwide appeal,
even though it was certain to attract some support from the CDU.[23]
Other reservations felt within the CSU itself about Strauss's idea
dwelt on the threat from a Bavarian CDU *Landesverband* to the
dominant political position of the CSU in Bavarian politics, on which
so many party careers depended, the difficulties facing the
establishment of a new national party organisation in West Germany
involving the need for extensive finance and available personnel, and
the likely loss of CSU membership in Bavaria.[24] The CSU leadership
therefore acted cautiously, refusing to become associated with

f   See above chapter 5 (c).

various 'initiatives' elsewhere in the Federal Republic to sponsor a 'federal CSU', while taking no active steps to discourage them. These 'initiatives' invariably arose from pockets of extreme right-wing activists, including disaffected Christian and Free Democrats, who looked to Strauss as a charismatic leader-figure and assumed a nationalist position on Ostpolitik. They proved to be temporary occurrences and made very little political impact, as shown by the record of the 'Circles of Friends of the CSU' (nicknamed 'Strauss fan clubs') in 1970, the German Union (DU) led by Friedrich Zoglmann, a former right-wing FDP leader, and the Fourth Party (AVP) initiative of 1975-6.

While the fortunes of personal-political and ideological elements in the CDU/CSU alliance reflected the degree of its intensity, the clinching factor which determined the changing character of that relationship was the question of the Government/Opposition role. The temporary rupture in CDU/CSU relations, which took place after Kohl's close failure to defeat the Left-Liberal coalition in the 1976 Bundestag Election, confirmed how much further solidarity between the two Christian Democratic parties was dependent on a return to power. Basic differences over Opposition policy and strategy had once again erupted shortly after the election early in October, with Strauss advocating absolute confrontation vis-à-vis the re-elected SPD/FDP Government and Kohl preferring the policy of the 'differentiating centre' of keeping open the possibility of an eventual coalition with the FDP.[25] With no possible compromise visible between the Opposition leaders, the majority of CSU Bundestag deputies under Strauss's leadership declared unilaterally their intention to form a separate *Fraktion.* The 'Crisis of Kreuth',[10] which lasted over three weeks during November-December 1976, was not merely another drama in the alliance repeating earlier occasions of friction, but evidence that the CDU/CSU relationship had reached a new level of disharmony.

First, there was an air of finality encouraged by the fact that this time, unlike 1972, Strauss, the prime mover, acted rather than threatened. His action, taken without any consultation of the CDU, produced an initial sense of shock in the latter which soon gave way to a feeling of outrage, which heightened solidarity within the CDU behind Kohl.[26] Kohl was therefore able to take a firm line by demanding that the Kreuth Resolution be revoked, and plans were prepared by the CDU leadership for establishing a new *Landesverband* of the party in Bavaria.[27] Secondly, this air of finality produced divisions within the CSU itself and a new attitude of defiance towards Strauss. Just as a large minority of CSU deputies had opposed the move,[11] so there were substantiated rumours of leading CSU politicians who might join a Bavarian CDU,[28] threats and indeed declarations of withdrawal of CSU membership in Bavaria[29] and open revolt by regional and district organisations of the CSU, especially in Franconia.[30] Thirdly, the alarming prospect of a final break in the CDU/CSU relationship occasioned speculation about the disruptive effect of this event on the stability of the West German party system. It was believed that the consequent alteration in the balance of political forces within that system would produce unavoidable pressures on the unity of the individual political parties.[31]

The sudden end to the crisis in mid-December, when Strauss revoked the Kreuth Resolution, could not erase the psychological rift which had appeared between the two parties, particularly as the unexpected renewal of the common Bundestag *Fraktion* was accompanied by scepticism in the CDU that a repeat performance, perhaps with a permanent rupture, could always happen in the future.[32] Strauss had recrossed the Rubicon, but at some cost to his political standing, while opinions about Kohl's success in 'saving the Union' divided between a favourable public response and some doubts among some CDU leaders about the strength of his leadership qualities as a factor in holding the CDU/CSU together in the future. In an immediate sense, Kohl had emerged the victor, but the inevitable personalisation of the affair could not detract essentially from its disruptive effect on CDU/CSU solidarity. The 'Crisis of Kreuth' had come extremely close to shattering morale in the CDU/CSU which had developed during the course of the Bundestag Election campaign. Indeed, the formal agreement to renew the CDU/CSU *Fraktion* under Kohl's chairmanship had emphasised more pointedly than in 1972 the right of the CSU to present a divergent position on basic policy issues and its independent status as a political party.[12]

The CDU/CSU alliance had by the mid-1970s become different in quality from what it had been during the 1950s, when both parties had been bound to the wheel of Adenauer's political fortune. Yet this alliance was never at any time a fully integrated relationship, and the CSU presented a version of Christian Democracy based on regional consciousness which developed in the course of time into a national-conservative force to the right of the mainstream CDU. This itself was a pertinent reflection on the loose nature of Christian Democratic ideology, for the CDU and CSU continued to proclaim adherence to

The Christian Social Union (CSU) 315

its values while growing apart as political parties. They had reacted differently to the new political environment of the 1960s and 1970s, with the CDU attempting painfully to adapt to changed conditions and the CSU reaffirming its fundamental beliefs. It was increasingly recognised that their growing political alienation might eventually lead to an organisational break, yet their long association over three decades has meant that any such event would damage electorally their respective claims as *Volksparteien*. At the heart of this dilemma was their development during this period as different kinds of political parties. This aspect of the problem will be considered further with respect to the leadership and organisational structure of the CSU.

(b)   Party Leadership: the Role of Franz-Josef Strauss

It has been evident from the foregoing discussion of the political relationship between the CDU and CSU that the personal element has been one of the major influences affecting its intensity. The importance of this factor has derived from the basic difference in the developing personal structure of leadership in both parties. For, while the CDU moved away from the charismatic/authoritarian style of Adenauer to one more collegial in approach to accord with increasing demands for programmatic discussion in the party, the CSU has experienced in some respects the reverse process. The CSU leadership changed hands several times from the late 1940s to the early 1960s, but since his election as party chairman in 1961 Strauss has developed a charismatic/ authoritarian style of leadership, which has been reinforced rather than weakened by the CDU/CSU's Opposition role from 1969.

There are several common features of the party leadership of Strauss[13] and that of Adenauer during the 1950s. Apart from their similar longevity of tenure as party chairmen, both political leaders based their political positions on their unquestionable success as electoral magnets for their parties, and used their charismatic authority · to impose their claims as supreme policy architects within their respective spheres. In both cases, their concentration of personal political power was accompanied by their élitist view of internal party democracy and the tendency of party congresses to assume a plebiscitary character. Indeed, Strauss's own enduring admiration for Adenauer — the only CDU leader for whom he has ever had a profound respect — has suggested a self-conscious parallel, for CSU publicity brochures on Strauss have stressed both Adenauer's eulogy of his qualities and his own nimbus in Bavaria as a political strategist.[14]

The analogy must, however, cease here, since there have been sufficient differences of circumstance and party structure to invalidate any deeper comparison. Strauss has been the dominant figure in only one of the two power bases of the CSU, its Bundestag representation, whereas the Bavarian government has not been his political preserve, and there has even been quiet resistance there to Strauss's authority. Strauss's projection of the CSU into national politics has brought him undoubted prominence, but he has not been able to consolidate his political authority through continuous performance in high executive office, as did Adenauer. While Adenauer could appear as the architect of his country's reconstruction after the War, Strauss's 'strong man' image has in the context of the 1960s and 1970s divided rather than mobilised support for him.

Whatever the differences between Adenauer and Strauss as political leaders, no political party in West Germany has since Adenauer's ascendancy been so identified with the figure of its chairman. The idea that Strauss embodies the CSU has been encouraged by his closest associates in the party.[15] But to what real extent can the CSU be called a 'Strauss party', for has the charismatic role of Strauss been reinforced by the structure of the party leadership? The mass media have been apt to describe Strauss's position in the CSU as 'all-powerful', but this question must be examined systematically by considering not only the institutionalisation of a strong party leadership, but also its history and the political position of Strauss himself.

A strong party leadership must ultimately depend on the attitudes towards authority, which predominate in the party concerned, but it can usually be facilitated by its reproduction in the institutional arrangements. An analysis, for example, of the CSU party executive (*Landesvorstand*) has shown a marked and continuous overweighty majority of *Land* ministers and (Federal and *Land*) *Fraktion* leaders and members,[16] of whom many among the latter owed their promotion to Strauss. The party statute changes of 1968 accentuated this concentration of *Landesvorstand* personnel on parliamentary figures rather than grass-roots representatives through the reduction of its size, thereby strengthening the lack of dualism between parliamentary and extra-parliamentary elements in this most important of the leadership organs.

The party organ which has acted as the formal channel of contact between leaders and activists has of course been the CSU Congress. Its meetings have shown an undeveloped state of internal party democracy, although progress towards policy discussion became slowly visible from the mid-1960s. CSU Congresses have primarily performed an acclamatory function, acting as a trampoline for Strauss's political gymnastics, with his major policy speech and re-election as chairman being the highlights of the occasion. The Bavarian showmanship which has coloured these events has been a more prominent feature than the modest efforts to promote serious debate on issues. From 1964, discussion forums were initiated with 'independent' (though usually pro-CSU) outside speakers selected by the leadership, and the proceedings of Congresses began to be published in the early 1970s with an increase in policy motions from local branches during these years.[33] The influence of greater programmatic discussion in the CDU encouraged by Biedenkopf, its new General Secretary, was already apparent in a small way at the 1973 CSU congress,[34] and the active involvement of the grass-roots with the formulation of the new CSU Basic Programme *(Grundsatzprogramm)* issued in 1976 was unprecedented.[35] Even so, the essential power of determining policy positions has remained with the CSU leadership and Strauss in person.

The history of the CSU leadership has shown clearly that the charismatic role of chairman has developed only under Strauss, who has held that office continuously since March 1961. If the decisive features of a charismatically-led political party are the unchallenged authority of the leader and his messianic political style, then the first three CSU chairmen would not qualify as examples. Josef Müller (1945-9) was too preoccupied with defending his forlorn attempt to impose an inter-confessional Christian Democratic approach on the CSU, while his successors, Hans Ehard (1949-55) and Hanns Seidel (1955-61), gave prior attention to their role as Bavarian minister-president. There existed concurrently other attractive figures in the party like Fritz Schäffer and Alois Hundhammer, not to mention Strauss himself, who made early bids for the chairmanship in 1952 and 1955. Strauss was fortunate for, when he eventually became CSU chairman, the party had overcome its political crisis of the mid-1950s, its organisational reforms had been implemented and it had laid the basis for becoming the dominant force in Bavarian politics.[g] The strict discipline implanted in the party structure through this organisational reform became a buttress of the party leadership, which has been further strengthened by personal reverence for Strauss among party activists.

Strauss's own conception of party leadership has attached primary

g   See below chapter 10 (c), pp. 323-4.

importance to loyalty from his colleagues and supporters. In a report to the CSU executive shortly after his election to the chairmanship in 1961, Strauss emphasised: 'I see the task of the party as tightening up organisation, propaganda and financing, and working together internally in a solid and loyal manner, so that the Union remains the dominating factor in the political life of Germany.'[36] Many years later, he commented in similar terms during a television interview with ZDF in reference to his differences with Franz Heubel, the CSU vice-chairman, in 1976:

> There are neither essential differences between us, nor is there a personal quarrel. An obvious prerequisite within the leadership level of a party must be mutual trust and loyal behaviour, so that one can achieve the strongest fighting power and the greatest possible solidarity.[37]

Loyalty has remained the constant theme relating to discord with other CSU leaders, for Strauss has reserved the right to interpret its application. One prominent case illustrating this early in Strauss's period as chairman was his dispute late in 1962 with Karl Theodor Freiherr von und zu Guttenberg, the CSU's spokesman on foreign issues in the Bundestag. Guttenberg was an independent character who was nevertheless close to Adenauer and enjoyed popular appeal among the CSU grass-roots.[38] His talks with SPD leaders about the possibility of a grand coalition in December 1962 shortly after Strauss's resignation over the Spiegel Affair were at the instigation of Adenauer, but led to accusations of disloyalty by Strauss, who claimed he was not informed of this matter. Disciplinary measures were initiated against Guttenberg, but ultimately no action was taken and the matter became closed.[39] Strauss has specifically stressed loyalty when taking a controversial decision. At the height of the crisis over ending the common Bundestag *Fraktion* with the CDU at the end of 1976, Strauss justified this move in the following way before the Bavarian Young Union:

> You cannot combine two things: fully informing all circles that want to be informed, together with total outward discretion . . . that would make a party ungovernable. Either I have so led the party that it has had an absolute majority for 15 years, or I haven't. For I must expect to be trusted to say what I need to say without its being regarded as detrimental, and not be prevented from saying

something because it would be destructive.[40]

Strauss's own personal political position, based especially on his role in Federal politics, has therefore been the decisive factor in his leadership of the CSU, for the party has not been fundamentally one which has been constructed in an authoritarian manner in the wide sense. It has suffered rather from an undeveloped state of internal party democracy, for which reason it is likely in the post-Strauss period that changes in this respect would have to come. At this point, it is useful to summarise the main reasons for the strength of Strauss's position. First, his ability to mobilise voters in Bavaria (though less successfully elsewhere in the Federal Republic) has wedded the CSU to him in spite of his occasional rhetorical derailments and reputation for political scandal. Strauss has become with his demagogic style the electoral Cassius Clay of the CSU, for his meetings have always drawn mass crowds, and he has learned to expect large and enthusiastic audiences.[41] Secondly, Strauss's prominence as a national politician has allowed him considerable freedom as supreme policy formulator within the CSU on issues of 'grand politics'. Viewed as the champion of Bavarian interests and values in Bonn, Strauss's role has been welcomed particularly by those *Land* political leaders of the CSU who have preferred to see him active at the national level. This political dualism in the CSU leadership with Strauss's regular absence in Bonn has facilitated his reputation as master strategist among the party's grass-roots.[42] His periodic speculations about a 'return' to Bavarian politics as minister-president have invariably aroused misgivings, especially as they have often been coupled with unflattering comments on the Bavarian government, much respected in CSU circles, and on the *Landesvater* figure of Alfons Goppel (minister-president since 1962). He has nevertheless been able to impose his will on the Bavarian cabinet over national questions, as with the Bavarian application to the Constitutional Court in 1973 against the General Treaty with the DDR. Thirdly, Strauss's lack of serious political rivals in the CSU has followed from both his unmatched electoral skill and his dominant personality in national affairs, for many other capable figures in the CSU have confined their activities to the *Land* political stage.

The CSU has therefore been a 'Strauss party' only at the national level, for virtually all key positions in the *Landesgruppe* in the Bundestag have been held by Strauss appointees. In so far as the CSU has gained prominence as a national political force under Strauss's leadership from the 1960s, the impression has been strengthened that the party as a whole has been the instrument of its chairman, so that its liberal wing has hardly been in evidence in West German politics. The dualism which has actually existed was illustrated clearly by the 'Crisis of Kreuth' late in 1976,[h] when Strauss was supported by the *Landesgruppe* (though not all its members) but faced a revolt within the party organisation. Indeed, this affair may well be seen as a noteworthy stage in the growing independence of the party in Bavaria vis-à-vis its chairman, just as the trend of democratisation at CSU Congresses, albeit slow, has been a pointer to future developments.

Strauss's relationship with his party has therefore been charismatic in nature, judging by his political style, his relations with other leaders as well as activists and his exclusive claims to national policy formulation. As his charismatic leadership has not been based essentially on an authoritarian institutional structure in the CSU, but rather on his dominance of the *Landesgruppe* and his own political authority in general, it would always be vulnerable to a serious decline in the latter coming in particular from electoral reverses in Bavaria associated with Strauss's name. Any decision by him to become Bavarian minister-president would demand some revision of his leadership position, depending on how far he would be using this post as a different power base in national politics or whether his move to Munich remained controversial within the CSU itself. It is necessary now to focus directly on the institutional structure of the party as a third dimension of the nature of the Christian Social Union.

(c)   Structural Character of the Party

The conclusion drawn from the foregoing two analyses is that the separate organisational history of the CSU has helped to emphasise it as a different kind of political party from the CDU, in spite of their common adherence to the values of Christian Democracy and their long-standing political alliance. Indeed, it has been the strong link between political and organisational factors, together with the increasing political divergence between the two parties, which has reinforced the separate development of the CSU. While bureaucratisation of the CDU's party machine has been associated with a move away from charismatic/authoritarian leadership (Adenauer style), as a consequence of its political decline in the 1960s and especially of its loss of power, in the CSU's case bureaucratisation and the development of charismatic/authoritarian leadership (Strauss style) occurred roughly at

h   See above chapter 10 (a), pp. 313-14.

the same time.

The basic problem which emerges when looking at the structural nature of the CSU is therefore how far the one development (charismatic leadership) has imprinted itself on the character of the other development (bureaucratisation). Bureaucratisation was initiated before the development of charismatic leadership, and at a much earlier stage than in the CDU, but for the same reason. The CSU's reaction to its loss of power in Bavaria in the mid-1950s resulted in organisational changes remarkably similar to those of the CDU in the 1970s, involving the upgrading of the party headquarters in Munich, the professionalisation of activist personnel and the beginnings of a deliberate membership recruitment drive. This adoption of a conscious organisation policy, aimed at re-establishing the party's electoral and political position, had nevertheless different consequences than those of the CDU for the party's structural character. First, the CSU's bureaucratisation was centralised, whereas in the CDU's case it had to take account of the deeply rooted federal structure, which was determined by the federal political system of West Germany. The organisation of the CSU has been based on one regional state only, so there have been no strong political pressures against a centralised party machine. Secondly, the balance of political weight inside the CSU since the party crisis of the mid-1950s has not been subject to internal pressures comparable to those affecting the CDU as a result of the 'change of power' in 1969, producing in the latter's case a greater awareness among the party as a whole. Although the CSU had relied on Adenauer's electoral appeal in the 1950s, it had by 1969 become less dependent than the CDU politically and psychologically on the office of Federal Chancellor. The CSU has on the contrary remained continuously in office as governing party of Bavaria since 1957 with increasing success in Landtag elections, especially since the 'change of power' in Bonn.[17] Thirdly, the organisational consequences of the reinforced monopoly of political weight which bureaucratisation brought for the CSU leadership have been seen most significantly in the passive nature of party membership. There has also been a dramatic rise in the membership total especially since 1969, promoted as in the CDU by a systematic membership campaign, but it has not so far resulted in much greater involvement of the membership in policy discussion.

The key to the separate organisational development of the CSU has lain in its Bavarian origins and character. The CSU revealed at first similar organisational features to the CDU, with the dominant role of local notables at the grass-roots and their prevalent anti-bureaucratic antipathy towards central control by a party machine, which derived particularly in rural Bavaria from fears of class warfare and its association with socialist party organisation.[43] On the other hand, the CSU was founded after the War as a separate party rather than *Landesverband* of the CDU, so the idea of a distinct organisational entity was present from the beginning, although it did not become fully established in the party until the late 1940s.[i] Josef Müller, the first chairman, attempted to create a strong party machine in Bavaria in order to fulfil his plans for forming the CSU as an instrument for overcoming social and confessional cleavages in that region.[44] His policy failed because of the challenge to his leadership, for the nature of party organisation was itself a subject of bitter dispute in the later 1940s, with the idea of central control being anathema to Fritz Schaffer, Alois Hundhammer and other former BVP leaders. The currency reform of 1948 had a similar effect on the CSU as on other political parties in the three western Occupation zones in reducing membership and weakening organisation, except that in the CSU's case party organisation was in such a precarious state that its collapse afterwards was immediate. The sharp reduction in organisational personnel forced the CSU at the grass-roots level exclusively into the hands of the notables.[45] The impression that the CSU was formed in the image of the pre-1933 Bavarian People's Party was justified all the more as the former's organisation network was well-established mainly in the Catholic southern regions of Bavaria.[18] CSU membership was very predominantly Roman Catholic and small-town-based like that of the BVP. In no sense, therefore, had the CSU succeeded in building a 'confessional bridge' — a central feature of Christian Democracy elsewhere in the Federal Republic — nor would this have been secured by developments on the Catholic side. The serious challenge to the CSU from the patriotic Bavarian Party (BP), whose strongholds were also in southern Bavaria, meant that the CSU was unable to monopolise the Catholic electorate.[19]

The political impact of the Bavarian Party from the late 1940s was one motive for party reform in the CSU, but the event which forced change on the latter was its expulsion from the Bavarian government by the coalition of four parties (SPD, FDP, BP and the refugee party, GB/BHE) led by the Social Democrat, Wilhelm Hoegner, from 1954-7. Until that time, pressures for reorganisation were not sufficiently

i   See above chapter 10 (a), pp. 304-5.

great to overcome prevalent attitudes of lethargy in the CSU indulged due to its governing role and typified by Hans Ehard (minister-president, 1946-54), who, like his contemporary, Adenauer, showed no serious regard for party organisational matters. The loss of control over the machinery of state finally decided the question. Ehard was replaced by Hanns Seidel, formerly Bavarian minister of economics, as party chairman, and the shock effect on the whole party was so traumatic that the new leadership embarked swiftly on a full-scale organisational policy. The new party business manager, Friedrich Zimmermann, who shortly became CSU General Secretary (1956-63), outlined the main aspects of this policy in his report to the party congress in October 1955. Noting that the party had to prepare itself for the eventuality of Adenauer's retirement, which would deprive the CDU/CSU of its stabilising authority and popularity, Zimmermann continued that it was necessary

> so to maintain and extend our party, that its share in political life and success cannot be endangered by the fickleness of public opinion. I am not in any sense overrating the possibilities of organisational work. For I believe that a good organisation of our party can give us the backing we need for the future, when worse times arrive.[46]

Another firm advocate of a strong party organisation then was Franz-Josef Strauss, who continued after his election as CSU chairman in 1961 to support efforts to improve further the state of the party machine.

The reform of party organisation initiated in the mid-1950s was above all electorally motivated, coming as a reaction to the loss of power in Bavaria and based on the assumption that in the projected post-Adenauer era it would no longer be sufficient to rely on the charisma of a leader figure. The reorganisation involved wide-ranging changes leading to the establishment of a centralised party machine, at the centre of which was the party headquarters *(Landesleitung)* in Munich. These changes were directed by the *Landesleitung,* which thereby acquired considerably more weight in the party than before. This process of bureaucratisation from above necessitated the restructing of the *Landesleitung* itself, with a substantial increase in its staff (from 14 to 100 during 1955-61), the improvement of its technical facilities, the rationalisation and elaboration of its sub-departments and the appointment of a General Secretary. Within the party as a whole efforts aimed at attracting qualified personnel as functionaries, the professionalisation of party activists through full-time paid appointments and, most significantly, the introduction of a new layer of machinery — the electoral district organisation *(Bundeswahlkreisorganisation)*.[47] It was maintained that honorary district party managers were no longer suited to the professional business of modern electioneering, and that full-time staff should oil the channels of contact between CSU deputies in Bonn and Munich and their constituencies, so as to make possible 'concentrated and embracing election campaigns'.[48] The constituency managers *(Bundeswahlkreisgeschäftsführer)* acquired in the course of time increasing numbers of tasks as the complexity of arranging election campaigns grew. They were paid a reasonable salary and were provided with an office, a business car and a secretary.[49] All these new organisational developments were financed centrally, but it took some years for them to amount to a fully integrated party machine, because of persistent resistance to changes from the local notables. This was inevitable because bureaucratisation meant imposing a sharp reduction on their role in the party.[20]

Although the party machine was established by the early 1960s, continuous efforts were made to improve its effectiveness in response to political demands during the decade that followed. The reform of the CSU remained essentially bureaucratic in character, for it was not associated with any significant growth of programmatic consciousness in the party, as for instance occurred in the CDU in the mid-1970s. The principal reason for the lack of such development was that the CSU soon began to make substantial electoral gains, starting with its staggering vote of 57.2 per cent in Bavaria in the Bundestag Election of 1957, thus solidifying the position of the leadership. That same year the party returned to power in Bavaria. Further changes in party organisation followed during the 1960s, under the General Secretaryships of Anton Jaumann (1963-7) and Max Streibl (1967-71). They included a greater emphasis on membership recruitment as a source for future activist personnel, more 'rational' election planning with the use of social scientific survey material, the enlargement of the party's publicity system, the adoption of computer methods and further restructuring of the *Landesleitung* in 1967 and again in 1971-2.[50]

Doubts were, however, expressed in the party leadership itself about the deeper impact of these organisational changes on party life. In his report as General Secretary in 1964, Jaumann deplored the lack of 'party consciousness', which he attributed to the CSU's 'bourgeois' and hence unassertive character, but nevertheless said that the main responsibility for the lack of efficiency of organisational work lay with the lower levels of the party.[51] The work of Gerold Tandler, a former leader of the Bavarian Young Union who was appointed CSU General Secretary in 1971, has concentrated on improving internal party communications between different levels of the CSU.[52] Tandler all the same suffered from critical comparisons with Biedenkopf, the rising star in the CDU in the mid-1970s, for not improving the genuine flow of information within the party.[53] This was not surprising since Tandler, like his predecessors, had not developed any individual political profile, emphasising as he did that the General Secretary must identify politically with the party chairman.[54] This has led to his reputation as 'the shadow of FJS', and 'the voice of his master'.[55] As appointees of the party chairman, CSU General Secretaries under Strauss have performed as managing directors of the party headquarters, or overlords of the party organisation, with no right to political leadership.

The CSU party machine developed to such an extent by the early 1970s that it became superior to that of the Bavarian SPD. The event which has most given it renewed stimulus in the 1970s has been the dramatic rise in CSU membership, which, as with the CDU, derived its momentum from the mobilisation of Opposition supporters following the 'change of power' in Bonn.[21] The CSU has sought to exploit the feeling of resistance to 'socialist' policies, which is particularly intensive in Bavaria, by systematic membership recruitment campaigns, as a result of which CSU membership doubled during 1969-76 from just over 70,000 to 140,000. In the decade before, membership drives had been sporadic and were geared to election campaigns,[56] although they were pursued with more determination during the later 1960s in reaction to the student protest movement and the Extra-Parliamentary Opposition. During the 1970s, the ordinary membership of the CSU has been encouraged by party headquarters to play a more active part in election campaigns as part of a general process of anti-Government mobilisation. In the party's handbook for CSU speakers for 1973, produced just after the 1972 Bundestag Election, it was urged:

This general activisation of members and sympathisers is worth using in the periods after the election, in order to meet the strengthened political pressure of the coalition parties. Furthermore, we must now prepare for the Landtag election of 1974. We must reckon with the fact that political altercation with the SPD/FDP will transfer more to the ideological level.[57]

Especially significant has been the large recruitment of young members from the late 1960s onwards. During the period 1970-6, for instance, the membership of the Bavarian Young Union doubled from 20,000 to 40,000.[58]

This mobilisation of new members for the CSU has had positive consequences for the party's electoral appeal, as shown by its results in the Bundestag Elections of 1972 and 1976 and the Landtag Election of 1974. In 1972, for example, the CSU won as many as 50.5 per cent of young voters in Bavaria[59] (not so far short of its general vote of 55.1 per cent there), although the trend elsewhere in the Federal Republic among young voters was decisively in favour of the Left-Liberal coalition in that election. One striking long-term feature of CSU support has on the other hand been the lack of working-class electoral support, also reflected in the composition of party membership, although there has been a mild increase since 1969. Generally speaking, the CSU's electoral strength and location of its members have, since it overcame the challenge from the BP, been strongly weighted towards the Catholic regions of southern Bavaria. It was also in these regions that its organisational reforms from the mid-1950s were most efficiently executed.[60] CSU membership has long had a strong rural/small town character with a high proportion of farmers and artisans (accounting for one-third of the total membership in 1964) and with a considerable predominance of Catholics (roughly 90 per cent of the membership). The major expansion in the 1970s of both membership recruitment and also voting support has occurred in the Protestant regions of Franconia, where in some areas it had previously been relatively weak.[61] The CSU's opportunity to appeal to Protestant voters came with the 'change of power' in 1969, which allowed it to present itself as a strong anti-socialist, nationalist force in a region where that mentality was strongly embedded. Signs of a breakthrough by the CSU in the city vote have also been apparent, especially in Munich where the party has systematically cultivated grass-roots feelings and exploited the local SPD's ideological divisions.[62] In both respects, the CSU made impressive gains in the Landtag Election of 1974. This significant take-off in both the electoral appeal and membership recruitment of the CSU may be seen as the consequence of the party's skilful exploitation of feeling in Bavaria against the SPD/FDP Government in Bonn.

The CSU has developed over time into a political party with a sophisticated and centralised organisation. This process of bureaucratisation during the two decades since the mid-1950s has involved above all a professionalisation of activist personnel, although local notables have not been entirely squeezed out of party life and retain an importance below the level of constituency organisation.[63] The two key factors in the organisational history of the CSU have been: the impact of political developments, as illustrated by the negative effects of the party's leadership feuds in the late 1940s, the threat to the CSU's existence posed by the Bavarian Party and its own loss of power in Bavaria and the mobilising effect of the national Opposition role in the 1970s, but in general the connection between political and the organisational factors has been shown by the CSU's strong electoral orientation; and, the second factor has been the party's essentially Bavarian character, for the source of its real strength has been its dominance of Bavarian politics, however much it has developed as a party of national importance. The structure of its membership has underlined this with its deeper roots in the traditional Bavarian regions of the southern part of the state, quite apart from the obvious fact that the party's organisation has been confined to Bavaria. The CSU has derived many benefits from its sway over Bavarian politics, including the advantages of patronage and its virtual monopoly of private contributions to political parties in Bavaria, which, together with state finance and membership dues, have accounted for the healthy state of CSU finances.[64]

There have been nevertheless two major limitations to the CSU's development as a political party. Its claim as a *Volkspartei* appealing across social barriers has been less strong than that of the CDU, because of its small working-class support (although that must be set in the context of the conservative Bavarian social structure), and (until the early 1970s) its limited appeal to Protestant voters. The other limitation is more serious, and differentiates it most of all from the reformed CDU of the mid-1970s. While the CDU has overcome its organisational deficiencies as the CSU did from the mid-1950s, it has also overtaken the latter in its encouragement of internal party democracy. The lack of this feature in the CSU has derived from the nature of its reorganisation process, which did not promote any development of wider policy discussion in the party, and from the charismatic and somewhat autocratic tendencies of its leader. Change could only come in this respect either if it were forced by the impact of electoral setbacks, or if a more liberal leadership were to assume office which would possibly lead to an alteration in the balance of political weight in the CSU.

Notes

[1]   For a detailed analysis of the early relationship between the CDU and the CSU, see Günter Müchler, 'Zum frühen Verhältnis von CDU and CSU' in *Politische Studien,* November/December 1972, pp. 595-613, as well as the author's Ph.D. thesis on the same subject (Munich University, 1973).

[2]   For a detailed analysis of the organisational character of the CSU *Landesgruppe,* see Günter Müchler, *CDU/CSU: das schwierige Bündnis* (1976), pp. 63-81.

[3]   E.g. the CSU slogan in Bavaria during the 1957 Bundestag Election campaign: 'Whether Sunshine or Shower, the German People vote for Adenauer'.

[4]   Fritz Schäffer, the CSU leader, was Minister of Finance in Adenauer's Cabinet.

[5]   Günter Müchler interprets the dual role of the CSU in this respect as that of both an 'in-group', exerting its influence within the alliance with the CDU, and an 'out-group', using its autonomy as a separate political party to behave in a manner similar to that of a coalition partner of the CDU (see his *CDU/CSU: das schwierige Bündnis* (1976), pp. 138-44, and also generally pp. 87-138 for a detailed discussion of the CSU's role in the Government formations of 1949, 1953 and 1957).

[6]   In spite of fluctuations in accordance with the CDU's electoral fortunes, its Bundestag vote in Bavaria ranged from 54.4 per cent to 57.2 per cent from 1957-69 inclusive.

[7]   See Erich Eisner, *Das europäische Konzept von Franz-Josef Strauss: die gesamteuropäischen Ordnungsvorstellungen der CSU* (1975), especially Part One, Chapter Two, for a clear discussion of the CSU's divergent views from the CDU over European policy.

[8]   The CSU had already begun to regard with suspicion programmatic changes in the CDU, beginning with the latter's Berlin Programme of 1968, which the CSU organ *Bayern-Kurier* described as 'basically changing' the party's character for 'under Adenauer it stood for the primacy of foreign policy'. In 1969 the same paper attacked the 'reform rigmarole' in the CDU and warned against a 'strategic Godesburg (*Bayern-Kurier,* 25 October 1969). Late in 1969, Strauss claimed: 'Our policy has stood the test, for we have nothing to repent and to regret − at best, we have succeeded in convincing the public more deeply about our policy' (quoted in Günter Müchler, *CDU/CSU: das schwierige Bündnis,* pp. 190-1).

[9]   Until 1972 the CSU could both fill the leadership positions in the *Fraktion* allotted to it proportionally, and participate in the election to leadership positions held by the CDU. Henceforth, the common election by both CDU and CSU deputies would be confined to that of *Fraktion* chairman (Günter Müchler, *op. cit.,* p. 182).

[10]   So named after Wildbad Kreuth, the town in Upper Bavaria, where the meeting of CSU deputies took place on November 19 at the

Hanns-Seidel-Foundation, the CSU affiliate organisation.

[11]   Of the 53 CSU Bundestag deputies, 50 were present at the meeting. 30 voted for the Kreuth Resolution, 18 against, there was one abstention and one invalid vote.

[12]   Called the agreement on 'The Bases of Political Co-operation between CDU and CSU', it insisted that there was no compulsion to vote en bloc *(Fraktionszwang)* and included the meaningful statement: 'The CSU is and remains an independent party, and will not become a *Landesverband* Bavaria of the CDU; as an independent party, it lays claim to a Federal-wide importance of the policy it represents' (see full text of this agreement in *FR*, 14 December 1976).

[13]   Franz-Josef Strauss, born 1915, has played a prominent part in national politics from the beginning of the Federal Republic. He has been a Bundestag deputy since 1949, and held various posts in CDU/CSU governments: Minister for Special Tasks (1953-5), for Atomic Energy (1955-6), for Defence (1956-62) and for Finance (1966-9). He was out of national office for four years following the Spiegel Affair of 1962. As a protégé of Josef Müller in the late 1940s, Strauss had risen fast in the CSU hierarchy, becoming head of party organisation in 1949. He became deputy chairman of the CSU in 1952, and nine years later its chairman. During the years of national Opposition since 1969, Strauss has specialised as CDU/CSU spokesman in financial policy.

[14]   E.g. see *FJS: das ist der private Strauss* (1972): 'Patron Dr Konrad Adenauer recognised the political talent of Strauss early, and valued it highly'; and the comment in *In Sachen Strauss* (1975) that 'citizens perceive increasingly that Franz-Josef Strauss possesses, apart from his level-headed appraisal of situations, a political eye for the future and will strive with action, energy and application, so that the Federal Republic again becomes an island of stability'.

[15]   E.g. the comment attributed to Friedrich Zimmermann, CSU General Secretary 1956-63 and CSU Bundestag *Landesgruppe* chairman from 1976, that 'without Strauss the CSU would be only half its value', and that of Gerold Tandler, General Secretary since 1971, that 'in primary matters there is an absolute identity between party and Strauss' *(Der Spiegel,* 6 November 1972, p. 36). The Strauss personality cult was further suggested by the series of mammoth celebrations of his 60th birthday in September 1975, when for instance records were sold of an interview with 'The Chairman' about 'his thoughts and memories' *(Die Zeit,* 19 September 1975). In 1971 the CSU had struck silver medals with Strauss's figure on one side and the Bavarian arms on the other.

[16]   Bundestag and Landtag deputies accounted for roughly 77 per cent of the *Landesvorstand's* members between 1967-74 (Alf Mintzel, *Die CSU: Anatomie einer konservativen Partei* (1975), pp. 492-3).

[17]   The CSU vote in Landtag elections has risen from 38 per cent in 1954 to:

1958 - 45.6%	1970 - 56.4%
1962 - 47.5%	1974 - 62.1%
1966 - 48.1%	

[18]   Apart from the cities of Munich and Augsburg, these accounted for nearly 70 per cent of the total membership in 1947 (Alf Mintzel, *Die CSU,* p. 180).

[19]   The highpoint of the BP's vote was 20.9 per cent in the Bundestag Election 1949, compared with 29.2 per cent for the CSU. The CSU had won 52.3 per cent in the Landtag Election of 1946 before the rise of the BP, falling by 24.9 per cent to 27.4 per cent in 1950 compared with 17.9 per

330 Christian Democracy in Western Germany

cent for the BP. Even as late as 1954 the BP won 13.2 per cent (CSU: 38 per cent) in the Landtag Election of that year. The BP had been allowed to engage in political activities in 1948, at the very moment when the CSU's central organisation collapsed. It was able to exploit feeling in the late 1940s that the CSU was not 'truly Bavarian' through its association with the 'Prussian' CDU.

[20] For a useful and detailed account of these organisational changes see Alf Mintzel, 'Die CSU in Bayern: Phasen ihrer organisationspolitischen Entwicklung' in *Politische Vierteljahresschrift*, October 1972, pp. 205-43.

[21] This overriding factor was emphasised in interviews the author had with Dieter Kiehl, CSU spokesman, in Munich, August 1976, and with Hermann Woesner, Passau district party manager, in Passau, September 1976.

References

1. On the BVP see Karl Schönhoven, *Die Bayerische Volkspartei 1924-1932* (1972); also, Dieter Posser, 'Nichts Neues aus Bayern: der Streit zwischen CDU und CSU hat historische Parallelen in *Die Zeit*, 8 December 1972.

2. On this, see Alf Mintzel, *Die CSU: Anatomie einer konservativen Partei* (1975), p. 252 and passim.

3. Quoted in Günter Müchler, 'Zum früheren Verhältnis von CDU and CSU' in *Politische Studien*, Nov./Dec. 1972, pp. 605-6.

4. *Ibid.*, pp. 607-8.

5. Quoted in Ernst Deuerlein, *CDU/CSU 1945-1957* (1957), p. 188.

6. See Müchler, *op. cit.*, pp. 609-10.

7. Wolfgang Dexheimer, 'Die CSU-Landesgruppe: ihre organisatorische Stellung in der CDU/CSU Fraktion' in *Zeitschrift für Parlamentsfragen*, No. 3, 1972, pp. 307-8.

8. *Ibid.*, pp. 308-10.

9. *Ibid.*, p. 312.

10. Quoted in Alf Mintzel, *Die CSU in Bayern* in J. Dittberner and R. Ebbighausen, *Parteiensystem in der Legitimationskrise* (1973), p. 422.

11. *Ibid.*, p. 422.

12. For a critical assessment of the CSU's long-term policy position on the German question, see Detlef Bischoff, 'Illusionen und Legenden: Die Deutschlandpolitik der CSU' in *Die Zeit*, 11 May 1973, as well as the same author's *Franz-Josef Strauss, die CSU und die Aussenpolitik: Konzeption und Realität am Beispiel der Grossen Koalition* (1973).

13. *Der Spiegel*, 19 May 1969, pp. 31-2.

14. For a discussion of the background of Strauss's plans on this question, see article by Klaus Bloemer, former foreign-policy adviser to Strauss, in 'Wer hat Angst vor FJS?' in *Die Zeit*, 12 April 1974.

15. *Der Tagesspiegel*, 20 December 1972, and *Der Spiegel*, 1 April 1974, p. 42.

16. Alf Mintzel, 'Die CSU-Parteitage im April und Juli 1970' in *Zeitschrift für Parlamentsfragen*, No. 3, 1970, pp. 366, 368.

17. E.g. *FAZ*, 4 March 1976.

18. *Parteitag: Dokumentation I, 15-17, Oktober 1971* (1971), p. 27.

19. *SZ*, 11 December 1972.

20. Günter Müchler, *CDU/CSU: das schwierige Bündnis* (1976), p. 180.

21. *SZ*, 28 November 1972; see also, Günter Müchler, *op. cit.*, pp. 174, 185-6.

22. *Die Zeit*, 8 December 1972 and *FAZ*, 2 December 1972.

23. E.g. see the poll by Emnid in *Die Welt*, 14 May 1973, and by the research

institute of the Konrad Adenauer Foundation in *Die Welt*, 26 November 1976.

24. *FR*, 30 March 1974; *Die Zeit*, 23 May 1975; and, *FAZ*, 17 November 1975.
25. Carl-Christian Kaiser, *Der verspielte Erfolg der Unionsparteien* in *Die Zeit*, 15 October 1976.
26. Carl-Christian Kaiser, 'Vereint gegen den Stoss aus Bayern' in *Die Zeit*, 3 December 1976.
27. *FR*, 23 November 1976 and *NZZ*, 23 November 1976.
28. See Eghard Mörbitz and Rudolf Grosskopff, 'Kohls künftiger Statthalter hat noch keinen Namen' in *FR*, 8 December 1976.
29. *Die Welt*, 24 November 1976.
30. *FR*, 27 November 1976 and *Der Spiegel*, 29 November 1976, pp. 23 ff.
31. For a discussion of this problem at the time, see Christian Graf von Krockow, *Der Unions-Bruch: die SPD geht schweren Zeiten entgegen* in *Die Zeit*, 26 November 1976.
32. *FR*, 14 December 1976.
33. Alf Mintzel, *Die CSU*, pp. 485-6.
34. See Hans-Joachim Noack, 'Ein leichter Wellenschlag bewegt die Basis' in *FR*, 1 October 1973.
35. *NZZ*, 16 March 1976 and *FAZ*, 13 March 1976.
36. Quoted in Alf Mintzel, *Die CSU-Parteitage*, p. 381.
37. *Die Zeit*, 25 June 1976.
38. See the profile of Guttenberg in *Die Zeit*, 21 April 1967.
39. *SZ*, 10 December 1962; *Die Zeit*, 28 December 1962; and *NZZ*, 4 March 1963.
40. *Der Spiegel*, 29 November 1976, p. 31.
41. See analyses of Strauss's election campaigns in *SZ*, 10 November 1972; *FAZ*, 16 September 1974; and *NZZ*, 30 September 1976.
42. *FAZ*, 17 November 1975.
43. Alf Mintzel, *Die CSU*, pp. 311-12.
44. *Ibid.*, p. 140.
45. *Ibid.*, p. 88.
46. Quoted in *ibid.*, p. 300.
47. *Ibid.*, pp. 309-10.
48. CSU-Landesleitung, *CSU: Porträt einer modernen Partei*, p. 13.
49. *Der Spiegel*, 6 November 1972, p. 46.
50. Alf Mintzel, *Die CSU*, pp. 318-27.
51. *Ibid.*, p. 314.
52. See report on CSU headquarters in *FAZ*, 30 November 1974.
53. *Der Spiegel*, 1 April 1974, p. 41.
54. *FAZ*, 30 November 1974.
55. See profiles of Tandler in *FAZ*, 13 May 1975 and *Die Zeit*, 17 October 1975.
56. *SZ*, 29 December 1960.
57. *CSU-Rednerdienst '73*, p. 7.
58. *Der Spiegel*, 13 September 1976, p. 76.
59. *Der Spiegel*, 1 April 1974, p. 42.
60. Alf Mintzel in J. Dittberner and R. Ebbighausen, *op. cit.*, p. 370.
61. Alf Mintzel, *Die CSU*, p. 385.
62. See article on the Munich CSU in *Die Zeit*, 8 November 1974.
63. Mintzel in Dittberner/Ebbighausen, *op. cit.*, p. 367.
64. See article on CSU finance in *Die Zeit*, 15 October 1971.

11 VOTER APPEAL AND ELECTION CAMPAIGNS OF THE CDU/CSU

The purpose of this chapter is not to review elections and voting behaviour comprehensively, on which there is ample literature,[1] but to discuss the nature of the CDU/CSU and its public impact. All *Volksparteien*, defined as large political parties with a consistent and substantial cross-sectional electoral appeal, are in reality characterised by a certain imbalance of their support from different sectors of the electorate. The CDU/CSU has been recognised as a *Volkspartei*, having established a wide electoral following within a decade after the Second World War, but it has, however, continuously shown a marked bias towards middle-class support among its electorate as well as at the membership level, as already seen.[a] From the 1960s its dominant electoral position was progressively challenged by the SPD, which has led to some revision of the CDU/CSU's standing as a *Volkspartei*.[2]

This chapter will examine the long- and short-term influences on the CDU/CSU's voter appeal, and how these reflect the sociological and organisational aspects of voting behaviour. In addition to surveying the CDU/CSU's voting strength among the various groups of the electorate during the generation since the War, it selects examples of Bundestag election campaigns during the parties' period in both Government and Opposition. This will highlight once more the Christian Democrats' role as a 'Chancellor's party', as well as touch on their strong electoral orientation. The resulting analysis has accordingly a bearing on the development of the party system in the Federal Republic of Germany, for one of the most crucial features of its evolution towards a 'two-and-a-half' party system has been the formation and maintenance of a unifying conservative force.

(a) Nature of Electoral Appeal

Any analysis of the social base of the CDU/CSU's voting strength must examine the extent of its breadth, and how consistently this strength has been maintained. Furthermore, its electoral position must be related to that of any rival political party which also acquires mass

---

a See above chapters 8 (a) on CDU membership and 10 (c), p. 326 on CSU membership.

support, in this case the SPD.

The Christian Democrats laid the foundations for their wide electoral base as successor party to the various Catholic and bourgeois parties of the Weimar period in the early years after the War.[b] The CDU/CSU was able to take advantage of the vacuum created by the collapse of the Third Reich, but its electorate remained unconsolidated for some years, and this became noticeable with the reappearance of smaller parties in the early 1950s.[c] The party, however, capitalised skilfully on its role in Government, and particularly on the figure of Adenauer, to establish its claim as the majority party, as became clear in the 1953 election and was confirmed in the dramatic result of 1957. Its position as a party with mass appeal, whose overall percentage of votes since 1953 has fluctuated between 44.8 and 50.2, is evident from the following table,[3] which includes a straight comparison with the SPD:

Table 6: Bundestag Election Results, 1949-1976

	1949	1953	1957	1961	1965	1969	1972	1976
CDU/CSU	31.0	45.2	50.2	45.3	47.6	46.1	44.8	48.6
SPD	29.2	28.8	31.8	36.2	39.3	42.7	45.9	42.6

The near equality between the votes of the two main parties in later elections has been explained with reference to long-term changes in social structure, whereby the CDU/CSU's traditional strongholds — such as older/rural/Catholic voters — are a declining element. The usual method of assessing the social base of a party's electorate is to unscramble its different component elements. This method is adopted here, though with some caution remembering that it is at best a 'crude' approach to the problem. Voting determinants provide a necessary guideline, but they must not suggest a static condition all the more as a decline in the intensity of party identification and a growth of voter mobility became evident in West Germany from the mid-1960s. Moreover, such long-term determinants cannot be considered too rigidly in isolation for they often overlap, not to mention that they present one side of the electoral picture. As Bone and Ranney aptly note, 'in every election the question of how any person will vote depends upon how his long-run and stable party preferences fit with

b   See above chapter 1 (c), pp. 49-50.
c   See above, chapter 2 (c), pp. 88-9.

his short-run and changing views on issues, and his opinions of the candidates who happen to be running at the moment'.[1]

1.   Confession

Confession has traditionally been the overriding factor influencing voting behaviour in Germany, which has historically been divided in this respect. The division of post-war Germany into two separate states has meant that the Catholic share of the population in the Federal Republic has been markedly higher than that in Weimar Germany, while on the other hand the trend of secularisation has progressively reduced somewhat the pungency of the confessional factor. The CDU/CSU's historically important attempt to build a 'confessional bridge' electorally must be judged in relation to these changes, for they have in turn assisted and limited the party's electoral dominance. Seeing that the original nucleus of the CDU/CSU's electorate came from former Centre Party/Bavarian People's Party Catholic voters, the greater proportion of Catholics gave it a strong starting-point. Even with the SPD's partial advance among Catholic voters in 1969 and 1972 (notably in the Bonn-Cologne-Aachen area), the CDU/CSU's main stronghold has remained the Catholic regions, as shown in the following table:[2]

Table 7: Areas with High/Low Proportion of Catholics

(a)	Areas with High Proportion		
		1969	1972
	CDU/CSU	55.6%	54.3%
	SPD	34.6	38.2
(b)	Areas of Low Proportion		
	CDU/CSU	40.9	39.9
	SPD	46.5	49.6

In 1976, the CDU/CSU succeeded in winning back from the SPD many of the Catholic voters lost to it in 1969-72, thus reinforcing this confessional picture. At the same time, the party succeeded in establishing a relatively strong base among Protestant voters from the 1953 Election, when its largest advances were in northern (i.e. Protestant) regions such as Schleswig-Holstein. There remain, however, two qualifying points about the factor of confession. First, the decisive influence has lain not so much between Catholics and

Protestants as such as between practising and nominal voters in both camps, with the former expressing a clear preference for the CDU/CSU.[4] Second, confession, like most other determinants, cannot be taken in isolation. The question of overlap is evident in the case of the sex determinant, for the overall preference for the Christian Democrats among women voters is particularly explained by their higher degree of religious practice. The urban/rural axis has been relevant too as stronger religious practice in smaller communities has helped to account for the CDU/CSU's dominance there, just as the party's variation of support between the regions has been determined considerably by their differing confessional character.

2.   Social Class and Occupation

A parallel tendency between class membership and political behaviour has been obvious, particularly since the relative weakening of confession as a voting determinant, but its relevance as a flexible rather than strict guideline is underlined by the impact of social structural changes and the varying expectations and perceptions of the political environment within any one class. Certain general features may, however, be noted. The most stable sectors of support for the two main parties have been the working class for the SPD, and the self-employed and farmers for the CDU/CSU, though even here social change has affected the degree of that support: notably, the decline of the agricultural class, the embourgeoisement of working-class voters, not to mention the impact of campaign mobilisation (which for instance worked in favour of the SPD among workers in 1972). The factor of class has been furthermore influenced by the campaign role of institutions like trade unions (in the case of blue-collar workers), and the Catholic Church (in the case of Catholic workers, as well as Catholics in general). In the latter instance, (strong) Catholic workers have maintained a certain loyalty to the CDU, following the tradition set by the Centre Party before 1933. The class factor has been influenced also by class mobility. This has applied above all to the urban vote, following the general movement to the cities, and within this group white-collar workers (employees and civil servants), who have been the most crucial element in recent elections because of their prominence among floating voters. The most significant gains achieved by the SPD at the expense of the CDU in 1969 were in this sector, with a further similar movement from the CDU to the FDP in 1972. Equally, white-collar workers have demonstrated a striking tendency to loosen their new attachment to the SPD in favour of both the CDU/CSU and the FDP in the mid-1970s, culminating in important gains in this sector by the CDU/CSU in the 1976 Election. The principal class limitation in the party's electorate has therefore been its limited appeal to working-class voters.

3.   Age

This determinant can be treated more simply, although clearly it has been conditioned by the factor of age within occupational categories. The CDU/CSU has traditionally relied on a strong preference among the older age groups, particularly among older women voters.[3] This has been related to a senescence trend (growing conservatism in later years), theories of generational loyalty (older voters remain grateful to Adenauer for 'rebuilding' Germany) and the central place of the 'security' theme in CDU/CSU publicity in successive elections with its special appeal to older voters. Greater interest has focused on this factor during the 1970s because of the progressive orientation of young voters (two-thirds of whom voted for the SPD and FDP in 1972), following the lowering of the voting age to 18 in 1970. This apparent sharpening of generational differences was modified in the mid-1970s with the preference for the CDU/CSU Opposition among the new group of young voters as the major feature of the so-called *Tendenzwende* of the mid-1970s.[4] In the 1976 Election, the CDU/CSU did much better among first voters than in 1972, gaining equal support among 18-21-year-olds compared with the SPD.[5] The principal conclusion to be drawn from this analysis is a relatively high degree of mobility among young voters, suggesting that any examination of their party political preferences must be made somewhat less on sociological grounds than is usually the case, and more in relation to shorter-term influences deriving from the impact of political events and of new political moods.

4.   Sex

The continuous female predominance among West German voters during the post-war period (still 54 per cent in 1976) has led to assertions that they have determined the outcome of Bundestag elections. The traditionally strong preference of women voters for the CDU/CSU, which in 1957 received 25 per cent more of their support than did the SPD, was emphasised as the principal reason for that party's electoral dominance. This assumption has had to be modified considerably in the light of the impact of social change with the emancipation process, the rise in female employment and the declining influence of the Church. Women began from 1969 to vote somewhat more similarly to men,[6] particuarly among the younger age groups where there was a noticeable trend to the SPD in 1969 and especially in 1972. Politically, this change has been encouraged by a marked governmental orientation ('Chancellor effect') among women voters, which started to favour the SPD once the CDU/CSU moved to Opposition. The picture of 'little old mothers' voting as a group for reasons of 'greater conservatism due to religiosity'[7] is therefore no longer quite so typical, although it was in any case subject to such cross-pressures as occupational affiliation, levels of church-going and confessional differences. The lower level of political interest has, however, remained generally evident among women compared with men voters, for, as one analysis of female voters at the time of the 1969 Election noted: 'For many female voters, social researchers discovered, the CDU is less a political party than a protective institution, which adheres to comfortable values, shelters marriage and family and lives in peace with the churches.'[8] In 1976, the growing similarity between male and female voters was reversed, with above-average SPD losses to the CDU/CSU among the latter.[9]

5. Regional

While less obvious a sociological determinant in voting behaviour, the regional aspect is nevertheless relevant in a country, which has witnessed significant regional variation in both voter movements and political traditions. The latter explain partly why certain *Länder* have proved to be strongholds for one party or the other, notably in the CDU/CSU's case the conservative bastions of Schleswig-Holstein in the north and Baden-Württemberg and particularly Bavaria in the south. There are various other aspects to be considered. The factor of overlap with other determinants has been evident, for variation in social structure between *Länder* has clearly influenced the parties' fortunes around the country. In North-Rhine Westphalia, for instance, not only has the population been divided between urban concentration in the Ruhr basin and the rural areas of Westphalia but the phenomenon of voter mobility is strongest here, which has helped to account for the close rivalry in this state between the CDU and SPD. For instance, the CDU's greatest losses in 1969 occurred in North-Rhine Westphalia. Speaking generally, both Kitzinger and Kaltefleiter found marked regional variations in CDU gains respectively in the 1957 and 1965 Elections.[10] One further reason for such variation which emerges from these studies has been the different regional structures of party strength, especially with respect to smaller parties which tended to owe their overall vote to a relatively good showing in certain areas. This factor affected the CDU more than the SPD, because supporters of smaller parties have more often than not been potential Christian Democratic voters. Kaltefleiter emphasised the failure of parties, such as the conservative GDP (Pan-German Party), to repeat their performance of 1961 four years later, as one cause of the CDU/CSU's success in increasing its vote in 1965.[11] Similarly, the movement of conservative Free Democrats away from the FDP in 1969 (following that party's left-liberal trend) prevented greater CDU/CSU losses in that election. This happened noticeably in Baden-Württemberg with its 'old liberal' tradition. Finally, the regional aspect of voting behaviour gained increased attention in 1972, when the CDU/CSU lost in all states except Hesse and Bavaria, leading to discussion of a 'North-South divide'.[12] This 'divide' was again evident in the different voting trends between North and South in the 1976 Election.[13] The area approach to CDU/CSU voting performance may of course be taken one stage further to the local level, which serves to underline not only local political traditions but also individual factors, such as the personality of candidates, the influence of personal/political rivalries in the locality and the state of local party organisation.[5]

The picture of CDU/CSU voting strength which emerges from this brief analysis is that of a political party which has since the early years of the Federal Republic maintained its position as a *Volkspartei,* although with some significant modifications. Kaltefleiter's conclusion based on the 1969 result, that the CDU/CSU was 'as before a *Volkspartei* in the sense that among its voters are representatives of all social groups, but the proportion of these groups has become somewhat unbalanced',[14] was confirmed by the 1972 Election. The CDU itself from the mid-1960s revealed a growing concern about its weak appeal in the cities,[15] but any arguments about the demise of the CDU/CSU vote on grounds of social structural change had of course to take into account the increase in social mobility and electoral volatility, which precluded any too rigid judgement. For instance, the CDU/CSU made inroads into the vote of some big cities in the 1976 Bundestag Election.[6]

Problems of generalisation in voting behaviour are further complicated by the fact that a party's electoral fortunes are also dependent on political circumstances, the condition of party organisation and morale at the time of individual election campaigns and the impact of the party's national leaders. These factors have usually played an important part in influencing the electoral behaviour of floating voters in particular.

(b)   Campaigns as the Chancellor's Party: the Bundestag Elections of 1957 and 1965

Election campaigns are an important indicator of the nature of a political party, for they can reveal how it projects itself to the voters at a time when its immediate future is at stake. This point has been especially relevant in the case of West Germany, where fixed election periods have encouraged long campaigns and where it is generally accepted that campaigns play an important role in determining voters' final preferences, if only by crystallising their perceptions of the parties and polarising their political behaviour. No two elections are the same, because general circumstances change and the composition of a party's leadership, which helps to colour its image among the electorate, may be different. The examples of 1957 and 1965 have been selected for two reasons: in view of the central feature of the Chancellor's role in CDU/CSU campaigns during the 1950s and 1960s, it is necessary to include a 'classic' case of an 'Adenauer election', while also looking at a campaign under a different leader when the party was still in office; the state of the parties in these two elections was significantly different — in particular, the Christian Democrats were at the highpoint of their electoral dominance in 1957, whereas by 1965 their position was under serious challenge from the SPD.

In spite of these differences of circumstance, certain overriding features of CDU/CSU campaigns were apparent, and established a consistency of pattern in electoral approach. First, the Chancellor figure was dominant in the party's self-projection. The CDU/CSU capitalised on the authority of the state, and chose to present the Chancellor of the day as the personal embodiment of its achievements in office — linking Adenauer with the international prestige acquired by the new West German republic,[7] while Erhard was obviously viewed as the 'father' of the economic miracle. This approach facilitated a simplified and effective message to the voters with the famous Adenauer poster of 1957 featuring simply his profile (Big-Brother style), and the similar Erhard poster of eight years later. Adenauer's election tour,[8] described by one foreign correspondent light-heartedly as having 'all the characteristics of an inspection by a colonial governor in a restive province',[16] was usually publicised locally with posters stating simply: 'HE comes'.[17] According to Bruno Heck, who organised that campaign, survey research showed that over half the population 'revered Adenauer like a monarch'.[18] Erhard, whose political style was very different from Adenauer's, nevertheless followed the strong precedent set by his predecessor when he carried through an intensive whistle-stop tour of the country in 1965 (described as the 'Palais Schaumburg on wheels'), urging people to 'elect not only a new Bundestag, but a new Chancellor'.[19] In both cases, this approach paid dividends. Kitzinger's study of the 1957 election shows that the CDU/CSU succeeded in the last weeks of the campaign in mobilising a large number of 'don't knows', who were attracted by Adenauer's personality and his party's record of 'continued and intensified political and economic success',[20] and that this helped to give the CDU/CSU its absolute majority on polling day. Equally, in the view of Kaltefleiter, it was the 'Chancellor voters' *(Kanzlerwähler)* who ultimately decided the 1965 result, despite the uncertainties created during the campaign by the polls' prediction of a neck-and-neck race between the two main parties.[21] The continued predominance of the Chancellor in CDU/CSU election campaigns (repeated again with Kiesinger in 1969) served to underline the basic psychological dependence of the party on its leader figure.

Second, a certain consistency of ideological tone was apparent in the CDU/CSU's Bundestag election campaigns. The main tenor of the party's effort to 'conceptualise' its image was clearly expressed in the principal slogans chosen for different elections: 'No Experiments' (1957), 'Our Security − CDU' and 'It is a Question of Germany' (1965), and 'Safely into the 70s' (1969). The leitmotiv of successive Christian Democratic appeals, apart from the emphasis on the Chancellor (e.g. 'It all depends on the Chancellor' in 1969), was the 'security' theme. The remarkable frequency of this theme suggested it represented, in CDU eyes, the condensation of party values for electoral purposes. The intention was to emphasise the party's role in guiding the nation's destiny (the state as protector), hoping thereby to exploit satisfaction with the *status quo*. This theme, especially as it was used in relation to the country's international position, has played a greater part in the politics of West Germany than in any other comparable industrialised nation.[22] It was allied with that other prominent aspect of CDU/CSU electoral propaganda, its anti-Communism, and served the party political purpose of combining all forms of socialism and thereby undercutting the SPD's legitimacy, as with Adenauer's claim in 1957 that the SPD in power would spell the 'ruin' of Germany. Another noteworthy feature of CDU/CSU campaigns was the tendency to refer back to past achievements in office. It became even more marked in the 1960s, when Adenauer was no longer at the helm and his memory was revived to maintain loyalty among traditional party voters.

Thirdly, the CDU/CSU developed an early awareness of the value of electoral cosmetics. While the SPD did not really begin to adopt such an approach until the 1961 Election, the Christian Democrats were already 'professional' in their long-term campaign planning during the 1950s, with their employment of publicity agencies and use of social survey data. Kitzinger described, with some accuracy, their campaigns as operating with 'all the centralised manoeuvrability of an advertising firm'.[23] Even early preparations for the 1957 campaign could be traced back to the post-mortem on the previous election, so that the strategy of the campaign had been exactly defined by the autumn of 1956.[24] The 1965 campaign operated under more difficult political circumstances, but even here leading party officials sought to counter their new vulnerability in the face of the strong SPD challenge by trying to gear their publicity machine to changing social attitudes.[25]

These three aspects of CDU/CSU campaign behaviour generally suggest a political party with an essentially conservative appeal, although one with flexibility in its mastery of modern electoral methods. The latter feature derived clearly from the CDU/CSU's pronounced electoral orientation and awareness. The SPD challenge was viewed by party leaders above all as an electoral problem, so much so that Bruno Heck visited the USA in the mid-1960s to study new electoral techniques,[26] and Helmut Kohl asserted at the Rhineland-Palatinate party congress in 1968 that the CDU should swallow any reluctance to adopt 'new thought-categories' in the wooing of voters.[27]

Election campaigns did indeed provide the highpoint of CDU/CSU organisational sophistication, but there must be a powerful limit to how far good organisation can control the pace of events in an election campaign. Influential and sometimes unforeseeable constraints affect the role of a party's campaign, such as the impact of election events[9] and the simple factor of human unpredictability. Elections are furthermore complex events for 'there are literally hundreds of different campaigns taking place simultaneously' (Richard Rose),[28] which would apply more to the West German case than it has done to Britain, because of the federal character of politics in the former case. Local constituencies continued to play a crucial role, as indeed have party-inclined pressure groups (such as Catholic associations for the CDU/CSU), even though the mass media have increasingly encouraged a generalised viewpoint of campaigns. Finally, the Christian Democrats' greatest electoral advantage, Chancellor appeal, had to be judged in conjunction with other factors, specifically the voters' changing perception of the party's 'issue-competence' (*Problemlösungs-kompetenz*), for it was precisely here that the SPD challenge in the 1960s made itself felt.[29] It was not surprising that their loss of the Chancellorship in 1969 was viewed by the Christian Democrats as the most serious weakening of their overall electoral position.

(c) Campaigns as Opposition Party: the Bundestag Elections of 1972 and 1976

These two campaigns in Opposition provided sufficient contrasts of candidate appeal, party organisation and morale and general political circumstances to make a comparison interesting and worthwhile. Indeed, the differences between the CDU/CSU's performance in both elections reflected a qualitative change in its public impact during the intervening years and therefore helped to account for their different results. During the 1972 Election, CDU/CSU supporters were distinguished by a 'spiral of silence' or reluctance to express publicly their party affiliation in contrast with supporters of the two coalition parties. This derived from a sense of representing a 'minority' vewpoint in a 'hostile' political environment at a time when the SPD and FDP presented themselves as more convincing spokesmen for the needs of the 1970s.[30] By the 1976 Election, the CDU/CSU had regained some initiative in keeping in line with public opinion trends and consequently was in a much stronger position to put the Government on the defensive.[10] This new punch in the CDU/CSU's public appeal partly reflected and was a consequence of its different performance in Opposition between the 1969-72 and 1972-6 periods, although it also resulted from the less favourable political position in which the Government found itself in the second election compared with the first.

The most obvious difficulty facing the CDU/CSU in 1972 and 1976, compared with the 1950s and 1960s, was that it could no longer build its campaigns on Chancellor appeal. The problem for the party in Opposition has been consistently illustrated by opinion polls showing the superior popularity of the incumbent Chancellor over that of the Chancellor candidate in successive elections, though in 1976 the popularity gap between Kohl and Schmidt was generally significantly less than that between Barzel and Brandt in 1972. The conventional strategy for an Opposition party has therefore been to present a 'team' of leaders in an effort to counter the appeal of the individual Chancellor. This method was adopted by the CDU/CSU in 1972, and supplemented by a 'regionalisation' of its personal appeal by concentrating at the *Land* level on popular party figures there.[31] This attempt failed to work because Brandt's evident charisma and the growing importance of television coverage in election campaigns demanded that attention focus on his opposite number among Opposition leaders. The main exception was the interest shown in the role of the CSU leader, Strauss, who inevitably attracted mass media attention because he was generally regarded as the stronger of the two Opposition personalities, which further highlighted the deficiencies of Barzel's public appeal.[d] Barzel's campaign appeared to be restrained and to lack verve, for he concentrated on indoor gatherings of the party faithful and was less active than Kiesinger had been in 1969 in terms of the number of meetings he addressed.[32] His performance on television, particularly in the last discussion between the four party chairmen,[33] was less impressive than that of both Brandt and Scheel. Generally, Barzel was unable to stimulate his party to break out of the defensive position in which it found itself during the campaign, especially over Ostpolitik, while the SPD could depend on its vastly superior image of competence in foreign and social affairs.[34] The Government moreover could exploit the publicity advantages of policy initiative, notably with the signing of the General Treaty with the DDR in the week before election day.

Kohl's campaign four years later had similarly to contend with the SPD's continued possession of the Chancellorship, although the advantages of incumbency proved less obvious than in 1972 in view of the impact of the difficult economic situation, the enhanced image of competence acquired by the CDU/CSU in the domestic field[35] and Schmidt's reluctance to 'personalise' his campaign. Kohl was inhibited like Barzel by the negative impact of Strauss's personality in the country at large, but he chose to follow the maxim that the Opposition Chancellor candidate must work harder than the incumbent Chancellor, and carried out an intensive programme of public meetings which drew on the strong 'sympathy bonus' which he enjoyed vis-à-vis Schmidt in the opinion polls.[36] Although lacking charismatic appeal, Kohl managed to project a 'human' image both through television and his

d See above chapter 5 (b), p. 195.

public appearances, where he usually restricted his speech to 20-30 minutes and concentrated on greeting people in the crowds.[37]

Kohl's decided electoral advantage compared with Barzel in 1972 was the enhanced state of his party and its effect on campaign organisation. Whereas Barzel's campaign had been weakened by the CDU's organisational deficiencies, particularly in the production of publicity material,[38] and a general lack of preparedness for the early election which was called in 1972, the CDU's campaign four years later was the result of a carefully constructed strategy of different stages leading from the mobilisation of party members early in 1976 to the 'hot phase' in September.[39] The improvements in party organisation since 1972, and above all the strong increase in party membership, provided both better facilities and greater manpower for the conduct of the campaign in 1976. A series of 'actions' was planned by the CDU from the beginning of 1976 and geared to the active involvement of all new members in the campaign, notably canvassing,[40] as well as efforts to attract further new members (e.g. the CDU poster 'Voting by itself is not enough − Get to grips with the Party'). By exploiting this growing reservoir of party activists, especially the willingness of new members to participate, the CDU was able to create a momentum which in turn reinforced party morale. The result was evident in the noticeable readiness of CDU members to argue their views with members of the public during the course of the 1976 campaign.[41] At another level, the smoothly run organisation of the CDU's (and CSU's) electoral machine was illustrated by its growing adoption since the early 1970s of 'American'-style campaigning techniques. This was a feature also of the other political parties, and by 1976 it had been developed to a sophisticated degree with stickers, campaign buttons, ballpoint pens, election records and balloons as well as the usual forms of glossy campaign literature.[11] It was a further reflection in a small way of the readiness of CDU/CSU members to declare openly their party political attachment in this election, although the 'Americanisation' of style had already been evident in the party's 1972 campaign.

There were furthermore differences of ideological tone between the CDU/CSU campaigns of 1972 and 1976. In the former case, the party selected as its main slogan 'We will build Progress on the Basis of Stability', which was intended as a modification of the traditional 'security' theme to include the demand for 'change'. Its campaign, however, projected old values like the social market economy and was widely criticised for its 'nostalgic' tone,[42] while various anonymous electoral 'initiatives' (*Bürgerinitiativen*) probably harmed the party's image by associating it too closely with business interests.[43] A post-mortem report by the Rhineland CDU later criticised the party for failing to present a 'convincing' formula to the voters, giving 'old answers to new questions' and generally offering a picture of itself as 'a party, which was striving after power with all means, without actually knowing for what purpose it wanted to use it'.[44]

Unlike the CDU/CSU slogan of 1972, that of 1976 – 'Freedom instead of/or Socialism' – succeeded in both mobilising party activists and putting the SPD on the defensive for part of the campaign. It expressed a staunch anti-Communist/Socialist attitude, of which a special feature was an attack on 'bureaucratisation' in society. Generally, the party's line in the campaign was featured in Kohl's set speech in that this combined traditional values like 'solidarity', patriotism and a pride in the party's history ('I am the successor of Konrad Adenauer') with the demand for 'a new beginning in German politics' and· a concern for the future of young people. While not particularly original in its thought content, the party's programme nevertheless managed to convey the impression of an alternative concept for the future to that of the governing parties, and it made an impact as disillusionment with the latter was easier to exploit after seven years in power compared with only three in 1972. Indeed, the CDU/CSU was able to take advantage in 1976 of the growth of a new conservative political mood since the earlier election.

Both 1972 and 1976 showed that elections can act both as catalysts of longer-term developments in the party, and as agents for political and organisational change in it. The earlier campaign was inhibited by the weakening effect on party morale of its difficulties in adjusting to the role of Opposition, and the campaign itself drew attention to deficiencies of organisation and leadership. The 1976 campaign by contrast could be seen as a culmination of the CDU's organisational and political renewal, which had occurred during the second Opposition period. The factors of party morale and state of party organisation were therefore closely related to each other. This problem became far more apparent during the Opposition years, for in the case of the 'Chancellor elections' in the 1950s and 1960s the personal element in the party's appeal provided the focus for its electoral activities. After 1969 with the loss of the Chancellorship, the CDU/CSU had to draw more than before on the party's internal resources of political mobilisation, although clearly the personality of the Chancellor candidate was still important. In adjusting to these different conditions,

the CDU/CSU's aim was to strengthen its public impact as the
basis for its regaining power, for the party's future depended
essentially on whether it returned to Government or remained for an
indefinite period in Opposition.

Notes

[1]   For a recent introductory survey in English, see Tony Burkett, *Parties and Elections in West Germany: the search for stability* (1975).
[2]   For instance, David Conradt, writing in the early 1970s, argued that the shift in the demographic composition of the Christian Democratic vote might mean that the traditional characterisation of the CDU/CSU as a broadly based 'catch-all' party was in need of revision, as it has become less of an 'integrating party of the middle', and more of a conservative-right party (David P. Conradt, *The West German Party System: an ecological analysis of social structure and voting behaviour, 1961-1969* (1972), p. 31).
[3]   This chapter concentrates on trends in Bundestag elections, for, while Landtag elections provide further evidence on the electoral strength of the parties, they have also normally registered an anti-government swing and can be coloured by special regional factors. This helps to explain why the SPD Opposition performed better in Landtag elections in the 1950s and earlier 1960s, and the CDU/CSU Opposition in the earlier 1970s.
[4]   See Erhard Blankenburg, *Kirchliche Bindung und Wahlverhalten* (1967) for a discussion of this aspect with reference to North-Rhine Westphalia in the mid-1960s.
[5]   An interesting example of such an approach is Bernhard Vogel and Peter Haungs, *Wahlkampf und Wählertradition, eine Studie zur Bundestagswahl von 1961* (1965). This looks at the case of Heidelberg, and examines the performance of the parties in that constituency in 1961 against the background of party development since the nineteenth century.
[6]   This was due in part to the movement of floating voters, but also to the weaknesses of SPD organisation in certain cases, notably in Munich. The CDU had already shown its capacity for attracting urban voters by winning the election for mayor of Stuttgart late in 1974. In the Hesse local elections in March 1977, the CDU made large gains in several major cities, including Frankfurt which the SPD had held since the Second World War.
[7]   Adenauer's speeches in the 1957 campaign were punctuated with frequent references to his meetings with foreign leaders.
[8]   For a colourful and detailed description of Adenauer's campaign in 1957, see cover story, 'Adenauer: Wie man Wähler gewinnt' in *Der Spiegel*, 11 September 1957, pp. 13-33.
[9]   E.g. the building of the Berlin Wall in 1961, with the negative implications this held for attitudes towards Adenauer's foreign policy by showing up the deficiencies of a firm anti-Communist stand.
[10] Cf. Biedenkopf's claim made at the mass rally at Dortmund on 5 September 1976 that 'The CDU, my friends, is on the offensive – we determine the themes of the election campaign'.

[11] The best example of this 'Americanisation' of campaign publicity found by the author during the 1976 Bundestag Election was the large bright red plastic briefcase handed out to each journalist on Kohl's campaign train in September. This contained among other things: a campaign biography of the candidate, a book on Adenauer, a CDU tie, a leather cup with three dice, a CDU T-shirt, a pack of cards with Kohl's face on some of them and various election posters.

References

1. Hugh Bone/Austin Ranney, *Politics and Voters* (1971), p. 13.
2. Analysis by Rudolf Wildenmann on ZDF television, 20 November 1972.
3. E.g. see Uwe Kitzinger's analysis of 1957 Election in *German Electoral Politics* (1960), esp. p. 291.
4. See analysis of party political preferences of young voters, 'Wechseln Jungwähler die Fronten?' in *Der Spiegel*, 5 April 1976, pp. 46-60.
5. See Infas analysis in *FR*, 5 October 1976.
6. Werner Kaltefleiter, *Zwischen Konsens und Krise: eine Analyse der Bundestagwahl 1972* (1973), p. 161 ff.
7. Kitzinger on the 1957 Election, *op. cit.*, p. 301.
8. *Der Spiegel*, 15 September 1969, article on women voters, p. 54.
9. See analysis in *Die Welt*, 5 October 1976.
10. See Kitzinger, *op. cit.*, pp. 280-4, and Kaltefleiter, 'Konsens ohne Macht? Eine Analyse der Bundestagswahl vom 19. September 1965' in *Verfassung und Verfassungswirklichkeit*, 1966, pp. 44-8.
11. Kaltefleiter, *Konsens*, p. 49.
12. R.E.M. Irving and W.E. Paterson, 'The West German Parliamentary Election of November 1972' in *Parliamentary Affairs*, Spring 1973, pp. 235-6.
13. See analysis in *Die Welt*, 5 October 1976.
14. Werner Kaltefleiter, 'The Impact of the Election of 1969 and the Formation of the New Government on the German Party System' in *Comparative Politics*, July 1970, p. 599.
15. E.g. see publications of Günter Rinsche, CDU Oberbürgermeister of Hamm, such as 'Die CDU in den Grosstädten' in Dietrich Rollmann (ed.), *Die Zukunft der CDU* (1968), pp. 192-210.
16. *The Times*, 26 August 1957.
17. *Der Spiegel*, 11 September 1957, p. 31.
18. Kitzinger, *op. cit.*, pp. 104-5.
19. See report by H.U. Kempski on Erhard's campaign in *SZ*, 8 September 1965.
20. Kitzinger, *op. cit.*, pp. 275-6, 301.
21. Kaltefleiter, *Konsens*, pp. 53-4.
22. Kaltefleiter in G. Gölter and E. Pieroth, *Die Union in der Opposition* (1970), pp. 14-15.
23. Kitzinger, *op. cit.*, p. 101.
24. *Ibid.*, p. 103.
25. E.g. see report on meeting of leaders of auxiliary organisations, April 1964, Archiv BGS.
26. *Die Zeit*, 2 June 1967.
27. Kohl speech, April 1968, in *14. Landesparteitag der CDU Rheinland-Pfalz* (1968), pp. 27-8.
28. Richard Rose, *Influencing Voters: a study of campaign rationality* (1967), p.24.

29.   On this point, see Kaltefleiter in Gölter and Pieroth, *op. cit.*, pp. 16-17;
      and H. Klingemann and E.U. Pappi on the 1969 Election in *Comparative
      Politics*, July 1970, pp. 543-6.
30.   See Allensbach survey on this question, published in *FAZ*, 27 January
      1973.
31.   See *Bericht der Bundesgeschäftsstelle*, presented to the CDU Congress in
      June 1973, p. 21.
32.   See report by H.U. Kempski on Barzel's campaign in *SZ*, 14 November
      1972.
33.   *FR*, 17 November 1972.
34.   Kaltefleiter, *Konsens*, p. 84.
35.   Werner Kaltefleiter, 'Der Gewinner hat nicht gesiegt: eine Analyse zur
      Bundestagswahl 1976' in *Aus Politik und Zeitgeschichte*, 11 December 1976,
      pp. 21-4.
36.   *Der Spiegel*, 23 August 1976, p. 17; see also, reports on Kohl's campaign
      in *NZZ*, 12 September 1976 and by H.U. Kempski in *SZ*, 27 September
      1976.
37.   Report on Kohl's campaign in *The Times*, 24 September 1976.
38.   *Wahlkampf 1972: Rechenschaftsbericht der Bundesgeschäftsstelle der
      CDU* (1973), pp. 33-5.
39.   Based on interview with Gerhard Pietsch, press spokesman of the Rhineland
      CDU, in Cologne, July 1976.
40.   See the series of special supplements on campaign preparations, giving
      details of these 'actions', in *Union in Deutschland*, 2 October 1975,
      23 October 1975, 12 February 1976 and 4 March 1976.
41.   E.g. *NZZ*, 12 September 1976; *Der Spiegel*, 23 August 1976, p. 22.
42.   Peter Haungs, 'Warum verlor die CDU/CSU die Bundestagswahl von 1972?'
      in *Der Bürger im Staat*, March 1973, p. 13.
43.   For a documentation on this, see Jörg Richter (ed.), *Klassenkampf von
      oben? oder Angstmacher von rechts* (rororo, 1973).
44.   See CDU Rheinland, *Bundestagswahl 1972* (1973).

CONCLUSION: GOVERNMENT OR OPPOSITION —
A QUESTION OF EXISTENTIAL IMPORTANCE

The approach of this study has been both historical and thematic, aiming at providing a comprehensive analysis of the CDU/CSU and its development in the context of the West German party system. It is proposed here to draw some concluding remarks about the impact of the Government and Opposition roles on the CDU/CSU and thereby to focus on its main features as a political force and summarise changes which have occurred in its composition, structure and outlook during the generation since its founding after the Second World War.

The principal emphasis of this book has been the effect of the Government and Opposition roles of the CDU/CSU, which remained continuously as a party of national office from the beginning of the Federal Republic in 1949 until the SPD/FDP coalition assumed power in 1969, thrusting the CDU/CSU into Opposition. The Government/ Opposition dimension is important for a number of reasons in the study of West German politics. First, and most directly relevant to this present study, the CDU/CSU developed as a governing force before it became a unified political party, and the strong dependence of the latter factor on the former was reinforced by the CDU/CSU's long uninterrupted period in power. Secondly, the political system of West Germany is executive-orientated in the sense that, within the scope of parliamentary democracy, a pronounced emphasis is placed on strong executive leadership by the Chancellor. Thirdly, this emphasis on the Chancellor has posed special difficulties for the Opposition, which has in addition suffered from historically determined problems of legitimacy. These latter two factors have continued to derive some force from traditional political thinking, which enhanced the role of 'the state' and undervalued societal forces of which the political opposition in the parliament is one of the most significant. Fourthly, a 'change of power' does not operate easily in the Federal Republic, depending as it does not on the ready alternation between large parties but on changes in coalition partners — a more complicated and long-term process. Fifthly, political debate in the Federal Republic has often resulted in an antagonistic polarisation of the main parties. All these factors have combined to make the role of Government versus Opposition a fundamental matter for the two main political parties in the Federal Republic.

The Government/Opposition dimension is however significantly modified by the federal structure of the state, which allows a party in opposition at the national level an outlet for executive action through office in *Land* government. Indeed, the tendency of a national Opposition party to mobilise its own voters more effectively in state elections than the party in power in Bonn can both act as a stimulant to the morale of its members and provide an important integrating force for its activities, thus mitigating the centrifugal forces inherent in being out of power.

The importance of the Government/Opposition roles for the development of the CDU/CSU can be illustrated by dividing its history broadly into four periods. First, the Period of Occupation (later 1940s) saw the CDU/CSU establish its political position, thus giving legitimacy to its claim to the governing role. Secondly, in the Period of Adenauer's Ascendancy (the 1950s) the CDU/CSU was dependent on the authority of the Chancellor and on its role in Government, while at the same time exploiting favourable political and economic circumstances, which additionally helped it to acquire a dominant political position. Thirdly, the Period of Transition (the 1960s) witnessed the CDU/CSU's gradual loss of its dominant position, yet it continued to depend heavily on its role in Government so there was little basic change in its political and organisational structure. Fourthly, the Period of Opposition (the 1970s) saw the loss of national office by the CDU/CSU although it continued to depend on the memory of the Government role until the shock of the 1972 Election forced the party (in particular the CDU) to depend more on its own political resources.

Thus, there has been throughout the period 1945-76 a fundamental interrelationship between the Government/Opposition role, the relative dominance of the CDU/CSU's political position and its political and organisational development. This was especially so with the CDU/CSU because it acquired national office and its dominant position early in its own history, so that it had little time to develop itself beforehand as a political party. This sequence of events had three significant consequences for its development. First, the CDU/CSU became electorally orientated in its activities and outlook to a greater extent than was normally the case with parties in parliamentary systems, because it had no or little tradition of political activism independent of its role in government. Secondly, these developments affected the CDU/CSU's ideological character in that it gained a reputation as essentially a 'pragmatic' political party because of the necessary adjustments and compromises it learned to make in office. The CDU/CSU's ideology lacked cohesion and was potentially divisive, because it tried to incorporate many different political tendencies from the German past. Consequently, its variegated ideological viewpoints did not provide the principal basis for the CDU/CSU's political activity, although certain consistent themes were evident in its outlook, such as anti-Communism/socialism, the social market economy and European integration. Thirdly, the CDU/CSU placed a very high value on the personal authority of its leadership, as the focus of integration which would counter the disadvantages of its loose internal structure. This was possible so long as the CDU/CSU not only possessed the Chancellorship, but also a leader of exceptional skills in Adenauer.

While the CDU/CSU successfully presented itself as the party of post-war reconstruction during the 1950s, it was unable to adapt to the changing political environment of the 1960s and gradually lost its dominant position in the face of the growing challenge from the SPD. Its lack of adaptation was manifested by repeated leadership crises during this decade beginning with Adenauer's slow decline, but it arose basically from internal differences over policy matters and the party's future course as well as the conservative influence of internal vested interests (which restrained various attempts at party reform). The party's continued dependence on the retention of national office for its political motivation, even though the Grand Coalition substantially reduced its role as the dominant party of government, posed obvious dangers for its future course. Hence, the loss of power and in particular the Chancellorship in 1969 created all at once a problem of 'existential importance' for the CDU/CSU, for its whole purpose as a political party was called into question.

While the aforementioned factors of historical circumstance applied to the CDU/CSU as a whole, the change in response to them was much more evident in the case of the CDU than the CSU (on the latter, see below). Several major changes have occurred in recent years, which had long been delayed because of the continued retention of the Government role. The forces for change, unleashed eventually after 1972, produced several significant developments. These can be divided for analytical purposes into two broad categories — the political, and the organisational — although they were essentially interrelated. On the political side, the party leadership was never able to repeat the uniqueness of Adenauer's dominance of his party, although it was affected nostalgically by this precedent; it underwent repeated crises of political confidence during the 1960s, especially as the party had been reared on firm personal authority, which was then lacking, but, from 1973 it began to adjust to a more collegial form of leadership. Other political developments included the promotion of internal party democracy (associated with the change in the form of leadership), which was illustrated by greater involvement of the party as a whole in policy discussion and a more participant membership. The notable organisational changes were improved co-ordination within the bounds of the party's federal structure, the search to enhance internal cohesion through the new form of leadership, the growth of an efficient and responsive party machine and a much increased membership.

The CSU was less affected as a political party by the change in the Government/Opposition dimension than was the CDU, because its own strengths in Bavarian politics gave it a greater resilience. These strengths included the long-standing support of the Bavarian electorate, its competent performance as the governing party of Bavaria and the strength of its organisation there. Indeed, one could go so far as to say that any classification of the CDU/CSU as a political force within the context of comparative studies of political parties has become progressively less possible, because there has been a qualitative change in the relationship of mutual dependence between the two Christian Democratic parties, largely as a result of the CDU/CSU's loss of its dominant position in Federal politics and of the impact of the Opposition role. Following their diverse reactions to the loss of national office in 1969 – the one producing a positive response, the other a hardening of attitudes (with the CSU) – solidarity between them has weakened progressively, emphasising their differences of policy orientation and form of leadership.

Consequently, the approaches of the CDU and CSU have diverged, thus intensifying their view of each other as rival political forces. The Government/Opposition dimension is, however, applicable to the CSU in the special context of Bavarian politics, for some changes, similar to those implemented in the CDU in the 1970s, particularly in the organisational field, occurred after its loss of power in *Land* politics in the mid-1950s. In the political field, the CSU has moved in many respects in a divergent direction to that of the CDU, notably in the nature of its leadership and the progress of its electoral strength. The main problem in evaluating the CSU is however the 'duality' of its role in Federal and *Land* politics.

Since the solidarity between the two Christian Democratic parties in West Germany has weakened, this must be considered the main potential threat to the cohesion of the CDU/CSU as a political force in the future, seeing that the CDU itself has overcome the most serious of its weaknesses of the 1960s – an inadequate organisation, a disputed leadership and an inflexible adherence to traditional policy outlook. The CDU has learned to rely more on itself as an 'autonomous' party in its own right rather than being simply the 'party of the government' it was in the 1950s. It is therefore an instructive example of a political party in a parliamentary system which has 'learned' from the role of Opposition, even though it was in power for such a long and continuous period. It was required to undergo this process of change and adaptation because the fundamental significance attached in West German politics to the Government vs. Opposition roles has meant that each in turn has had a greater impact on the CDU/CSU than would be the case in many other West European democracies. Furthermore, it cannot be assumed that the new political self-confidence acquired by the CDU from the mid-1970s will be maintained should it remain in Opposition beyond the legislative period inaugurated by the 1976 Election. For all these reasons, a return to power in Bonn is of 'existential importance' for the CDU/CSU, both for its future as a political force in West Germany and for its own internal solidarity.

NOTE ON SOURCES

The material for this book has been drawn from four sources: academic publications on the subject; party documentation; the press; and, interviews. Together, they have provided the author with a sound, and indeed plentiful, basis for writing a book about the CDU/CSU, even though there are obvious limitations of direct evidence when working on a contemporary subject.

First, there has been a relative lack of academic interest in the CDU/CSU, although the early history of the CDU was well covered by the work of H.G. Wieck and Arnold Heidenheimer during the 1950s. The author has used these publications, and supplemented them with material acquired from other sources, notably various monograph studies (published and unpublished), Ph.D. theses and articles in journals and periodicals by academics, journalists and party members. Much of this material was available in the library of the Bundestag. A welcome exception of late to this general lack of interest has been the appearance of the study by Mintzel on the organisational development of the CSU, which the author has consulted in addition to other forms of evidence on the CSU's political activities (the book by Müchler was obtained while revising the manuscript). Both these works are important, especially as the CSU has been either neglected or treated as an appendage of the CDU.

Secondly, party documentation has been useful for the study of the CDU's electoral activities and organisational matters in particular. This consisted chiefly of memoranda, reports, correspondence among the regional organisations and between them and the Federal headquarters, as well as party publications. They were located to some extent in the CDU party archives (documentation department of the *Bundesgeschäftsstelle der CDU*), but predominantly in the different *Landesverband* offices. The author was allowed free access in nearly all cases, and consulted the archives of the following selected *Landesverbände:*

Westphalia-Lippe (Dortmund)
Rhineland (Cologne)
Baden-Württemberg, and north Württemberg (Stuttgart)
North Baden (Karlsruhe)

Württemberg-Hohenzollern (Weingarten)
Lower Saxony, and Hanover (Hanover)
Hamburg (Hamburg)
Hesse (Wiesbaden)
Saar (Saarbrücken)

The amount and quality of material varied considerably between them, with Westphalia-Lippe having the best organised and most abundant archives and those in Stuttgart and Cologne also valuable. In two cases, earlier material had been destroyed following the reorganisation of *Landesverbände* offices. There are now efforts to centralise much of this documentation in the Konrad Adenauer Foundation in Bonn (including the transfer of the archives of Westphalia-Lippe). The various state archives, with which the author corresponded, yielded little material on the party, except the Hauptstaatsarchiv at Düsseldorf (especially for the archives of the Rhineland CDU). *Nachlässe* of early party figures were consulted, the main one being that of Leo Schwering (Stadtarchiv Köln), but an extensive use of them was not regarded as necessary in view of the scope of this book (they covered mainly the Occupation period). The Adenauer papers at Rhöndorf are not available, and are not likely to be for some time to come.

Thirdly, the press was the most voluminous source available. The excellent press archives at the Bundestag proved a very useful base, although the author also relied on his own files collected over the Opposition years since 1969. The documentation department at the *Bundesgeschäftsstelle der CDU* was another important location of press material. Political parties in the Federal Republic are relatively 'open' institutions, so that party affairs are reasonably well documented, particularly on policy matters and leadership questions. The author was able to use this source fruitfully, bearing in mind the party political inclinations of the West German press and cross-checking information with other sources and, when necessary, interviewing journalists as well as politicians.

Fourthly, interviews were a worthwhile and interesting exercise to gain additional information, and test assumptions made from reading evidence. In most cases, party members were very willing to discuss aspects of the subject during the course of research. The author also benefited from numerous informal discussions with party members and non-party members alike.

LIST OF INTERVIEWS

The author is grateful to the following members of the CDU/CSU for granting him interviews:

Wolfgang Bergsdorf, Head of CDU Chairman's Office, in Bonn, September 1973, September 1974 and July 1976.

Warnfried Dettling, Head of Planning Group, Bundesgeschäftsstelle der CDU, in Bonn, August 1976.

Arved Deringer, CDU Bundestag Deputy 1957-69, in Cologne, April 1973.

Bruno Dörpinghaus, General Secretary of the Arbeitsgemeinschaft der CDU/CSU 1947-51, in Bornheim/Bonn, September 1973.

Heinz Dziedziezak, Spokesman of Lower Saxony CDU, in Hanover, November 1972 and September 1973.

Peter Egen, Federal Business Manager of the Evangelischer Arbeitskreis der CDU/CSU, in Bonn, September 1973.

Karl Enderes, District Branch Manager of CDU Rhein-Sieg-Kreis, in Siegburg, August 1976.

Ludwig Erhard, Federal Chancellor 1963-6, in Bonn, September 1973.

Arnold Fratzscher, General Secretary of Lower Saxony CDU 1946-66, in Hanover, September 1973.

Johann Baptist Gradl, Chairman of Exil-CDU, in Bonn, September 1974.

Willi Gehring, District Branch Manager of CDU Saarbrücken, in Saarbrücken, August 1973.

Franz Grandel, Business Manager of North Württemberg CDU, in Stuttgart, August 1973.

Dieter Haassengier, General Secretary of Lower Saxony CDU, in Hanover, September 1973.

Bruno Heck, Federal Business Manager of CDU 1952-8 and General Secretary of CDU 1967-71, in Bonn, September 1973.

Jürgen Heidborn, personal assistant to Richard von Weizsäcker, in Bonn, September 1973 and September 1974.

Thomas Jansen, personal assistant to Rainer Barzel, in Bonn, August 1973 and September 1974.

Dieter Kiehl, Spokesman of CSU, in Munich, November 1972 and August 1976.

Josef Konnertz, District Branch Manager of CDU Rhein-Sieg-Kreis

356

1945-72, in Cologne, August 1973 and Siegburg, July 1976.

Konrad Kraske, Federal Business Manager of CDU from 1958 and General Secretary of CDU 1971-73, in Bonn, September 1974.

Paul Krauskopf, official of the Baden-Württemberg CDU Landes-geschäftsstelle, in Stuttgart, August 1973.

Franzheinrich Krey, Land Business Manager of Rhineland CDU, in Cologne, August 1973.

Karl Lamers, former District Branch Chairman of CDU Rhein-Sieg-Kreis, in Bad Godesberg, September 1976.

Hans Leveling, Head of Organisation Department of Lower Saxony CDU, in Hanover, September 1976.

Josef Müller, Chairman of CSU 1945-9, in Munich, September 1973.

Gerhard Pietsch, Press Spokesman of Rhineland CDU, in Cologne, July 1976.

Eduard Prosch, Land Business Manager of CDU Hamburg, in Hamburg, September 1973.

Günter Rinsche, Mayor of Hamm since 1964, in Hamm, August 1973.

Josef Rösing, CDU Bundestag Deputy, in Bonn, September 1973.

Ulrich Scholtz, official of Baden-Württemberg CDU Landesgeschafts-stelle, in Stuttgart, August 1973.

Kurt Sieveking, Mayor of Hamburg 1953-7, in Hamburg, September 1973.

Lothar Späth, Chairman of CDU Fraktion in Baden-Württemberg Landtag since 1972, in Stuttgart, August 1976.

Hans Terlinden, Land Business Manager of CDU Rhineland-Palatinate, in Mainz, August 1973.

Klaus Wagener, official of CSU Landesleitung, in Munich, September 1973.

Willy Wagner, District Branch Manager of CDU Mainz, in Mainz, August 1973.

Reinhard Weiss, Head of Organisation Department of CDU Westfalen-Lippe, in Dortmund, August 1973 and August 1976.

Bodislav Wentzel, former personal assistant to Peter Lorenz, in Hamburg, September 1976.

Hermann Woesner, District Branch Manager of CSU Passau, in Passau, September 1976.

Werner Wolf, official of the Hesse CDU Landesgeschäftsstelle, in Wiesbaden, August 1973.

The author also thanks the following journalists for interviews:

Siegmund Alf (Süddeutsche Zeitung)
Reinhard Appel (Süddeutsche Zeitung)
Norman Crosland (Guardian, later The Economist)
Richard Davy (The Times)
Klaus Dreher (Süddeutsche Zeitung)
Hanns Funk (Stuttgarter Zeitung)
Hans Kepper (Frankfurter Rundschau)
Dan Van Der Vat (The Times)

BIBLIOGRAPHY

Baring, Arnulf, *Aussenpolitik in Adenauers Kanzlerdemokratie* (Munich, 1969)

—, (ed.) *Sehr Verehrter Herr Bundeskanzler! Heinrich von Brentano im Briefwechsel mit Konrad Adenauer* (Hamburg, 1974)

Becker, Dierk-Eckhard and Wiesendahl, E., *Ohne Programm nach Bonn, oder Die Union als Kanzlerwahl-Verein* (rororo, 1972)

Blankenburg, Erhard, *Kirchliche Bindung und Wahlverhalten: die sozialen Faktoren bei der Wahlentscheidung Nordrhein-Westfalen 1961-1966* (Olten, 1967)

Bracher, Karl Dietrich, 'Das Bonner Parteiensystem' in Bracker (ed.), *Nach 25 Jahren: eine Deutschland-Bilanz* (Munich, 1970)

Bucheim, Karl, *Geschichte der christlichen Parteien in Deutschland* (Munich, 1953)

Burkett, Tony, *Parties and Elections in West Germany: the search for stability* (London, 1975)

Conradt, David, *The West German Party System: an ecological analysis of social structure and voting behaviour, 1961-1969* (London, 1972)

Conze, Werner, *Jakob Kaiser – Politiker zwischen Ost und West, 1945-1949* (Stuttgart, 1969)

Deuerlein, Ernst, *CDU/CSU, 1945-1957: Beiträge zur Zeitgeschichte* (Cologne, 1957)

Dexheimer, Wolfgang, *Koalitionsverhandlungen in Bonn, 1961-1965-1969: Zur Willensbildung in Parteien und Fraktionen* (Bonn, 1973)

—, 'Die CSU-Landesgruppe: ihre organisatorische Stellung in der CDU/CSU Fraktion' in *Zeitschrift für Parlamentsfragen*, No. 3, 1972, pp. 307-13

Dittberner, Jürgen and Ebbighausen, Rolf, *Parteiensystem in der Legitimationskrise: Studien und Materialien zur Soziologie der Parteien in der Bundesrepublik Deutschland* (Opladen, 1973)

Domes, Jürgen, *Mehrheitsfraktion und Bundesregierung: Aspekte des Verhältnisses der Fraktion der CDU/CSU im zweiten und dritten Deutschen Bundestag zum Kabinett Adenauer* (Cologne, 1964)

Dreher, Klaus, *Der Weg zum Kanzler: Adenauers Griff nach der Macht* (Düsseldorf, 1972)

Egen, Peter, *Die Entstehung des Evangelischen Arbeitskreises der*

359

CDU/CSU (Ph.D. thesis, undated)

Eisner, Erich, *Das europäische Konzept von Franz Josef Strauss: die gesamteuropäischen Ordnungsvorstellungen der CSU* (Meisenheim am Glan, 1975)

Elschner, Gerhard, 'Zwanzig Jahre Christlich Demokratische Union: Reflexionen über Eigenart und Struktur' in *Civitas, Jahrbuch für christliche Gesellschaftsordnung*, Vol. 4 (Mannheim, 1965), pp. 167-89

Fratzscher, Arnold, *Die CDU in Niedersachsen: Demokratie der ersten Stunde* (Hanover, 1971)

Gölter, Georg and Pieroth, Elmar, *Die Union in der Opposition* (Düsseldorf, 1970)

Günther, Klaus, *Der Kanzlerwechsel in der Bundesrepublik: Adenauer – Erhard – Kiesinger* (Hanover, 1970)

Hacke, Christian, *Die Ost- und Deutschlandpolitik der CDU/CSU: Wege und Irrwege der Opposition seit 1969* (Cologne, 1975)

—, 'Die Ost- und deutschlandpolitische Argumentation der CDU/CSU seit 1973' in *Aus Politik und Zeitgeschichte*, 23 August 1975

Heidenheimer, Arnold, *Adenauer and the CDU: The rise of the leader and the integration of the party* (The Hague, 1960)

—, 'Federalism and the Party System: the case of West Germany' in *American Political Science Review*, September 1958, pp. 809-28

—, 'Foreign Policy and Party Discipline in the CDU' in *Parliamentary Affairs*, Winter 1959-60, pp. 70-84

—, 'German Party Finance: the CDU' in *American Political Science Review*, June 1957, pp. 369-85

—, 'Der starke Regierungschef und das Parteiensystem: der "Kanzler-Effekt" in der Bundesrepublik' in *Politische Vierteljahresschrift*, 1960-1961, pp. 241-62

—, 'La Structure Confessionelle, Sociale et Régionale de la CDU' in *Revue Française de Science Politique*, 1957, pp. 626-45

Hereth, Michael, *Die parlamentarische Opposition in der Bundesrepublik* (Munich, 1969)

Kaack, Heino, *Geschichte und Struktur des deutschen Parteiensystems* (Opladen, 1971)

Kaltefleiter, Werner, 'Konsens ohne Macht? Eine Analyse der Bundestagswahl vom 19. September 1965' in *Verfassung und Verfassungswirklichkeit*, 1966, pp. 14-62

—, 'In Wechselspiel der Koalitionen: eine Analyse der Bundestagswahl 1969' in *ibid.*, Vol. I, 1970

Kaltefleiter, Werner, *Zwischen Konsens und Krise: eine Analyse der Bundestagswahl 1972* (Bonn, 1973)

Kitzinger, Uwe, *German Electoral Politics* (London, 1960)

Knorr, Heribert, 'Die Grosse Koalition in der parlamentarischen Diskussion der Bundesrepublik, 1949-65' in *Aus Politik und Zeitgeschichte*, 17 August 1974

Konrad-Adenauer-Stiftung (ed.), *Christliche Demokraten der ersten Stunde*(Bonn, 1966)

——, *Konrad Adenauer und die CDU der britischen Besatzungszone, 1946-1949* (Bonn, 1975)

Kramer, Gertrud and Johannes, 'Der Einfluss der Sozialausschüsse der Christlich-Demokratischen Arbeitnehmerschaft auf die CDU' in *Aus Politik und Zeitgeschichte*, 13 November 1976

Kühr, Herbert, 'Probleme innerparteilicher Demokratie in der CDU' in *Aus Politik und Zeitgeschichte*, 24 August 1974

Loewenberg, Gerhard, 'Parliamentarism in Western Germany: the functioning of the Bundestag' in *American Political Science Review*, March 1961, pp. 87-102

——, 'The Remaking of the German Party System' in M. Dogan and R. Rose (ed.), *European Politics: A Reader* (London, 1971) pp. 259-80

Mayntz, Renate, 'Oligarchic Problems in a German Party District' in D. Marvick (ed.), *Political Decision-Makers* (Glencoe, 1961) pp. 138-92

Merkl, Peter, 'Equilibrium, Structure of Interests and Leadership: Adenauer's Survival as Chancellor' in *American Political Science Review*, 1962, pp. 634-50

Mintzel, Alf, *Die CSU: Anatomie einer konservativen Partei, 1945-1972* (Opladen, 1975)

——, 'Die CSU in Bayern: Phasen ihrer organisationspolitischen Entwicklung' in *Politische Vierteljahresschrift*, October 1972, pp. 205-43

Müchler, Günter, *CDU/CSU: Das schwierige Bündnis* (Munich, 1976)

——, 'Zum früheren Verhältnis von CDU und CSU' in *Politische Studien*, 1972, pp. 595-613

Narr, Wolf-Dieter, *CDU/SPD: Programm und Praxis seit 1945* Stuttgart. 1966)

Oberreuter, Heinrich (ed.), *Parlamentarische Opposition: ein internationaler Vergleich* (Hamburg, 1975)

Politische Akademie Eichholz der Konrad-Adenauer-Stiftung (ed.),

Dokumente zur Christlichen Demokratie (Bonn, 1969)

Pridham, Geoffrey, 'Christian Democracy in Italy and West Germany: a comparative analysis' in M. Kolinsky and W.E. Paterson (ed.), *Social and Political Movements in Western Europe* (London, 1976), pp. 142-74

——, 'The CDU/CSU Opposition in West Germany, 1969-72: a party in search of an organisation' in *Parliamentary Affairs*, Spring 1973, pp. 201-17

——, 'A "Nationalisation" Process? Federal Politics and State Elections in West Germany' in *Government and Opposition*, Autumn 1973, pp. 455-72

——, 'The Ostpolitik and the Opposition in West Germany' in Roger Tilford (ed.), *The Ostpolitik and Political Change in Germany* (Farnborough, 1975), pp. 45-58

Pütz, Helmuth, *Die CDU: Entwicklung, Aufbau und Politik der Christlich Demokratischen Union Deutschlands* (Düsseldorf, 1976)

Radunski, Peter, 'Zum Generationswechsel in Parteien: die Junge Union als Sprungbrett für politische Karrieren in der CDU' in *Reale Utopien*, Schriftenreihe des Instituts für Internationale Solidarität, Vol. 6 (Mainz, 1970), pp. 139-67

Rollmann, Dietrich (ed.), *Die CDU in der Opposition: eine Selbstdarstellung* (Hamburg, 1970)

——, *Die Zukunft der CDU: Christlich-Demokratische Konzeption für die Zukunft* (Hamburg, 1968)

Schäfer, Gert and Nedelmann, Carl, *Der CDU-Staat: Analysen zur Verfassungswirklichkeit der Bundesrepublik* (Munich, 1967)

Schulz, Gerhard, 'Die CDU: Merkmale ihres Aufbaus' in *Parteien in der Bundesrepublik: Studien zur Entwicklung der deutschen Parteien bis zur Bundestagswahl 1953* (Stuttgart, 1955), pp. 3-156

——, 'Die Organisationsstruktur der CDU' in *Zeitschrift für Politik*, No. 2, 1956, pp. 147-65

Schwering, Leo, *Frühgeschichte der Christlich-Demokratischen Union* (Recklinghausen, 1963)

Storz, Henning, *Aussenpolitik als Gesellschaftspolitik: die aussenpolitische Konzeption der CDU mit besonderer Berücksichtigung der Zeit der Grossen Koalition, 1966-1969* (Ph.D. thesis, Berlin, 1973)

Varain, Heinz Josef, *Parteien und Verbände: eine Studie über ihren Aufbau, ihre Verflechtung und ihr Wirken in Schleswig-Holstein, 1945-1958* (Cologne, 1964)

Veen, Hans-Joachim, *Die CDU/CSU-Opposition im parlamentarischen Entscheidungsprozess* (Munich, 1973)

—, *Opposition im Bundestag: ihre Funktionen, institutionellen Handlungsbedingungen und das Verhalten der CDU/CSU Fraktion in der 6. Wahlperiode 1969-1972* (Bonn, 1976)

Wieck, H.G., *Christliche und Freie Demokraten in Hessen, Rheinland-Pfalz, Baden und Württemberg 1945-1946* (Düsseldorf, 1958)

—, *Die Entstehung der CDU und die Widergründung des Zentrums im Jahre 1945* (Düsseldorf, 1953)

INDEX

Adenauer, Konrad
  early CDU leader 27-8, 29-30, 33,
    51, 52, 70-1, 124; and confession
    27-8, 42-3; anti-Communism of 30,
    57; and party organisation 48-9,
    95-6, 243, 249, 250, 259;
    candidacy for Presidency (1959)
    58, 59, 96, chap. 2 (d), 114,
    115-16; government formations
    59-62, at party Congresses 65-6,
    90-5, 122, 129; elected party
    chairman 67; use of patronage 72;
    health and age 73, 76, 94, 96, 98,
    99, 114, 127, 129; and Bundestag
    Fraktion 74-5, 76-7, 78, 135,
    136-7, 139, 153; Western policy
    75-6, 77-9, 85-8, 91, 199; and
    federalism 83-4; challenge to
    authority 94-5; question of
    succession to chap. 2 (d) *passim*,
    122, 124; relations with
    Erhard chap. 2 (d) *passim*,
    113, chap. 3 (c) *passim*,
    147-8, 151, 153; CDU's
    dependence on 113, 137-8, 144;
    prospect of his retirement 113;
    attitude to party reform 118,
    119-20, 120-1, 123, 126, 133;
    party tribute to 119; as
    campaigner 124, 138, chap. 11 (b);
    retirement as Chancellor 137-8;
    as divisive figure in party 144, 153;
    as 'Gaullist' 150, 152, 155;
    and Grand Coalition 158;
    retires as party chairman 159;
    attitude to Opposition 188;
    relationship with CSU 304,
    307, 308, 311, 318, 323, 328;
    and regional party leaders 312;
age factor, members and voters 278-9,
    287, 326, 336
Ahlen Programme (1947) 25, 31, 227,
    292, 298, 299
Ahlers, Conrad 172
Albers, Johannes 63, 298
Albrecht, Ernst 211, 229, 232, 235
allied occupation policy 47-8
Altmeier, Peter 105, 249

anti-communism, and CDU/CSU
  29-30, 31, 57, 77, 176, 180, 200,
  202, 230, 243, 340, 345, 346,
  351
Arbeitsgemeinschaft der CDU/CSU
  44, 49, 64, 241
Arnold, Karl 43, 60, 62, 63, 73, 82,
  90, 94-5, 109, 138, 139, 298

Baden, CDU in 24, 48, 87, 277;
  see also Baden-Württemberg,
  CDU in
Baden-Württemberg, CDU in 156,
  247-8, 268, 269, 277, 279, 283,
  286, 287, 337, 338; *see also*
  Baden, CDU in; Württemberg,
  CDU in
Barth, Karl 39
Barzel, Rainer 109, 124-5, 127-8,
  128-9, 138, 149, 153, 160-1,
  162-3, 164, 171-2, 175, 177,
  181, 183, 184, chap. 5 (b)
  passim, 188, 189, 190, 191, 199,
  202, 204, 208, 211, 212, 213,
  214, 217, 232, 233, 234, 263,
  268-9, 284, 296, 312, chap.
  11 (c)
Basic Law 32, 70, 81, 105
Basic Policy Commission
  (*Grundsatzkommission*) 228,
  235
Bausch, Paul 41, 49, 107, 174
Bavarian Party (BP) 36, 50, 305,
  322, 326, 327, 329-30
Bavarian People's Party (BVP)
  21, 36, 304, 305, 322
Benda, Ernst 189, 261
Bergsdorf, Wolfgang 216
Berlin, CDU in 23, 30, 37, 39, 48,
  51, 53, 256, 267, 268, 277,
  279
Berlin Programme, of CDU 177-80,
  192, 211, 214, 227, 233, 288,
  328
BHE, refugee party 88, 322
Biedenkopf, Kurt 208, 209, 210,
  212, 213, 214, 216-17, chap.
  6 (d), 233, 234, 235, 244-5, 262,

365